ENDGAME

Bobby Fischer's Remarkable Rise and Fall—

from America's Brightest Prodigy to the

Edge of Madness

FRANK BRADY

Crown Publishers

New York

Library of Congress Cataloging-in-Publication Data

Brady, Frank, 1934–

Endgame : Bobby Fischer's remarkable rise and fall—from America's brightest prodigy to the edge of madness / by Frank Brady.

p. cm.

1. Fischer, Bobby, 1943–2008. 2. Chess players—United States—Biography. 3. Chess—Collection of games. I. Title

GV1439.F5B68 2010

794.1092—dc22

[B]

2010033840

ISBN 978-0-307-46390-6

eISBN 978-0-307-46392-0

Printed in the United States of America

Book design by Leonard W. Henderson

Jacket design by David Tran

Jacket photograph © Stephen Green—Armytage/*Sports Illustrated*/Getty Images

1   3   5   7   9   10   8   6   4   2

First Edition

To Maxine,
always my talisman

CONTENTS

AUTHOR'S NOTE

AS SOMEONE WHO knew Bobby Fischer from the time he was quite young, I've been asked hundreds of times, "What was Bobby Fischer *really* like?" This book is an attempt to answer that question. But a warning to those who turn these pages: Paradoxes abound. Bobby was secretive, yet candid; generous, yet parsimonious; naive, yet well informed; cruel, yet kind; religious, yet heretical. His games were filled with charm and beauty and significance. His outrageous pronouncements were filled with cruelty and prejudice and hate. And though for a period of decades he poured most of his energy and passion into a quest for chess excellence, he was not the idiot savant often portrayed by the press.

As Virginia Woolf observed in her one attempt at writing a life story, that of artist Roger Fry: "A biography is considered complete if it merely accounts for six or seven selves, whereas a person may well have as many as one thousand." Many lives, and then second and even third acts, constitute the drama of Bobby Fischer, but my attempt here was to delineate just *one* of Fischer's kaleidoscopic personalities—that of a genius, an inwardly tortured warrior—and within that framework to capture his shifting identities and roles. The renowned psychologist Alfred Binet noted that if we could look inside the mind of a chess player we would see there "a whole world of feelings, images, ideas, emotions and passions." And so it was with Bobby: His head was not merely filled with chess bytes, phantom computer connections on a grid of sixty-four squares, but with poetry and song and lyricism.

I ask forgiveness for my occasional speculations in this book, but Fischer's motivations beg to be understood; and when conjecture is used, I inform the reader of my doing so. To vivify Bobby's extraordinary life I sometimes use the techniques of the novelist: elaboration of setting, magnification of detail, fragments of dialogue, and revelation of interior states. But always my use of those devices is based on my research, recollection, and study of the man. I want readers—whether they play chess or not—to feel as though they're sitting next to Bobby, on *his* side of the chessboard, or in the privacy of his home, experiencing the rush of his triumphs, the pain of his defeats, and the venom of his anger.

I've been following Bobby Fischer's life story from the first time we met—at a chess tournament when he was a child and I was a teen—all the way to his grave in the remote and windswept countryside of Iceland. Over the years we played hundreds of games together, dined in Greenwich Village restaurants, traveled to tournaments, attended dinner parties, and walked the streets of Manhattan for hours on end. He was light-years ahead of me in chess ability, but despite the yawning gap that separated us, we found ways to bond. I knew his family and had many talks about Bobby with his mother.

Though Bobby and I were friends, with a tempestuous relationship that remained on for years and eventually was off, I was also a privileged *official* witness to his greatness. As a director of one of the first rated tournaments he played in as a child, I noted his steadfastness. As an arbiter when he accomplished his historic 11–0 clean sweep at the 1963–64 U.S. Championship tournament, I stood by his board and observed his pride of accomplishment. And as the initial arbiter for Bobby when he was banned from traveling to Cuba for the Havana International Tournament and forced to play remotely by Teletype entry, I spent hours alone with him in a closed room of the Marshall Chess Club, watching how his deep concentration was being compromised by fatigue.

Although *Endgame* includes many incidents to which I was an eyewitness or in which I participated, the book is not in any way my memoir, and I've tried to remain invisible as much as possible. Through original research, analysis of documents and letters heretofore untapped, and hundreds of interviews over the years with people who knew or had a different perspective on Bobby, I've tried to capture the story of how he not only transformed himself, but also how, through a mysterious alchemy, he affected the image and status of chess in the minds of millions. And also how, unexpectedly, he saw his life become intertwined with the Cold War.

Mainly as a result of Bobby's charisma and his widely publicized contretemps, his winning the World Championship created more furor and attention—and more awareness of the game by the general public—than any other chess event in history. Bobby had an uneasy relationship with his extraordinary celebrity and ultimately grew to despise it. It was the public's intrusive gaze that caused him, in later years, to lead a determinedly reclusive, almost hermetic life.

For this book, I obtained access to portions of the KGB and FBI files on Bobby and his mother; the files not only provided me with insights but also with specific information that corrects previously published versions of Bobby's life (including my own).

In the course of researching *Endgame,* I came across an autobiographical essay—never published—that Bobby wrote when he was in his teens, rough-hewn for sure, but introspective nevertheless, which in many ways gave the "story behind the story" of his life at that time, especially how he viewed his ascent and how he was treated by various chess organizations. Information that I found in this essay helped to rectify existing misconceptions. In addition, I obtained access to the personal archives of his chess mentor, Jack Collins, and of Bobby's mother, Regina Fischer. These invaluable troves of letters, photos, and clippings have been an important source for this book. Reading a letter from Bobby to Jack Collins, written decades ago, is almost like bringing Bobby back to life.

Whether one admires or despises Bobby Fischer—and it's quite easy to do both simultaneously, as these pages will show—I hope that his story proves that while he was a deeply troubled soul, he was also a serious and great artist, one who had a passion to *know.*

We may not—and perhaps *should* not—forgive Bobby Fischer's twisted political and antireligious assaults, but we should never forget his sheer brilliance on the chessboard. After reading this biography, I would suggest that the reader look to, and study, his games—the true testament to who he was, and his ultimate legacy.

There was a boy, a chessplayer once, who revealed that his gift consisted partly in a clear inner vision of potential moves of each piece as objects with flashing or moving tails of colored light. He saw a live possible pattern of potential moves and selected them according to which ones made the pattern strongest, the tensions greatest. His mistakes were made when he selected not the toughest, but the most beautiful lines of light.

From *The Virgin in the Garden,* by A. S. Byatt

1

Loneliness to Passion

I CAN'T BREATHE! I can't breathe!" Bobby Fischer's screams were muffled by the black hood tied tightly around his head. He felt as if he were suffocating, near death. He shook his head furiously to loosen the covering.

Two Japanese security guards were holding him down on the floor of the brightly lit cell, one sitting on his back and pinning his arms to his sides, the other holding his legs—Lilliputians atop the fallen Gulliver. Bobby's lungs were being compressed, and he couldn't get enough air. His right arm felt as if it had been broken from the scuffle that had happened moments before; he was bleeding from the mouth.

So this is how I'll die, he thought. *Will anyone ever know the truth about how I was murdered?*

He pondered in the darkness, incredulous that a supposedly revoked passport had turned him into a prisoner. The scenario had evolved rapidly. It was July 13, 2004. After spending three months in Japan, he was about to embark for the Philippines. He'd arrived at Tokyo's Narita Airport about two hours before his flight. At the ticket counter, an immigration officer had routinely checked his passport, entering the number: Z7792702. A discreet bell sounded and a red light began to flash slowly. "Please take a seat, Mr. Fischer, until we can check this out."

Bobby was concerned but not yet frightened. He'd been traveling for twelve years between Hungary, Czechoslovakia, Germany, the Philippines, Japan, Austria, and other countries, clearing customs and crossing borders without incident. Extra pages had to be added to his passport because there was no room left to stamp the dates of his entries and exits, but this task had already been completed at the American embassy in Bern, Switzerland, in November 2003.

His worry was that the U.S. government might finally have caught up with him. He'd violated State Department economic sanctions against Yugoslavia by playing a $5 million chess match against Boris Spassky in Sveti Stefan, Montenegro, in 1992, and an arrest warrant had been issued at that time. If he went back to the United States, he'd have to stand trial, and the penalty, if he was convicted, would be anywhere from ten years in prison to $250,000 in fines, or both. A friend had called the State Department in the late 1990s and asked if Bobby could return home. "Of course he can," said the spokesperson, "but as soon as he lands at JFK, we'll nail him." As a man without a country, Bobby eventually chose to settle in Hungary, and he had never heard another word from the American government. With twelve years having passed, he figured that as long as he stayed away from the United States, he'd be safe.

He sat where he was told, but fear began to take hold. Eventually, an immigration official asked Bobby to accompany him downstairs. "But I'll miss my flight." "We *know* that" was the peremptory reply. Escorted by security guards down a long, dark, and narrow hallway, Bobby demanded to know what was going on. "We just want to talk to you," the official said. "Talk about what?" Bobby demanded. "We just talk" was the answer. Bobby stopped and refused to move. A translator was called in to make sure there was no confusion. Bobby spoke to him in English and Spanish. More security guards arrived, until approximately fifteen men surrounded the former chess champion in a grim, silent circle.

Finally, another official appeared and showed Bobby an arrest warrant, stating that he was traveling on an invalid passport and that he was under arrest. Bobby insisted that his passport was perfectly legal and had two and a half years to go before it expired. "You may call a representative of the U.S. embassy to assist you," he was told. Bobby shook his head. "The U.S. embassy is the problem, not the solution," he muttered. His fear was that a State Department representative might show up at the airport with a court order and try to have him extradited back to the United States to stand trial.

He wanted to call one of his Japanese chess friends for help, but Immigration denied him access to a phone.

Bobby turned and started to walk away. He was blocked by a guard. Another guard tried to handcuff him, and he started twisting and turning to thwart the process. Several of the guards began hitting him with batons and pummeling him with their fists. He fought back, kicking and screaming, and he managed to bite one of the guards on the arm. Eventually, he went down. A half dozen guards hoisted him into the air and began carrying him by his arms and legs. Bobby continued squirming to get loose as the guards struggled to take him to an unknown destination. He kicked frantically, almost yanking his hands free. It was then that they put the black hood over his head.

Since Bobby knew that his passport was valid, what was going on? His comments about Jews and the crimes of the United States had stirred things up, but as an American citizen wasn't he protected by the First Amendment? Anyway, how could his opinions have anything to do with his passport?

Maybe it was the taxes. Ever since his unsuccessful 1976 suit against *Life* magazine and one of its writers for violation of a contract, he'd been so disgusted with the jurisprudence system that he refused to pay any taxes.

Gasping for air, Bobby tried to enter a Zen state to clear his mind. He stopped resisting and his body became relaxed. The guards noticed the change. They released his arms and legs, stood up, ceremoniously removed the hood, then left the cell. They'd taken his shoes, his belt, his wallet, and—much to his dismay—the buffalo-leather passport case that he'd bought in Vienna years back. But he was alive . . . at least for the moment.

When he looked up, he saw a nondescript man with a video camera quietly filming him through the bars. After a few minutes the man vanished. Bobby spit out a piece of a tooth that had been chipped, either from one of the punches or when he was thrown to the floor. He put the remnants in his pocket.

Lying on the cold cement floor, he felt his arm throb with pain. What was the next move and who would make it? He drifted off to sleep.

♖

Forty-eight years earlier, August 1956

Visualizing his white pawn two squares in front of his king on an imaginary chessboard, thirteen-year-old Bobby Fischer announced his first move to his opponent, Jack Collins: "Pawn to king four." Bobby was using a form of chess notation that described the movement of the pieces to various squares. As he spoke, he made a slight, unconscious movement of his head, an almost imperceptible nod, as if pushing the unseen pawn forward.

Collins, a diminutively proportioned man whose stunted legs had left him unable to walk, was propelled in a wheelchair along the crowded New York City street by a black manservant named Odell. The man was so strong that, in the days before handicap ramps, he could lift Collins and the chair all at once—up and down the stairs of homes or restaurants. Odell never talked much, but he was friendly and fiercely loyal to Collins, and from the time he met Bobby he'd felt a deep affection for the young boy.

Walking next to Collins was his slightly younger sister, Ethel, a plump but pretty registered nurse who was almost always by his side. She adored her brother and gave up everything—even marriage—to care for him. Although Jack and Ethel had just met Bobby that summer, they were fast becoming parental substitutes for him.

The Fellini-esque quartet spoke in an arcane language and made references to people with feudal titles who lived centuries ago. As they walked the long Brooklyn block from Lenox Road and Bedford Avenue to sometimes clamorous Flatbush Avenue, they attracted the curiosity of passersby. But they were unembarrassed, involved in a world of their own, one that bridged many continents and thousands of years and was inhabited by kings and courtiers, rajahs and princes. The group's destination was the Silver Moon Chinese restaurant.

"Pawn to queen bishop four," responded Collins in a basso profundo that could be heard across the street.

Just as an accomplished musician can read a score and hear the music in his head, a master chess player with a strong memory can read the record of a game and see it in his mind's eye. Composer Antonio Salieri was moved to tears of joy by reading some of Mozart's scores before they were performed. In the same way, some chess players can be emotionally stirred by mentally replaying a brilliant game by a great master.

In this case, Fischer was not only visualizing a game without benefit of board, pieces, or printed score; he was creating it, composing it as a motion picture in his mind. As he and Collins strolled down Flatbush Avenue, they were playing what is called "blindfold chess," a form of the game practiced throughout the ages. There are accounts dating back to A.D. 800 of nomadic Arabs playing a kind of boardless and sightless chess while riding on camels. For many chess players—and especially for those people who don't know the game—witnessing two players competing without sight of a board can evoke astonishment. The uncanny feats of memory on display can seem almost mystical.

Collins was more than well schooled in strategic theory. He was the co-author of the then latest edition of the modern bible of chess, *Modern Chess Openings,* which contained thousands of variations, positions, analyses, and recommendations. Bobby, who was becoming Collins's pupil, had been studying past and present chess games for years and had begun to dip into Collins's library of hundreds of books and periodicals.

It was humid, threatening to drizzle. Earlier in the year Fischer had become the U.S. Junior Champion at a tournament in Philadelphia, and he'd just returned from the U.S. Open Championship in Oklahoma City, the youngest player, at thirteen, ever to compete in the event. Collins was a former New York State Champion, a veteran tournament player, and a renowned teacher of the game. He was forty-four years old.

The odd couple continued to play their invisible game. Bobby mentally controlled the white pieces, Collins the black. As the contest seesawed, each player acted the role of predator and prey.

Bobby had always been short for his age, and still only stood five-four, but he was just beginning to stretch out of his clothes and sprout up. By the time he was eighteen, he'd reach a height of six-two. He had bright hazel eyes and a shiny, toothy smile with a slight gap between his two front teeth. His beaming grin was that of a happy child who wanted to be liked, or at least to be engaging. On this night he wore a polo shirt, brown corduroy slacks—even though it was August—and battered black-and-white, $5 sneakers. His voice was slightly nasal, perhaps because he needed to have his tonsils and adenoids removed. His hair was a tufted brown crew cut, as if his mother, Regina, or his sister, Joan, had clipped it one day and a comb hadn't touched it since. Bobby looked more like a farm boy from Kansas than a kid from the streets of Brooklyn.

He usually stayed a few steps ahead of Collins and the others, wanting to go faster but grudgingly slowing up to announce his moves or to receive his teacher's reply. Bobby's answer to Collins's move was always instantaneous, his response bursting from somewhere deep in his unconscious as he visualized bishops speeding along the diagonals, knights catapulting over pieces and pawns, and rooks seizing crucial squares. Occasionally, he'd split his mental gymnastics, leaving his imaginary board to swing a fantasy baseball bat and knock an invisible ball into the left-field stands of the Ebbets Field in his mind. Even more than a chess champion, young Bobby Fischer wanted to be Duke Snider, the legendary Brooklyn Dodgers baseball player.

It was astonishing that Fischer, at thirteen, could excel at blindfold chess. Many seasoned players fail to master it. The boy didn't *prefer* to play without sight of the board; it was just that he wanted to be involved in the game every spare minute, and the twenty-minute walk to the Silver Moon from the Collins home was just too long to go without a game. He didn't seem to be distracted or annoyed by the honking traffic or the cacophony of music and voices spilling out onto the avenue.

Even at this young age, Bobby had already played thousands of games, many in a form called "speed chess" or "blitz." Instead of the usual one to two hours, speed chess often takes only ten minutes to complete; five minutes or less if the players want to challenge themselves even more. Sometimes the rule is that each move must be completed in no more than a second. In such cases, there's virtually no time to reflect, to engage in that familiar inner dialogue: *If I move my bishop here, and he moves his knight there, then maybe I should move my queen there—no, that won't work! Then he'd take my pawn. So instead I'd better move . . .* Bobby's years of playing intense speed games helped lead to his ability to instantly comprehend the relationships of the pieces on the board.

Walking down that Brooklyn street, Fischer and Collins exchanged knowing glances as they played. It was as if they were engaged in a secret ritual. As they approached the restaurant, each felt an unspoken pressure to finish the contest, but there wasn't enough time. Just as they drew up to the front entrance, when some twenty-five moves had been made, Collins offered Bobby a draw. It was intended as a gentlemanly gesture, but Bobby looked hurt, almost insulted. To him a tie was equivalent to a loss, and he judged his position to be superior. He wanted to fight. Nevertheless, in deference to his mentor, he grudgingly agreed to a draw. He almost sang out his response: *"Okaaay."* Then his mind immediately shifted to what awaited: his favorite Chinese meal of Egg Drop Soup, Chicken Chop Suey, pistachio ice cream, and inevitably, a large glass of milk.

Regina Wender Fischer, Bobby's mother, was born in Switzerland and moved with her family to the United States when she was just two years old. In her late teens—already graduated from college—she traveled to Germany to visit her brother, who was stationed there as a sailor in the U.S. Navy. In Berlin she was hired by the American geneticist Hermann J. Muller (who later won a Nobel Prize in physiology), to act as his secretary and governess for his child. Muller and Regina had met when she took courses at the University of Berlin, and they respected each other: She admired his brilliance and humanism, and he valued her because she knew German, could take shorthand, and was a speed typist. Also, she was bright enough to understand and accurately type his complex chemical and genetic ruminations. Muller encouraged her to study medicine and to follow him to Russia when he received research appointments both in Leningrad and Moscow—she ultimately remained in touch with him for more than fifty years. She became a student at the First Moscow Medical Institute from 1933 to 1938.

There was another person, an associate of Muller's, who also made the journey to Russia. A biophysicist, the associate was then known as Hans Gerhardt Fischer, but he'd changed his name from Leibscher to make it sound less Jewish as anti-Semitism took hold in Germany. Fischer secured a position at the Moscow Brain Institute, and in November 1933 he and Regina, who was then twenty, fell in love and were married in Moscow. A few years after the marriage their daughter Joan was born. With anti-Semitism flourishing in the USSR under Joseph Stalin, the young couple realized they and their infant were in danger. Although Regina had spent six years studying to be a physician, she left before completing her degree, took the baby to Paris, and settled there, working as a teacher of English.

She and Hans Gerhardt had separated before they left Moscow, although they were still legally husband and wife. As it became probable that Germany would soon invade France, Regina, who held American citizenship, arranged to take Joan to the United States, but Hans Gerhardt, who'd moved to Paris to be near his daughter, was a German and therefore wasn't permitted entry into the United States. Facing an uncertain fate, he left Europe and eventually settled in Chile. Regina divorced him for nonsupport in 1945, when she was living in Moscow, Idaho. The coincidence of a marriage and then a divorce both occurring in cities named Moscow was ironic enough to make headlines in local newspapers.

Regina Fischer had no long-term residence during the early 1940s. Rather, she carted Joan from place to place as the United States struggled with the end of the Depression and the country's entry into the Second World War. She and her daughter lived barely above the poverty level. In June 1942, Regina became pregnant with her second child—Bobby—and she sent the five-year-old Joan to St. Louis to stay with Regina's father, Jacob Wender, during her pregnancy. When Bobby was born at the Michael Reese Hospital in Chicago on March 9, 1943, Regina was homeless. She named her newborn Robert James Fischer, and Hans Gerhardt Fischer was listed as the father on the birth certificate, despite the fact that he'd never entered the United States. After spending about a week in the hospital, Regina and her baby moved into the Sarah Hackett Memorial House, a hospice for single mothers who lacked funds to provide for the welfare of themselves or their infants. Once there, Regina called her father and told him to bring Joan back to Chicago to join them, but the hospice refused to provide housing for the older child. When Regina refused to move, she was arrested by an officer of the Chicago Police Department for disturbing the peace, and she, Bobby, and Joan were forced to move out. She waived a jury trial, was ordered to have a psychiatric examination, and was found not guilty by a judge. The psychiatrist's bizarre report stated that Regina had a "stilted (paranoid) personality, querulous, but not psychotic." She immediately landed a job as a typist for the Montgomery Ward company and moved to an inexpensive one-room flat on the South Side of Chicago—2840 South Lake Park Avenue, Bobby Fischer's address during the first weeks of his life.

As Regina struggled to raise her children as a single parent, she begged for money from Jewish welfare agencies and other social institutions, from her father, Jacob Wender, and from anyone else whom she felt she could approach. Money was forthcoming, but it was never enough and it came too slowly. Always struggling financially and without support from a husband, Regina, during the war years, went wherever she could find work. One of Bobby's first memories, when he was just a toddler, was of living in a trailer "out west." "Out west" could have meant California, Idaho, Oregon, Illinois, or Arizona. The family lived in all of those places before moving to New York. Regina's flexibility and desperation led her to a surprising gamut of jobs. She was a welder, schoolteacher, riveter, farm worker, toxicologist's assistant, and stenographer, all throughout the early and mid-1940s.

Six-year-old Bobby studied the maze. His effort lasted only a few seconds. He lifted his stubby number-2 yellow pencil and began to trace the route to a damsel imprisoned in a castle cell in the puzzle's center. To rescue her, the knight, armed with a lance, would have to determine the proper starting point to get to the damsel, and then move her from her prison to the concluding space without crossing a line. At first, Bobby entered the maze at the top right corner. Working his way hurriedly through the alleys, circles, roundabouts, and barriers, he found himself trapped in a dead end, deadlocked and defeated.

He quickly erased his work, put down his pencil, and studied the problem before him, deciding that if he began the journey at a different corner of the puzzle, he might find access to the damsel's cell. He let his eyes examine each of the remaining starting-point possibilities—top left, bottom left, and bottom right—and then, in a form of backward reasoning, tracked the path from the princess to the knight. After several minutes, he saw that there was one path and one path only that led to the maiden—starting at bottom left. Now understanding the maze's algorithm, he took up his pencil again, cut though the Gordian knot, and completed the task.

His next task, to get to the treasure left by a gold miner in a more intricate and difficult maze, at first defeated him when he tried to solve it prematurely, without sufficient study. He flung his pencil down in frustration and grabbed a brown crayon, but this time he paused. Soon the answer became clear, and he felt silly that he hadn't seen the solution immediately. "Look, Joanie!" he said proudly to his eleven-year-old sister. She nodded in approval.

Parcheesi was a game that held Bobby's interest for a while. He liked moving his tiger and elephant pawns through his opponent's blockades, but he became furious if, owing to a toss of the dice, he was captured and sent back to "Start." Other board games, such as Trouble and Sorry, were also problematic: If a touch of bad luck stymied his plans, he became angry and would abandon the game. Ultimately, he rejected all games of chance.

To keep rambunctious Bobby occupied—in today's parlance he might be referred to as hyperactive—Regina bought books such as *50 Peppy Picture Puzzles for Girls and Boys*, and *Pencil Puzzles: Sharpen Your Pencil, Sharpen Your Wits*, which contained mazes, picture puzzles, and word games. Bobby would always go first to the mazes. Later, he became enamored of Japanese interlocking puzzles and dimensional wooden puzzles shaped in the form of an automobile or an animal. He would disassemble the fifteen or so pieces and spread them at random on the table or floor, then see how fast he could reassemble them. Speed of accomplishment was as important to him as solving the puzzles' mystery.

In early 1949 Regina Fischer took the least expensive housing she could find when she moved the family—Bobby, Joan, and herself—to East 13th Street in Manhattan, facing the kitchen back entrance of the famed Luchow's restaurant, where many of the best chess players would occasionally dine. The Fischers could never afford to eat there. The apartment's entrance was marred by a rusty fire escape running up the front, and there was only one small bedroom—but the rent was $45 a month.

Located downstairs on the same street was what is known in New York City as a "candy store." The small shop sold newspapers, magazines, toys, games, ice cream, sundries, and of course, candy. In March of 1949, on a rainy day when Bobby had just turned six, his sister, Joan, looking for yet another game to amuse or occupy her restless little brother, bought a plastic chess set for $1 at the candy store. The hollow pieces were barely taller than an inch, and the set came with a folding cardboard chessboard that had red and black squares. Neither Joan nor Bobby had ever seen a chess set before, but they followed instructions printed on the inside of the top of the box, with Joan acting as instructor even as she figured out the rules for herself. After describing which piece was which by name, the rules went on to explain the intricacies of how each piece moved: "The Queen moves as many squares in any direction as is possible, the Knight moves in an L shape and can jump over other pieces or pawns," etc. Only a few other rudimentary hints were offered, such as that white should move first, and the object of the game was to checkmate, but not actually capture, the king.

"Nobody we knew ever played chess and we never saw anyone playing it," Fischer would later write. It's impossible to say with certainty whether Bobby actually won the first game he played, but it's likely he did, given his propensity for solving puzzles quickly and the fact that his first opponent was his sister, who didn't particularly take to chess. "At first it was just another game," remembered Bobby, "just a little more complicated." Joan, tied to her homework—she was an honor student—quickly became uninterested in chess and didn't have time for it, so Bobby taught his mother the moves. Bobby said later: "She was too busy to take the game seriously. For example, she'd try to peel potatoes or sew up a hole while she was playing, which, of course, annoyed me very much. After I'd beat her, I'd turn the board around and go on playing her side until I beat her a second time. Both of us got tired of this, and I was looking for someone to play chess with all the time."

That six-year-old Bobby was beating thirty-six-year-old Regina and eleven-year-old Joan, as brilliant as both were, is significant in understanding his rapidly evolving mastery of chess, and himself. It gave the boy confidence and built his self-esteem. The problem was that neither mother nor sister ever really wanted to play. "My mother has an anti-talent for chess," Bobby once told an interviewer. "She's hopeless."

Since Bobby couldn't find a worthy opponent, or *any* opponent for that matter, he made himself his principal adversary. Setting up the men on his tiny board, he'd play game after game alone, first assuming the white side and then spinning the board around, with some pieces often tumbling onto the floor. He'd scramble after them, place them quickly back on their squares, and then play the black side. Trying to outwit himself required an unusual turn of mind. Black, for example, knew what white was going to do, and vice versa, because black *was* Fischer and so was white. So the only way the game made any sense to Bobby was to study the board anew after every single move, pretending he was playing a real opponent. He tried to forget what he'd just planned to do when he was playing the other side. Instead, he sought to discover any trap or pitfall lurking in his "opponent's" position and respond accordingly. To some, such a regimen might seem simplistic or maddening, even schizophrenic. However, it did give Bobby a sense of the board, the movement and role of the pieces, and the choreography of how a game of chess could develop. "Eventually I would checkmate the other guy," he chuckled when he described the experience years later.

In the fall of 1950, Regina moved the family out of Manhattan and across the bridge to Brooklyn, where she rented an inexpensive apartment near the intersection of Union and Franklin streets. It was only temporary: She was trying to get closer to a better neighborhood. Robbed of her medical degree in Russia because of the war, she was now determined to acquire a nursing diploma. As soon as she enrolled in the Prospect Heights School for Nursing, the peripatetic Fischer family, citizens of nowhere, moved once again—its tenth transit in six years—to a $52-a-month two-bedroom flat at 560 Lincoln Place in Brooklyn. Never shy about asking for what she or her children needed, Regina recruited neighbors to help her transport, box by box, the family's sparse belongings across Eastern Parkway a few blocks, to what she expected would be a somewhat more lasting home. Though the small apartment was a third-floor walkup, its proximity to the nursing school enabled Regina to look after her children while attending classes. Bobby and Joan each had a room to themselves, and Regina slept in the living room on what was called a daybed. This apartment was also in a better neighborhood. Flatbush was middle-class Jewish, beginning to be populated by other ethnic minorities, and in closer walking distance to lush Prospect Park and the Botanical Gardens, as well as one of the city's finest libraries, at Grand Army Plaza.

Bobby, then seven years old, hated his new environs. When cold or rainy weather forced him inside, he could find no place to play in the building, and even on nicer days Regina showed a reluctance to let her son play in the streets unsupervised. Occasionally, Bobby and another boy who lived in the building would rush up and down the stairwells and landings, playing tag, but they were chastised so often by the landlord that an embargo on any kind of noisy physical activity was handed down in writing by the building's management. Bobby loved to climb onto his bed and then jump off to see how far away he could land. Farther and farther he'd soar, making note of his progress. The tenants downstairs complained of the banging noise coming through the ceiling, and bed-to-floor leaping was declared off-limits as well. When Bobby got older and started doing calisthenics, management objected to that, too. Years later Bobby commented, "If anyone asked me what I owe my [interest in] chessplaying to, I could say it was the landlord."

Bobby grudgingly tolerated being in the care of Joan, five years his senior, whenever his mother was at school or work. Regina was constantly active, working as a stenographer on those days that she had no nursing classes. During the times she had no work, she collected an unemployment check of $22 a week. She was intensely involved in political activities as well, but she always saw to it that when Bobby was little there was food to eat and that someone—Joan, a neighbor, a friend—watched over her son.

Regina knew that Bobby was intellectually gifted, but at first she didn't considered him a "prodigy." Certainly, he could figure out some things faster than she could. He quickly saw patterns and analogies that helped him jump to reasoned conclusions, such as figuring out that if a bank was closed on one street because of a holiday, then a bank on another street would likely be closed too.

The problem with Bobby was a social one: From a very early age he followed his own rhythms, which were often antithetical to how other children developed. An intense stubbornness seemed to be his distinguishing feature. He was capable of ranting if he didn't get his way—about foods he did or didn't like, or when to go to bed (he liked to stay up late), or when to go out or stay home. At first Regina could handle him, but by the time Bobby reached six, he was dictating policy about his own regimen. Bobby wanted to do what *he* wanted to do—and to choose when, where, and how to do it.

"When he was seven," Joan said in an interview, "Bobby could discuss concepts like infinity, or do all kinds of trick math problems, but ask him to multiply two plus two and he would probably get it wrong." Although this was likely an exaggeration, it's clear that Bobby hated memorizing things that failed to engage his interest, and multiplication tables fell into that category. The story that he could understand number theory and the complexity of prime numbers and their infinite results but not perform simple multiplication is analogous to the myth of Einstein not being able to do his own income tax.

Regina visited guidance centers and agencies for gifted children, sometimes alone and sometimes with Bobby in tow, to determine whether they could offer tips for getting her son through school and helping him connect with other children. Of primary importance to her was education. She felt that Joan was being intellectually stimulated at home, but that the creative ferment she always attempted to foster was having little effect on Bobby. He took no interest in the stacks of books that Regina, an avid reader, always had in the house. She was a college graduate, almost a medical doctor but without the degree, a former teacher and a perpetual student, and her home was a gathering place for the intelligentsia she'd meet at school or through her political groups. At night and on weekends, there were often lively discussions around her kitchen table, sometimes with friends—mostly Jewish intellectuals. The subjects often revolved around politics, ideas, and cultural issues. Arguments raged over Palestine and Israel and the possibility that Eisenhower might run for president. When within a month two great educators, Maria Montessori and John Dewey, died, the talk was of writing and advanced reading skills and whether they were good for the very young. Bobby and Joan were present, but though Bobby may have absorbed some of what was said, he never participated. Years later, he blurted out that he'd "hated" all of that kind of talk.

From the time he was six until he was about twelve, Bobby spent almost every summer at camp somewhere in the tri-state area around New York City. That first or second summer, at a camp in Patchogue, Long Island, he found a book of annotated chess games. When he was pushed to remember the book's title some fifteen years later, Bobby said that it *might* have been *Tarrasch's Best Games of Chess*. He then named Siegbert Tarrasch, a German player, as "one of the ten greatest masters of all time." Whatever the book was, Bobby figured out how to follow the games, which were presented move by move using descriptive chess notations (e.g., P–K4 for "Pawn to King Four").

The rest of camp was occasionally fun. Bobby rode a horse named Chub, played with a black-and-white calf, engaged in an occasional softball game, and made a boat in the arts-and-crafts class—but he still couldn't relate to the other children. After a full month away, using one of the pre-addressed and stamped postcards given to him by Regina, he issued a plaintive appeal in large block letters: MOMMY I WANT TO COME HOME.

Soon after, Bobby forgot about chess for a while. Other games and puzzles entered the household, and the chess set, with some pawns missing, was stored in a closet. After about a year, however, chess reentered his mind. In the winter of 1950, when he was seven years old, he asked Regina if she'd buy him another, larger chess set for Christmas. She bought him a smallish, unweighted wooden set that was housed in a sliding, unvarnished wooden box. Although Bobby immediately opened his gift, he didn't touch it for about a month. He had no one to play with.

He was often alone. When he came home from school, it was usually to an empty apartment. His mother was at work during the days and sometimes in the evenings, and his sister was generally busy in school until later in the afternoon. Though Regina was concerned about her son, the simple truth was that Bobby was a latchkey child who craved but was not given the maternal presence that might have helped him develop a sense of security. Moreover, Regina's financial circumstances had caused the family to move so frequently that Bobby never gained a sense of "neighborhood." And it didn't help that there was no father present.

Regina tried giving her son the approval that every child needs, and the wings to find himself, by encouraging him to engage in sports, take part in family excursions, and do better in school. But as time went on, Bobby just kept journeying more and more into himself, once again reading chess books and playing over games from the past. The possibilities of chess somehow made his essential loneliness and insecurity less painful.

Regina believed that she could learn and excel at anything, except perhaps chess, and that her children also had the capacity to master anything. The social workers that she confided in invariably suggested that she enroll Bobby in a small private school where he could receive closer attention and where he could develop at his own pace. Money was always an issue for her though, and she couldn't afford to enroll him in a school that demanded tuition. She received no child payment or alimony from Hans Gerhardt Fischer, but she did receive occasional checks for $20—not totally insignificant in those years—that arrived sporadically but often weekly, sent by Paul Nemenyi— like Gerhardt Fischer, a physicist. Nemenyi was a friend whom Regina had first met when she was a student at the University of Colorado in Denver and then later reconnected with in Chicago. He may have been Bobby's biological father. The patrimony has never been proven one way or the other. Regina not only denied that Nemenyi was Bobby's father, but once stated for the record to a social worker that she'd traveled to Mexico in June 1942 to meet her ex-husband Hans Gerhardt, and that Bobby was conceived during that rendezvous. However, a distant relative of Bobby's suggested that the reason Regina listed Hans Gerhardt as the father on Bobby's birth certificate was that she didn't want Bobby to be known as a bastard. "It *does* appear that Paul Nemenyi was the real father," the relative said. It's also possible that Regina didn't know who Bobby's father was if she was having an affair with Nemenyi around the time the Mexican assignation with Gerhardt Fischer occurred.

In an attempt to find other boys who might want to play with Bobby, Regina wrote to the chess editor of the *Brooklyn Eagle* to see if he knew of any seven-year-old players. She referred to her son as "my little chess miracle." The editor, Hermann Helms, a great old chess master, replied that she should bring Bobby to the Grand Army Plaza library on a particular Thursday evening in January 1951, so that the boy could play in a simultaneous exhibition to be given by several chess masters.

Normally, a simultaneous exhibition is given by *one* master who walks from board to board, competing against multiple players. The boards are arranged in the shape of a square or horseshoe. When the master reaches each of the boards, the player makes his move and the master responds before quickly moving to the next board.

Bobby, accompanied by his mother, entered the high-ceilinged rotunda of the Grand Army Plaza library and was momentarily surprised by what he saw. Circling the room were locked glass cases displaying unusual and historic chess sets, loaned to the library from private collectors for the occasion. The cases also contained a variety of popular chess books and some incunabula printed in German. There was a ceramic set of chessmen inspired by Tenniel's illustrations of *Alice's Adventures in Wonderland;* two sets from displaced persons' camps, one carved by hand and another made of woven straw; each set had taken more than five hundred hours of work to produce; and a set from Guatemala that was reminiscent of pre–Spanish New World architecture. This was all quite fascinating for the general spectator, but Bobby Fischer hadn't come to look at chess sets. "They did not interest me too much," he remembered. He'd come to play.

On that evening masters were performing in rotation, one playing for about an hour, followed by another who'd take his place. When Bobby sat down to play with his own new wooden set, the master who came to his board was Max Pavey, a thirty-two-year-old radiologist who'd been champion of both Scotland and New York State and who was playing at the top of his form. Pavey was the first master Bobby ever played. It's also likely this was his first serious game of chess against a player with tutored expertise. What was occurring at that moment was analogous to a seven-year-old playing a few games of tennis with his peers, then taking to the court against a still-active John McEnroe.

A crowd of spectators gathered around the board as the diminutive Bobby faced the self-assured, tweed-jacketed Max Pavey. The boy was so serious about what he was doing that the game attracted more and more onlookers. He kneeled on his chair to get a more panoramic view of the pieces.

Bobby remembered his experience in solving puzzles. He must not move too quickly; he knew that the solution was there waiting to be found, if only he had time, time, more time. Pavey, who excelled at playing rapidly—he'd recently captured the title of U.S. Speed Chess Champion—seemed to zoom around the room hardly studying the other boards as he made his moves, returning to Bobby's game in such a short time that the child couldn't calculate as deeply or as carefully as he wanted. That night there were only eight players, making it more difficult for each to contend with the master than if there'd been scores of players, who would have slowed Pavey's progress.

The master was much too strong. In about fifteen minutes, puffing on his pipe, Pavey captured Bobby's queen, thereby ending the game. He graciously offered his hand to the boy and with a gentle smile said, "Good game." Bobby stared at the board for a moment. "He crushed me," he said to no one in particular. Then he burst into tears.

Despite his phenomenal memory, Bobby as an adult could never remember the moves of that game with Pavey. A friend's offhand mention that Bobby probably had every expectation of winning his first game against a chess master elicited a strident rebuke: "Of course not!" He did say that Pavey probably had "gone easy" on him and that he was amazed that he'd even lasted a quarter of an hour against him. That he was passionate enough to cry demonstrated his growing intensity concerning the game. Even at seven he didn't consider himself an amateur. He later admitted that the game had a great effect in motivating him.

One spectator at the exhibition that evening was Carmine Nigro, a short, bald man in his early forties; Bobby described him as "cheery."

Nigro studied the Pavey-Fischer game intently. He liked the moves that Bobby was making. They weren't scintillating, but they were sensible ones, especially for a beginner. With the utmost concentration, Bobby seemed to block out everything and everyone around him. When the game concluded, Nigro approached Regina and Bobby and introduced himself as the newly elected president of the Brooklyn Chess Club. He invited Bobby to come to the club on any Tuesday or Friday night. No, there would be no membership dues for the boy, Nigro assured Regina. She took him to the club, which was located in the old Brooklyn Academy of Music, the very next evening.

2

Childhood Obsession

WHEN SEVEN-YEAR-OLD BOBBY, accompanied by his mother, walked into the Brooklyn Chess Club for the first time on a Friday night in January 1951, he was an anomaly. He was, in fact, the first child permitted to enter. Even the appearance of Regina Fischer was unusual: There were no other women present, and at that time there were no female members on the club's roster, as was the case at many other clubs in the United States.

As the new president of the club, Carmine Nigro announced that Bobby was his guest and would be accepted as a member. No one had the temerity to disagree. It was a tradition in many chess clubs, not only in the United States but throughout the world, that children were not to be heard, and certainly not seen. Even Emanuel Lasker, who ultimately became World Chess Champion, was as a child denied membership in his local club in Germany, despite his evident talent.

The Brooklyn Chess Club, established just after the Civil War, was one of the most prestigious in the nation. It was housed in the impressive and stately Brooklyn Academy of Music, where Enrico Caruso and Geraldine Farrar had sung. The club had distinguished itself by competing every year in the Metropolitan Chess League, often defeating dozens of clubs throughout the New York area. Nevertheless, Bobby seemed unafraid of the cigar-smoking adepts hunched over their boards.

The room was quiet except for the occasional rap of a chess piece slammed to the board in anger. At the conclusion of a game, a player might ask, "If I'd played the rook instead of the bishop, what would you have done?" or mutter indignantly, "I overlooked a mating net: You're lucky to get a draw." Invariably, the tones were hushed, even when the speaker was annoyed. Bobby looked on in wonderment, understanding some of the jargon and trying to comprehend the rest.

The problem that developed for Bobby almost instantly that night was more in the minds of his potential opponents. None of the club's veterans wanted to play a boy, especially since Bobby looked to be about five. A chorus of nervous, fretful snickers ran through the high-ceilinged room when it was suggested they "give Bobby a chance." The predominant feeling was: *It's bad enough to lose to a peer, but what if I lose to a seven-year-old? The embarrassment! The loss of reputation!* After coaxing from Nigro, a few of the older players relented and gave Bobby a game or two.

Most were experienced tournament competitors, some even approaching the strength of Max Pavey. As it developed, they had nothing to fear though: Bobby lost every game that night.

Despite his defeats, Bobby kept coming back for more. He became a dedicated member, and a bit of a novelty. The tableau of a little boy engaged in mental combat with a judge, doctor, or college professor some eight or ten times his age was often greeted with mirth and wonder. "At first I used to lose all the time, and I felt bad about it," Bobby said later. He was teased unmercifully by the conquering players. "Fish!" they'd bleat, using the chess player's derisive term for a really weak player, whenever Bobby made an obvious blunder. The epithet hurt even more because of its similarity to his own name. Bobby himself despised the term. Later he'd refer to a poor player as a "weakie"—or, less commonly, a "duffer" or "rabbit."

Nigro, an expert player of near master strength, sensed potential in the boy, and aware that Bobby was without a father, he assumed a mentoring position. He became the boy's teacher and invited him on Saturdays to his home, where he'd match him up with his son Tommy, just a shade younger than Bobby though a slightly better player. Tommy didn't mind playing chess with Bobby, but he didn't want to take lessons from his father. On those teaching days, Nigro would greatly increase his son's allowance if he'd sit still long enough to learn chess tactics.

As soon as Bobby began to understand the basics of chess, Nigro went over specific ways to conduct the part of the game known as the opening, where the first few moves can decide or at least influence the outcome of the contest. These initial moves and "lines" follow well-charted paths that have been chronicled for centuries, and players who want to improve their game attempt to understand and memorize them. Because there are a myriad of such variations, it's difficult for most players to internalize even a small portion. For example, there are 400 different possible positions after two players make one move each, and there are 72,084 positions after two moves each—not all good, it must be added. But Bobby approached with dedication the daunting task of learning many of the substantive ones. Referring to the difficult regimen, he later said, "Mr. Nigro was possibly not the best player in the world but he was a very good teacher. Meeting him was probably a decisive factor in my going ahead in chess."

Nigro had no problem teaching Bobby. The boy could hardly wait for his weekly lesson, and eventually he began to defeat Tommy. "I started going to Mr. Nigro's house on Saturdays," Bobby later wrote, "as well as meeting him on Fridays at the Club. My mother was often on duty on weekends at her job as a nurse, and was glad to have me go [to Mr. Nigro's house]."

In 1952, still not yet turned nine, Bobby made his first entrance into competitive chess. A group of Nigro's protégés won the first match with a score of 5–3; the score of the second match has been lost or forgotten. Auspiciously, Bobby won his first game and drew his second against ten-year-old Raymond Sussman, the son of a dentist, Dr. Harold Sussman, a nationally rated master from Brooklyn. Dr. Sussman was also an amateur photographer, and he captured some portraits of Bobby that worked their way into the Fischer oeuvre years later. Fittingly, Sussman also became Bobby's dentist. "He had a great set of teeth," Sussman remembered.

That summer and fall, Bobby also spent time playing against his grandfather's septuagenarian cousin Jacob Schonberg, who also lived in Brooklyn. Regina would take the boy with her when she nursed Schonberg and Bobby would play his great-cousin as the old man sat in bed. Years later Bobby could not remember how strong Schonberg was or how many games the two played, but one could tell by the inflection in his voice that he was affected by the experience, not so much by the playing of the games, but by the encounter with a family member, however distant. It was a ritual that was all too rare for him.

Carmine Nigro was a professional musician, and taught music in a number of styles. Since Bobby was such a sponge in absorbing the intricacies of chess, Nigro tried to foster in him an interest in music. Since the Fischers didn't own a piano, Nigro began giving Bobby accordion lessons, lending him a somewhat battered "twelve-bass" instrument so he could practice at home. Soon Bobby was playing "Beer Barrel Polka" and other tunes and felt competent enough to give performances at more than one school assembly. After about a year, though, he concluded that the amount of time he was spending practicing the accordion was impinging on his chess studies. "I did fairly well on it for a while," Bobby said, looking back, "but chess had more attraction and the accordion was pushed aside."

Until he was ten, Bobby's regimen was fairly routine: He played at the Brooklyn Chess Club every Friday night, with Regina sitting on the sidelines, reading a book or doing her nursing homework. Late Saturday morning Nigro would pick him up in his car, and if Tommy Nigro was uninterested in playing, which was more often than not, Nigro would drive Bobby to Washington Square Park in Greenwich Village to get the boy some competition at the open-air chess tables. Nigro also had another agenda: At first, Bobby was somewhat of a slow player, and the chess players in the park were just the opposite. Nigro felt they wouldn't tolerate Bobby's sometimes languorous tempo, so he'd be forced to quicken his play and therefore his thinking.

To boost his competitiveness Bobby spent hours after school at the Grand Army Plaza library reading almost every chess book on the shelves. He became such a fixture there, and displayed such seriousness, that a photograph showing him studying appeared in the library's newsletter in 1952 with a caption identifying him. It was the first time that his photograph appeared in print. Within a few months, he found that he could follow the games and the diagrams in the books without the use of a board. If the variations were too complex or lengthy, he'd check the book out, and at home, sitting in front of his chess set, he'd replay the games of past masters, attempting to understand and to memorize how they'd won—or lost.

Bobby read chess literature while he was eating and when he was in bed.

He'd set up his board on a chair next to his bed, and the last thing he did before going to sleep and the first thing he did upon awakening was to look at positions or openings. So many peanut-butter-and-jelly sandwiches, bowls of cereal, and plates of spaghetti were consumed while Bobby was replaying and analyzing games that the crumbs and leavings of his food became encrusted in the crenellated battlements of his rooks, the crosses of his kings, the crowns of his queens, and the creases in the miters of his bishops. And the residue of food was never washed off. Years later, when a chess collector finally took possession of the littered set and cleaned it up, Bobby's reaction was typically indignant: "You've ruined it!"

He even maintained his involvement with the game while bathing. The Fischers didn't have a working shower, just a bathtub, and Bobby, like many young children, needed to be urged to take at least a weekly bath. Regina established a Sunday night ritual of running a bath for him, practically carrying him to the tub. And once he was settled in the water, she'd lay a door from a discarded cabinet across the tub as a sort of tray and then bring in Bobby's chess set, a container of milk, and whatever book he was studying at the time, helping him position them on the board. Bobby soaked sometimes for hours as he became engrossed in the games of the greats, only emerging from the water, prune-like, when Regina insisted.

The neurons of Bobby's brain seemed to absorb the limitations and possibilities of each piece in any given position, storing them for future reference. They remained there, tucked into his memory, deep within a cave of abstract thoughts: information and ideas about pawns and squares to be used, discarded, or ignored—all in perfect cadence and synchronicity. Studying the games of masters from the past and present, Bobby seemed to appropriate and learn from many: the intuitive combinational ability of Rudolf Spielmann, the accumulation of small advantages as demonstrated by Wilhelm Steinitz, the almost mystical technique José Capablanca had of avoiding complications, the deep but beautiful murkiness of Alexander Alekhine. As one chess master said of him: "Bobby virtually inhaled chess literature. He remembered everything and it became part of him." The boy—and then the man—had one salient cognitive goal, although he didn't express it openly: He wanted to *understand*.

He enjoyed playing over what are called miniature games, short encounters of usually twenty moves or less, as if they were musical exercises, works of art unto themselves, usually with only one pervasive idea.

Beginner's books such as *An Invitation to Chess* and other primers were quickly discarded as Bobby then became engrossed in advanced works such as *Practical Chess Openings* and *Basic Chess Endings;* the two volumes of *My Best Games of Chess* by Alexander Alekhine; and a then newly published book, *500 Master Games of Chess.* He was also particularly interested in the collection titled *Morphy's Games of Chess,* which displayed the great player's tactical ingenuity and his adherence to three general principles: rapid development of one's pieces, the importance of occupying or capturing the center squares of the board, and mobility—the necessity of keeping lines, ranks, files, and diagonals open. Bobby absorbed these lessons and would act on them for the rest of his life. He once told master Shelby Lyman that he'd read thousands of chess books and retained the best from each.

It should be stressed that these works wouldn't have been easy to read even for an experienced adult player: They aren't accessible unless a person has the drive to excel in the abstraction of chess. That an eight- or nine-year-old boy had the power of concentration to get through them was highly unusual. That the same boy was able to understand and absorb what he read was nothing short of remarkable. Later, Bobby would increase the degree of difficulty by reading chess books in multiple languages.

In the realm of academics Bobby's level of achievement was more erratic. Aside from summer camps, the first classes Bobby ever attended were at the Brooklyn Jewish Children's School, a kindergarten, where he was taught songs by rote for Hanukkah and Purim, in both English and Yiddish, a language he didn't know. He couldn't relate to the other children. At first, he couldn't figure out the purpose of a dreidel—a four-sided spinning top that's played with during the Jewish holiday of Hanukkah. He didn't like the idea that he had to wear a uniform—a white shirt and pressed pants. And in the restroom he may have seen that his penis was different from the rest: He wasn't circumcised. After a few weeks Regina withdrew him from the school. Although she was Jewish, she wasn't religiously observant; Bobby never had a bris (the circumcision ceremony usually performed on the eighth day after birth for Jewish boys), and he later claimed that he'd received no training in Judaic customs or theology and was never taken to a synagogue for religious purposes. He may have simply failed to recall it.

Attempts by Regina and Joan to engage Bobby in schoolwork were usually fruitless. Bobby could concentrate on puzzles or chess for hours, but he fidgeted and grew restless when confronted with reading, writing, and arithmetic. Attending the Brooklyn public schools was also problematic. He was a loner and invariably separated himself from the other children, possibly because of acute shyness or fear of competition. By the time he reached the fourth grade, he'd been in and out of six schools—almost two a year—leaving each time because he wasn't doing well in his studies or couldn't abide his teachers, classmates, or even the school's location. In frustration, Regina registered Bobby in a school for gifted children. He lasted one day and refused to go back.

Eventually, she found a school that was an appropriate match for her problematic son. In the fall of 1952, when Bobby was nine, Regina secured scholarship enrollment for him in Brooklyn Community Woodward, a progressive grade school of approximately 150 children. Housed in a stately brownstone that had originally been a private home, it was one of the loveliest school buildings in Brooklyn. The school's philosophy of education was based on the principles of Johann Heinrich Pestalozzi, an eighteenth-century Swiss educator who opposed memorization exercises and strict discipline, and concentrated on the individual's development though a series of experimental techniques. The school promoted the concept of *Anschaung,* a personal way of looking at things that was inherent and individual to every child. The seats and desks weren't permanently fixed in place as they were in most schools, and the children were encouraged to forget the distinction between study and play. To learn early American history, for example, students dressed in costumes of the era and were taught how to spin yarn, hook rugs, and use quill pens.

Bobby's way was chess, and what it meant to him. He was already showing talent for the game, and he was accepted by Community Woodward with the understanding that he'd teach the other students to play, and also as a result of his astronomically high IQ test score of 180.

A bright spot in his social and physical development at Community

Woodward occurred when he was chosen to be on the baseball team, and he began to emerge from his shell. He fell in love with the game, could hear the roar of the crowds from nearby Ebbets Field, the home of the Brooklyn Dodgers, while at school or at home, and on class trips attended games at the stadium. He had a knack for fielding and batting, but although he was fast, he wasn't a particularly coordinated runner on the bases. "He incited a great deal of interest in chess here," one of his teachers said later. "He easily beat everybody, including the chess-playing members of the faculty. No matter what he played, whether it was baseball in the yard, or tennis, he had to come out ahead of everybody. If he'd been born next to a swimming pool he would have been a swimming champion. It just turned out to be chess."

One day Bobby bounded up the three flights of stairs to the safety of his home, only to find it empty. Joan was still in school, staying late for the Biology Club; Regina was in a nursing class, to be followed by library work and then a night shift after that. He found a note, penned in a small, blue spiral-bound pad, propped up on a chair in the kitchen:

> *Dear Bobby—Finish off the soup and rice. Milk in refrig. I may get back after 3 to drop off groceries, and will then go back to study. Love, M.*

Being alone in the apartment was the default position of Bobby's life from the time that Regina felt her son could be left by himself without supervision, and this persistent solitude might well have been a catalyst for his deeper involvement in chess. As he sat in front of the chessboard, often at the kitchen table, with a chess book spread open, the pieces became his companions, the book his mentor. Neither the loneliness nor the learning was easy for him, however. He would have liked to have had a friend, some other boy that he could play and share adventures with, but since chess was already occupying most of his time, interest, and thoughts, that potential friend would have had to not only know how to play chess but play it well enough to engage Bobby's attention and loyalty.

A certain compulsion forced him to continue to search for the secrets of the chessboard, and this preoccupation commanded his attention for hours on end. He was happy when the glare of the winter light ceased to pierce the broken shade of the kitchen window; it interfered with his thinking. When his sister Joanie or mother Geenie—as they were known by their friends—would come home in the late afternoon or early evening, they'd sometimes find Bobby in the dusk of the apartment, unaware or not caring that the lamps were unlit, staring at the board and lost in a reverie of tactics or strategies.

Even though Regina felt Bobby was fairly independent, she was worried that he was home alone too much, and she had been seeking someone to childsit for him, to be sort of a companion. Money was a problem: Even a token payment to a caretaker was difficult to raise. So she had placed the following advertisement in the campus newspaper of Brooklyn College, not far from the Fischer home:

Baby sitter wanted for schoolboy, 8½. Evenings, some weekends, in exchange for room, kitchen privileges. Sterling 3-4110 7 to 9PM.

A young math student replied—he even knew how to play chess—but for unknown reasons he didn't take the job. Bobby remained alone.

Unlike Joan, Bobby seemed to have little interest in school, and whenever Regina helped him with his homework he typically gave it short shrift, impatient to go back to chess. She had great difficulty coping with his imperiousness: "I want to play *chess*!" he'd demand, with all the pomposity of a crown prince talking to a servant. And off he'd go to his chessboard, without his mother's permission, leaving his school assignments in abeyance.

It's not that Bobby rejected the studiousness displayed by his sister and mother. Rather, he was bent on the acquisition of another skill: chess. The difference was that it was more important to him to study how to win with rook and pawn than to learn the three branches of government or where to move the decimal point in long division. The three Fischers, prototypes of Talmudic scholars, were always studying: Joan her textbooks; Regina her medical tomes; and Bobby the latest chess periodical. The apartment was often as silent as a library.

One of Bobby's few non-chess interests emerged unexpectedly during his eighth year in the summer of 1951, when Regina sent him to the Venderveer

Nursery School, a day camp in Brooklyn. Despite its name, the school accepted older children for its summer camp, and the program provided a place for Bobby to go once the school year ended. Either Regina or Joan would drop him off in the morning and fetch him in the late afternoon. Bobby fully expected to hate the camp—or at least dislike it—but he found that he enjoyed many of the physical activities it offered. Most important to him was Venderveer's large outdoor pool, where he learned to swim.

Thereafter every summer, when he was in one of the camps he attended and when he wasn't studying chess, Bobby would train to take various Red Cross swimming tests, easily qualifying as an "Intermediate" and then "Advanced" swimmer. A true Piscean, he loved the water, especially if swimming meant competing with the other children in races. He was fast, determined, and alert, and the instant the swimming coach blew the whistle Bobby would kick off, often landing in the water when the other swimmers were still in mid-dive. Swimming gave him the chance to move and exercise his body, to uncramp it from the stiffening stillness of sitting with a chessboard or a book. He discovered that he loved moving through the water, and he found that he loved competition itself, whether swimming or playing chess. There seemed to be virtually nothing else he enjoyed doing.

Regina began to fear for Bobby's future if he didn't take his schoolwork seriously. More than that, she was worried that his interest in chess was becoming obsessive. She believed he was so engrossed in the game that he was never quite in touch with the reality around him, so addicted to chess that he would not—could not—control it, and that eventually, because of the exclusion of everything else, this accidental interest might ruin his life.

For Regina, discussing Bobby's overcommitment to chess with Nigro was a hopeless endeavor. If anything, Nigro was constantly encouraging him to play more, to study, to enter tournaments. Bobby became Nigro's protégé and chess companion. A caring man who was aware of Regina's strained financial state, he never charged her for the lessons he gave Bobby, whether chess or music. Nigro and Bobby began to play clocked games together, at two hours each—the official speed of tournament chess—and with each encounter Bobby seemed to become stronger, which made him study even more, until he was beating Nigro in the majority of games.

Much to Bobby's consternation, Regina insisted that he have a psychological evaluation to determine whether something could or should be done to temper his relentless preoccupation with the game. When she brought the boy to Dr. Harold Kline at the Children's Psychiatric Division of the Brooklyn Jewish Hospital, Bobby was less than cooperative. Sensing this, Dr. Kline didn't give him any of the battery of personality, intelligence, or interest tests usually used to assess a child. He simply talked to the boy. "I don't know," said Bobby sullenly, when asked why he spent so much time playing chess and not on his schoolwork. "I just go for it." With just a word of advice to Bobby about not neglecting his schoolwork, he asked the boy to step outside. Dr. Kline told Regina that she shouldn't worry about Bobby, that children often became intrigued, virtually obsessed, with games, toys, sports, and other things, and that after a while they either lose interest or step away from such heavy involvement. No, he didn't think that Bobby was neurotic, and he didn't recommend therapy. "Neurotic" was a word that really explained nothing, he added, pointing out that Bobby was not hurting himself or others, chess was probably stretching his mind, and she should allow him to play as often as he liked. Her son's resistance to schoolwork was a mild disorder that many children go through, but his study of chess, an intellectual activity, was supplanting it. Perhaps, he added, she could fashion some of his schoolwork as a sort of game, which might pique his interest.

Not fully comforted, Regina sought a second opinion. She learned of a psychiatrist who was a chess master, Dr. Ariel Mengarini, a nonanalytic neuropsychiatrist who worked for the government. Mengarini was so in love with chess that he identified with Bobby's passion. He confessed to Regina his own fanaticism for the game and also something else she didn't want to hear about Bobby: "I told her that I could think of a lot worse things than chess that a person could devote himself to and that she should let him find his way."

Gradually, Bobby's performance at the Brooklyn Chess Club began to improve. It took him a few difficult and sometimes discouraging years, but eventually he was winning the majority of his games. For their part, his opponents were impressed with his tenacity and clear signs of progress. "I'd already gone through most of the books in the public library near us and was beginning to want chess books of my own," Bobby said later, reflecting back on the period. Nigro gave or loaned him books, and Regina permitted him to purchase a book now and then, whenever she had some spare cash. Bobby's allowance of 32 cents a day didn't afford him much of an opportunity to buy books—and even as he grew older and his per diem was raised to 40 and then 60 cents, the money was spent on chocolate milk for lunch and a candy bar after school.

Whenever Nigro was finished reading his copies of *Chess Review* and *Chess Life,* he gave them to Bobby, who became fascinated with both periodicals, not only for their multitude of engaging and instructive games and descriptions, but because they gave him the chance to read about the great champions in chess. Sitting with those magazines, it was as if he were studying the chess equivalent of Plutarch's lives of the Roman generals or Vasari's lives of the artists. Quite simply, they inspired.

Then, in the summer of 1954, Bobby had an opportunity to see in action some of the greats he'd been reading about. It turned out that the Soviet team would be playing for the first time on United States soil.

In that era of anti-Communist hysteria, when anyone in America who read Karl Marx's *Das Kapital* or wore a red tie was thought to be a Communist, the president of the U.S. Chess Federation, Harold M. Phillips, a lawyer who'd defended Morton Sobell in the Rosenberg espionage case, confided almost with relish that he expected to be called in front of Senator McCarthy's House Un-American Activities Committee hearings and accused of being a Communist simply because he'd tendered the chess invitation to the Russians. It never happened.

It's important to stress the difference between Soviet and American chess teams at that time. The Soviets were all not just professional players, but grandmasters, the designation given to the highest-rated chess masters who have distinguished themselves in international tournaments. Tsar Nicholas II originally bestowed the title in 1914; it was being used in 1954 and is still awarded today.

The Soviet players were subsidized by their government and in many cases given dachas as retreats where they could study and train for matches. Back then, these grandmasters commanded as much prestige in Soviet society as a movie star or an Olympic athlete does in contemporary America. When Mikhail Botvinnik, who became World Chess Champion, arrived at the Bolshoi Opera House, he was given a standing ovation. In the mid-fifties, the Soviet Chess Federation had four million members, and playing chess wasn't just required in elementary schools but compulsory in after-school activities; youngsters who possessed talent were given special training, often working one-on-one with grandmasters who were tapped to groom the next generation of world beaters. One Soviet tournament registered more than seven hundred thousand players. In the USSR, the playing of chess was considered more than just a national policy. It was deeply ingrained in the culture, and it seemed that everyone—man, woman, and child; farmer, civil servant, or doctor—played chess. The impending clash between the Soviets and the Americans thus had Cold War implications.

Three days before the match an editorial in *The New York Times* observed: "It has become painfully obvious to their opponents that the Russians bring to the chessboard all the fervor, skill and manifest devotion to their cause that Foreign Minister Molotov brings to the diplomatic conference. They are out to win for the greater glory of the Soviet Union. To do so means public acclaim at home, propaganda victories abroad." Chess was not merely a game to the Soviets; it was war, and not as cold as might have been thought.

The U.S. Chess Federation then had only three thousand members, no national program to promote chess or train children, and only boasted one grandmaster, Samuel Reshevsky. His status netted him a grand total of $200 a month, a stipend meted out by a few admiring patrons. In addition, he made approximately $7,500 a year giving exhibitions and lectures. It was falsely rumored that he didn't even own a chess set.

In many ways the looming match was analogous to a team of National Basketball Association all-stars playing a college team. There was always the possibility that the collegians would win, but statistically their chances would be much lower than a thousand to one.

On Wednesday, June 16, Bobby, wearing a short-sleeved polo shirt, arrived at the Roosevelt Hotel escorted by Nigro, to witness the first round of the historic match. It was the first time the boy had ever been in a hotel, and he looked up at the large clock at the head of the stairs, then noticed some familiar faces entering the Grand Ballroom. He recognized various members of the Brooklyn Chess Club and also a few regulars from Washington Square

Park. He dutifully took his seat in the auditorium, as though he were at the Academy Awards of chess, scanning the stage "wide-eyed with amazement," as Nigro noted.

On the stage, in front of a velvet curtain, were two flags: the Stars and Stripes and the unmistakable and portentous crimson Soviet banner with its hammer and sickle. Beneath them, spanning the breadth of the stage, were eight demonstration boards, where the moves of the games were to be displayed. The eight tables, with chess sets and boards, were at the ready for the players. There were eleven hundred spectators, more than for any previous chess event in U.S. history.

And then there were the players, gathering onstage, waiting for the signal from the referee to take their places and commence their games. Soviet player David Bronstein asked for a glass of lemon juice—no, not lemonade, but real lemon juice, he insisted—which he downed in what looked like one gulp. Someone remarked that the Americans looked nervous, as indeed they should have: Aside from their previous two defeats to remind them of the odds against victory, there was the Soviets' recent routing of the Argentine team in Buenos Aires and the French team in Paris. Donald Byrne, the United States Open champion, said he was so on edge that he spent the entire day before the match trying not to think of chess, reading the romantic prose of Nathaniel Hawthorne.

Eventually, after some speech making about the contribution of chess toward a possible détente between the Soviet Union and the United States, play got under way. Nigro noted with proud amusement that his protégé was watching carefully and absorbing everything he could.

Did Bobby fully comprehend the political implications of the match? Did feelings of patriotism surge within him and was he rooting hard for his country to win? Did he wish—dream—that one day he'd be up on a similar stage playing against the world's finest players? He never made a statement about the match, but it's likely that the answer to at least the latter question was yes.

Aside from the games themselves, which he followed assiduously, Bobby noticed other things: chess players congregating in all the corridors and public rooms of the hotel discussing and analyzing the games, chess books and portable sets at the ready, and many people leaving observation posts only briefly to buy tuna fish and ham-and-cheese sandwiches at a small newsstand in the lobby. When Bobby spotted Reuben Fine—perhaps America's second strongest player—in the audience, he became especially excited, since Fine's books had become almost chess bibles for Bobby. Dr. Fine wasn't playing for the United States because he had retired from play in 1948. But there was Dr. Max Pavey up on the stage—the man Bobby had played in a simultaneous exhibition three years previously—ready to play for his country.

When Nigro introduced Bobby to writer Murray Shumach of *The New York Times,* the boy shied away and just looked down at his shoes. Allen Kaufman, a master player, also met Bobby for the first time that day and more than a half century later reminisced: "He seemed to be a nice kid, somewhat shy, and I had no idea that I was talking to a future World Champion." The next day, Shumach wrote humorously of the assembled onlookers at the match: "Chess spectators are like Dodger fans with laryngitis—men with rampant emotions but muted voices."

Not *totally* voiceless, as it developed. As the games became more complex, the spectators, many of whom followed each game with their tiny pocket sets or leather chess wallets, discussed the vagaries of the positions in whispers. The cumulative effect of the sound was that of a mild winter wind or the roll of a summer surf. At times, when a dubious or complex combination was played, or when the diminutive American Reshevsky took one hour and ten minutes *on one move,* twenty-two hundred eyebrows seemed to rise in unison. If the noise in the hall became too intrusive, Hans Kmoch, the ultra-formal bow-tied referee, would stare angrily out at the audience and issue a stern, Dutch-accented *"Quiet, please!"* Stung by the rebuke, the spectators would look momentarily embarrassed and quiet down for a few minutes.

Bobby enjoyed being in the hall, and kept a scorecard as if he were at Ebbets Field. The eleven-year-old carefully penciled in the results for each game: zeroes for losses, ones for wins, and halves for draws. He attended all four rounds, unaware that in just a few short years he'd be facing, in separate tournaments and matches on different continents, fourteen of these same sixteen players from the United States and the USSR, a conglomeration of the finest players in the world.

Aside from following the action in the ballroom, Bobby liked the analysis room. There, out of earshot of the contestants, top players were discussing and analyzing in depth every game, move by move, as it was played. Bobby wasn't confident enough to offer an opinion as to what move a player should or shouldn't make, but he was delighted that he could predict some of the moves before they were made and could understand after the fact why others were played.

Finally, after four days of play, the United States team had taken a humiliating beating, falling to the Soviets 20–12. At the final round, the applause from the American audience appeared to be sincere and respectful, but privately, a plaintive cry went up among many of the chess players: "What's wrong with American chess?" An editorial in *Chess Life* lamented the loss of the vanquished team and tried to explain it: "Once again in the USA vs. USSR Team Match we behold reiterated proof that the gifted amateur is rarely, if ever, the equal of the professional. No matter how talented by natural heritage, the amateur lacks that sometimes brutal precision that marks the top professional as master of his trade, that almost instinctive pre-vision which comes only from constant practice of the art under all conditions and against all sorts of opposition." With heavy hearts, Nigro and Bobby rode the subway home to Brooklyn. If Bobby took anything away from that match, it was the knowledge that the Soviet players were the best in the world. It was a realization that made him fairly seethe with purpose.

The following year, in July 1955, a return match in Moscow was even more distorted in favor of the Soviets: The Americans lost again, this time 25–7. Banner headlines in newspapers across the globe ballyhooed the match, however, and the American players had their picture splashed across the front page of *The New York Times,* as well as other newspapers throughout the world. The amount of ink was attributable to the fact that Nikita Khrushchev and Nikolai Bulganin paid a surprise visit to a garden party held in Moscow for the American chess team. There Khrushchev issued a policy statement to the effect that the Soviet Union was solid as never before, and he was willing to pursue détente between both countries as long as the United States agreed to talk "honestly."

During that same summer of the Americans' annihilation by the Soviets, Bobby Fischer, now twelve, was engaged in his own battles on the board, playing in a tournament in Greenwich Village. The scene at the outdoor chess tables in Washington Square Park was a mélange of urban vitality and color. In contrast to the subdued, almost meditative pairings at the Brooklyn Chess Club, the park's contests were waged by a fast-talking and disparate group of chess hustlers, Village bohemians, and tournament-strength players who enjoyed competing in the open air, sometimes from sunup to sundown. Intriguingly, the chess tables crossed class barriers: One might find Wall Street bankers playing against homeless men from Skid Row, or Ivy Leaguers facing down high school dropouts. As for the park itself, it was an American version of a Middle Eastern bazaar, with folk singers, storytellers, beggars, political dissidents, soapbox orators, and even the occasional snake charmer. The "anything goes" atmosphere encouraged audacity and inventiveness.

Despite the park's nonconformity, during the 1950s organized tournaments and other games were played there almost every day, even in winter, with players wrapped in mufflers and hats, awkwardly moving their pieces with gloved hands. "At first I couldn't get a game," Bobby said, looking back on his days at the park. "The players were all adults, mostly old men in fact, and didn't care to waste their time on a boy. Mr. Nigro introduced me around and when I got better it was easier to get a game." Bobby's recollection of a homogenous cast of "old men" was probably skewed by his child's perspective at the time. In reality, the tables were populated by players of all ages; there just weren't many children as young as him.

In the park in those days chess clocks to time the games weren't often used, but a form of speed chess called "blitz" (the German word for "lightning") was quite popular. In this variation, players had to move immediately as soon as an opponent made his move. If a player didn't respond after more than a few seconds, the opponent—or a designated timekeeper—would shout "Move!" and if the demand wasn't complied with, that player would lose the game. Many shouts of "Move!" could be heard on any given day in the park. Bobby played this form of chess at Nigro's insistence and wasn't particularly good at it, but it did quicken his appraisal of the position at hand and forced him to trust his instincts.

As Bobby's participation in the summer of 1955 Washington Square Park tournament got under way, he took his place on a wooden bench and began moving his pieces on the stone tables embedded with lightly colored red and gray squares. As soon as the action on the board began to grow tense or complicated, the boy would grow more pensive and often have to kneel on the bench to get a better perspective. Pink and white petals from late-blooming cherry trees would occasionally float down onto the board, and some would gently land on his head. Dog owners out for a stroll would continuously pass by, pulling on leashes and calling out commands to keep their animals from scurrying under the tables and sniffing the ankles and shoes of the players. Kibitzers, always free with mostly unwanted advice, would often have to be chased away by the tournament organizer José Calderon.

During the games, Nigro would ritually head off for a few minutes to a nearby restaurant and return with a hamburger, French fries, and a chocolate milk shake for Bobby, who'd consume the lunch absentmindedly, his eyes always on the board. Bystanders commented softly to Nigro on how steadfast and serious the boy appeared. Once, thirty minutes after his lunch, Bobby, unaware that he'd already eaten, whispered, "Mr. Nigro, when is the food coming?"

The 1955 Washington Square tournament included sixty-six players of all different strengths and talents. Since the entry fee was only 10 cents (the $6.60 collected was sent to the American Red Cross as a donation), anyone could enter. So there were rank beginners who barely knew the moves, seasoned club players who'd been playing chess all of their lives, and a sprinkling of masters. So involved was Bobby in his games that he never noticed that some of the top players en route to Moscow for yet another return USA-USSR match had stopped by to watch, and a few were even following one of his games.

Bobby won a series of contests against weaker players, but as he progressed up the tournament ladder, he confronted stiffer opposition and started to lose. Harry Fajans, a tall, pencil-thin master with poor posture, who was a member of the Marshall Chess Club, one of the most renowned chess institutions in the country, related that when he beat Bobby in that Washington Square tournament, the boy began to cry. When questioned about the incident years later, Bobby was highly indignant and vehemently denied it.

The rounds of the tournament stretched into October, and toward the final weeks it was often cold and rainy. Bobby, dressed in a light zip-up jacket that wasn't warm enough, pressed on despite the discomfort, his pieces occasionally sliding off the cement tables slick with rain. "We were glad when it was over," Fischer remembered.

He finished fifteenth, and was awarded a ballpoint pen, perhaps because he was the youngest player. He later recounted: "I felt bad when the pen was handed to me, because it looked like the ones that I was always buying for a quarter or a half dollar." A few weeks later, however, while walking with his mother past a drugstore, she pointed out an identical pen for sale in the window. It had a price tag of $10.00. "I felt better," quipped Bobby.

As a result of his participation in the tournament, Bobby for the first time saw his name published in a major newspaper, a harbinger of the vast publicity he'd attract for the rest of his life. *The New York Times* ran a small story about the results, crammed in the back of the paper, on the obituary page. The headline proclaimed, EASTMAN WINS AT WASHINGTON SQUARE—BOY 12, NEAR TOP.

Although Charles Eastman had won the event, it was Bobby who received the most ink. The *Times* extolled: "Many in the crowd of 400 onlookers seemed to think the best show was given by Bobby Fischer. Despite competition from his more mature and experienced adversaries, he was unbeaten until yesterday, when he came within 15 players of the championship."

When Bobby's maternal grandfather, Jacob Wender, died, the yellowed *Times* article was found among his papers. Bobby commented with both wistfulness and sting: "My grandfather had shown little interest in [me] and knew nothing about chess." Still, the irony wasn't lost on him. He sensed that the old man was probably proud of him from the very beginning of his chess career, but never told him.

3

Out of the Head of Zeus

URING THE SUMMER of 1955 Bobby serendipitously happened
upon a gathering place for chess aficionados and, in so doing, raised
his game to a whole new level. Nigro would often take him to
Manhattan's Central Park, where they'd rent a boat for an hour or two and
then paddle up, down, and around the placid lake, through the lily pads,
looking like fin de siècle oarsmen in an Impressionist painting. Bobby did
most of the rowing, which broadened his shoulders.

One Saturday afternoon, as they walked out of the park on their way
home, Bobby noticed a brass plaque affixed to the front of an elegant stone
building on Central Park South, a posh street bordering the park. The en-
graving read simply, MANHATTAN CHESS CLUB. The sign startled the boy,
and as he stared at it, his attention was drawn to an open window on the
ground level. Bobby stood there for a moment, agape: He was just inches
away from two players sitting at a table inside, intently moving pieces across
a board. The men were attempting to get a breath of fresh air during one of
the dog days of summer. The club looked inviting. Bobby turned sheepishly
to Nigro. "Can we go in?" His teacher said simply, "Let's try."

"We were looking for [a way] to get out of the heat," Bobby remembered.
"As soon as I saw the sign I wanted to go in, and the minute I went in, I liked
it." The club was decorated with trophies; oil paintings of legendary players
such as Lasker, Morphy, and Capablanca; photographs of contemporary
masters; and bookcases filled with works on chess strategy. There were about
a dozen games taking place when they entered. Bobby saw no children.

Walter Shipman, one of the club's directors, walked over to the newcomers as they hesitated in the doorway. A twenty-six-year-old novice attorney who later became an international master, he greeted the Brooklyn pair and immediately matched Bobby with a player. Bobby quickly downed his opponent, who called to another player to try his hand with the boy; and he, too, was defeated. Soon, not yet aware that they were in the presence of a prodigy but realizing that Bobby was someone exceptional, the club's players started gathering around his board and asking him questions. "Where did you learn how to play chess?" "How old are you?" "Where do you live?" "Where'd you learn that opening?"

Bobby was making his debut among the elite chess fraternity of New York. They observed that unlike most beginning players (although he wasn't really a beginner; he'd been playing at the Brooklyn Chess Club for four years, since he was eight) Bobby could see the totality of the board. It wasn't that he made the best choice each and every move, but he was almost never forced into playing or being on the receiving end of a one- or two-move unsound combination: a "cheapo," the term for a "cheap move."

Shipman, who was rated among the top twenty players in the United States, grasped the boy's potential. Eagerly, he played him a series of blitz games at one second a move, and Bobby won about a third of them. Shipman remembered: "I was so impressed by his play that I introduced the 12-year old to Maurice Kasper, the president of the club and a millionaire garment maker, whose beneficent offer of a free junior membership was immediately accepted by Bobby." Bobby became the youngest member in the club's history. Kasper told him that he could come every day if he wished. Bobby beamed. He was like a little kid being set free in a candy store.

The Manhattan Chess Club was the strongest chess club in the country and the second oldest. It was founded in 1877, three years after the Mechanics' Institute Chess Club of San Francisco, and for many years it included almost every great player that the United States produced. Chess enthusiasts from out of town and even from other countries, hearing of the club's almost mythic history, moved to New York just to become members of the Manhattan, to improve their skills and have a chance to play against the greats. Its popularity was analogous to the way artists flocked to Paris in the 1920s to hone their craft under the tutelage of the masters there. The club had been the site of two World Championship matches (Steinitz-Zukertort in 1886 and Steinitz-Gunsberg 1890–91) and had hosted the annual United States Championship tournament since the 1930s. A preponderance of the members were Jewish, a group that had pursued the game for centuries and was highly proficient at it. More than one million Jews, most of them immigrants, lived in New York City at that time, and many had brought with them their love for chess. In 1974, Anthony Saidy wrote in *The World of Chess* that "perhaps half of all of the greatest players of the past hundred years have been Jews." When asked whether he was Jewish, Bobby replied, "Part. My mother is Jewish."

On the rare occasions when no worthy opponents were available at the Manhattan during the daytime, Bobby would wander into Central Park and play under the open sky at the stone chess tables near the Wollman skating rink. During one long, exasperating endgame, it began to rain, and neither he nor his opponent would let the storm stay their appointed task of finishing the game. Bobby thought and played, pondered and moved, all the while becoming drenched. When he finally arrived home, his clothes soaked, his sneakers squeaking and swishing water, and his hair looking as if he'd just stepped from a shower, Regina was furious. But her anger never lasted long.

The Manhattan Chess Club was organized into four groups, based on playing strength. The strongest was the rarefied "A" group where the masters and experts resided; then there was the "A-Reserve," consisting of potentially strong players, followed by the "B" group and finally the "C" category, which incorporated the lowest-rated or weakest players, many of whom were hoping to work their way up the ladder. In the first few weeks of his membership, Bobby enrolled in a tournament for C players and won it easily. He advanced to the B group and played tournaments within that section until he eventually won and was promoted to the A-Reserves. Ultimately, in not quite a year, he finished first in that group as well.

Soon he was going to the club every day, staying there from early afternoon until late at night. Regina wanted him to go to summer camp as he had before, but Bobby wouldn't hear of it. For him, the Manhattan Chess Club was nirvana, and although he hadn't yet developed a grand plan about dedicating his life to chess, he loved the feeling of winning and wanted to be near the game all the time. The Brooklyn Chess Club only afforded him the chance to play on Friday nights and an occasional Tuesday—the two nights of the week they met—for a total of about four hours on any given evening. At the Manhattan, though, he could play twelve hours a day, seven days a week.

The game not only engaged Bobby's mind, it tempered his loneliness, and while playing, he felt more alive. Since it was the summer and there was no school, he'd rise late, after his mother and sister had left the apartment, eat breakfast alone at a diner, and take the subway into Manhattan to go to the club. Regina would constantly monitor him, bringing him liverwurst sandwiches wrapped in tinfoil and a container of milk for dinner, lest Bobby, engrossed in his games, skip his evening meal. At about midnight every night, she'd appear at the club and almost have to drag him back to Brooklyn, the pair taking the one-hour subway ride home together.

Throughout that summer and during the next few years, Bobby began making chess friends at the club. At first his friendships were mostly with older players—but perhaps as a result of Bobby's now being a member, or because of a shift in the club's policy, promising players Bobby's own age or just a few years older were permitted to join, and these, finally, were children he could relate to. Many would remain lifelong friends or competitors-in-arms. William Lombardy, who'd go on to win the World Junior Championship and enter the pantheon as a grandmaster, was six years older than Bobby and at first beat him most of the time. He was an intense and brilliant young man who possessed a great positional sense. Bernard Zuckerman, who was almost as studious as Bobby in analyzing games, especially the strategy of opening moves, was born just days apart from Bobby and ultimately would become an international master. Asa Hoffmann—like Bobby, born in 1943 and the son of two Park Avenue lawyers—became a master and was also adept at other board games, such as Scrabble and backgammon, in addition to chess, and acquired a reputation as a "money" player: that is, his ability often increased in proportion to the wager or prize. Jackie Beers, a short young man with a charming smile and a ferocious temper, earned Bobby's respect because Beers could sometimes hold his own with him in speed games; and James Gore, a tall redheaded boy who dressed conservatively even as a teen and who adopted a condescending attitude toward anyone he defeated, had a great influence on Bobby. All of these young players would eventually be surpassed by Fischer, but they tested him with daring alternative variations, and his play sharpened as a result.

Bobby would play as many as a hundred speed games against his friendly foes on any given day. Eventually, as the boys blossomed into their teens and then became young men, Bobby emerged as a leader of sorts: Whatever he wanted they gave him; wherever he went they followed. "One more," he'd say voraciously, setting up the pieces, and no one refused him. Dr. Stuart Margulies, a master, who was several years older than Bobby, said in retrospect, "I adored playing with Bobby, just *adored* it!" Playing with Bobby was like reading the poetry of Robert Frost or taking a long hot bath. You came away feeling better for it. Perhaps you learned something, or perhaps the concentration required calmed you, even if you did lose a preponderance of games. Players would often smile when they resigned a game to Bobby, showing admiration for his brilliance.

One of the first grandmasters whom Bobby met at the club was Nicholas Rossolimo, the U.S. Open Champion and former champion of France. The day they met, Rossolimo was sitting on a sofa, eating a bagel with lox and cream cheese, and he spoke to Bobby with his mouth full. Because of that—and Rossolimo's pronounced accent—Bobby couldn't understand a word. Nevertheless, the boy was impressed at being in the presence of a champion, and awed that Rossolimo would deign to talk to him, mumbler though he was.

Within a few months after joining the club, Bobby, together with Lombardy and Gore, dominated the weekly speed tournaments, which limited players to ten seconds a move. Eighty-year-old Harold M. Phillips, a master and member of the board, wistfully likened Bobby's style of play to that of Capablanca, whom he remembered well from when the young Cuban joined the club at seventeen in 1905.

Although Bobby's life now revolved around the Manhattan, there were other pawns to capture. Nigro brought his student to the 1955 United States Amateur Championship, held at the end of May, during the Memorial Day weekend. Because players of master strength weren't eligible to enter, the tournament encouraged the participation of weaker and less experienced players. It was a Swiss System tournament (in which players with like scores keep getting paired until a winner emerges after a specific number of rounds are played), with each contestant playing six games. The tournament was held at a resort at Lake Mohegan, north of New York City, in Westchester County.

As Nigro drove out of the city, he and Bobby held their usual conversation, the boy questioning theories he'd read and asking about the strength or weakness of moves that he or an opponent had made during games at the Manhattan Chess Club. After a while, Bobby switched to questions about the weekend's tournament. Who did Nigro think would enter? How strong would the other players be? How did he think Bobby would do?

Sensing that Bobby felt insecure, Nigro tried to reassure the boy and explained how important it was for him to gain competitive experience. Bobby became quieter, finally biting his nails and staring out the window at the scenery as their car turned off the highway onto the road that cut through the fields alongside the lake to the resort.

When they arrived at the tournament site, and Nigro was about to pay the $5 entry fee and enroll Bobby as a member of the U.S. Chess Federation, as was required of all participants, Bobby lost either his nerve or his will and said he didn't want to play. He said he'd seen people swimming in the lake and rowing boats. He'd rather do that, he felt. There was also a tennis court! Nigro tried to bring his attention back to the reason they were there. Bobby argued that since the hotel room was already paid for (only $3 a night for each person, a special rate given to tournament participants) and they were going to stay the weekend anyway, he wanted to take advantage of the sports possibilities.

Nigro realized that Bobby was trying to stave off what he feared would be an inevitable loss. He persuaded the boy to change his mind and urged him to the board. Bobby played, but because of either his wavering confidence or interest, his efforts resulted in a minus score. Years after, Bobby recalled that he was unhappy with the outcome and took to heart Nigro's advice: "You can't win *every* game. Just do your best *every* time."

A few months later, determined to make up for his poor showing, Bobby mailed in his registration to play in the U.S. Junior Championship in Lincoln, Nebraska. Nigro couldn't take time off from his teaching schedule to accompany him, nor could Regina leave her job and studies, especially since she'd been home ill with a chronic lung problem for three weeks. So Bobby elected to go alone.

He stood impatiently at a ticket window in Pennsylvania Station where Regina was attempting to buy him a ticket to Nebraska via Philadelphia.

She'd saved the money for him to go and was determined to get him there. The plan was for Bobby to take the train to Philadelphia and meet another player, Charles Kalme, who was also going to attend the U.S. Junior. The two could then travel the almost 1,400 miles together. "How old is your son, ma'am?" the ticket agent asked. Told that the boy was twelve, the agent refused to sell her a ticket. "He's too young to travel all that distance alone." "But you don't understand," she argued. "He must go! It's for his chess!" The agent peered over his glasses and looked at Bobby. "Why didn't you tell me the boy was going for medical care?" Years later, Bobby laughed in reminiscing about the incident: "And he sold us the ticket without further talk. He thought there was something wrong with my *chest*!" With some trepidation Regina sent her little chess duckling on his way, but not before draping a large U.S. Army surplus dog tag around his neck, engraved with his name, address, and telephone number. "In case . . . ," she said. "Don't take it off!" And he didn't.

Charles Kalme, a Latvian-born sixteen-year-old, was a handsome and polite boy who'd spent years in a displaced persons' camp and was the reigning U.S. Junior champion. He and Bobby played dozens of fast games during the two-day trip and analyzed openings and endgame positions. Kalme, considerably stronger, was respectful of Bobby's passion.

Unfortunately for the participants in the U.S. Junior, the city of Lincoln was embroiled in a heat wave of more than one hundred degrees during the run of the tournament, and Civic Hall, the ballroom where play took place, seemed to have little if any air-conditioning. Going into the ten-round tournament, twelve-year-old Bobby was the youngest of twenty-five players. One contestant was thirteen, and there were several twenty-year-olds, all rated quite highly. Ron Gross, slightly older and more experienced than Bobby, later reflected back on Bobby's performance there: "Fischer was skinny and fidgety but pleasant in a distracted way. He wasn't a bad loser. He would just get real quiet, twist that dog tag even more and immediately set up the pieces to play again." Regina called Bobby every day at an arranged time to see if he was all right, and when she received the telephone bill at the end of the month, it came to $50, more than she was paying for rent.

Bobby, dog tag entwined, managed to compile an even score, with two wins, two losses, and six draws, fretting afterward that "I didn't do too well." But he was awarded a handsome trophy for achieving the best score of a player under the age of thirteen. "I was the *only* player under 13!" Bobby was quick to point out. The trophy was quite large and heavy, yet he insisted on carrying it back to Brooklyn rather than have it shipped. "It gave me a big thrill," he remembered, despite not having won it for exceptional play. His traveling companion, Charles Kalme, repeated his win of the previous year and was crowned the champion once again. He didn't return to the East Coast right after the tournament, so Bobby journeyed alone, this time by bus, looking out the window sometimes, but mostly analyzing games on his pocket set.

As Bobby was becoming more involved in the world of chess, he attracted the attention of a wealthy and unusual man named E. Forry Laucks. A chess player himself, Laucks liked to surround himself with other players, many of them offbeat and highly talented. He was always generous to Regina in assisting Bobby with small amounts of money—$25 to $100—for tournament entry fees and other expenses. During the spring of 1956, Laucks gathered a group of chess players for a thirty-five-hundred-mile motor trip throughout the southern United States and ultimately to Cuba, stopping off at towns and cities for a series of matches with local clubs.

So that twelve-year-old Bobby could participate in the barnstorming jaunt to Cuba, Regina allowed him to withdraw from school temporarily. Her thinking was that the trip would be educational, exposing her son to new places and different people. However, she agreed to Bobby's participation only if she could serve as his chaperone. Laucks didn't know or care that Regina, and therefore Bobby, was Jewish, nor did Regina seem too concerned about Laucks's neo-Nazi (someone called him "an old Nazi") allegiance. The idea of travel, especially to the politically explosive country of Cuba, stimulated Regina's wanderlust. Permission from the Community Woodward School was forthcoming for Bobby's three-week absence, and the boy was delighted to be on the road playing chess instead of being in the classroom.

Laucks frequently wore a small, black-enameled lapel pin bearing a gold Nazi swastika. Amazingly, it never seemed to attract much attention. He didn't wear it all the time, but often enough, and it didn't seem to inhibit him when he went to a Jewish delicatessen to get his favorite sandwich of pastrami on rye, or when he was talking to Jewish chess players. One player, William Schneider, said he was embarrassed when he and Laucks—sporting his swastika—were driving back from a tournament and they stopped at a Jewish restaurant. No one said anything about the swastika, or even seemed to notice it. In addition to the pin, Laucks often wore—weather permitting— a small-brimmed Alpine fedora with a feather in the band, adorned with emblems from the countries to which he'd traveled. He ostentatiously dressed in lederhosen at times, and for a few years even sported a Hitlerian mustache. When he entered a tournament, dressed in a khaki shirt and pants and dark tie and displaying that mustache, it was as if a doppelgänger of Der Fuehrer had been incarnated. In his home he hung Nazi flags in prominent locations and displayed airplane models of Messerschmitts and Junkers as well as an oil painting of Adolf Hitler and other memorabilia from the Third Reich.

Laucks was inarguably one of the most eccentric people in the New York chess community, with conflicting values and erratic behavior. But despite his Nazi trappings, he rarely talked about his political beliefs. His financial patronage of teams and players could always be relied upon, and he was the sponsor of many chess events, some major. He'd also formed a fully functioning chess group—the Log Cabin Chess Club—that met in the finished basement (decorated to look like a log cabin) of his spacious house in West Orange, New Jersey. A number of players, some outcasts or close to homeless but with master-level playing ability, actually lived—on and off—in the house with him. Laucks's wife and two children lived in another house, in Old Lyme, Connecticut, and Laucks rarely visited them, preferring to stay in New Jersey with his chess cronies.

Aside from her self-serving desire to travel, Regina insisted on being part of the tour because she didn't trust one of its participants: the shifty-eyed Norman T. Whitaker. He was a disbarred lawyer who'd served years in Alcatraz and Leavenworth for a variety of crimes and confidence schemes, including the extortion of more than $100,000 by claiming (falsely) that he knew the whereabouts of the missing Lindbergh baby. Whitaker, known as "The Fox," the name he was referred to in the Lindbergh duping, had also been imprisoned for car theft and for raping a twelve-year-old girl. When he was in his sixties, he proposed marriage to a fourteen-year-old. Regina worried that his pedophiliac tendencies might apply to boys as well as girls, and she didn't want him to be alone with Bobby on the trip. Why Whitaker was accepted as a part of the Log Cabin team or in the chess community at all is a difficult question to answer, beyond noting that at the time of Laucks's journey Whitaker was still a powerful player at age sixty-six, and in his prime he had been one of the strongest players in the nation. He also had a charming way about him, as do most confidence men. His chess prowess and velvet tongue may have blinded some people to his despicable past, proving the adage that sometimes chess players make strange team fellows.

In contrast to Whitaker, one of the chess caravan's more delightful players was Glenn T. Hartleb, an expert-level Floridian. A tall, gentle man with steel-rimmed glasses and a perpetual smile, Hartleb greeted everyone he met—champion or patzer, beginner or veteran, child or octogenarian—by bowing low and saying with deep reverence, *"Master!"* When asked why he used this salutation, he said, "In life we are all masters," countering a past champion's chestnut, "In life we are all *duffers.*"

The disparate team crammed into Laucks's unreliable 1950 Chrysler station wagon, which contained everyone's luggage, chess sets and boards, food, and sleeping bags—some of it precariously strapped on top—and like the Joad family in *The Grapes of Wrath,* gunwales straining, shock absorbers depressed to their limits, they were ready. "Let's *schuss*!" said millionaire Laucks jovially, using his favorite expression, and off they sped at seventy miles an hour down the turnpike for a hair-raising trip (Laucks was a dangerously careless driver). Bobby sat up front between the fascist and the con man.

As the Cabineers roamed through the South, stopping at towns for either prearranged or hastily organized matches, Whitaker as best player would invariably play board one, and Bobby board two. Bobby, feeling as though he were playing hooky from school, had a good time competing in the matches, usually at the relatively leisurely time limit of sixty moves in two hours. Most of his competition was stiff but nothing he couldn't handle. While in the car, he also played hundreds of games with his fellow team members, and with the exception of his games against Whitaker, he usually won.

"I want to see the alligators," Bobby piped up as they drove through the

Everglades. "Let's stop—I want a soda," he could also be heard to say frequently. His little-kid complaints, including the traditional "Are we there yet?" annoyed some team members, and behind his back they began referring to him as "The Monster."

The trip was not entirely expense-free for the Fischers. Although Laucks, with his great wealth, could have covered everyone's expenses, he'd frugally pick and choose where, when, and how he wanted to spend his money. On some occasions, the team would stop at a fairly expensive restaurant and he'd announce to everyone, "Order anything on the menu you want, but *no alcohol*." At other times Bobby and Regina had to pay for themselves.

While in the South, Bobby was getting his first exposure to racial prejudice. Blacks were still not allowed to sit at the counters. Bobby had to ask his mother what it meant when he saw a drinking fountain that was labeled COLORED ONLY. Regina was furious at the prejudice she was witnessing, but no one else seemed to care.

One of the men on the trip began to hint to the others that he was ready to seduce Regina and that he thought she was a willing seductee; he became a laughingstock one night when she adamantly refused him entrance to her room.

Crammed in the car, the group sometimes tired of chess talk and reminisced about other adventures, real or imagined. Whitaker cracked at least one joke a day, usually tasteless: "I know a woman who will pay me one thousand dollars to see me in the nude: She's blind." Bobby often asked for explanations. "See me later, kid; I'll tell you," someone would pipe up.

During the six-hour trip on the ferry from the Duval Street dock in Key West to Havana, Bobby and an older player, Robert Houghton, played blind-fold chess, visualizing the evolving game and calling out their imaginary moves; but when they reached nine or ten moves and the game became more complicated, the positions began to dissolve in Houghton's mind and he couldn't continue. To Bobby, the positions were as clear as if he had the game set up on a board in front of him. After a few additional attempts sans board and pieces, the invisible match was abandoned and they played on the portable set. Bobby won dozens of quick games during that session, not losing one.

Havana in 1956 was a feisty, corrupt city. Tourist agents called it "The

Pearl of the Antilles," but it was more provocatively referred to by others as "the sexiest city in the world." Filled with gambling casinos, brothels, and streetwalkers, and with rum costing only $1.20 per bottle, the city had a reputation for debauchery. More than 250,000 American tourists went to Havana that year, most to have a wanton weekend or two. The Cabineers, however, were in Havana to play chess, and although it's possible that some of the men went to the infamous Shanghai Theater or to other shadowy places at night, the team members played a match almost every day.

The major team match against the Capablanca Chess Club was disappointing for the Americans: though Bobby and Whitaker won their games, the five other Americans lost. Bobby gave a twelve-board simultaneous exhibition against members of the club and won ten and drew two—"just for fun, not for money," he was quick to explain. He later summed up his experience: "The Cubans seem to take chess more seriously. . . . They feel more the way I do about chess. Chess is like fighting, and I like to win. So do they."

The New York Times took notice of the Log Cabin tour with a headline: CHESS TEAM ENDS TOUR. The story pointed out that the Cabineers ended the tour with a minus score; they won 23½ games and lost 26½, but Whitaker and Bobby were the leading scorers in the club matches at 5½–1½ each, excluding Bobby's ten wins in his simultaneous exhibition.

After Bobby's three-week adventure, returning to Brooklyn and to school was anticlimactic. Nevertheless, the boy enjoyed getting back to the familiarity of the unregimented school and to the opportunity to play with his friends at the Manhattan Chess Club. In retrospect, he said he enjoyed his four years at Community Woodward, mainly because the unstructured routine enabled him to "get up and walk around the room if you wanted" and to dress any way he liked ("ordinary polo shirts, dungarees or corduroy pants"). He also enjoyed his status as the school's resident chess player. Instead of Bobby's adapting to the teachers or the administration, the staff ended up adapting to him. When graduation from eighth grade occurred, however, in June 1956, Bobby elected not to attend the ceremony, because he didn't want to give up an afternoon of chess and because he disliked "any kind of formality and ceremony." He was thirteen and intended to spend the summer studying and playing chess. Although he'd be entering high school the following September, that transition, exciting to many youngsters, was of little interest to him.

♖

Jack Collins, one of the great teachers of chess, lived with his sister Ethel in Brooklyn and was host to a chess salon in his apartment called the Hawthorne Chess Club, which met there regularly. It was open and free to just about anybody who wanted to play—or study—the game with him, although he did charge a token fee to some for individual lessons. He was kindhearted, highly self-educated, and had an uproarious sense of humor. Some of the greatest players in the United States were Collins's pupils, such as the Byrne brothers and William Lombardy. Collins's apartment was stocked with hundreds of chess books, chess paintings and statues, and furniture and draperies decorated with chess figures; it was a virtual chess museum. Jack had exchanged a few words with Bobby when they met in Asbury Park, New Jersey, at the U.S. Amateur Championship during Memorial Day weekend in 1956. At that meeting Collins had invited Bobby to come to the apartment, and two weeks after, the boy appeared. Collins wrote about Bobby's first visit to his home:

> Bobby Fischer rang my doorbell one afternoon in June 1956. I opened the door and a slender, blond, typical thirteen-year-old American boy dressed in a plaid woolen shirt, corduroy trousers, and black-and-white sneakers, said simply: "I'm Bobby Fischer."
>
> I had seen him once before, and I replied, "Hi, Bobby, come on in." We went into the living room and sat down at the chess board. I knew he was rather shy and I am not always easy at first meetings either. So, it seemed the best thing to do was to become immediately involved in the thing we both loved best—chess. I happened to have a position from one of my postal instruction games set up on the board. It was a difficult position, and I had just been analyzing it for about half an hour. I nodded at it and asked, "What do you think about this position, Bobby?"
>
> Bobby plunged right in. Within seconds he was stabbing out moves, trying combinations, seeking won endings, and rattling off variations, his fingers barely able to keep pace with his thoughts. He found several hidden possibilities I had not seen. I was deeply im-

pressed. Of course, I had heard of his remarkable talent. But this was the first time I realized that he was really a prodigy and might become one of the greatest players of all time.

Just as Bobby had fairly leaped into—and established residence at—the Manhattan Chess Club the previous summer, he soon became a regular presence at Collins's salon. The chess teacher's place was only a few blocks from Erasmus High School, and Bobby would dash from the school during lunch hour and free periods, play a few games with Collins while eating his sandwich taken from home, then hurry back to school. At three p.m. he'd return and spend the rest of the day over the board, eventually having dinner with Jack and Ethel, more often than not eaten while the two friends were still playing or analyzing. Bobby would continue at the board through the evening, until Regina or Joan would come and escort him home. Bobby and Jack played thousands of games—mostly speed—analyzed hundreds of positions, and solved dozens of chess problems together. Bobby also became a constant borrower of books from the Collins library. The short, stunted man confined to a wheelchair and the growing boy went to movies, dined in restaurants, attended chess events at clubs, and celebrated birthdays and holidays together. The Collins apartment became a home to Bobby in every way, the boy being thought of as part of the family.

Was Jack Collins, in fact, Bobby's most important teacher, overshadowing Carmine Nigro? The question should be raised, since Bobby later in life said he'd learned nothing from Collins. In truth, Bobby's quick dismissal of Collins's contribution may have been delivered out of cold, ungrateful pride. Certainly, Collins replaced Carmine Nigro as Bobby's mentor after Nigro moved to Florida in 1956, the year that Bobby and Collins met. Bobby would never see Nigro again.

Collins was one of the finest players in the United States, and for a number of years was rated in the top fifty; Nigro never reached anywhere near that achievement. Bobby said that he always felt Nigro was more of a friend than a teacher, but that he was a very good teacher. Nigro was a professional teacher and was quite formal in his instructional technique, while Collins, as talented and caring as he was, employed a Socratic approach. With pupils, he'd often just set up a position and say, "Let's look at this," as he did that first day with Bobby, and then ask the player to come up with a plan or series of alternatives, making the student think. He did this with Bobby hundreds of times. Nigro and Collins both acted fatherly toward the boy, but Collins's relationship lasted more than fifteen years. Nigro's, though admittedly occurring at a formative time in Bobby's life, lasted just five.

When Bobby returned from a tournament, he'd often rush to see Collins and go over his games with him. Collins, a shrewd analyst, would comment on the moves that Bobby did and didn't play. Learning was taking place, but not in the traditional way. Collins's approach wasn't "You must remember this variation of the King's-Indian Defense, which is much stronger than what you played"—rather, he relied on a kind of osmosis. International master James T. Sherwin, a New Yorker who knew both Fischer and Collins well, had this to say when he heard of Bobby's later dismissal of Collins's influence on him: "Well, I think that's a little hubristic; it must have been said in a moment of pridefulness. Bobby *must* have learned from Collins. For example, Jack always played the Sicilian Defense, and then Bobby started playing it. I think the remark was a young man's way of saying, 'I'm the greatest. No one ever taught me anything and I received my gifts from God.' I think Jack helped Bobby psychologically, with chess fightingness, just being tough and wanting always to win."

Collins also noticed what Nigro had observed the year before: Bobby's habit of procrastinating during a game, loitering over the board, taking just a little too long to make an obvious move. To help the boy overcome these self-defeating tendencies, Collins ordered a clock from Germany with a special ten-second timer, and he insisted that Bobby play with it to practice thinking and moving more rapidly.

Collins, for his part, said that he never "taught" Bobby in the strictest sense. Rather, he pointed out that "geniuses like Beethoven, Leonardo da Vinci, Shakespeare and Fischer come out of the head of Zeus, seem to be generally programmed, know before instructed." Essentially, Collins was saying that Bobby Fischer's talent *was* God-given, innate, and all Collins could do was serve as a guide or bystander, offering encouragement and nurturing the boy's prodigious gifts. He was also a loyal friend.

♖

Fischer, who much later in life would gain notoriety for his anti-Jewish rhetoric, always said that although his mother was Jewish, he had no religious training. It is not known whether Bobby, on or near his thirteenth birthday of March 9, 1956, participated in the formal Jewish ritual of Bar Mitzvah, reading Hebrew from the Torah at a synagogue. However, his chess friend Karl Burger said that when he played twelve-year-old Bobby in the park on Rochester Avenue in Brooklyn, the boy "was studying for his Bar Mitzvah." Also supporting the belief that Bobby had experienced the ritual was the fact that, many years later, he gave an old chess clock and chess set to his Hungarian friend Pal Benko, a grandmaster. Bobby had been keeping them among his belongings and told Benko that they were gifts he'd "received for his Bar Mitzvah."

It's possible that Bobby was simply given the gifts on his thirteenth birthday, even though there was no actual coming-of-age Bar Mitzvah ceremony. (Regina's strained circumstances may even have played a role: There are usually year-long fees for catenation, the instruction given to a twelve-year-old to ready him for the ritual.)

When he reached the age of thirteen, Bobby may have truly felt that he was an adult who had to take charge of himself, and that his destiny was no longer in anyone's hands but his own. Certainly, he did seem to exhibit a newfound maturity, and when it came to playing chess, his skills seasoned to some extent as he began playing more resolutely.

A significant improvement occurred in his learning curve in 1956, when he was thirteen. Bobby's intense study of the game and incessant playing came to remarkable fruition. During the annual amateur Memorial Day tournament that May, he placed twenty-first. Only five weeks later, during the July 4 weekend, he captured the United States Junior Championship at a tournament held at the Franklin Mercantile Chess Club in Philadelphia. Only four months had passed since his thirteenth birthday and Bobby had become the youngest chess master in history and one of the strongest young players in the country.

Many factors could have contributed to his meteoric rise at the time: meeting Jack Collins and playing countless games with him and with Jack's acolytes, almost all masters who came to the Collins salon throughout the summer; his year of facing competition at the Manhattan Chess Club; the knowledge he'd accumulated from steadily studying chess books and periodicals for almost five years; and a gestalt of understanding regarding the game that, through a combination of study, experience, and intrinsic gifts, coalesced in his mind.

But there were personal elements as well. Losses that he'd experienced in tournaments created a fierce determination to win. ("I just can't bear thinking of defeat.") And somewhere along the way, he became more reconciled to the need to take chances. In the end it may have boiled down to what the poet Robert Frost once said about a successful education: "Just hanging around until you have caught on."

♖

Just two weeks after that July 4 weekend tournament, the 1956 United States Open Championship was going to be held in Oklahoma City. It would have many more contestants, including some of the best players in the United States and Canada.

While Bobby had no hope of placing among the top contenders, he was eager to continue his winning streak, aware that the opportunity to compete against stronger players would sharpen his game. Regina balked. She was concerned that he'd exhaust himself playing in a third tournament within two months. It was also impossible for her to take time off to accompany her son on the long trip to Oklahoma, and she worried about his going alone.

Bobby was adamant. If he could go to Nebraska by himself, he argued, why couldn't he go to Oklahoma City? Regina reluctantly agreed, but raising enough money for his expenses was, as always, a problem. She persuaded Maurice Kasper of the Manhattan Chess Club to give her $125 toward Bobby's expenses (the travel fare was $93.50), and she contacted the tournament organizing committee to arrange to have Bobby stay at someone's home to save on the cost of a hotel. A player's wife agreed to keep an eye on the boy and provide most of his meals. Before leaving, to help raise money for his trip, Bobby played a twenty-one-game simultaneous exhibition in the lobby of the Jersey City YMCA, winning nineteen, drawing one, and losing one, with some one hundred spectators following his games. Each player paid a dollar, with two free entries allowed. Bobby's profit: $19. Scrimping to make up the balance, Regina sent him off to Oklahoma.

By far the strongest tournament Bobby had ever played in, the U.S. Open was held in the Oklahoma Biltmore Hotel, a somewhat palatial facility that seemed out of context in a Great Plains town, although the décor of American Indian and buffalo paintings reminded the competitors that they were in cowboy country.

Bobby, still small for his age (he appeared to be only nine or ten), became a novelty at the Open. He was interviewed twice on local television, profiled by newspapers, and by the *Oklahoman* magazine, and continued to draw crowds to his table. A flash of photographers seemed always on hand to snap his picture.

One hundred and two players competed in the twelve-round tournament, spread over two weeks. Bobby's opponents were not necessarily the strongest in the tournament, nor were they the weakest. He drew with several masters, defeated some experts (players a rank below master), kept his resolve, and ended up not losing a game—which was a record for a thirteen-year-old at a U.S. Open. When the pieces were cleared, he was tied with four other players for fourth place, just one point away from the winner, Arthur Bisguier, a fellow member of the Manhattan Chess Club. His official U.S. Chess Federation rating calculated after the event was astronomically high—2375—confirming his status as a master and ranking him number twenty-five in the nation. No one in the United States, or in the world, had ever ascended so quickly.

It was late in August 1956, and Bobby had followed his Oklahoma success with a trip to Montreal. Once again, Regina had arranged for him to stay in someone's home; this time it was with the family of William Hornung, one of the tournament's supporters. The eighty-eight players in the First Canadian Open may have composed a stronger roster than had been fielded at the United States Open a few weeks earlier. Canada's best players came out in force.

Some of America's youngest but strongest stars had ventured north of the border to play. As usual, Bobby was the youngest of the New York City contingent, which included Larry Evans, William Lombardy, and James T. Sherwin (who played ten straight speed games with Bobby in between rounds, and lost every one: "It was then that I decided that he was really too strong for me," Sherwin remembered).

In the fourth round, Bobby became involved in a 108-move extravaganza, a chess ultra-marathon that stretched to more than seven hours. In the contest he was pitted against Hans Matthai, a German immigrant to Canada. The game, which turned out to be the longest of Bobby's career, ended as an interesting draw.

After the game was drawn, he wondered if there'd been anything he'd overlooked. There was just *something* about the position, an echo of an idea distantly heard. Could he have established a won game, even at the point just before it was drawn?

That night, in a deep but restless sleep, a dream came to him and the position appeared over and over again—seemingly hundreds of times. Just before waking, the solution came to Bobby as a kind of apparition. There *was* a win there.

Bobby woke and sat bolt upright. "I've got it!" he said aloud, not knowing that anyone else was in the room. Mrs. Hornung had just tiptoed into the bedroom to wake Bobby and tell him breakfast was ready. She witnessed his epiphany. Still wearing his pajamas, he bounced barefooted into the living room to where he knew there was a chess set ready for action and began working on the endgame that he'd struggled with the previous day. "I knew I should have won!" he fairly screamed.

Freud held that dream content usually consists of material garnered from incidents, thoughts, images, and emotions experienced during or preceding the day of the dream. Some players in the midst of a tournament do dream about their games that night, and in these nocturnal reveries some actually solve an opening trap, an endgame finesse, or some other aspect that's been troubling them, waking with a fresh and practical idea. Former World Champion Boris Spassky once said that he dreamt about chess, and David Bronstein, a World Championship candidate, talked about playing whole games in his sleep—ones he could reproduce the next morning. Mikhail Botvinnik claimed that during his World Championship match with Vasily Smyslov, he awoke one night, walked naked to his board, and played the move that he was dreaming about in his adjourned game.

Dreaming about chess didn't happen often with Bobby. But when it did, the result was always something he could use in a future game, or the explanation of what he could have done in a lost or drawn game. In one interview he said that he most often dreamt about detective stories, which could be intricate games in themselves. Since chess had become such a motivating force in his life, he might have been incapable of dreaming about the game, or any game, *except* in symbolic form—that is, his psyche might have automatically defaulted to characters instead of pieces, plots and counterplots instead of variations on the board, murders in place of checkmates.

Bobby's last-round draw against Frank Anderson, the Canadian champion, was a nail-biter . . . literally. When he wasn't gnawing on the fingers of his left hand, he began biting his shirt, actually chomping pieces out of it and leaving holes.

He finished with a score of 7–3, tied for second place, a point behind first prize, and he won $59, which he pocketed without revealing his windfall to his mother.

Larry Evans won the prize as First Canadian Open Champion. Knowing that Evans had a car and was driving back to New York, Bobby asked for a ride. Evans was kind enough to agree. Bobby paid no attention to the stunning scenery or to Evans's equally stunning wife, who sat in the backseat to allow the boy to sit up front. Instead, during the entire eight-hour trip, Bobby plied the champion with questions: "Why do you play the Pirc, and against Anderson?" "Did Sherwin have winning or drawing chances against you? How?" "Didn't Mednis have a win against you? Why did he accept the draw? He could have made the time limit." Evans recounted, "I had no idea that I was talking to a future world's champion, just a very young master with great intensity. It was the beginning of a long and sometimes turbulent friendship."

A week after he returned from Canada in August, Bobby bought a ticket to a night baseball game at Ebbets Field to see his beloved Brooklyn Dodgers play the Milwaukee Braves. He wasn't disappointed: not only did the Dodgers win, but he was treated to a spectacle courtesy of Jackie Robinson. One of the great base stealers, Robinson danced around second base to worry and nettle the pitcher; when the pitcher tried to throw him out, the ball went over the head of the second baseman and Robinson sped home to score a run.

Bobby was feeling grown-up, mainly as a result of his summer travels to

New Jersey, Philadelphia, Oklahoma, and Montreal, but also because of the accolades he was receiving and his growing status in the chess world. He was thirteen. If he could defeat adults at chess, why shouldn't he be treated as an adult? He asked his mother if she'd stop coming to the chess club to take him home at night. It embarrassed him. "OK," she said, "I'll stop coming, and you can come home by yourself, but only on two conditions: You must be home by no later than ten p.m. on a school night and no later than midnight on a weekend night, *and* you must learn jujitsu to defend yourself." Regina didn't want Bobby to be mugged or hurt in a half-deserted subway station as he worked his way alone at night from Manhattan to Brooklyn. Bobby reluctantly agreed to the terms of the deal. As it developed, he never took a jujitsu lesson, though. Regina discovered that lessons would cost a minimum of $8 an hour—money she just didn't have. Their agreement had been made, however, and from that time on Bobby went home by himself. The only untoward incident he had was that someone once stepped on his newly polished shoes—on *purpose,* he said.

"*Me llamo* Robert Fischer."

During his first weeks in high school, right after he returned from Montreal, Bobby had not studied the introduction to his Spanish text, *El Camino Real,* had failed to attend two of his classes, and now was faced with his first ten-question quiz. Despite his trip to Cuba and his attempt to speak pidgin Spanish, he couldn't translate or come up with the answers to such questions as "Where is the train station?" or "How much does the banana cost?" so he only answered six of the questions—all incorrectly—and left the others blank.

In the Fischer household failing a language exam was a major infraction. In and out of college, Regina had formally studied Latin, Hebrew, Russian, German, French, and Spanish. She was fluent in many of these tongues (and got by in Yiddish) and was continually taking language courses in adult education centers to sharpen her skills. Joan took Spanish and German in high school and was adept in both. "Industry!" Regina yelled at Bobby, with the not-so-subtle implication that if he spent just a fraction of the time on his studies that he devoted to chess, he'd be a stellar student. She continually emphasized to him the importance of knowing other languages, especially if he intended to play chess in foreign lands. He understood. But to accelerate his progress, she began to speak to him in Spanish, coaxed him to take up his text, and tutored him, and within a short while he was receiving high grades. Eventually, he became fluent in Spanish.

Erasmus Hall High School in Brooklyn was one of the largest in New York and one of the oldest in the nation. With more than five thousand students, it was a factory of learning. Entering in the fall of 1956, Bobby felt comfortable there, although much less so than at Community Woodward. He later said that at Erasmus he was adorned with a cloak of anonymity: "As practically nobody in the school played chess, the other students did not know I was a chess player, which suited me fine, and I took care never to say anything about it either." At least that's what Bobby *thought*. The other students *did* know who he was. Indeed, it was difficult to not take notice of him: The New York newspapers regularly ran stories and photos of the prodigy; he gave several simultaneous exhibitions that drew publicity; he sparkled out from the cover of *Chess Review;* he even appeared with Arlene Francis on NBC's *Home* show. As for his classmates and their lack of acknowledgment, Bobby said, "I didn't bother them and they didn't bother me." He seemed unaware that fellow student Barbra Streisand, the future singer, had a secret schoolgirl crush on him. She remembered that "Bobby was always alone and very peculiar. But I found him very sexy." Bobby's remembrance of Streisand? "There was this mousey little girl . . ." His teachers, at least some, were annoyed by his aloofness and lack of interest in the lessons at hand.

October 1956

Scattering fallen leaves as he rushed down the tree-lined street, thirteen-year-old Bobby vaulted up the red-carpeted stairs of the Marshall Chess Club two steps at a time and entered the Great Hall. It was not his first visit. Indeed, he'd already begun making frequent visits to the Marshall, New York's other major chess club, where he enjoyed a heady feeling of being where he belonged, of possibly writing his own page into chess history.

The club—which was located on Tenth Street, between Fifth and Sixth avenues, one of Manhattan's most attractive neighborhoods—had been quartered in this venerable brownstone (built in 1832) since 1931, when a group of wealthy patrons, including one of the Roosevelts, bought the building so that their beloved Frank J. Marshall, the reigning U.S. Champion, who would hold the title for twenty-seven years, would always have a place to live with his family and to play, teach, and conduct tournaments. Walking down the street with its rows of stately brownstones festooned with window boxes of flowers, and a private boarding stable on the same block, Bobby could have easily felt he was transported back to the Gas Light or Silk Stocking era of the nineteenth century.

Most of the world's most renowned masters had visited the club—it was steeped in the echoes of legendary games, epic battles, hard-fought victories, and heartfelt defeats. Indeed, its only peer in the United States was the Manhattan Chess Club, forty-nine blocks to the north. In team matches, the Manhattan usually, but not always, came out on top.

Looking somewhat like a British officers' club, the Marshall was wood-paneled, with plush burgundy velvet curtains, several fireplaces, and oak tables fitted with brass lamps. It was at this club that Cuba's brilliant José Raúl Capablanca gave his last exhibition, where World Champion Alexander Alekhine visited and played speed chess, where many of the most gifted international grandmasters gave, and continue to give, theoretical lectures. Artist Marcel Duchamp lived directly across the street and was an active member of the club, and became a great fan of Bobby's. The Nobel Prize winner Sinclair Lewis took lessons there. If a motion picture location scout were searching for an idealized chess club, the Marshall might be his pick.

Certainly, there was a sense of decorum that permeated the club, even when it came to dress. Bobby's habitual mufti of T-shirt, wrinkled pants, and sneakers was considered an outrage by Caroline Marshall, Frank Marshall's widow and the long-standing manager of the club, and on several occasions she informed him of his sartorial indiscretion, once even threatening to bar him from the premises if he didn't dress more appropriately. Bobby ignored her.

He was at the Marshall that night in October to play in the seventh round of an invitational tournament, the Rosenwald Memorial, named for its sponsor, Lessing J. Rosenwald, the former chairman of Sears Roebuck who was an important art collector and chess patron. The invitation came as a result of Bobby's having won the U.S. Junior Championship three months earlier, and the Rosenwald was the first important invitational and adult all-masters tournament of his career. The other eleven players were considered some of the finest and highest rated in the United States, and the club members were excited by the event. Bobby's opponent that night was the urbane college professor Donald Byrne, an international master, former U.S. Open Champion, and a fiercely aggressive player. Dark-haired, elegant in speech and dress, the twenty-five-year-old Byrne invariably held a cigarette between two fingers, his hand high in the air, his elbow resting on the table, in a pose that gave him an aristocratic demeanor.

Regina accompanied Bobby to the club, but as soon as he began to play she left to browse at the nearby Strand Bookstore, whose shelves contained millions of used books. She knew it would probably be hours before Bobby's game would be over and she'd have to return.

To that point Bobby hadn't won a game in the tournament, but he'd drawn three, and he seemed to be getting stronger each round, learning from the other masters as he played. In chess tournaments, contestants are not only assigned opponents, they're also given, for each round, a color: black or white. Where possible, the tournament director alternates the colors, so that a player will play with the white pieces in one game and with the black in the next. Since white always moves first, having that color can provide a player with a distinct advantage in that he can make immediate headway on a preferred strategy. Alas, against Byrne, Bobby was assigned the black pieces.

Having studied Byrne's past games in chess books and magazines, Bobby knew something of his opponent's style and the strategies he frequently used. So Bobby decided to use an atypical approach—one unusual for Byrne to face and for Bobby to try. He played what was known as the Gruenfeld Defense.

Bobby knew the basics of the opening but hadn't yet mastered all of its intricacies. The point was to allow white, his opponent, to occupy the center squares, making the pieces a clear target that would be vulnerable to Bobby's attack. It wasn't a classical way to approach the game, and it leads to a very different configuration as the game progresses; but Bobby took the chance.

Because he hadn't memorized the sequence of moves, Bobby had to figure out what to do each time it was his turn, and he became time-troubled early on. Increasingly nervous, he bit his nails, toyed with his hair, sat on his folded legs, then kneeled on the chair, put his elbow on the table, and rested his chin first on one hand and then on the other. Byrne had just defeated Samuel Reshevsky, the strongest American grandmaster in the tournament, and his chess ability was not to be disrespected. Bobby wasn't panicked, but he was decidedly uneasy.

Kibitzers began gathering around his board, and each time Bobby had to get up to visit the tiny restroom in the back of the club, he almost had to fight his way through the scrum. It interfered with his concentration: Normally, an ongoing game resonated within him even if he left the table. "The onlookers were invited to sit right next to you and if you asked them to leave or be quiet they were highly insulted," Bobby recalled. He also noted that the warm Indian summer weather and the press of a large number of people made the room stifling. Bobby's complaints were heard by the club's organizers, but too late to do anything about it that night. The next summer the Marshall put in its first air conditioner.

Despite his discomfort, Bobby plunged ahead with the game. Surprisingly, after only eleven moves, he'd almost magically built a positional advantage. Then, suddenly, he moved his knight to a square where it could be snapped off by his opponent. "What is he *doing*?" said someone to no one in particular. "Is this a blunder or a sacrifice?" As the onlookers scrutinized the position, Bobby's ploy became obvious to all: Although not profound, it was cunning, perhaps ingenious, and even brilliant. Byrne dared not take the knight; though he would have won an important piece, ultimately it would have led to Bobby's victory. The tournament referee described the electricity that Fischer's audacious choice created: "A murmur went through the tournament room after this move, and the kibitzers thronged to Fischer's table as fish to a hole in the ice."

It was exactly the madding crowd that Bobby wished would stay afar. "I was aware of the importance of the game," recalled Allen Kaufman, a master who was studying the game as Bobby played it. "It was a sensational game and everyone was riveted on it. It was extraordinary: The game and Bobby's youth were an unbeatable combination."

As the game progressed, Bobby had only twenty minutes remaining on his clock to make the required forty moves, and he'd so far completed just sixteen of them. And then he saw it: Using a deeper insight, he realized that there was an extraordinary possibility that would change the composition of the position and give a whole new meaning to the game. What if he allowed Byrne to capture his queen, the most powerful piece on the board? Normally, playing without a queen is crippling, almost tantamount to an automatic loss. But what if Byrne, in capturing Bobby's queen, wound up in a weakened position that left him less able to attack the rest of Bobby's forces and less able to protect his own?

The idea for the move grew on Bobby slowly, instinctually at first, without any conscious rationale. It was as though he'd been peering through a narrow lens and the aperture began to widen to take in the entire landscape in a kind of efflorescent illumination. He wasn't absolutely certain he could see the full consequences of allowing Byrne to take his queen, but he plunged ahead, nevertheless.

If the sacrifice was not accepted, Bobby conjectured, Byrne would be lost; but if he *did* accept it, he'd also be lost. Whatever Byrne did, he was theoretically defeated, although the game was far from over. A whisper of spectators could be heard: *"Impossible! Byrne is losing to a 13-year-old nobody."*

Byrne took the queen.

Bobby, now so focused that he could hardly hear the growing murmur from the crowd, made his next moves percussively, shooting them out like poison darts, hardly waiting for Byrne's responses. His chess innocence gone, he could now see the denouement perhaps twenty or more moves ahead. Yet, other than the rapidity with which he was responding to Byrne's moves, Bobby showed little emotion. Rather, he sat still, placid as a little Buddha, stabbing out one startling move after another.

On the forty-first move, after five hours of play, with his heart slightly pounding, Bobby lifted his rook with his trembling right hand, quietly lowered the piece to the board, and said, *"Mate!"* His friendly opponent stood up, and they shook hands. Both were smiling. Byrne knew that even though he was on the wrong end of the result, he'd lost one of the greatest games ever played, and in so doing had become part of chess history. A few people applauded, much to the annoyance of the players whose games were still in progress and cared not that history had been made just a few feet away. They had their own games to worry about. *"Shh! Quiet!"* It was midnight.

Hans Kmoch, the arbiter, a strong player and internationally known theoretician, later appraised the meaning and importance of the game:

> A stunning masterpiece of combination play performed by a boy of 13 against a formidable opponent, matches the finest on record in the history of chess prodigies. . . . Bobby Fischer's [performance] sparkles with stupendous originality.

Thus was born "The Game of the Century," as it was dubbed by Hans Kmoch.

Bobby's game appeared in newspapers throughout the country and chess magazines around the world, and international grandmaster Yuri Averbach, among others, took notice, as did all of his colleagues in the Soviet Union: "After looking at it, I was convinced that the boy was devilishly talented." The British magazine *Chess* relaxed its stiff upper lip, calling Bobby's effort a game of "great depth and brilliancy." *Chess Life* proclaimed Bobby's victory nothing short of "fantastic."

"The Game of the Century" has been talked about, analyzed, and admired for more than fifty years, and it will probably be a part of the canon of chess for many years to come. In the entire history of the game, in terms of its sheer brilliance, not only by a prodigy but by anyone, it might only compare to the game in Breslau in 1912 when spectators showered the board with gold after Frank Marshall—another American—also employed a brilliant sacrifice and beat Levitsky. In reflecting on his game a while after it occurred, Bobby was refreshingly modest: "I just made the moves I thought were best. I was just lucky."

David Lawson, a seventy-year-old American whose accent betrayed his Scottish birth, was one of the spectators that night. Earlier he'd invited Regina and Bobby to dinner after the conclusion of the game, whenever it was finished, whoever won. A tiny man, Lawson was a collector of chess memorabilia and had a particular interest in the diminutive Paul Morphy,

America's first (though unofficial) World Champion. Lawson saw a connection between Fischer and Morphy in their precocious rise, although Bobby had yet to prove himself the world's—let alone America's—greatest player. Lawson was an opportunist, and although he was soft-spoken and possessed Old World manners, his invitation wasn't proffered completely out of courtesy. He'd wanted to acquire one of Bobby's score sheets in the boy's own handwriting to add to his collection, and by coincidence he chose to attend the Byrne-Fischer encounter, not knowing, of course, that the game would become one of the most memorable in the two-thousand-year history of chess.

Lawson's preference for dinner was Luchow's, the German restaurant that had been far beyond the Fischer family's means when they'd lived across the street from it some seven years before. But since it was past midnight, the kitchen was closed, so the trio repaired instead to an all-night local eatery on Sixth Avenue, the Waldorf Cafeteria—a Greenwich Village hangout for artists, writers, and roustabouts. It is here that the story of the score sheet becomes cloudy. Normally, in important tournaments, a score sheet is backed up with a carbon copy, the original going to the tournament organizers or referee for safekeeping should there be a subsequent dispute of any kind. The carbon is retained by the player. That night Bobby kept his copy—the carbon—which he wouldn't part with for many years. Indeed, upon request, he'd take out of his pocket the folded and slightly worn sheet and show it to admirers. So what happened to the original?

Kmoch, the arbiter, sensing that Bobby was a champion in the making, had already begun collecting the prodigy's original score sheets as if they were early Rembrandt sketches. And somehow, most likely by paying for it, Lawson acquired from Kmoch the original "Game of the Century" score sheet, which bore Kmoch's notation in large red-penciled numerals: 0–1 (indicating the loss for Byrne, the win for Fischer). Eventually, upon Lawson's death, the score sheet was purchased by a collector, sold again, and for the last number of years it has rested with yet another collector. In today's market, the estimated auction price for the original score sheet is $100,000.

Bobby's remuneration from the American Chess Foundation for his sparkling brilliancy? Fifty dollars.

It was his fourteenth birthday, a typically windswept March afternoon, bone-dry and cold, and as Bobby worked his way along Central Park South toward the Manhattan Chess Club, to the most important match of his burgeoning career, he was shivering from the wind, not from fear. It was a good feeling to get inside the well-heated club.

His opponent, Dr. Max Euwe, from Holland, was waiting. Fifty-six years old, conservatively dressed, and well over six feet tall, he appeared a giant next to Bobby. Aside from the four decades that separated their ages, they were a study in opposites. Euwe, a doctor of philosophy and a professor of mathematics at the Amsterdam Lyceum, was a former World Champion, having defeated his predecessor in 1935 with a studied and logical approach to the game. He was an even-tempered, soft-spoken, and mature grandmaster who represented the old guard, and over a lifetime of tournament warfare he'd played many of the game's legendary figures. His gentle demeanor aside, he thrived on combat, and improbably, given his academic and chess prowess, he'd once been the European heavyweight amateur boxing champion. Bobby, in contrast, was nervous and volatile, the chess arriviste of Brooklyn, a colt of a player, and as it was beginning to develop, the spearhead of the coming generation of American players. He was pleased that he'd won the U.S. Junior Championship the previous summer, but above all, he'd begun to have increased confidence in himself after his celebrated "Game of the Century." In just six months that game had established him as more than just a curiosity: He was now a new star in the international chess galaxy. As much as Bobby wanted to play Euwe, the renowned doctor was just as intrigued by the prospect of playing the prodigy.

Bobby greeted Dr. Euwe with a polite handshake and a gentle smile. Billed as a "friendly" contest—no titles were at issue—the two-game exhibition match was sponsored by the Manhattan Chess Club to give Bobby an opportunity to play against a world-class master. The stakes were pitifully small: $100 overall, $65 to the winner, and $35 for the loser.

Sitting at the chess table, the professor and the teenager created an almost comic tableau. Euwe's long legs could barely fit underneath, and he sat obliquely, somewhat casually, as if he wasn't truly a part of the action. In contrast, Bobby—all seriousness—had to sit upright to reach the pieces, his elbows just finding their way to the top of the board. A small crowd, hardly an audience, gathered around to follow the moves.

Euwe, in grandmasterly fashion, thoroughly outplayed Bobby until they reached the twentieth move, at which point Bobby, realizing that his position was hopeless, toppled his king in resignation. Feeling humiliated, Bobby burst out of the club in tears and ran to the subway. For his part, Euwe didn't evince much pride in his swift victory, since he felt that Bobby "was only a boy." He then quickly added, "But a promising one!"

The next day Bobby was back promptly at 2:30 p.m. for the second and final game of the match. This time he had the slight advantage of playing with the white pieces, which allowed him to employ his favorite opening strategy. Since he'd lost the day before, he was determined not to lose again. After an exchange of pieces, he emerged with a pawn ahead in an endgame that looked as though it would lead to a draw. When Bobby offered to trade rooks, Euwe responded by offering him a draw on the forty-first move. Bobby pondered for a long while and, with no apparent winning chances left, reluctantly agreed.

To wrest a draw from a former World Champion was neither small cheese nor minor chess, but Bobby was unhappy since he'd lost the match, 1½-½. Oddly, in the more than fifty years since, although virtually all of Bobby's games have been analyzed and published—good games and bad; wins, draws, and losses—the complete score of the Fischer-Euwe draw has not only gone unpublished, but the game itself has gone unheralded in the chess press.

Contrary to the popular press's portrayal of Regina Fischer as the absent mother who left Bobby alone to rear himself, she was actually a doting and caring parent who loved her son and was concerned about his welfare. Raising two children as a single parent and trying to complete her own education, she just didn't have much time to spend with Bobby, nor did she have enough income to provide all the things she wanted to give him. One writer has claimed that the two didn't speak to each other for more than thirty years; that's simply false. They were always in touch, even when she remarried and went to Europe to finish her medical degree when Bobby was in his twenties. They shared messages, phone conversations, and gifts throughout their entire lives, all delivered with love, even though they might have been continents apart.

Most biographers have failed to make the salient point that the Fischer family was exceedingly poor—bordering on poverty, in fact—and every decision about which tournaments to enter, where to play, even which chess books and periodicals to buy came down to a question of money or lack thereof. During the 1950s and 1960s, the time of Bobby's initial and then most intense ascent, an expenditure of just $5 was considered burdensome by both mother and son. It could be that this penury was the catalyst for Bobby's often-criticized "greediness" later in his career. Bobby, on his way up the chess ladder, at one point wrote, "Many people imagine that the chess club or some other chess organization would take care of my travel expenses, buy chess literature for me, or in some other way finance me. It would be nice, or it would have been nice, but it just happens not to be so."

As worrying as the family's financial state was to Regina, her concerns about Bobby's mental health, personality, and behavior eventually became preoccupying. Aside from taking Bobby to meet a psychologist, and her talk with the doctor about what to do with her son, she was always trying to guide Bobby to broaden himself through attending cultural events, engaging in sports, meeting other children, reading, and paying attention to his academic studies. She was pleased that Bobby found self-esteem in chess. What concerned her was that his life lacked balance; she worried that his chess single-mindedness wasn't healthy.

In 1956, Dr. Reuben Fine, an American who was one of the world's best chess players from the 1930s through the 1940s, wrote a monograph entitled *Psychoanalytic Observations on Chess and Chess Masters,* which was published as Volume 3 of *Psychoanalysis,* a journal of psychoanalytic psychology. Afterward, it became available as a separate seventy-four-page book, with a red-and-white chessboard cover. A certain amount of skepticism and even resentment was felt by many of the chess players who took the time to read it. Regina Fischer bought a copy and read it carefully; the book was found in Bobby's library years later, but whether *he* ever read it is unknown.

Fine, a devoted Freudian (he'd go on to write two book-length studies of Freud's theories and a history of psychoanalysis), took the position that chess is symbolically related to the libido and has Oedipal significance: "The King stands for the boy's penis in the phallic stage, the self-image of man, and the father cut down to the boy's size."

He also devoted a chapter to the psychoses of four chess masters, selected from the millions of normal people who'd played seriously over the years. This imbalance provoked criticism for its promotion of the belief that all chess players are seriously addled.

Regina was impressed enough with the book, however, and with Dr. Fine's chess credentials (he was an international grandmaster and had been a contender for the world title) to think he might be able to help Bobby, or at least temper the boy's slavish devotion to the game. She wanted her son to do well in high school, enter a prestigious university, and get down and do some real work.

Regina arranged for Dr. Fine to telephone Bobby and invite him to his home just for an evening of chess. Bobby was well aware of Fine's chess reputation, having played over his games; he also owned and had read several of his chess books. Bobby was suspicious, however. He didn't want psychological probing. Fine assured him that he just wanted to play a few games with him.

Reuben Fine was not a therapist in the strict sense of the word, but he *was* a renowned psychoanalyst. His theory was that the problems of many troubled patients rested in forgotten psychic traumas, and through free association and the interpretation of dreams the key to the problems could be unlocked. The cure was usually a long process—sometimes lasting years—starting first with childhood memories and even, if possible, memories formed in utero.

Fine's office was located in a huge apartment on the Upper West Side of Manhattan. One wing of it was his home, which he shared with his wife and three children; the other part consisted of an analysis room, complete with a Freudian fainting couch, and a group room next door. Patients underwent a minimum of one hour a week of analysis at $55 a session, and some participated in group sessions in the evening. Fine would sit in on the groups for one hour, say nothing, and observe how the members interacted with one another, and then for the final hour he'd quit the room and the group would continue alone. He'd then briefly discuss that session the next time each patient appeared for psychoanalysis. With Bobby, Fine wanted to first gain the boy's trust and respect by playing chess, and then begin classical Freudian analysis, in tandem with the group process.

So that Bobby wouldn't think he was being psychoanalyzed, Fine avoided bringing the boy into his analysis room at first, instead inviting him to the home wing of the apartment. Bobby met Fine's wife Marcia and their children, and then he and Fine played speed chess for an hour or two. The psychoanalyst was then one of the fastest players in the country, perhaps even stronger than Bobby had anticipated. Fine would later write that Bobby "was not yet strong opposition. My family remembers how furious he was after each encounter, muttering that I was 'lucky.'"

After about six weekly sessions of chess, at the point when Fine believed Bobby had bonded with him, the psychoanalyst nonchalantly started a conversation about what Bobby was doing in school. Bobby was on his feet in seconds, recognizing that he'd been duped. "You've tricked me," he blurted out, and stalked out of the apartment, never to go back. Fine later remarked that whenever the two saw each other after that, at a chess club or a tournament, Bobby would give him an angry look "as though I had done him some immeasurable harm by trying to get a little closer to him."

Although there may be some substance to Fine's implication that Bobby's hostility was all about the psychoanalyst's attempt to "get closer," to peel back his layers, the main reason that Bobby never talked to him again was Fine's *deception,* and his use of chess to accomplish it. In a boastful statement, Fine wrote "that it becomes one of the ironic twists of history that of the two leading American chess masters of the twentieth century one almost became the psychoanalyst of the other." *Hardly.*

Bobby, for his part, didn't think that anything was wrong with him. At thirteen, his behavior at chess tournaments and in clubs was quite benign, but like many teenagers, he was sometimes too loud when talking, clumsy when walking past games in progress, unkempt in grooming, and a perennial "bobber" at the board. There was nothing in his actions, however—at *that* time—that indicated serious problems or advanced neurosis.

Perhaps Fine's monograph gave impetus to the press; whenever they did chess stories, reporters would look for a certain amount of aberration among the players. Bobby, therefore, frequently became a victim of a twisted interpretation of his personality. When he was interviewed by a reporter, he was often asked patronizing or offensive questions ("How come you don't have a girlfriend?" . . . "Are all chessplayers crazy?"), and it became clear to him that they were going to slant the story to make him appear weird. "Ask me something usual," he once said to a reporter, "instead of making me look unusual." To another he talked about newspapermen in general: "Those guys always write bad stories about me. They say I'm stupid and that I have no talent in anything except for chess. It's not true."

Some articles proclaimed Bobby an idiot savant, with emphasis on the first word rather than the second. *Chess Life*, indignant at the disrespect shown Bobby, came to his defense, calling such articles "Fischer-baiting" and proclaiming them "utter nonsense."

Of course, Bobby *was* obsessed with chess and spent hours playing and studying it, but perhaps not any more than musical prodigies practice their craft. And he did have other interests, including sports. He saw as many hockey games as he could, was an active tennis player, skied, swam, and belonged to a Ping-Pong club in Manhattan. Science interested him most of all. What he was *not* interested in was hypnotism and prehistoric animals, as some pop-culture articles indicated.

The press was sometimes negative enough to cause those around Bobby to revise their opinion of him. Some players at the Manhattan Chess Club began huffing that he was a meshuggener—a Yiddish term of disparagement suggesting he was "a little crazy." But others, also using Yiddish, referred to him as a *gaon*, a genius.

Despite all the discussion about Bobby, including the nicknames and the petty comments leveled at him, he just continued to play and study the game that he loved. During that one year, from 1956 to 1957, Bobby's official rating soared. Just fourteen years old, he was now officially ranked as a chess master, the youngest person ever to achieve that ranking in the United States. By the rules of the U. S. Chess Federation he could no longer play in amateur tournaments, which was fine by him. Bobby always wanted to play the strongest players possible, seeing it as a way to hone his abilities. And every time he defeated a player with a higher rating, his own rating rose.

In July, four months after the match with Euwe, he traveled to San Francisco to play again in the U.S. Junior Championship, which he won for the second year in a row. For each Junior Championship win he was awarded a typewriter, as well as a trophy and a parchment certificate with his name imprinted. As a result of now owning *two* typewriters, he began to teach himself how to touch-type from a typing book, covering the letters with tape to memorize their positions, locating the starting position, and then checking to see if what he typed made any sense. He could quickly locate the keys that he wanted—memory was never a problem with him—but he never learned to build up real speed without first peeking at the keyboard.

On top all of the prizes he was winning, he defeated grandmaster Samuel Reshevsky at an exhibition at the Manhattan Chess Club, although Bobby later recalled that it was not much of an accomplishment: Reshevsky was blindfolded (and Bobby was not) and they played at ten seconds a move. It was, however, his first grandmaster scalp.

After winning the United States Junior in San Francisco, instead of going back home to Brooklyn and then journeying out again to Cleveland to play in the United States Open, Bobby stayed on the West Coast. That gave him three weeks to relax, play chess, and travel around California. Several other boys from the tournament traveled with him and he visited Los Angeles and Long Beach, where he stayed in the home of chess player/entrepreneur Lina Grumette and swam in her pool. An elegant public relations agent, Grumette conducted a regular chess salon in her home, which players paid to attend. During the 1940s she'd been one of the strongest female players in the United States. When she met Bobby, she took a maternal interest in him, and she became one of his few lifelong friends, ultimately playing an important part in his career.

After their three-week hiatus, the young players borrowed an old automobile from the editor of the *California Chess Reporter,* Guthrie McClain. Since most were too young to have a driver's license, William G. Addison, a twenty-four-year-old who also was going to play in Cleveland, got behind the steering wheel and they headed east to the tournament. The car kept breaking down, and everyone chipped in to have it repaired so that they could keep going. Riding through the hot desert with no air-conditioning led to petty arguments, and a fistfight broke out between Bobby and Gilbert Ramirez (who'd taken second place in the United States Junior). Bobby bit Ramirez on the arm, leaving scars that remain fifty years later. (Ramirez proudly displays them, as if to say, "This is the arm that was bitten by Bobby Fischer.") Eventually, the car broke down entirely and had to be abandoned. The boys arrived in Cleveland by bus on the evening before play began at the U.S. Open.

Before he was to play his first game, Bobby was rated at 2298, making him among the top ten active players in the country. There were 176 players in the two-week, twelve-round tournament. For his first round, Bobby was paired to play white against a Canadian player who'd registered in advance and paid his entry fee but was nowhere in sight. When the tournament began, Bobby made his first move and pressed his clock, which then started counting down against his invisible opponent. After an hour of waiting, the game was declared a forfeit, and Bobby received a gratis point. Curiously, later in the tournament that "free" point almost led to his downfall. In his next five games, Bobby won three and drew two; one of the draws was with twenty-seven-year-old Arthur Bisguier, the defending United States Open Champion and one of the strongest players in the nation.

In the second half of the tournament Bobby won five games straight, and it was certain that he'd be among the prizewinners. But could he win the title? Several players in the tournament had come down with the flu—including Bobby's teacher, Jack Collins—and had to forfeit games. Bobby tried to keep himself fit by getting enough sleep, eating healthfully, and staying in his room as much as possible, away from the other players. As it developed, the flu forfeits didn't affect Bobby's pairings or score.

In the final round Bobby had to face Walter Shipman, the man who'd first welcomed him at the Manhattan Chess Club. Shipman had a reputation as a fearsome and stubborn player. The game didn't evolve to Bobby's liking, so he offered Shipman a draw on the eighteenth move. It was quickly accepted. Bobby had a score of 10–2 and hadn't lost a game. Arthur Bisguier, the highest rated player in the tournament, also finished with a score of 10–2. Who then was to be the United States Open Champion?

Bobby, Bisguier, and about twenty other players and spectators stood around the tournament director's desk as he applied the tie-breaking system to determine the winner. The ideal way to break a tie is to have a play-off between the two players. However, in American tournaments, where hotel ballrooms are rented and contracted for a specified period and players have made arrangements for flights home, it's necessary to apply a tie-breaking system to determine the winner. There are many such systems used in tournaments, and they're as complicated as abstract mathematical theorems. Few are applied without controversy.

While they were waiting for the results, Bisguier asked Bobby why he'd offered the draw to Shipman when he had a slight advantage and the outcome wasn't certain. If Bobby had *won* that game, he would have been the tournament's clear winner, a half point ahead of Bisguier. Bobby replied that he had more to gain than lose by the decision. He'd assumed that Bisguier would either win or draw his own game, and if so, Bobby would have at least a tie for first place. That meant a payday of $750 for each player, a virtual gold mine for Fischer. Recognizing Bobby's greater need for money than the capture of a title, however prestigious, Bisguier noted: "Evidently, his mature judgment is not solely confined to the chessboard."

The tournament director continued to make calculations, finally looking up and declaring that Bisguier had won. Bobby, crestfallen, recalled: "I went to the phone booth and called my mother to tell her the bad news. In the booth next to me was Bisguier, phoning his good news to his family." After that, both players returned to the tournament hall to watch the conclusions of the other games.

After two hours had passed during which people congratulated Bisguier as the champion, the tournament director announced that he'd made a mistake in the calculations. Under the Median System of tie-breaking, which was to be used in all tournaments conducted by the United States Chess Federation, all of the scores of all of the opponents of the players who are tied are totaled, the top two and the lower two are deleted, and whoever played the highest rated (and therefore more difficult) opponents would be declared the winner. Under this system, Fischer emerged a half point higher than Bisguier. But wait a minute, argued Bisguier: Fischer's first game was won by a forfeit; his opponent didn't show up, so he didn't even play the game! If that game was discounted, he claimed, then *he* would be the winner. The counterargument was that the forfeited player in the first round was of such a low rating that it would have been almost statistically impossible for Bobby to have lost the game, and the result would have been discounted anyway. Back to the telephone booths.

This time, Bobby told Regina the good news, admitting that even though he was splitting the prize money with Bisguier, "it was the title that really mattered." One wonders, then, why he didn't fight for the win against Shipman and win the title outright.

No one as young as Bobby had won the United States Open before, and no one had ever held the United States Junior and Open titles concurrently.

When Bobby returned to New York, both the Marshall and Manhattan chess clubs conducted victory celebrations, and he was lauded as America's new chess hero. Even Bisguier, not prolonging any resentment, proclaimed Bobby Fischer as the strongest fourteen-year-old chess player who had ever lived.

After a summer of chess, Regina insisted that Bobby devote more attention to his sporting interests. So he swam at the YMCA and began to take tennis lessons, while also playing on the free city-owned courts. He hated going to the free courts, since it took two buses to get to the closest one, and then he'd have to wait sometimes for more than an hour to get a game. Nevertheless, he continued to play into late fall, until the weather became too cold and damp. Mother and son looked into his joining an indoor tennis club for the winter months, but when they discovered there was an initiation fee and a $10-per-hour charge, "it was, of course, ridiculous for us to consider," Bobby lamented.

Returning home from school one afternoon in September, Bobby sorted through his mail. He'd started to receive fan letters and requests for photos, autographs, even some selected game scores to autograph and inscribe—not just from the United States but from different corners of the globe. The letters didn't pour in at the level experienced by Hollywood stars, but hardly a day would go by that several pieces of request mail did not arrive at 560 Lincoln Place. Additionally, Bobby regularly received unsolicited advice from fellow chess players, as well as offers from companies that wanted him to sponsor products. Sporadically, Bobby would select a letter at random and reply with a personal note. To speed up the "fan relations" process, Regina had Bobby's photograph placed in an inexpensive greeting card on which was printed his signature, and she'd mail that out to the various requesters. She also responded to the commercial offers, but for reasons of his own, Bobby showed almost no interest in them, whatever the price offered.

One letter he almost skipped over came in an envelope on which was imprinted the Manhattan Chess Club logo. When he opened it, all he could do was smile:

Mr. Robert J. Fischer
560 Lincoln Place
Brooklyn, 38, N.Y.

New York, September 24, 1956

Dear Mr. Fischer:

You are hereby invited to participate in the Lessing J. Rosenwald Tournament for the United States Championship, co-sponsored by the United States Chess Federation and the American Chess Foundation.

This tournament will also be the official Zonal Tournament of FIDE in its World's Championship competition.

The tournament will be held in New York City at the Manhattan Chess Club from December 15, 1957, to January 6, 1958. There will be fourteen participants. The playing schedule is enclosed herewith.

Please advise us at your earliest convenience but not later than October 10, 1957, whether or not you will participate in this tournament. If we do not receive your acceptance by October 14, 1957, we will assume that you are declining this invitation.

THE TOURNAMENT COMMITTEE

M.J. Kasper, Chairman
Walter J. Fried
I.A. Horowitz
William J. Lombardy
Edgar T. McCormick
Walter J. Shipman

As the newly reigning United States Open Champion, and a participant in the Rosenwald the previous year, Bobby had anticipated getting this invitation for the 1957 tournament. What particularly intrigued him, though, was that this tournament would be the qualifying tournament for the Interzonal, which was the beginning of the path to the World Championship. Interzonal tournaments were only held every four years, and this coming year happened to be *the* year. He should have been thrilled with the invitation, but he faced a conflict, and thus was forced to puzzle out what to do.

The problem was that the Rosenwald overlapped with the great Hastings Christmas Congress in England, the annual international tournament that, over the years, had seen some of the greatest chess legends capture first prize. Bobby had been invited to that tournament and wanted to enter its elite winner's circle. It would be his first real trip abroad, and his first international event, and it would be against some of the world's finest players.

He couldn't decide what to do.

After he had talked the situation over with his mother and his friends at the club, his mind was finally set. Youth believes it has no limits, and shows little patience. In the end Bobby could not tolerate a denial of his destiny. He notified the Rosenwald Committee that he'd accept their invitation to compete for the United States Championship—the prelude, he hoped, to eventually capturing the World Championship as well.

In December, just before play began in the United States Championship, Bisguier predicted that "Bobby Fischer should finish slightly over the center mark in this tournament. He is quite possibly the most gifted of all players in the tournament; still he has had no experience in tournaments of such consistently even strength." Bisguier's crystal-ball divination seemed logical, but of course Bobby *had* had experience from the previous year's Rosenwald. And although many other tournaments in which he'd played may not have included the very top players in the country, there were enough that skirted the summit. Throughout 1956 (when Bobby traveled some nine thousand miles to compete in tournaments) and through 1957, he never stopped playing, studying, and analyzing.

It seemed that his strength grew not just from tournament to tournament and match to match, but from day to day. Each game that he played, or analyzed, whether his or others', established a processional of insight. He was always working on the game, *his* game, refining it, seeking answers, asking questions, pulling out his threadbare pocket set while in the subway, walking in the street, watching television, or eating in a restaurant, his fingers moving as if they had a mind of their own.

The New York winter wind began to blow snow flurries through the trees of Central Park as Bobby entered the Manhattan Chess Club for the first round of the United States Championship. Immediately, a buzz of awe passed among the spectators, some of whom called out—as if Jack Dempsey had entered the ring—*"There's Fischer."*

Perhaps Bisguier was right. The field *did* seem stronger than the previous year. Players who turned down the invitation in 1956 accepted readily in 1957, as Bobby had, because of the importance of the tournament. Almost all of the fourteen entrants wanted an opportunity to go to the Interzonal, and it was rumored that some had entered to take a crack at Bobby Fischer. It was a chance to play against a growing legend.

Bobby walked to his board and silently sneered at the chess timer. It looked like two alarm clocks side by side and had a plunger on its flanks for each player. Bobby disliked the timer because it took up too much room on the table—plus, you had to push the plunger forward to stop your clock and start your opponent's. That took too much time, especially when a player faced time pressure and every second counted. In contrast, the new BHB clocks from Germany featured buttons on top, which made them much faster to operate: As one's hand quit the piece, in a swift motion one could hit the button with one's retracting hand, thereby saving a second or two. There was rhythm that could be established with top-button clocks, and Fischer had become a connoisseur of that kind of clock. Nevertheless, in the 1957 championship he put up with the old push-plunger clunkers.

Bobby started off with a win against Arthur Feuerstein, defeating the young up-and-comer for the first time. Bobby then drew with Samuel Reshevsky, who was the defending champion, in an extremely intense game—and the fourteen-year-old was on fire after that, at one point amassing five wins in a row.

Bobby's last-round opponent was the rotund Abe Turner, a perpetual acting student whose great claim to thespian fame was that he'd been a contestant on Groucho Marx's television program, *You Bet Your Life*. Turner, who exhibited an *opéra bouffe* appearance but was a slashing and dangerous player, had beaten Bobby in the previous year's Rosenwald. So Bobby was especially careful when playing him. After only a few minutes, though, Turner, in his high-pitched voice, offered Bobby a draw on the eighteenth move. Bobby accepted and then nonchalantly walked around the club as the other games were still being contested. He'd amassed 10 ½ points, and just as at the United States Open, he hadn't lost a game. The peach-faced Lombardy, who wasn't in the running for the title, was playing the venerated Reshevsky, and the Old Fox stood at 9 ½ points. If Reshevsky defeated Lombardy, he'd equal Bobby's score and they'd be declared co-champions: In this championship there were no tie-breaking systems or play-offs. To while away the time, and perhaps to feign indifference until the deciding game was finished, Bobby began playing speed chess with a few of his chess friends. Occasionally, he'd wander over to the Lombardy-Reshevsky game and scan it for a few seconds. Eventually, after making one of these trips, he declared matter-of-factly, as if there was no room for debate, "Reshevsky's busted." Lombardy was playing the game of his life, steamrolling over Reshevsky's position. When it was entirely hopeless, Reshevsky removed his lighted cigarette from its holder, pursed his lips, and resigned. Bobby came over to the board and said to his friend, "You played tremendously." The twenty-year-old Lombardy smiled and said, "Well, what could I do? You forced me to beat Sammy!" With Reshevsky's loss, fourteen-year-old Bobby Fischer was the United States Chess Champion.

4

The American Wunderkind

THE ODYSSEY BECAME more than just a routine or a habit. It was a ritual, a quest for chess wisdom. After classes during the school year, on Saturdays, and all throughout the summer when he wasn't playing in tournaments—on the days that he didn't go to the Collins home—Bobby would walk to the Flatbush Avenue subway station and take the train across the East River into Manhattan, exiting at Union Square. He'd stride south on Broadway to Greenwich Village, and make his way to the Four Continents Book Store, an emporium of Russian-language books, music recordings, periodicals, and handmade gifts such as nested *martryoshka* dolls. It has been confirmed through the Freedom of Information Act that the FBI conducted an investigation and surveillance of the Four Continents from the 1920s to the 1970s, amassing fifteen thousand reports, photos, and documents on whoever entered, exited, or bought from the store, looking for potential Communist sympathizers or Soviet agents. In the 1950s, when Bobby frequented the establishment, the Bureau was particularly active, hoping to supply information to the House Un-American Activities Committee.

The Four Continents stocked a small but potent collection of chess books, as well as the latest copies of *Shakhmatny Bulletin,* a newly launched Russian-language periodical. This chess magazine contained theoretical articles and reports on the latest games from around the world, mostly games involving players from the Soviet Union. Fischer learned when the new copies would arrive each month, and within a day or two of their appearance he'd be at the Four Continents to purchase the latest edition. To others he proclaimed *Shakhmatny Bulletin* "the best chess magazine in the world."

He'd play over the magazine's featured games assiduously, following the exploits of eighteen-year-old Boris Spassky, the chess comet who'd won the World Junior Championship in 1955. He also studied the games of Mark Taimanov, the 1956 champion of the Soviet Union—and a concert pianist—who introduced novelties in opening play that Fischer found instructive. Thumbing through copies of each edition, Bobby made a mental note of which openings being played around the world won more games than others and which seemed too unorthodox. He also noted the games that ignited his interest toward further exploration. The games of the masters that he discovered in *Shakhmatny* became his models; later, some of these masters would emerge as his competitors.

At the Four Continents, Bobby bought a hardcover Russian-language copy of the *Soviet School of Chess* for $2. A classic of contemporary chess literature, it had been issued as a propagandistic treatise to highlight the "rise of the Soviet school to the summit of world chess [as] a logical result of socialistic cultural development." Even as a teenager, it's likely that Bobby was able to separate the not-so-subtle Soviet attempt at indoctrination from the sheer brilliance of the games and what he learned from them. He was in awe of the acuity and the rapid, intuitive understanding of the Soviet players, inarguably the best in the world at that time. When Bobby was fourteen, he gave an interview to a visiting Russian journalist from *Shakhmatny v SSSR (Chess in the Soviet Union)* saying that he wanted to play the best Russian masters, and elaborated: "I watch what your grandmasters do. I know their games. They are sharp, attacking, full of fighting spirit."

Bobby browsed and shopped at the Four Continents for years, and nothing attracted him more than a book he'd heard spoken about in almost reverential whispers: Isaac Lipnitsky's *Questions of Modern Chess Theory*. For chess players, the book became an instant classic the moment it was published in 1956, and copies were scarce. A chess-playing friend, Karl Burger, ten years older, who went on to become a medical doctor and an international master, first told Bobby about the tome, feeding the boy's imagination about the wisdom it contained. Bobby was eager to read it but had to place a special order through the Four Continents. Only months later did it arrive, poorly printed on cheap paper and filled with typographical errors.

Bobby cared nothing about the book's physical appearance, though. He pored over the pages, as if he were a philosophy student attempting to understand Immanuel Kant's *Critique of Pure Reason*. He struggled with the Russian and continually asked his mother to translate some of the prose passages that accompanied the annotations of the moves. She didn't mind at all and was, in fact, delighted that he was learning some Russian. For his part, Bobby was astonished at how much insight he absorbed from the book.

Lipnitsky stressed the connection between commanding the center squares of the board and seizing the initiative through the mobilization of the pieces. It's a simple notion, almost rudimentary, but accomplishing this in an actual game can be quite difficult. Lipnitsky didn't just fling concepts at the reader, but rather gave clear and logical examples of how to do what he recommended. In his own games Bobby began employing some of Lipnitsky's suggestions and adopted a plan called the Lipnitsky Attack when playing against the Sicilian Defense. Years later, he'd quote Lipnitsky's precepts in his own writings.

After spending perhaps an hour in the Four Continents in pursuit of the best in current chess literature, Bobby would cross the street to the Dickensian shop of the phlegmatic Dr. Albrecht Buschke, where he sought an entrée into the past. The shop was located deep within the innards of an old office building that, one hundred years earlier, had been the Hotel St. Denis, the place where Paul Morphy, America's unofficial World Champion, had stayed when he played in the First American Chess Congress. For Bobby, the building was a totemic destination since it also contained the offices of the U.S. Chess Federation, housed in what had been the St. Denis's bridal suite.

Buschke's lair was no larger than a small bedroom. It smelled of mold, was redolent of antique paper and bindings, and was permeated with a perennial gray cloud from Buschke's cigar. Used chess books were everywhere, hidden in every conceivable crevice, many stacked from floor to ceiling or on top of chairs, or weighing down and bending the shelves. Some were haphazardly strewn across the floor; none seemed to be in thematic order. If a customer questioned the proprietor about a book's price being too high, he had the perverse habit of saying, "Oh, I'm sorry," erasing the price that had been penciled in, and autocratically adding a new one that was higher!

Bobby pored over Buschke's holdings for hours, looking for that one book, that one magazine, that one luminous game that might lead him to enlightenment. And he bought some books that were many decades old, such as Rudolf von Bilguer's *Handbuch* and Wilhelm Steinitz's *Modern Chess Instructor*. The serendipity of finding a book he hadn't known about was delicious, as was the pleasure of discovering the expected—a book he knew he wanted if only he could find it in Buschke's labyrinth.

Bobby's funds were meager, but the good doctor would often give him a discount price, a policy he shared with absolutely no one else. When Bobby won the U.S. Championship, Buschke gave him a $100 gift certificate, and he took months to select his gift books, picking nothing but the best.

From Buschke's, Bobby would sprint around the corner to the University Place Book Shop, just a pawn's throw away. The store had a chess collection—at prices lower than Buschke's—combined with a specialization in Caribbean and radical literature. It was at that store that Bobby met a short man named Archie Waters, who wasn't only a chess player but also the World Champion of a variation of draughts called Spanish Pool Checkers, played for money in Harlem and other urban neighborhoods. Waters, a journalist by profession, had written two books on the variation, both of which he presented to Bobby—eventually, he'd teach the boy the intricacies of the game and become a lifelong friend. Bobby obligingly studied Waters's books and other checkers books, but he never entered a tournament. He enjoyed checkers but found it far less of a challenge than chess. The only thing the two games had in common, he said, was the board of light and dark squares.

Within the chess world, Bobby at fourteen was something of a celebrity, and the general media were also finding his anomalous background good copy for their publications: a poor kid from Brooklyn who seemed interested only in chess, carelessly—or certainly, casually—dressed, talking in monosyllables, and beating the most renowned adepts of the day. Each story generated more publicity, and Regina, while conflicted about her son's prospects, tried to help Bobby by capitalizing on the attention. Her oft-quoted statement that she'd tried everything she could to discourage her son from playing chess "but it was hopeless" had been blurted out in an offhand moment in an attempt to deflect the blame she was receiving for not broadening him. The truth is, she knew that Bobby's self-chosen raison d'être was to become the world's best at chess, and like any mother wanting her child to achieve his dreams, she supported him, ultimately becoming his pro bono press agent, advocate, and manager.

From that point forward, there wasn't a tournament Bobby played in or an exhibition he conducted that wasn't pre-ballyhooed by a press release Regina sent to the media. She also compiled the addresses and telephone numbers of the major radio and television stations, newspapers, and magazines in New York City, and if her press release didn't work in generating coverage, she called, wrote personal letters, or—like a true stage mother—visited the newsrooms to promote her son. I. A. Horowitz, the editor of *Chess Review,* claimed that she was a "pain in the neck" for always appealing to him for more publicity for Bobby. She even tried to get on various radio and television quiz shows herself, hoping to bring home some money for being a successful contestant. She was pre-interviewed for television quiz shows such as *Top Dollar* and *Lucky Partners,* but despite her high intelligence and erudition she was never chosen.

That Regina was apt to put Bobby's interests above her own and, out of love, signed on to Bobby's dream of chess dominance is hinted in a letter she wrote back when her son had been vacillating between attending the Hastings Christmas Tournament and playing for the U.S. Championship. To Maurice Kasper, president of the American Chess Foundation, she wrote: "I hope Bobby will become a great chess champion some day because he loves chess more than anything else."

During tournaments, either in the United States or abroad, she'd often send Bobby letters, cables, and telegrams of encouragement and advice, such as: "I see you are 1½ so far after two rounds, which is terrific. Keep it up but don't wear yourself down at it. Swim, nap."

Eventually, through Regina's persistence, Bobby received an invitation to be a possible contestant on the most popular show on television, *The $64,000 Question.* The idea was that he'd be answering questions about chess. Several other players were also invited to audition for the proposed show, which would present questions that would focus on the history and lore of the game. Fourteen-year-old Bobby showed up at CBS's Television Studio 52, garbed in his characteristic corduroy pants and flannel shirt buttoned at the collar and displaying an attitude that was one part assurance and one part skepticism.

The way the show worked was that contestants would choose a category, such as movies, opera, baseball, etc., and answer questions that would become exponentially more difficult and ultimately more valuable. The first correct answer was worth $2, then $4, then $8, doubling week after week until the sum of $64,000 was reached, if ever. If a contestant reached the $8,000 plateau and failed to answer that question correctly, he or she was given a new Cadillac as a consolation prize, worth about $5,000 at that time.

The $64,000 Question was so popular that even President Eisenhower watched it every week, telling his staff not to disturb him during its time slot. On the Tuesday nights when the show was broadcast, crime rates fell, and attendance at movie theaters and restaurants dropped. It seemed as if all of America was watching the show, and successful contestants were becoming celebrities in their own right. If chess were chosen as a category for the show, the result could greatly promote the game to the public. The chess fraternity, at least in New York, was all aquiver over the possibility.

Regina Fischer was also atypically giddy about Bobby's prospects, and Bobby, for his part, was excited about using his immense knowledge of the game and the possibility of going all the way, emerging with $64,000 (equivalent to about a half million dollars in today's wealth), thereby solving the family's financial woes.

In the audition, everything went well at first. Bobby correctly answered question after question, until he was asked in what tournaments Yates defeated Alekhine. Bobby thought for a long while, then told his interrogator that it was a trick question, because Yates had never defeated Alekhine.

Surprised because Bobby's answers had been unerringly correct up to that point, the quiz show representative told the boy that Yates had beaten Alekhine in two tournaments: in Hastings in 1922, and in Carlsbad the following year. Bobby was furious, unwilling to admit that he was mistaken.

Yates did defeat Alekhine in those tournaments. Nonetheless, it was not as a result of Bobby's peevishness or slip of the mind that the producers decided against initiating a chess-devoted category segment. The idea died because of the arcane nature of the game. Ultimately, the producers concluded that there just weren't enough people interested in chess to maintain a large enough viewing audience.

Bobby took some of the blame himself. His dreams of wealth quickly slipped away, and he wrote, humbly: "I guess none of us were smart enough to pass inspection. It made interesting conversation while it lasted, anyway."

Returning home one afternoon from her hospital shift, Regina was approached in front of her apartment house at 560 Lincoln Place by two sunglassed men, conservatively dressed. "Mrs. Fischer? Regina Fischer?"

"Yes?" she said.

The men flashed their credentials: They were FBI agents.

"What's this about?"

"May we go inside? We don't like to talk on the street."

"Before I do anything," said Regina, "tell me what you want."

"We just want to ask you some questions."

Regina demurred: "I don't want to answer anything unless I have my lawyer present."

"What are you afraid of? Do you have something to hide?"

"I'm not afraid of anything," Regina answered, "and I have nothing to hide. I just don't want to talk to you unless I have my lawyer with me."

With that, she walked proudly away, entered the vestibule of her building, and trudged upstairs. She was shaking, not because she was concealing anything, but because of the scenario that had just taken place: two law enforcement agents, men who towered over her relatively tiny frame of five feet, four inches, coming at her in a confrontational way in the street.

Regina's political activities—any or all of which could be considered "subversive," taking into account the near hysterical anti-Communist climate of the day—were fodder for the FBI: her six years in Moscow, her mercurial ex-husband in Chile, her work at defense plants, her association with rabble-rousers, her affiliation with left-wing political organizations, and her active participation in protests—such as a vigil she joined on the night of the execution of the convicted spies Ethel and Julius Rosenberg. Had she done anything illegal? Were any of her friends spies? She questioned herself, and then called her lawyer, before telling Joanie and Bobby what had happened.

To her relief, there were no further overt visits from the FBI. What Regina didn't know, however, was that since 1942 the Justice Department had suspected her of being a Soviet espionage agent. Consequently, there was a sweeping investigation taking place of her activities, past and present, spearheaded by FBI director J. Edgar Hoover.

The confidential FBI report on Regina dramatically points up the degree to which McCarthy-inspired paranoia gripped America at that time:

SECRET

It is to be noted that subject is a well-educated, widely traveled intelligent woman who has for years been associated with communists and persons with procommunist leanings. She would appear to be a person who would be ideologically motivated to be of assistance to the Russians. In view of the foregoing and in light of her recent contact of an official of the Soviet Embassy, it is desired that this case be re-opened and that investigation be instituted in an effort to determine if subject has in the past or may presently be engaged in activities inimical to the interest of the United States. Investigation of Fischer is not to be limited to developing additional data concerning her recent contact of XXXXXX. It is desired that the investigation of subject be most searching and pointed towards ascertaining the nature of her present activity and the identity of her associate.

The telephone in the Fischer home was tapped. Undercover agents rifled through Joan Fischer's records at Brooklyn College. Regina was shadowed. Her fellow nurses and neighbors were questioned. Her high school and college records were examined, and her former teachers and administrators were questioned. Even the second wife of Jacob Wender, Bobby's grandfather, was investigated. The investigation would continue for almost a half century and produce some 750 pages of reports, costing the American taxpayers hundreds of thousands—if not millions—of dollars, all ending with a whimper, nary a bang, since nothing definitive was ever found about any espionage activity on Regina's part. "My mother," said Joan Fischer, "is a professional protester." Other than that, the FBI eventually considered Regina Fischer harmless to the security of the United States.

An ironic twist to this red-hunting saga developed when the FBI learned from an informer that Regina had been "kicked out" of the Communist Party—if indeed she'd ever been a member; the informer claimed she'd been active from 1949 to 1951. Supposedly, she'd been ejected for failing to be a "faithful Party member." If that was, in fact, the case, the Bureau reasoned that Regina might be eager to retaliate against the Communists, by being "cooperative and furnishing information regarding persons who were active in the Party and other current information she may possess." If the Bureau had acted on this notion, Regina Fischer might have actually become a counteragent, a spy, for the U.S. government. It would have been a suitable career for her, considering her penchant for intrigue, politics, and travel. No approach to her was ever made, however.

Bobby kept telling his mother that he wanted to go to Russia to try his hand against the best players in the world. Besides his trip to Cuba and his participation in a tournament in Canada when he was twelve, he'd never been out of the country, and Regina, a peripatetic, almost obsessive traveler, was eager for her son to go abroad. But where was the travel money to come from?

She sent a letter directly to Premier Nikita Khrushchev, asking him to extend an invitation to Bobby for the World Youth Festival. While waiting for a reply, Bobby applied for a passport and then submitted an application for a visa to enter Russia. A year later the visa request was granted, and all that was needed was the money for air transportation and expenses. The idea was that Bobby would spend the summer, or part of it, in Russia so as to train before playing in the Interzonal, which was to be held in Yugoslavia.

Agents and informers continued to spy on the Fischers, and the idea that Big Brother could always be watching haunted Regina. Such continued suspicion on her part—which had a valid basis—greatly influenced her children.

She was worried that the FBI might come again, perhaps when she wasn't at home, and begin questioning Bobby. If they were trying to build a case against her, any scrap of information that Bobby might give them could possibly be used against her. She began to train him as to what to say should the investigators appear: "Bobby, if they come, and ask you *any* questions—even your age or where you go to school—just say, *'I have nothing to say to you.'* Don't change the words; do you understand? *'I have nothing to say to you.'*"

She made him repeat the phrase over and over again until she was sure he had it right. In retrospect, Bobby said that it was probable that she had learned the phrase from other people who had been investigated by the FBI, as the most effective tactic. "I think it was terrible that they might have questioned a little boy: I was only ten or twelve at the time." As it developed, Bobby was never questioned, but the fear had been implanted.

As a further protection for Bobby, Regina bought fairly expensive leather covers for his Russian chess books so that the titles could not be read by agents or possible informants and cause trouble for him as he was studying the books while traveling to and from Brooklyn on the subway.

One morning when Bobby was in geometry class, a student from the principal's office appeared with a note for Bobby's teacher. It said that Bobby had been invited to be a contestant on the television show *I've Got a Secret* at four-thirty that afternoon. It was the week after his fifteenth birthday. The show was a guessing game to determine a contestant's "secret," in this case not that Bobby or his mother might be a Communist, but that he was United States Chess Champion. On the broadcast, looking shy and fearful, he held up a mock newspaper specially printed by the show, with a headline that blared, TEENAGER'S STRATEGY DEFEATS ALL COMERS. When the emcee mentioned that his young guest, introduced as "Mister X," was from Brooklyn, someone shouted "Hooray!" and Bobby beamed. When he was asked by a panel member whether what he did, as his secret, made people happy, he quipped: "It made *me* happy," sparking appreciative laughter from the audience (who were in on the secret). Bobby stumped the panel.

Determined to get Bobby to Moscow, Regina had appealed to the producers to help her come up with a ticket not only for her son but also for his sister Joan to accompany him. Perhaps through their phone tap, the FBI learned about the Moscow trip. They dispatched a young-looking undercover agent, posing as a reporter for a college newspaper, to "interview" the public relations representatives at the Goodson-Todman Productions, producers of *I've Got a Secret*. The agent remained throughout the broadcast but did not reveal his true identity.

Since Sabena Airlines was one of the show's sponsors, it was agreed that two round-trip tickets would be given to Bobby as a promotional gift. Without his knowledge, and much to his delight, at the end of the broadcast he was given the tickets to Russia, with a stopover in Belgium, Sabena's home country. So ebullient was he over finally being able to get to the country of his dreams, he tripped with youthful awkwardness on the microphone wire while making his exit from the stage, but managed to keep his balance. At the show's conclusion the FBI immediately phoned their contact in Moscow to make sure Bobby's activities were monitored while he was behind the Iron Curtain.

Someone at the Manhattan Chess Club asked Bobby what he'd do if he were invited to a state dinner while in Moscow, where he'd have to wear a tie; Bobby had never been seen wearing one. "If I have to wear a tie, I won't go," he answered honestly.

It was the first time he'd been in an airplane. Bobby and Joan had a three-day stopover in Brussels and visited Expo 58, one of the greatest international fairs of all time ("The eighth wonder of the world," Bobby wrote to Jack Collins, describing the 335-foot Atomium monument whose nine steep spheres formed the shape of a cell of an iron crystal). While the Belgians were sampling Coca-Cola for the first time, Bobby, avoiding Joan's watchful eye, drank too many bottles of Belgian beer and the next day experienced his first hangover. Nevertheless, he played some seven-minute games—which he won—with the tall and elegant Count Alberic O'Kelly de Galway, an international grandmaster. Bobby also ate as much soft ice cream—another first at the fair—as he could consume. After a few days of fun and education in Brussels, the Fischers were ready to leave, but not before a minor fracas occurred. When checking in, Bobby had rudely voiced objections to the hotel staff over the accommodations they were to have (he didn't want to share a room with his sister), and as they were checking out he was severely criticized by the management, who'd given up the room as a complimentary gesture and were short of space due to the fair. The self-confident fifteen-year-old paid no heed to their discontent and discourteously stormed out.

Before boarding the plane to Russia, Bobby plugged cotton into his ears to reduce the pressure (which had bothered him on the trip from New York to Brussels) and also to block out engine noise so that he could quietly work out variations on his pocket chess set.

Met at the Moscow airport by Lev Abramov, the head of the chess section of the USSR, and by a guide from Intourist, Joan and Bobby were ushered to Moscow's finest hotel, the National. It was an apt choice, since one of the Bolshevik leaders who worked out of there after the Revolution of 1917 was Vladimir Lenin, an active chess player who fostered a continuing interest in the game among the Russian people.

The Fischers enjoyed the amenities of a relatively opulent suite, with two bedrooms and an unobstructed view—across Mokhovaya Street—of the Kremlin, Red Square, and the splendor of the towers of St. Basil's. As part of the celebrity treatment, Bobby was also given a car, driver, and interpreter. Three months before, the Russians had feted another young American: twenty-three-year old Van Cliburn, who'd won the Soviet Union's International Tchaikovsky piano competition and, in so doing, helped momentarily temper the Cold War rivalry of the two countries. Bobby didn't expect to earn the same acclaim, nor did he think he'd melt any diplomatic ice. Nonetheless, Regina thought he should be afforded equal respect and attention. Although many chess players believed that Bobby could emerge as America's answer to the Sputnik, Regina was thinking in more practical terms: She'd read that Van Cliburn had called his mother in Texas each night while he was in Moscow and as a perk wasn't charged for the international telephone call. "Call me," she wrote to Bobby. "It's on the house." He didn't.

His respect for the Soviet players, from what he knew of their games, was immense, and at first, the reality of being in Russia was like being in chess heaven. He wanted to see how the game was taught and played at the state-supported Pioneer Palaces. He wanted to read and purchase Russian chess literature and visit the clubs and parks where chess was played. But mostly he wanted to duel with the best in the world. His mission was to play as many masters as possible and to emulate the Soviets' training regimen for the Yugoslav tournament. Fortune, however, seemed to have other plans.

There was no way that the Soviet chess regime would allow an American to observe their training methods or to share in their chess secrets—especially when the very same players Fischer hoped to train with would be competing against him in a few weeks. The Soviet chess establishment thought of Bobby as a *novinka*—a novelty—but, also, someone ultimately to be feared. They certainly weren't going to aid his attempt to defeat them at their own national pastime.

An itinerary and schedule were established for the Fischers, which included a tour of the city, a sightseeing introduction to the buildings and galleries of the Kremlin, and a visit to the Bolshoi Ballet, the Moscow Circus, and various museums. For Bobby, it was a chance to gorge himself on Russian history and culture. He had little interest, though, in such figures as Ivan the Terrible or Peter the Great or Joseph Stalin or Leo Tolstoy or Alexander Pushkin. He'd come to Moscow to play chess, to cross pawns with a serious Russian tournament player. And every spare minute he spent there he wanted to be engaged in chess, hopefully playing with the highest-rated masters in the country. Moscow was the city where the great tournament of 1925 had been played; where Alekhine had become a grandmaster; where most of the world's top masters played, learned, and lived; where the World Championship had been held only a few months prior. For Bobby, Moscow was the Elysium of chess, and his head was spinning with the possibilities.

Spurning Abramov's offer of an introduction to the city, Bobby asked to be brought immediately to the Tsentralny Shakhmatny Klub, the Moscow Central Chess Club, said to be one of the finest in the world. Virtually all of the strongest players in Moscow belonged to the club, which had been opened in 1956 and boasted a library reported to consist of ten thousand chess books and over one hundred thousand index cards of opening variations. Bobby simply couldn't wait until he saw it all.

Upon arriving at the club's headquarters on Gogolsky Boulevard, Bobby was first introduced to two young Soviet masters, both in their early twenties: Evgeni Vasukov and Alexander Nikitin. He began playing speed chess in rotation with both, in a hallway on the first floor of the club, and won every game. Lev Khariton, a Soviet master, then a teenager, remembered that a crowd gathered. Everyone wanted to see the American wunderkind. "There was a certain loneliness about him hunched above the board," said Khariton.

"When can I play Botvinnik [the World Champion]?" Bobby asked, using a tone that was almost a demand. "And Smyslov [Botvinnik's most recent challenger]?" He was told that because it was summer, both men were at their dachas, quite a distance from Moscow, and unavailable. It may have been true.

"Then what about Keres?"

"Keres is not in the country."

Abramov later claimed that he'd contacted several grandmasters but had made little progress in finding an opponent of the caliber that Fischer was insisting on. True or not, Abramov was becoming more than annoyed by Bobby's brashness and frequent distemper. Bobby begrudgingly met the weight lifters and Olympians he was introduced to, but he seemed bored by it all. The Russians began calling him *Malchick* or "Little Boy." Although it was an affectionate term, to a teenager it could be considered an insult. Bobby didn't like the implication.

Finally, Tigran Petrosian was, on a semi-official basis, summoned to the club. He was an international grandmaster, known as a colorless player but he was almost scientifically precise, and one of the great defensive competitors of all time. He was also an extraordinarily powerful speed player. Bobby knew of him, of course, having played over his games from the Amsterdam tournament of 1956 and also from seeing him from afar at the USA-USSR match in New York four years earlier. Before he arrived, Fischer wanted to know how much money he'd receive for playing Petrosian. "None. You are our guest," Abramov frostily replied, "and we don't pay fees to guests."

The games were played in a small, high-ceilinged room at the end of the hallway, probably to limit the number of spectators, which had grown to several dozen while Bobby was playing the younger men. The contest with the Russian grandmaster was not a formal match, but consisted of speed games, and Petrosian won the majority. Many years later, Bobby indicated that during those speed games Petrosian's style of play had bored him "to death," and that was why he'd wound up losing more than he won.

When the Soviet Union had agreed to invite Bobby to Moscow, and generously pay all expenses for him and his sister, he was granted a visa that was good for only twenty days. Regina, though, wanted him to stay in Europe until the Interzonal in Portorož began, and because of a lack of funds she was trying to get both his visa and his guest status extended. She wanted him to have a European experience and sharpen his use of foreign languages, which she kept insisting was so vital for his education. Plus, she knew that he wanted to play chess against the better Soviet players as training before he entered the Interzonal. It wasn't to happen, however.

When Bobby discovered that he wasn't going to play any formal games, but simply speed chess, he went into a not-so-silent rage. He felt that he wasn't being respected. Wasn't he the reigning United States Champion? Hadn't he played "The Game of the Century," one of the most brilliant chess encounters ever? Hadn't he played a former World Champion, Dr. Max Euwe, just a year earlier? Wasn't he the prodigy predicted to become World Champion in two years?

A certain monarchic attitude seized him: How could they possibly refuse *him,* the Prince of Chess? This was no trivial setback, no mere snub; it was, to Bobby, the greatest insult he could imagine. He reacted to that insult, from his point of view, proportionately. It seemed obvious to him that the reason the top players wouldn't meet him was because, on some level, they were frightened of him. He likened himself to his hero Paul Morphy, who for the same reason, on his first trip to Europe in 1858 exactly one hundred years before, was denied a match with the Englishman Howard Staunton, then considered the world's greatest player. Chess historians and critics believed that twenty-one-year-old Morphy would have easily beaten Staunton. And fifteen-year-old Fischer firmly believed that if he were given a chance to meet Mikhail Botvinnik, the World Champion, the Soviet player would be defeated.

As the reality set in that Bobby would not soon—not in the next several days, at least—be meeting the giants of Russian chess and triumphing over them, and that while in the Soviet Union he'd receive no financial reward for his playing, the Soviets ceased to be his heroes; rather, they became his betrayers, never to be forgiven. He made a comment in English, not caring that the interpreter could hear and understand it—something to the effect that he was fed up "with these Russian pigs." She reported it, although years later Abramov said that the interpreter confused the word "pork" for "pigs" and that Bobby was referring to the food he was eating at a restaurant.

Certainly, Bobby didn't help himself with a postcard he sent to Collins: "I don't like Russian hospitality and the people themselves. It seems they don't like me either." Before the postcard was delivered to New York, it was read by Russian censors, and Bobby's intemperate response found its way into the Soviet press. Fischer's request for an extended visa was denied, and what would be his lifelong, not-so-private war with the Soviet Union had commenced.

Bobby's situation aside, it was becoming difficult at that time for *any* United States citizen to remain in Moscow. In mid-July, one hundred thousand irate Soviet citizens, inflamed by the government-controlled press, besieged the American embassy on Tchaikovsky Street, demanding that the United States withdraw its troops from Lebanon. Windows were broken, and outside the building an effigy of President Eisenhower was burned.

The situation was serious enough that Gerhardt Fischer, Bobby's father of record, feared Joan and Bobby might be in great danger. Using his South American name of Gerardo Fischer, he wrote in German to Regina from Chile voicing his worries. He fretted that the children might have been kidnapped because no one had heard from them. He asked Regina what she was going to do to get Joan and Bobby out of the country. He said that if he didn't hear soon, he'd try to do what he could, but he also added—somewhat mysteriously—that he didn't want to get into trouble himself.

Just as Regina was beginning to panic, she received a cable from the Yugoslavian chess officials stating that they would not only receive Bobby and Joan as early guests before the Interzonal, but they'd also set up training matches for Bobby with top players. For her part, Joan Fischer, who'd gotten into some spats with her brother over his behavior while in Moscow, accompanied him to Belgrade but left after two days to spend the rest of the summer with friends in England. Fifteen-year-old Bobby was, thus, left to fend for himself—but not for long. He was surrounded by chess officials, players, journalists, and the merely curious, and within hours of touching down in Yugoslavia he was at the board playing, analyzing, and talking chess.

Bobby's training match opponent in his first formal game on European soil was Milan Matulovic, a twenty-three-year-old master who would become infamous in the chess world for sometimes touching a piece, moving it, and then—realizing it was either a blunder or a weak move—returning the piece to its original square, saying, *"J'adoube,"* or "I adjust," and moving it to another square or moving another piece altogether. The *"j'adoube"* statement is the customary announcement when a player wishes to center or adjust one of his or his opponent's pieces, but according to the Laws of Chess this must be done *before* touching the piece, or the mover risks yielding a forfeit. French players would often say, *"Pièce touchée, pièce jouée"* ("if you touch a piece, you move it"). Matulovic *"j'adoube*d" his pieces *after the fact* so often that years later he earned the nickname "J'adoubovic." In contrast, Bobby was strictly observant of this rule and said *"j'adoube"* first whenever he touched a piece to straighten it. Once he was even heard to say it, with a smile on his face, when he casually jostled someone at a tournament.

In his first encounter with Matulovic, Bobby ignored the Yugoslav's mischievous disregard of the rules and lost the game. So with three games left to play, Bobby told Matulovic he'd no longer accept any bogus *"j'adoube*s." Bobby won the second game, drew the third game, and won the fourth, and therefore won the match at 2 ½–1 ½ . Both of Bobby's wins were hard fought and went to fifty moves before his opponent resigned. Matulovic may have been a trickster, but he was also one of his country's finest players, not easily defeated. Bobby felt that this victory was significant enough to write to Collins about.

Bobby then played one of the most colorful Yugoslavian masters, Dragoljub Janosevic, a heavy drinker, womanizer, and poker player, and more of a Damon Runyon character than a stereotypical chess player. He was a forceful and attacking opponent, but in a two-game match, Bobby held his own and drew both games.

Bobby cracked open his suitcase, weighed down with about fifty pounds of books and chess magazines, and prepared for the tournament to come, going over lines and variations, and analyzing the tactics of the opponents he'd be facing. Of the twenty players he was to meet, he'd competed against only three: Benko, Sherwin, and Petrosian. But the other seventeen were no strangers. For years he'd been studying the nuances of their games: their styles, opening preferences, strengths and weaknesses. For example, he knew how Fridrik Olafsson almost always drifted into time trouble and so might not play the end game so precisely; how Bent Larsen could be counted on to trot out a forgotten opening from long ago as a surprise. These unexpected jolts from Larsen were difficult to prepare for, but Bobby's continuous study of the old masters left him relatively forearmed. There wasn't one player in the upcoming Interzonal that Bobby wasn't somewhat prepared to meet.

For reference, there was his talismanic Lipnitsky on which to rely, and the latest edition of *Modern Chess Openings,* which had thousands of games and variations. He confronted the board in the evenings after dinner, with his transistor radio playing whatever kind of music he could tune in to, and he usually continued his study until dawn, falling asleep as it became light. He rarely woke until sometime in the early afternoon. The only times he left the hotel were to play the two matches and once when a good friend, Edmar Mednis (a young American player en route to another tournament and only in the city for one day), visited him and convinced him to take a long walk through several of Belgrade's parks.

Moving from the historic and somewhat somber city of Belgrade to Yugoslavia's resort town of Portorož, on the coast of the Adriatic Sea, to play in the Interzonal didn't appear to have much effect on Bobby. He seemed to be uninterested in the beach that was just steps away from the hotel, or the outdoor cafes that faced the Gulf of Trieste and played host to both locals and tourists, who'd gather in the evenings for al fresco dining and a view of the stunning sunset. During the month that he played in the tournament, Bobby was rarely seen outside of the hotel: He spent most of the time holed up in his room, weighing strategy and tactics.

Twenty-one players from a dozen countries had qualified to play in this march, toward an opportunity to earn a place at the next plateau. The six players with the highest scores would then be joined by two top players who were seeded into the ultimate play-off, the Candidates (also known as the Challengers) tournament. The winner would then play a match with the reigning World Champion, Mikhail Botvinnik, to seek the title. Although the Interzonal was Bobby's first international tournament, he wasn't alone in this status; twenty-two-year-old Mikhail Tal of Riga, who'd twice won the USSR championship, was also playing in his first international. Some pundits, not just from the Soviet Union, were forecasting Tal to be the winner. Top players in the United States predicted that Bobby wouldn't qualify for a place in the Candidates this time. He was just too young to conquer enough of the tournament veterans—each with years of experience in international competition.

Folke Rogard, the Swedish president of the World Chess Federation, welcomed the players, their seconds and trainers at the formal opening ceremonies, saying, "It is sufficient evidence of the widespread popularity of the
game of chess in the last few decades and the way the strength of play has
grown in pace with it, that the Interzonal tournament at Portorož can compare in respect of strength of play with many of the grand tournaments which
we recall from an earlier period."

Bobby, though, seemed to feel that he'd make short work of his competitors. He predicted that he'd wind up as one of the Candidates and that his
method of qualification would be to beat all of the "small-fry" or "patzers"
and then draw with all of the top players. The flaw in this plan was that there
were really no feeble players in the tournament; they were all, if not world
class, then at least of national or international renown.

Bobby's aide or so-called second at the tournament was his close friend
and fellow Jack Collins student William Lombardy, a portly twenty-year-old
seminarian who was studying to become a Roman Catholic priest. Lombardy had captured the World Junior Championship by winning every game,
and he was a formidable player. He was so solid in his ability, so sure of himself on the board, that Fischer once described him as playing "like a house."
At that time in the United States, Lombardy was in ability only slightly behind Fischer himself.

In chess, a second's job is to be an attendant, advisor, advocate, and majordomo for the player he serves. Many seconds pay particular attention to the
openings of the other players and attempt to scout out any weaknesses. They
then report back, round by round. Perhaps the *most* important role for a
second is analyzing adjourned positions jointly with the player. Sometimes
this means all-night sessions, so that the player has a variety of tactics to
employ when play is resumed the next day. Soviet players were traditionally
serviced by a team of seconds, each performing an assigned task. For example, there could be an endgame specialist, an opening theoretician, a physical
trainer, a "go-for," and sometimes a psychologist.

Acting and looking older, and being highly intelligent, Lombardy treated
Bobby in a parental and nurturing way. From Portorož he wrote to Regina of
his charge: "Bobby brushes his teeth daily but has more difficulty in taking a
bath." Lombardy also conveyed his initial impressions of Portorož:

If you have never seen a great international tournament such as the one in Portorož, then you might be interested in hearing something about this great chess classic. Extraordinary things happen in connection with such an event that do not exactly have anything to do with tournament itself. The Portorož tourney is of a type that should make for interesting and exciting chess as only six are permitted to go to the World Championship Challengers Tournament. It seems, however, to work *au contraire*. A great tension hangs overhead. The players are nervous, and many get into extreme time pressure. As a result, the games have not been especially brilliant for a tournament of this class.

Regina wrote to Joan that she was worried Lombardy might be damning Bobby with faint praise. "He's good at that," she wrote. But there was no evidence that Lombardy, known for his acerbic tongue, was antagonistic toward Bobby. On the contrary, the older player always showed the younger one affection and respect, often sending him friendly little notes and asides. The two young men shared almost all of the major holidays together, usually at the Collins home. James T. Sherwin, the other American in the Interzonal, recalled that Lombardy was supposed to be *his* second as well. "Bobby really didn't need Lombardy since their styles were so dissimilar. Lombardy was an enormously gifted, intuitive positional player but not a well-prepared player like Bobby. Bobby's strength was the inexorability of his tactics."

One difficulty arose when Lombardy had to leave the tournament for several days and attend the World Chess Federation annual meeting as the U.S. representative, leaving Bobby without a second. Bobby had two adjournments to play and analyze by himself. He lost to Olafsson and drew with Tal.

In a pre-tournament conversation with Bent Larsen of Denmark and Fridrik Olafsson of Iceland, Lombardy reported the following remarks about his friend Bobby:

Larsen: Fischer is one baby I am going to spank.

Olafsson: Don't be too sure. Be careful!

Larsen: Don't worry, I can take care of myself.

Scrubbed clean at Lombardy's behest, Bobby was dressed in a dark shirt and starched khaki pants for the first evening of play. His opponent was the stocky Oleg Neikirch of Bulgaria, one of the oldest players in the tournament (he was forty-four) and considered, by Bobby's standards, a small-fry. Nevertheless, perhaps because of first-night board fright, Bobby underestimated his opponent but was lucky to coax a draw from Neikirch, even though Bobby had an inferior game. With tongue in cheek, Neikirch explained his draw offer: "It's sort of embarrassing to defeat a boy. Back in Bulgaria I would be the laughing-stock of everybody." But it would be more embarrassing to *lose* to a boy, clucked the scoffers. As for the *New York World-Telegram,* it proclaimed that Bobby's managing to avoid a loss in his first European tournament "highlighted a noteworthy turn in chess history."

Bobby's play was spotty in the first several games of the tournament, as he attempted to find his chess legs. After the Neikirch game, he won one, lost one, and drew one. FISCHER OFF FORM IN DEBUT ABROAD, blared a headline in *The New York Times.* It wasn't until the sixth round, at which point Bobby had barely compiled an even score, that he was tested by one of the true greats of the game, David Bronstein of the Soviet Union.

Bronstein looked like what one might picture a chess player to look like. Bald-pated, with horn-rimmed glasses, and often dressed in a black suit and white shirt, he was actually the prototype of the grandmaster character Kronsteen in the James Bond film *From Russia with Love* (except that Kronsteen had hair), and the game played on-screen in that film was based on a real one Bronstein had played against Spassky. But despite his mien of seriousness and inapproachability, Bronstein was friendly, animated, and liked by virtually all the other players, owing to his cordiality, immense knowledge of the game, and a certain intellectual eccentricity. He was a fiercely attacking player, but at the board he'd often seem as if in a trance. In one game he actually stared at the position for fifty minutes before making a move. On paper and through reputation, Bronstein and Smyslov, both of whom had played against Botvinnik for the World Championship, were considered the favorites at Portorož (though some contended Tal should be a favorite as well). Bronstein had tied Botvinnik in their 1951 match for the World Championship, but Botvinnik retained the title as sitting champion. The rules of the

World Chess Federation required a challenger to *win* the match, not merely draw it, to gain the title.

Because of a lack of air-conditioning in the hall, both Fischer and Bronstein arrived in short-sleeved shirts: white for Bronstein, beige for Fischer. Fischer had publicly announced before the tournament that there might be one player who could defeat him: Bronstein. And, in fact, Bobby had diligently prepared for his opponent's onslaughts.

Fischer's and Bronstein's places at the table were indicated by a small American flag on Bobby's side and an equally small Soviet flag on the opposite side. Fischer plunged into the game with his trusted and thoroughly analyzed opening, the Ruy Lopez, instantly seizing the initiative and generating pressure in the center squares.

The game was a struggle, however, and he found himself in time trouble. It wasn't the tactical possibilities that made him consume time, but the long, drawn-out endgame position, rife with complications. He desperately wanted to win against Bronstein for many reasons: to prove to himself that he could do it; to prove to others, especially those in the tournament, that he was capable; to demonstrate to the world that he was as great a chess player as anyone. But the clock, the clock! Time was ebbing.

To limit the time that a game of chess may take—and to establish equality between players so that, for example, one doesn't take hours to make a move and the other only minutes—a special chess clock is used in tournaments. Actually, *two* clocks are utilized, one for each player. In that way players can budget their time in whatever way they wish. For example, they can take a few seconds on one move and perhaps thirty-five minutes on another—as long as all the moves are made within the period specified by the tournament organizers. In this Interzonal, the time limit was forty moves in two and a half hours and sixteen moves per hour thereafter. When a player made a move, he depressed a button on top of his clock, which stopped his device and started his opponent's. Both players were required to keep a record of their moves to prove, if necessary, that they'd complied with the time limit.

With only seconds to spare, Bobby just barely made his fortieth move against Bronstein before his flag fell, which otherwise would have caused him to be forfeited. He played one more move, and the game was then adjourned to be resumed the next day. That evening, he and Lombardy went over the endgame position, which consisted of both Bobby and Bronstein having a rook, a bishop, and an equal number of pawns. Although this position would result in a draw in most cases, the two young American colleagues searched for hours for any possibility that Bobby could squeeze out a win when play resumed.

The next day, when Fischer and Bronstein continued the game, both men parried for twenty more moves. Bronstein lost a pawn and began to check Fischer's king over and over again. Fischer could make no headway. The game was declared a draw through the special rule of repetition—that is, when a position comes about three times, not necessarily in succession, the game is automatically a draw.

A cynic once said that the most difficult part of success is finding someone who is happy for you. That wasn't the case with Bobby's draw against Bronstein. At the Marshall Chess Club, where players were analyzing the Interzonal games as they were cabled in from Portorož, there was near-delirium when word arrived of the draw. *"Bronstein?!"* people were saying incredulously, almost whooping, as if the Soviet player were Goliath, and Bobby as David had stood up to him piece for piece, pawn for pawn. *"Bronstein!? The genius of modern chess!"* The impossible had occurred: A fifteen-year-old had managed to draw against perhaps the second or third strongest player in the world. So great was the impact of that game that club members began planning a party for the returning hero, even if he hadn't actually qualified as a Candidate yet. In their minds people began rehearsing champagne toasts. And the process of mythologizing Bobby commenced in earnest. Stories were offered of how a certain club member had once played Bobby when he was a child, or was an eyewitness when he played "The Game of the Century," or shared a hot dog and orange drink with him at the Nedick's stand in Herald Square.

Expectations now changed, not only for Bobby's future, but for American chess itself. Could this precocious Brooklyn boy not just become a Candidate but possibly *win* the tournament? Was American chess about to soar on the wings of Bobby's fame? *"Bronstein!"*

Although it was only the sixth round out of twenty-two, for Bobby everything that followed from Bronstein was an emotional anticlimax. He tried to keep his focus, but it was difficult. On days off in Portorož, during the rare times he wandered into public view, Bobby was continually asked for his autograph or to pose for a photo. At first he liked the attention, but it annoyed him that the attention was constant, and he grew to hate it. At least twice, he was swallowed up in a throng of fans, and in both cases he became almost hysterical in his attempts to wrest himself free. He set a self-imposed policy: He'd sign autographs only *after* each game (as long as he didn't lose or wasn't upset over how he played) and only for a period of about five minutes, for the chess players assembled there. Sometimes, he'd sit in the theater seats after a game, and literally hundreds of people would hand their programs to him for his reluctantly scrawled signature.

Eventually, he asked the tournament organizers to rope off the area around his board, because the crowds would gather and gape, often for hours at a time, while he was playing. He complained that he couldn't concentrate. When he was in the streets, he'd ask autograph requesters if they played chess, and if they didn't, he refused to sign and disdainfully walked away. Continually besieged by newsmen, photographers, and autograph hunters, he finally put a stop to it all: By the midpoint of the tournament he wouldn't pose for a photo, sign his autograph, or answer any question.

Aside from his heroics against Bronstein, the tournament wasn't going quite the way Bobby had planned. He lost or drew to some of the "small-fry," including multiple players from Argentina, Hungary, and Czechoslovakia. However, his draws against superstar Tal; his erstwhile Moscow Chess Club opponent Tigran Petrosian; and Svetozar Gligoric of Yugoslavia were all great accomplishments, as was his win against Larsen of Denmark. Years later, Fischer would judge the Larsen game one of the best he ever played. "Fischer won with amazing ease," bleated *Chess Review*.

Against Olafsson Bobby fared more poorly. He didn't try to rationalize that loss (though he did think that he could have won the game). Writing to Collins, he explained: "I never should have lost. . . . I played the black side of Lipnitsky's thing [and here he gave the moves]. Anyway, I had a good opening. He sacked [sacrificed] the exchange for a pawn, but after winning the exchange, I blundered, and the game was about even. But (again) I got into time pressure, and played a series of weak moves in a row, and by adjournment he had two connected passed pawns which could not be stopped."

Bobby's last game of the tournament was with Gligoric, one of the strongest players outside of the Soviet Union. If Bobby lost that game, and others won who were only a half point behind him on the cross table (a scoreboard-like tally of who played whom and the results), he wouldn't be invited to the Candidates tournament. Because of his high score, Gligoric was already assured a berth in the Candidates, so he could easily offer Fischer an early "grandmaster draw" and coast to a successful denouement. Instead, he played for a win, sacrificing a knight, but ultimately winning back three pawns in exchange. Bobby withstood a relentlessly harassing attack, but always found a way to defend. On Gligoric's thirty-second move, the Yugoslav looked up from the board and said, *"Remis?"* Fischer knew the French word for "draw," and he immediately consented. "Nobody sacrifices a piece against Fischer," he brashly declared, grinning slightly as he said it.

Drawing his last game and coming in sixth, Bobby Fischer became the youngest chess player ever to qualify to play in the Candidates tournament, and the youngest international grandmaster in the history of the game. Some were even calling him the Mozart of chess. Normally quite restrained in its chess reporting, *The New York Times* was exuberant in running a salute to Bobby on its editorial page:

A CHEER FOR BOBBY FISCHER

Chess fans all over the United States are toasting Bobby Fischer and we are happy to join in the acclaim. At 15, this youngster from Brooklyn has become the youngest international grand master in chess and has qualified for next year's tournament to decide who shall meet Mikhail Botvinnik for the world's chess championship. Those who have followed Bobby's stirring matches in the competition just concluded in Yugoslavia know that he gave an exhibition of skill, courage and determination that would have done credit to a master twice his age. We are rightfully proud of him.

Though he'd only been gone from the United States two months, Bobby had taken from his competitive experiences more than just bragging rights. His new maturity was noticeable. When asked by a reporter in Portorož whether he was looking forward to playing the World Champion, he said, "Of course I would like to play Botvinnik. But it's too early to talk about that. Remember, next year I will have to attend the tournament of Candidates before I can think of meeting Botvinnik." Reflecting for a moment, he added, "One thing is certain—I am not going to be a professional chess player."

Bobby felt manhandled in both Moscow and Portorož, and his receiving only $400 for six weeks of effort at the Interzonal ("Every chess game is like taking a five-hour final exam," he said) discouraged him. The fact that he was now an international grandmaster and was eligible to compete for the World Championship made him feel accomplished, but he wondered how he could possibly make a living playing chess. Outside of the Soviet Union, where chess masters were comfortably supported by the state, no chess player could survive on his tournament winnings. There *were* some Americans who were chess professionals, but none made a living from tournament winnings alone. Rather, they put food on the table by teaching chess, giving exhibitions, operating chess parlors, selling chess sets, and writing books and magazine articles that received small advances.

It was an insecure life.

Bobby was met at Idlewild (which was later renamed John F. Kennedy International Airport) by his mother, sister Joan, and Norman Monath, an editor at Simon & Schuster who was putting the final touches on Bobby's first book of annotated games, called appropriately *Bobby Fischer's Games of Chess*. "He looks as skinny as a rail," Regina said upon beholding her famous son, and she almost burst into tears. All four tumbled into a limousine, and on the ride to Brooklyn, Monath talked to Bobby about the book, getting his opinion as to whether the publication date should be postponed slightly, until such time as his twenty Interzonal games could be included. In its original conception, the book had only contained thirteen games and the working title was just that: *Thirteen Games*. The plan was to focus it on Bobby's efforts in the 1957 U.S. Championship, with the teenager annotating each game. Later "The Game of the Century" from 1956 was added. By including the Interzonal games, the book would acquire some needed bulk and, presumably, be more valuable. Even *with* the Interzonal games, the finished tome was only ninety-six pages. *Thirteen Games*, had it remained as thirteen games only, would have appeared to be just a shade more than a monograph.

Upon arriving at Lincoln Place, Bobby charged up the three flights of stairs, unpacked his satchel, gave his mother a scarf that he'd bought in Brussels ("That looks Continental," he said in a courtly manner, when she tried it on), and, within twenty minutes, was out the door. Monath had him dropped off at the Collins house, and in a matter of seconds, Bobby and Jack were analyzing his games from the tournament. Bobby stayed for hours, and the Collins regulars began to drift in to offer their congratulations, have something to eat, and discuss the losses to Benko and Olafsson. The evening was capped off with Bobby playing dozens of five-minute games with almost all assembled, one by one.

Bobby entered his junior year at Erasmus several days late, and since his five courses were especially demanding, owing to his having to study for a Regents exam associated with each, he quickly fell behind in his work. The officials at the school were accommodating, however, and instead of chastising him for his sometimes shoddy work, they awarded him a gold medal for becoming the youngest grandmaster in history. Additionally, Bobby was profiled in the school newspaper, the *Dutchman,* adding to his student-as-celebrity status.

Six days after Bobby's arrival back in the United States, the Marshall Chess Club followed through on its intentions and held a reception for him with more than one hundred members in attendance. The president of the club, Dr. Edward Lasker, welcomed everyone, thanked them for coming, and then began a litany of Bobby's many accomplishments. Bobby, however, was hardly paying attention. Rather, he was playing speed chess at a side table with several of the young masters, who congregated around him.

To watch Bobby play speed chess was an entertainment in itself, aside from his depth of play. To him, speed games were like playground basketball or street stickball: trash-talking was definitely allowed. At the board, playing a speed game, Bobby was truly in his element, like Michael Jordan soaring for the hoop. Typically, he would crack his knuckles and pursue a humorous strategy of intimidation:

"Me?! You play that against Me?!"

"Crunch!" "Zap!"

"With that I will crush you, *crush* you!"

[In a feigned Russian accent] "You are cockroach. I am elephant. Elephant steps on cockroach."

He would pick up a piece and practically throw it at a square, almost as if he were tossing a dart at a bull's-eye; invariably, it would land in the center of the square. His fingers were long and nimble, and as he moved, his hand quitting the piece with a flourish, he looked like a classical pianist playing a concerto. When he made a weak move, which was rare, he'd sit bolt upright and inhale, emitting a sound like a snake's hiss. On the few occasions when he *lost* a speed game, he'd just push the pieces to the center of the board in disgust, his nostrils flaring as if he smelled a bad odor. He maintained that he could tell the strength of a player by the way he handled the pieces. Weak players were clumsy and unsure; strong players were confident and graceful. Sometimes, during a five-minute game, Bobby would get up from the board while his clock was running, go to the soda machine, buy a soft drink, and stroll back to the table, having "wasted" two or three minutes. He'd still win.

A week later Bobby was back at the Marshall to play in the weekly speed tournament—christened the "Tuesday Night Rapid Transit" in homage to the New York City rapid transit subway system. Bobby tied for first with Edmar Mednis, both players scoring 13–2. Not so ironically, the one game Bobby lost was to his mentor Jack Collins.

Bobby's relationship with Collins was complex. To Collins, Bobby represented a second existence—the boy's career was a vicarious entry to a level of chess mastery he himself would never achieve. But Collins also showed Bobby a father's love, taking pride in all of his accomplishments. He claimed to view Bobby as a surrogate son.

Bobby viewed their relationship differently. He didn't regard Collins as a father substitute, but as a friend, despite their thirty-year difference in ages. He considered Jack Collins's sister Ethel a friend as well, and he could be even more affectionate toward her at times. Bobby always felt comfortable with both, and at one point when Regina was about to embark on one of her perennial long-term journeys, she suggested that Bobby live with the Collinses. Their apartment was small by American standards, however—even for two people. Adding a third would have been impossible, so the idea never went beyond Regina's wish.

What Collins *didn't* know was that Bobby would occasionally snipe at him behind his back. The criticisms were purely chess-related. Despite the fact that Collins could occasionally beat Bobby in speed games and even in clocked training games (they never met over the board in a formal tournament), Bobby's opinion of his mentor's prowess—as indeed happened with him and other players—became inexorably linked to what his official rating was.

"What's your rating?" is one of the first things players ask each other on meeting for the first time, and whichever player has the lower rating is likely to get a snobbish reaction from the other and even be shunned, as if belonging to another caste. Fischer's rating reached an average high of 2780. Collins's rating never rose higher than 2400, light-years apart in winning predictability. If the separation in rating points had been minimal, Bobby's opinion of Collins might not have been so deprecatory. Raymond Weinstein, a strong international master and a student of Collins, wrote that he'd been in awe of his teacher until he heard Fischer's unkind remarks about him.

In addition to the rating disparity between mentor and student, Bobby didn't like that Collins was getting publicity from being his teacher, and that other young players were flocking to him for lessons, eager to become the next Bobby Fischer. Bobby, perhaps because of the indigence of his childhood, hated the idea of people making money off his name. As New York master Asa Hoffmann once put it: "If someone was willing to pay $50 for a Bobby Fischer autograph, and you were going to make $5 for introducing the autograph seeker to him, Fischer would want that $5 too, or else he was willing to forfeit the $50."

5

The Cold War Gladiator

MIKHAIL TAL'S STARE was infamous, and to some ominous. With his deep brown, almost black eyes, he'd glare so intently at his opponents that some said he was attempting to hypnotize them into making a vapid move. The Hungarian-American player Pal Benko actually donned sunglasses once when he played Tal, just to avoid the penetrating stare.

Not that Tal needed an edge. The twenty-three-year-old Latvian native was a brilliant player. Twice champion of the USSR, he'd won the 1958 Portorož Interzonal, becoming a front runner to play the incumbent title-holder, Mikhail Botvinnik, for the World Championship in 1960. Tal's style was filled with wild, inspired combinations, intuitive sacrifices, and pyrotechnics. Handsome, erudite, and a packet of energy, the Latvian was a crowd-pleaser and the darling of the chess world. His right hand was deformed, but it didn't seem to diminish his self-assurance.

Fischer was growing more self-assured, but his style was strikingly different: lucid, crystal-clear, economical, concrete, rational. J. H. Donner, the gigantic Dutch grandmaster, noted the contrast: "Fischer is the pragmatic, technical one. He makes almost no mistakes. His positional judgment is dispassionate; nearly pessimistic. Tal is more imaginative. For him, overconfidence is a danger that he must constantly guard against."

The European crowds who were watching preparations begin for the Candidates tournament liked Bobby too, but for different reasons: Americans weren't supposed to play as *well* as he did. And at sixteen! He was a curiosity in Yugoslavia, a chess-obsessed country, and was continually pestered for autographs and interviews. Lanky, with a loping gait, and dressed in what some Europeans thought was Western or Texan clothing, he was described as being "laconic as the hero of an old cowboy movie."

Bobby had tolerated Tal's stare when they first met over the board in Portorož. That game had ended in a draw. More recently, in Zurich, three months before this Candidates showdown, they'd drawn once again, with Bobby coming in third, a point behind the first-place Tal. But now the stakes were much higher—the Candidates results would determine who played for the World Championship—and Fischer wasn't going to let an obnoxious eye-jinx keep him from his destiny.

The Candidates tournament, spread throughout three Yugoslavian cities—under the beneficence of the dictator Marshal Josip Tito, an avid amateur chess player—was a quadruple round-robin among the world's best eight players, meaning that each would have to play everyone else four games, alternating the black and white pieces. It was a grueling schedule and would last more than six weeks. Four of the players—Mikhail Tal, Paul Keres, Tigran Petrosian, and Vasily Smyslov—were from the Soviet Union. Three others—Gligoric, Olafsson, and Benko—were indisputably among the world's best. Fischer was the only American, and to many he was the tournament's dark knight. In a moment of youthful bravado, though, he declared in an interview that he was counting on winning. Leonard Barden, a British chess journalist, claimed that Fischer was asked so often what his result would be that he learned the Serbo-Croatian word for "first": *prvi*.

During the contest, Fischer habitually dressed in a ski sweater and un-pressed pants, and left his hair matted as if unwashed, while the other play-ers donned suits, shirts, and ties, and were scrupulous about their groom-ing. With thousands of spectators appraising each player's sartorial—as well as strategic—style, the match moved from Bled to Zagreb and ended in Belgrade.

Bobby's second, the great Danish player Bent Larsen, who was there to help him as a trainer and mentor, instead criticized his charge, perhaps smart-ing from the rout he'd suffered at Fischer's hands in Portorož. Not one to keep his thoughts to himself, Larsen told Bobby, "Most people think you are unpleasant to play against." He then added, "You walk funny"—a reference, perhaps, to Fischer's athletic swagger from years of tennis, swimming, and basketball. Declining to leave any slur unvoiced, he concluded, "And you are ugly." Bobby insisted that Larsen wasn't joking and that the insults "hurt." His self-esteem and confidence seemed to have slipped a notch.

But that made him no less combative.

Still enraged from the disrespectful way he felt he'd been treated during his visit to Moscow a year before, Bobby began acting the role of a Cold War gladiator. At one point, he declared that almost all the Soviet players in the tournament were his enemies (he made an exception of the redheaded Smyslov, who displayed a gentility toward him). Years later, records released by the KGB, the Soviet intelligence agency, indicated he was right. One Russian master, Igor Bondarevsky, wrote that "all four of [Fischer's] Soviet opponents did everything in their power to punish the upstart." Tal and Petrosian, close friends, quickly drew all of their games, thereby conserving their energy. Although not illegal, indulging in the so-called grandmaster draw—in which neither player strives to win but, rather, halves the point after a few inconsequential moves have been made—bordered on unprincipled behavior.

Bobby, for his part, was livid at the seeming collusion: "I will teach those dirty Russians a lesson they won't forget for a long time," he wrote from the Hotel Toplice. That resolution would become a lifelong crusade.

At his first game against Tal, in Bled, Bobby was already at the board when the twenty-three-year-old Mischa arrived just in time to commence play. Bobby stood and Tal offered his right hand to shake. Tal's hand was severely deformed, with only three large fingers appended, and since his wrist was so thin, the malformation resembled a claw. Bobby, to his credit, didn't seem to care. He returned the gesture with a two-stroke handshake, and play began.

Within a few moves, though, Bobby's mood soured. He became annoyed at Tal's comportment at and away from the board. This time "the stare" began to rankle him. Tal, in a seeming bid to increase Bobby's irritation, also offered a slight smile of incredulity after each of the American's moves, as if he were saying: "Silly boy, I know what you have in mind—how amusing to think you can trick me!"

Fischer, deciding to use Tal's tactics against him, tried producing his own stare, and even flashed Tal an abbreviated, sneering smile of contempt. But after a few seconds, he'd break eye contact and concentrate on more important things: the action on the board, the sequence of moves he planned to follow, or the ways to counter the combination Tal seemed to be formulating.

Tal was an encyclopedia of kinetic movement. All in a matter of seconds, he'd move a chess piece, record the action on his score sheet, position his head within inches of the clock to check the time, grimace, smile, raise his eyebrows, and "make funny faces," as Bobby characterized it. Then he'd rise and walk up and down the stage while Bobby was thinking. Tal's coach Igor Bondarevsky referred to his charge's movements as "circling around the table like a vulture"—presumably, a vulture ready to pounce.

Tal chain-smoked and could consume a pack of cigarettes during the course of a game. He also had the habit of resting his chin on the edge of the table, peering *through* the pieces and peeking at his opponent, rather than establishing a bird's-eye view by sitting up straight and looking down, which would have provided a better perspective on the intricacies of the board. Since Tal's body language was so bizarre, Fischer interpreted it as an attempt to annoy him.

Tal's gestures and staring infuriated Fischer. He complained to the arbiter, but little was done. Whenever Tal rose from the board, in the middle of the game, when Fischer was planning his next move, he'd begin talking to the other Soviet players, and they enjoyed whispering about their or others' positions. Although he knew some Russian, Bobby had trouble with the declensions and usage. He'd hear the words *ferz'* ("queen") or *lad'ya* ("rook"), for example, and he couldn't tell whether Tal was talking specifically about *his* position. All he knew was that it was maddening. Bobby couldn't understand why the chief arbiter didn't prevent this muttering, since it was forbidden by the rules, and he told the organizers that Tal should be thrown out of the tournament. That Soviet players had for decades been talking to one another during games with no complaints didn't help Bobby's cause.

Fischer was also perturbed that when a game was finished, many of the players would immediately join with their opponents to analyze their completed games, right on the stage, just a few feet from where he was playing rather than in the postmortem analysis room. The buzz distracted his attention. He wrote a complaint about the chattering and handed it to the chief arbiter:

After the game is completed, analysis by the opponents must be prohibited to avoid disturbing the other players. Upon completion of the game, the Referee must immediately remove the chess pieces from the table to prevent analysis. We recommend that the organization prepare a special room for post-mortem analysis. The room must be completely out of earshot of all of the participants.
  Robert J. Fischer, International Grandmaster

As it turned out, though, nothing was done. No other players joined in the protest, because most were guilty of doing the very thing Fischer was opposing.

Bobby was fast gaining a reputation as a constant complainer, the Petulant American, a role most of the players found distasteful. They believed he'd invariably blame tournament conditions or the behavior of the other players for a loss.

Whether or not Bobby *was* hypersensitive, he did suffer from hyperacusis—an acute senstivity to noise and even distant sounds—and it was clear that Tal, in particular, knew just how to rattle him. The Russian would look at Bobby from near or far, and begin laughing, and once in the communal dining room he pointed to Bobby and said out loud, "Fischer: cuckoo!" Bobby almost burst into tears. "Why did Tal say 'cuckoo' to me?" he asked, and for the first and perhaps only time during the tournament, Larsen tried to console him: "Don't let him bother you." He told Bobby he'd have an opportunity to seek revenge . . . on the board. After that, a local Bled newspaper published a group of caricatures of all eight players, and a souvenir postcard was made of the drawings. Bobby's portrait was particularly severe, with his ears akimbo and his mouth open, making him look as if he were . . . well, cuckoo.

Sure enough, in the drawing, next to the portrait of Bobby was a little bird perched on his board. It was a cuckoo.

Spectators, players, and journalists began asking Bobby how he could take two months off, September and October, during the school year to play in a tournament. Finally it was revealed: He'd dropped out of Erasmus Hall. It had been crushing for Regina to have to sign the authorization releasing the sixteen-year-old from the school. She hoped she could talk him back into classes somewhere, someday, after he finished playing in the Candidates tournament. As an inducement to get him to change his mind about dropping out, the assistant principal of Erasmus, Grace Corey, wrote to Bobby in Yugoslavia, telling him how well he'd done on the New York State Regents examinations. He'd earned a grade of 90 percent in Spanish and 97 percent in geometry, making for "a really good year."

Good grades or not, an image began to attach itself to Bobby. As a result of the publicity about his schooling, or lack thereof, Fischer was beginning to be thought of as a *nyeculturni* by the Russians, unschooled and uncultured, and they began to tease him. "What do you think of Dostoyevsky, Bobby?" someone queried. "Are you a Benthamite?' another asked. "Would you like to meet Goethe?" They were unaware that Bobby had read literature in high school, and for his own enjoyment. He liked George Orwell's work, and for years held on to his copies of *Animal Farm* and *1984;* he also read and admired Oscar Wilde's *The Picture of Dorian Gray.* Voltaire's *Candide* was a favorite, and he'd often talk about the comic parts. Tal asked Bobby if he'd ever gone to the opera, and when Bobby burst into the refrain from "The March of the Smugglers," from Bizet's *Carmen,* the Russian was temporarily silenced. Bobby had attended a performance of the French opera with his mother and sister at the Metropolitan Opera House in New York shortly before going to Europe. He also owned a book that told the stories of all the great operas, which he'd dip into from time to time.

Unfortunately, cultured or not, Bobby played poorly in the tournament at first. He was frustrated at being down two games to none against Tal, who never passed up a chance to annoy his younger opponent. Just before Bobby and Tal were to play a third time, Bobby approached Alexander Koblentz, one of Tal's trainers, and said sotto voce, as menacingly as he could: "If Tal doesn't behave himself, I am going to smash out all of his front teeth." Tal persisted in his provocation, though, and Fischer lost their third game as well.

It was a situation where a youthful player like Bobby could spiral down irretrievably, playing himself into an abyss. But he took momentary charge of his psyche, despite his losses, and began to feel optimistic. After defeating a cold, he placed himself in the abstract world of Lewis Carroll and the universe of reversal and wrote: "I am now in quite a good mood, and eating well. [Like] in *Alice in Wonderland.* Remember? The Red Queen cried *before* she got a piece of dirt in her eye. I am in a good mood *before* I win all of my games."

"Let's go to a movie," Dimitrije Bjelica said to Bobby the night before he was to play Vasily Smyslov. Bjelica was a Yugoslavian chess journalist; he was also nationally known as a television commentator on soccer. He'd befriended Bobby in Portorož and was sympathetic to his complaints, and he thought a movie might take Bobby's mind off his problems. As luck would have it, though, the only English-language film being shown in Belgrade was *Lust for Life,* the lush biopic of the mad nineteenth-century Dutch painter Vincent Van Gogh.

Bobby agreed to the outing, and right after the scene when Van Gogh cuts off his ear in despair following a foolish quarrel with Paul Gauguin, Bobby turned to his companion and whispered: "If I don't win against Smyslov tomorrow, I'll cut off *my* ear." Fischer, playing brilliantly with the black pieces the next day, won his first game ever against the Russian, a former World Champion. The parallels of Bobby's life to Van Gogh's go only so far, however. Bobby's ear remained intact.

For Bobby, an unfortunate pattern emerged after that. If he managed to win a game from an opponent, on the next day he'd often lose to someone else. He defeated Benko then lost to Gligoric. After a win against Fridrik Olafsson, he lost to Tal again. Bobby saw his chance at a title shot fading away, and he didn't want to end up like Terry Malloy—the character played by Marlon Brando in one of Bobby's favorite movies, *On the Waterfront*—with "a one-way ticket to Palookaville."

Bobby lost games he should have drawn and drew contests he should have won. He dropped ten pounds, and not because he wasn't eating. The hotel doctor prescribed a tonic that did nothing to improve his condition. His pocket money was running low after he lost seven traveler's checks, and he was having trouble extracting more from his mother, at one point calling her a "louse" because she wouldn't make up the shortfall: "You know I am very good with money," he complained. Larsen, whom Bobby described as "sulky and unhelpful," kept discouraging him, telling him that he shouldn't expect to place higher than the bottom rank of those competing. When Larsen repeated this line publicly and it was published in the Belgrade newspaper

Borba, Bobby was enraged and humiliated. Larsen was his second, he was being paid $700—equivalent to about $5,000 today—and Bobby expected him to be something of a cheering squad, or at least not a public Cassandra.

He was losing to Tal, but some of his other games won accolades. Harry Golombek, the chief arbiter, said that Fischer was improving as the event progressed, and he surmised that "were the tournament [to go] 56 rounds instead of the 'mere' 28," Bobby's best days would lie ahead. "He is no match for Tal but his two victories over Keres and his equal score with Smyslov are sufficient in themselves to prove his real Grandmaster class."

World Champion Mikhail Botvinnik misdiagnosed the young American's struggles when he wrote, "Fischer's strong and weak points lie in that he is always true to himself and plays the same way regardless of his opponents or an external factor." It's true that Bobby rarely altered his style, which gave his opponents an advantage because they knew in advance what kinds of openings he'd play, but Botvinnik didn't know of the rage that Bobby was experiencing because of the disruptive atmosphere being created by Tal.

Bobby began to plot. Tal had to be stopped, if not on the chessboard, then in some other way. Tal, he said, had purposely made him lose three games in a row using unfair tactics, robbing him of first place: "He actually cheated me out of a match with Botvinnik," he wrote in a letter to his mother.

Whether it was a clinically paranoid musing, malice aforethought, or merely a boyhood fantasy, no one can know, but Bobby began to wonder and scheme and penned his plan of reprisal against Tal: "Should I poke him in the eye—both beetlely eyes, maybe—with my pen? Perhaps I should poison him; I could gain entrance to his room in the Hotel Esplanade and then put the poison in his drinking glass." Despite his dreams of revenge, which he never put into effect, he played valiantly in the fourth game, a contest that he vowed to the press he'd win, no matter what sleight of chess Tal would deliver on or off the board.

Bobby tried a psychological tactic himself during that game, despite his oft-quoted demurral, "I don't believe in psychology—I believe in good moves." Normally, he'd make his move on the board, punch his clock, and record the move on the score sheet. In this game, though, on his twenty-second move, he suddenly altered his sequence, and instead of first moving a piece, he went to his score sheet and, in recording the move he was contemplating, switched to a Russian system of notation. He then offhandedly placed his score sheet on the table so that Tal could see it, and while the clock remained running, he watched Tal to gauge his reaction.

Tal, wearing an atypical poker face, recognized what he thought was a winning move for Fischer, and he wrote later: "I would very much have liked to change his decision. So I calmly left my chair and began strolling the stage. I joked with someone [Petrosian], took a casual look at the exhibition board and returned to my seat with a pleased appearance." Since Tal looked as if he were comfortable with the impending move, Fischer momentarily thought he might have blundered. He crossed out his move on the score sheet, made another move, and checked Tal's king instead. It was a mistake.

Bobby closed his eyes to counter any further Talian shenanigans—he didn't have to see his position, since it was imprinted in his mind—and tried to block out any other distractions. He concentrated his energies on finding a single move, or a variation, a tactical feint that would help him emerge from the dark waters of his position, all the while trying to avoid the temptation to move a piece or pawn to a fatal square.

Alas, nothing worked. He was lost. Tragically, emotionally, existentially, it was chess death. He cried, and didn't attempt to hide his tears. Tal won the fourth and final encounter, and with it the tournament. It would lead to the Championship of the World.

"I love the dark of the night. It helps me to concentrate," Bobby once remarked. With his sister now married and his mother off on a peace march from San Francisco to Moscow, the Brooklyn apartment was all his—deliciously so, he felt. He only had his dog, Hoppy, a quiet mutt who limped, to keep him company. Alone, the teenager could think and do whatever he wanted, without familial or social constraints. So that he didn't have to change the sheets in the apartment's beds so often, and to give himself a different perspective, he rotated where he slept. Next to each bed, resting on a chair, was a chess set. Flopping down on the selected bed of the evening, he'd glance at the board and muse: Should he look into the Four Pawn attack against the King's Indian, which presented him with difficulty in speed games? Should he study endings, especially deceptive rook-and-pawn configurations? Maybe he should just go over some of the thirteen hundred high-level games played at the 1958 Munich Olympiad.

Questions like these arose every night before he fell asleep, only to be interrupted for forty-five minutes on most nights when his favorite radio program was being broadcast.

"The Bahn Frei Polka" by Eduard Strauss—with the trumpet call to the racetrack starting gate that blasted as a preamble—would jolt him awake if he'd begun to nod off. This *Jean Shepherd Show* theme song had been recorded by Arthur Fiedler and the Boston Pops orchestra, and the equestrian feel to the piece made Bobby feel good the instant he heard it. "It sounds like circus music," he once said in a joyful mood, and it was one of the liveliest dances ever composed by Johann's son. But it wasn't the music that was so important to Bobby. It was the cantankerous, curmudgeonly talk show humorist Jean Shepherd who entranced him.

More than a loyal follower of the show, Bobby was a fanatic. When the broadcast—variously described as part kabuki, part commedia dell'arte— started in 1956 on WOR Radio, Bobby listened to almost every show when he was in New York. Shepherd was an acquired taste: He told tales in novelistic form about his childhood in the Midwest, his life in the army, and his adult misadventures in New York City. He cracked jokes, wailed old barroom songs (he had a terrible voice), and played the toy kazoo, the lowliest of musical instruments. Most of his shows were hilarious, others so dark that they sounded maniacal, and he had a studied laugh, not quite a cackle— more a pseudo chuckle—that made him sound deranged. Still, he emerged as if he were a modern-day Mark Twain or a J. D. Salinger. His tales had a bite and a message and could be delivered over and over again.

Bobby sent Shepherd notes, attended live performances that the radio host gave at a Greenwich Village coffeehouse called the Limelight, and visited him at his studio at 1440 Broadway. After the show, the two would engage in a New York City ritual. They'd walk two blocks north and eat hot dogs at Grant's on the corner of Broadway and Forty-second Street, at the edge of "the Crossroads of the World," Times Square. Shepherd remembered that they didn't converse much, just ate. Once, Bobby did talk about a player he was to face in a tournament and kept saying over and over again, "He's stupid," without revealing who the player was or explaining why he felt that way.

Sporadically, Shepherd would mention Bobby on the air. While Shepherd didn't play chess, he admired the *idea* of Bobby Fischer and what he was accomplishing. *"Bobby Fischer,"* he'd whisper conspiratorially as if he were just talking to one person, not tens of thousands. "Just *imagine*. This really nice kid, this great chess player, maybe the greatest chess player who *ever* lived. When he plays chess he is . . . *mean*! I mean, *really* mean!" On a few occasions Shepherd helped fund-raise for the U.S. Chess Federation, the nonprofit membership organization. He did it for Bobby.

Bobby preferred listening to the radio rather than watching television. One advantage of the former was that while he was listening he could also be glancing at a board. He'd also heard that television emitted possibly harmful electronic rays and he was skittish about spending too much time in front of the ubiquitous tube. He loved the intimacy of radio. When Shepherd was on the air, Bobby would darken his room and have a one-way conversation that eased his loneliness. There, beside the glowing yellow night-light of his radio dial, chessboard at his side, chess books and magazines spread around the room, he'd let his thoughts drift.

When Shepherd went off the air, Bobby continued to twist the dial searching for other broadcasts and shows. Sometime he'd settle for pop music, which, if the volume was turned down low, still allowed him to concentrate on his board analysis. At other times, he'd hear late-night preachers, often of a fundamentalist bent, giving sermons and talks, usually about the meaning and interpretation of the Bible.

Intrigued, Bobby began listening more and more to religious radio programs, such as the revivalist Billy Graham's *Hour of Decision*, which featured sermons calling for listeners to give up their lives and be saved by Jesus Christ. Fischer also followed *The Lutheran Hour* and *Music and the Spoken Word*, a performance by the Mormon Tabernacle Choir that contained inspiring messages. On Sundays, Bobby made a habit of listening to the radio all day, flipping up the dial and back. During one of these electronic perambulations he found what he was searching for: a broadcast by the charismatic Herbert W. Armstrong, on what was called the *Radio Church of God*. It was a condensed church service that included songs and hymns as well as a sermon by Armstrong, often about the naturalness and practicality of the scriptures. "He seems so sincere," Bobby later remembered thinking. "He has all the right principles: dedication, hard work, perseverance, never giving up. He's dogged; he's persistent." These were the same qualities Bobby brought to the game of chess. He wanted to know more.

One of the tenets of Armstrong's creed was that you can't trust the role that doctors have assumed. In one of the sermons in which Bobby became engrossed, Armstrong preached:

> We take the broken bread unworthily if, and when, we take it at communion service and then put our trust in doctors and medicines, instead of in Christ—thus putting another god before Him! So, many are sick. Many die!
>
> If God is the Healer—the *only* real Healer—and if medical science came out of the ancient heathen practice of medicine-men supposed to be in the good graces of imaginary gods of medicine, is there, then, no need for doctors?
>
> Yes, I'm quite sure there is. But if all people understood and practiced God's truth, the function of the doctor would be a lot different than it is today. Actually, there isn't a cure in a car-load—or a train-load—of medicine! Most sickness and disease today is the result of faulty diet and wrong eating. The true function of the doctor should not be to usurp God's prerogative as a healer, but to help you to observe nature's laws by prescribing correct diet, teaching you how better to live *according to nature's laws*.

Taken by Armstrong's argument, Bobby sent away for copies of the sermon and distributed it to his friends.

Armstrong's Radio Church of God grew into an international undertaking, the Worldwide Church of God, and eventually claimed more than one hundred thousand parishioners and listeners. Bobby felt comfortable with the church since it blended certain Christian and Jewish tenets such as Sabbath observation from Friday sundown to Saturday sundown, kosher dietary laws, belief in the coming of the Messiah, keeping of Jewish holy days, and rejection of Christmas and Easter. In very little time, he became almost as absorbed in the Bible and "the Church" as he was in chess. On Saturday nights, after his Sabbath devotion, he'd usually go to the Manhattan Chess Club or to the Collins home and play chess all evening, and though he sometimes didn't return home until nearly four a.m., he still felt that he should pray for an hour. He also began a correspondence course in "Biblical understanding" that had been created by the Church and was often tied in to world events as interpreted by Armstrong. There was a self-administered test at the end of each week's lesson. A typical question was:

> What is the basic cause of war and human suffering? A. The inordinate lusts of carnal man. B. False political ideologies such as Communism and Fascism. C. Poverty. D. Lack of educational and economic opportunity.
> The correct answer: "A" [Bobby's answer as well.]

Eventually, Bobby sent 10 percent of his meager chess earnings to the Church. He refused to enter tournaments whose organizers insisted he play on Friday night, and he began a life of devotion to the Church's tenets, explaining: "The Holy Bible is the most rational, most common-sense book ever written on the face of the earth."

He began carrying a blue-covered cardboard box wherever he went. When asked what was in it, without answering he'd give a look that said in essence, "How can you possibly ask me that question? I'm deeply hurt and insulted." Week after week, wherever he went—be it chess club, restaurant, cafeteria, or billiard parlor—there was the blue box. Finally, in the mid-1960s, at a restaurant off Union Square, Bobby went to the restroom and left the box on the table. His dinner companion couldn't resist. Despite feeling guilty at invading Bobby's privacy, he slid the top off the box. Inside, was a book with a title embossed in gold: *Holy Bible.*

During this time, owing to his newfound piety, Bobby used no profanity. One evening when he and a friend were having ice cream sodas at the Howard Johnson's restaurant on Sixth Avenue and Greenwich, a woman in her late teens kept coming in and out of the restaurant. Either drunk or high, she kept up a continuous babble of four-letter words. Bobby became very upset. "Did you hear that?" he asked. "That's terrible." He couldn't bear listening to her any longer. "Let's leave," he said. And the two friends walked out, leaving their sodas unfinished.

6

The New Fischer

THE PLEADING WAS EMBARRASSING to witness. "C'mon, Bobby. Let me pick you up. C'mon." Silence on the other end of the phone. "We can just hang out." Dead air. "We can play some Five-Minute, or go to a movie." A young chess master, a few years Bobby's senior, was calling from the office phone of the Marshall Chess Club, attempting to talk Fischer into getting together. "Or take a taxi. I'll pay for it." It was two in the afternoon and Bobby had just woken up. His voice, when he finally answered, sounded tinny and sluggish, the words drawled so that each syllable was stretched into two. His volume was loud, though—loud enough for everyone in the office to hear. "I don't know. No. Well, what time? I have to eat." The caller's optimism surged. "We can eat at the Oyster Bar. You like that. C'mon." Success. An hour and a half later sixteen-year-old Bobby was having his first meal of the day: filet of sole and a large glass of orange juice.

As he walked through Grand Central Terminal toward the restaurant, Bobby probably wasn't recognized by most of the people he passed, but to his host—and almost all other chess players—having a meal with Fischer was like dining with a movie star. He was becoming a super-celebrity in the world of chess, but the more fame he achieved, the more unpleasant his behavior became. Inflated by his successes on the board, his ego had begun to shut out other people. Gone was Charming Bobby with the electric smile. Enter Problematic Bobby with the disdainful attitude and frequently flashed warning scowl. Increasingly, Bobby viewed it a favor merely to be seen with him.

And it didn't matter if he rebuffed or rejected a person, because someone else was sure to phone with yet another offer to play chess, see a movie, or eat a fish dinner. Everyone wanted to be in his company, to be part of the Bobby Fischer Show, and he knew it. One mistake, disagreement, or mistimed appointment on the part of a friend was enough for Bobby to sever a relationship. And banishment from his realm would last forever; there were always others who'd take the offender's place.

If you didn't play chess, it was nearly impossible to enter Bobby's world, and yet his disrespect seemed to be directed more at weak players than those who didn't know how to play the game. The latter could be forgiven their ignorance, but a weak player—which, by definition, included almost anyone he could beat—had no excuse. "*Anyone* should be able to become a master," he said with certainty.

Ironically, given his regal attitude, nothing seemed to be going right for Bobby in the fall of 1959. He'd been home barely a month from the Candidates tournament in Yugoslavia, and he was tired—never really weary of the game itself, but fatigued from his excruciating two-month attempt to become Botvinnik's challenger. He was psychically injured from not winning the tournament, and he couldn't eradicate the sting of his four bitter losses—robberies, he called them—to Tal.

Too, as always, there was the problem of money. Those still close to Bobby asked the obvious question: If he was one of the best players in the world, or certainly in the United States, why couldn't he make a living practicing his profession? While the average American salary at that time was $5,500 annually, Bobby, who certainly didn't consider himself *average*, had made barely $1,000 for a year's work. His prize for playing in the Candidates tournament had been only $200. If there just wasn't substantial tournament money to be had, why couldn't the American Chess Foundation sponsor him? It backed Reshevsky, even sending him to college. Was it because Bobby wasn't devoutly Jewish, while Reshevsky was Orthodox? Virtually all of the directors of the foundation were Jewish. Were they exerting subtle pressure on him to conform? To go back to school? Did they not respect him because he was "just a kid"? Was it because of the way he dressed?

Telegrams and phone calls kept pouring into Bobby through the end of November and the first weeks of December. Some of the correspondents asked whether he was going to defend his United States Championship title in the Rosenwald tournament. He really didn't know. A letter finally arrived in early December that announced the pairings. It listed the twelve players who were invited—Bobby included—and detailed who'd play whom on which dates, and what color each player would have in each round. Bobby went into a slow fume. *Public* pairing ceremonies were the custom, he loudly pointed out, in all European and most international tournaments.

The Rosenwald organizers, catching Bobby's implication that they'd colluded to make the pairings more favorable for some, expressed outrage at his protest. "Simple," said Bobby in response, "just do the pairings over again . . . this time publicly." They refused, and the sixteen-year-old Bobby threatened a lawsuit. *The New York Times* picked up on the dispute and ran a story headlined CHESS GROUP BALKS AT FISCHER DEMAND. The fracas escalated, and Bobby was told that a replacement player would take his place if he refused to play. Finally, the contest of wills ended after officials agreed that if Bobby would play this time, they'd make the pairings in public the following year. It was enough of a concession for Bobby, and he agreed to play. Ultimately, he'd won the battle.

In the past, Bobby had been perturbed by the constant criticism he received for his mode of dress. For example, an article in the Sunday newspaper supplement *Parade,* read by tens of millions, published a photograph of him giving a simultaneous exhibition with the caption: "Despite his rise to fame, Bobby still dresses casually. Note his dungarees and [plaid] shirt in contrast to his opponents' business suits and ties." Such potshots, he felt, diminished him—however subtle they might be. They detracted not only from who he *incontestably* was—a grandmaster and the United States Champion—but who he *believed* he was—the strongest player in the world.

Later, Pal Benko, whom Bobby had played in the Candidates tournament, would claim to be the one who talked Bobby into changing the kind of clothes he wore. He introduced Bobby to his tailor in the Little Hungary section of Manhattan so that the teenager could have some bespoke suits made. How Bobby could afford custom-tailored clothing is a mystery. Possibly, the money came from an advance he received for his book *Bobby Fischer's Games of Chess,* which was published in 1959.

When Bobby arrived at the Empire Hotel in December 1959 for the first round of the U.S. Championship tournament, he was dressed in a perfectly tailored suit, a custom-made white shirt, a Sulka white tie, and Italian-made shoes. Also, his hair was neatly combed, completing an image makeover so total that he was barely recognizable. Gone were the sneakers and ski sweaters, the mussed hair, the plaid cowboy shirt, and the slightly stained corduroy trousers. Predictably, the press began talking about "the New Fischer," interpreting Bobby's sartorial upgrade as a sign that he'd crossed into young manhood.

Bobby's competitors tried to hide their astonishment at the teenager's transformed appearance. As play progressed, though, they were stunned in a different way. By the end of the tournament, the suavely bedecked Bobby had played all eleven games without a single loss. Fischer had not only retained his title as United States Champion, he'd accomplished something unprecedented: For the third year in a row, he'd marched to the title without being defeated in any of the pairings.

There was a financial windfall, too. Bobby received $1,000 for his tournament win—and the Fischer family's pocketbook bulged further when Bobby's maternal grandfather, Jacob Wender, passed away, leaving $14,000 of his estate to Regina. It was enough—if invested wisely—for the frugal Fischers to live on for several years.

Indeed, Regina was prudent in her plans for the money. Joan had already married a man of means and was at the beginning of a nursing career, so Regina wanted to make sure that whatever income the inheritance generated would take care of Bobby and herself. She set up a trust fund with Ivan Woolworth, an attorney who worked for the Fischers pro bono. He was made the sole trustee, charged with investing the money in the best and most profitable way he could devise. Under the plan, Regina received $160 per month to help cover her personal needs. Since she was planning to move out of the apartment to attend medical school, perhaps in Mexico or in East Germany, she wanted the rent to be paid for Bobby for as long as he remained at 560 Lincoln Place. So he received $175 per month—enough to cover the rent, gas, and electric—plus a little extra. Additional money was added to the trust by Regina and Bobby over time, and the interest on the money invested allowed Bobby to live rent free for years, with some pocket money left over for himself.

Despite the small annuity, Bobby, to get by, had dinner almost every night at the Collins home and took advantage of lunch and dinner invitations from chess fans and admirers. Until he grew much older, he was never known to pick up a restaurant check, suffering what a friend called "limp wrist syndrome."

♜

In March of 1960 seventeen-year-old Bobby flew to Mar del Plata, the seaside resort on Argentina's Atlantic coast, south of Buenos Aires. Known for its art deco architecture and expansive boardwalk, the city had a proud tradition of hosting international tournaments. Argentinean players were as enthusiastic about the game as the Russians and the Yugoslavs, and Bobby was treated with respect wherever he went. The only downside of being in Mar del Plata was the incessant rain and the cold wind from the sea. Regina, ever irrepressible and somehow aware of the adverse weather, shipped a pair of galoshes to her son and admonished herself for not insisting that he take his leather coat when he left the States.

Bobby thought he'd easily walk through the Mar Del Plata tournament until he learned that David Bronstein and Fridrik Olafsson were also going to play, in addition to the twenty-three-year-old grandmaster from Leningrad, Boris Spassky. But it wasn't Spassky or Olafsson who really worried Fischer. It was Bronstein.

A week before he left for Argentina, Bobby and the author of this book had dinner at the Cedar Tavern in Greenwich Village, hangout of avant-garde artists and Abstract Expressionists, and one of Bobby's favorite eating places. The night we were there Jackson Pollock and Franz Kline were having a conversation at the bar, and Andy Warhol and John Cage dined at a nearby table—not that Bobby noticed. He just liked the pub food the restaurant served—it was a shepherd's pie kind of a place—*and* the anonymity that came from sitting among people who preferred gawking at art celebrities to taking note of chess prodigies.

We slid into the third booth from the bar and ordered bottles of beer— Lowenbrau for Bobby, Heineken for me. The waitress didn't question Bobby's age, even though he'd just turned seventeen and wasn't legally old enough to drink in New York State (eighteen was then the age limit). Bobby knew the selection without looking at the menu. He tackled an enormous slab of roast prime rib, which he consumed in a matter of minutes. It was as if he were a heavyweight boxer enjoying his last meal before the big fight.

He'd just received in the mail the pairings chart and color distribution from Mar del Plata. Bad news: He was to have black against both Bronstein and Spassky.

During a lull in the conversation—lulls were typical while spending time with Bobby, since he didn't talk much and wasn't embarrassed by long silences—I asked, "Bobby, how are you going to prepare for this tournament? I've always wanted to know how you did it." He seemed unusually chipper and became interested in my interest. "Here, I'll show you," he said, smiling. He then slid out of his side of the booth and sat next to me, cramming me into the corner. Next, he retrieved from his coat his battered pocket chess set—all the little pieces lined up in their respective slots, ready to go to war.

As he talked, he looked from me to the pocket set, back and forth—at least at first—and spat out a scholarly treatise on his method of preparation. "First of all, I'll look at the games that I can find of all of the players, but I'm only going to really prepare for Bronstein. Spassky and Olafsson, I'm not that worried about." He then showed me the progression of his one and only game with Bronstein—a draw from Portorož two years earlier. He took me through each move that the two had made, disparaging a Bronstein choice one moment, lauding another the next. The variety of choices Bobby worked through was dazzling, and overwhelming. In the course of his rapid analysis, he discussed the ramifications of certain variations or tactics, why each would be advisable or not. It was like watching a movie with a voice-over narration, but with one great difference: He was manipulating the pieces and speaking so rapidly that it was difficult to connect the moves with his commentary. I just couldn't follow the tumble of ideas behind the real and phantom attacks, the shadow assaults: "He couldn't play *there* since it would weaken his black squares" . . . "I didn't think of this" . . . "No, was he *kidding*?"

The slots of Bobby's pocket set had become so enlarged from thousands of hours of analysis that the half-inch plastic pieces seemed to jump into place kinesthetically, at his will. Most of the gold imprint designating whether a given piece was a bishop, king, queen, or whatever had, from years of use, worn off. But, of course, Bobby knew without looking—just by touch—what each piece represented. The tiny figurines were like his friendly pets.

"The problem with Bronstein," he went on, "is that it's almost impossible to beat him if he plays for a draw. At Zurich he played twenty draws out of twenty-eight games! Did you read his book?" I was snapped back into the reality of having to converse. "No. Isn't it in Russian?" He looked annoyed, and amazed that I didn't know the language: "Well, learn it! It's a fantastic book. He'll play for a win against me, I'm sure, and I'm not playing for a draw."

Resetting the pieces in seconds, again almost without looking, he said, "He's hard to prepare for because he can play any kind of game, positional or tactical, and any kind of opening." He then began to show me, from memory, game after game—it seemed like *dozens*—focusing on the openings that Bronstein had played against Bobby's favorite variations. Multiple outcomes leaped from his mind. But he didn't just confine himself to Bronstein's efforts. He also took me on a tour of games that Louis Paulsen had played in the 1800s and Aaron Nimzowitsch had experimented with in the 1920s, as well as others that had been played just weeks before—games gleaned from a Russian newspaper.

All the time Bobby weighed possibilities, suggested alternatives, selected the best lines, discriminated, decided. It was a history lesson and a chess tutorial, but mainly it was an amazing feat of memory. His eyes, slightly glazed, were now fixed on the pocket set, which he gently held open in his left hand, talking to himself, totally unaware of my presence or that he was in a restaurant. His intensity seemed even greater than when he was playing a tournament or match game. His fingers sped by in a blur, and his face showed the slightest of smiles, as if in a reverie. He whispered, barely audibly: "Well, if he plays *that* . . . I can block his bishop." And then, raising his voice so loud that some of the customers stared: "He won't play *that*."

I began to weep quietly, aware that in that time-suspended moment I was in the presence of genius.

Bobby's prediction at the Cedar Tavern was realized at Mar del Plata. When Bronstein and Bobby met in the twelfth round, the Russian *did* play for a win, but when the game neared its ending, there were an even number of pieces and pawns remaining on each side, and a draw was inevitable. By the conclusion of the tournament, Fischer and Spassky were tied for first place. It was Fischer's greatest triumph in an international tournament to date.

And then there was the Argentinean disaster two months later. Of all the cities Bobby had been to, Buenos Aires was his favorite: He liked the food, the people's enthusiasm for chess, and the broad boulevards. Yet something went uncharacteristically wrong with Bobby's play during his stay there, and the rumor that circulated, both then and for years after, was that he was staying up until dawn—on at least one occasion with an Argentinean beauty—allowing himself to become physically run-down, and not preparing for the next day's opponent. The worldly Argentinean grandmaster Miguel Najdorf, who wasn't playing in the tournament, introduced Bobby to the city's nightlife, not caring that he was undermining the boy's possibility of gaining a top spot in the competition. And with the bravado of a seventeen-year-old, Bobby assumed that he had the energy and focus to play well even after very little sleep, night after night. Unfortunately, when he found himself in extremis at the board and called on his chess muse to save him, there was no answer.

Whatever the reason for his poor play (when pressed, he said the lighting was atrocious), Bobby as the brilliant Dr. Jekyll morphed into a weakened Mr. Hyde, a shell of a player. In the twenty-player tournament, he won only three games, drew eleven, and lost the rest. *Bewildering.* Anyone can have a bad tournament, but Bobby's past record had been one of ascendancy, and his 13½–1½ result at Mar del Plata just a short time before had left his fans predicting that he'd take top honors at Buenos Aires.

For Bobby, the defeat was devastating. It's bad enough to fail, but far worse to see another succeed at the very accomplishment you'd hoped to achieve. Samuel Reshevsky, his American archrival, had tied for first with Viktor Korchnoi. A group photograph of the players taken at the end of the tournament shows Bobby with unfocused eyes, apparently paying no attention to the photographer or the rest of the players. Was he thinking about his poor performance? Or was he perhaps considering that, just this once, his determination to win hadn't been strong enough?

He'd agreed to play first board for the United States that year at the World

Chess Olympics, which was to be held in Leipzig, East Germany, in October of 1960, but American chess officials were claiming that they didn't have enough money to pay for the team's travel and other expenses. A national group called the People-to-People Committee was attempting to raise funds for the team, and the executive director asked Bobby if he'd give a simultaneous exhibition to publicize the team's plight. The event was held at the Rikers Island jail complex, which stands on a 413-acre plot of land in the middle of New York's East River. At the time the facility housed some fourteen thousand inmates, twenty of whom Bobby played. Unsurprisingly, he won all the games.

Unfortunately, though the exhibition did garner coverage in local newspapers, not one story mentioned the *reason* for the event: to bring attention to the American team's financial straits. But if the State Department and American chess organizations couldn't help, Regina Fischer thought *she* could. Probing into the activities of the American Chess Foundation, she demonstrated that some players (such as Reshevsky) received support while others (such as Bobby) did not. A one-woman publicity machine, she sent out indignant press releases, as well as letters to the government demanding a public accounting.

Although Bobby desperately wanted to go to Leipzig to play in his first Olympics, he began to seethe over his mother's interference, and on at least one occasion he openly took her to task when she made a public appearance at a chess event. *She* felt she was helping her son; *he* felt she was simply being a pushy stage mother.

While picketing the foundation's offices, Regina caught the attention of Ammon Hennacy, a pacifist, anarchist, social activist, and associate editor of the libertarian newspaper the *Catholic Worker*. He suggested that Regina undertake a hunger strike for chess. She did so for six days and garnered yet more publicity. Hennacy also talked her into joining the longest peace march in history, from San Francisco to Moscow, and she agreed. While on the march she met Cyril Pustan, an Englishman who was a high school teacher and journeyman plumber. Among other areas of interest, their political beliefs and religion—both were Jewish—meshed perfectly, and eventually they married and settled in England.

When, ultimately, Bobby walked into the lobby of the Astoria Hotel in

Leipzig, he was greeted by a man who resembled a younger and handsomer Groucho Marx: Isaac Kashdan, the United States team captain. Kashdan and Bobby had never met before, but the former was a legend in the chess world. An international grandmaster, he was one of America's strongest players in the late 1920s and 1930s, when he played in five chess Olympics, winning a number of medals. Having been warned that Bobby was "hard to handle," Kashdan was concerned that the young man might not be a compliant team member.

Bobby may have sensed the team captain's wariness, because he turned the conversation to Kashdan's chess career; the teenager not only knew of the older man's reputation, he was also familiar with many of his past games. Kashdan responded to Bobby's overture and later commented: "I had no real problem with him. All he wants to do is to play chess. He is a tremendous player." Although separated in age by almost four decades, the two players became relatively close and remained so for years.

One of the highlights of the Olympics came when the United States faced the USSR and Bobby was slated to play Mikhail Tal, then the World Champion. Fischer and Tal met in the fifth round. Before making his first move, Tal stared at the board, and stared, and stared. Bobby wondered, rightly so as it developed, whether Tal was up to his old tricks. Finally, after ten long minutes, Tal moved. He was hoping to make Fischer feel completely uncomfortable. But his effort to unsettle the American failed. Instead, Bobby launched an aggressive series of moves, waging a board battle that was later described as both a "slugfest" and a "sparkling attack and counter-attack." The cerebral melee ended in a draw, and later both players would include the game in their respective books, citing it as one of the most important in their careers.

That seventeen-year-old Bobby had held his own against the reigning World Champion didn't go unnoticed, and players at the competition were now predicting that in a very short time, Bobby would be playing for the title.

By the end of the Olympics, the Soviet Union, which had fielded one of the strongest teams ever, came in first and the United States eased into second. Bobby's score was ten wins, two losses, and six draws, and he took home the silver medal.

At the closing banquet someone mentioned to Mikhail Tal that Bobby, who'd been studying palmistry, was reading the palms of other players, almost as a parlor game. "Let him read mine," said Tal skeptically. He walked over to Bobby's table, held out his left hand, and said, "Read it." While Bobby stared at Tal's palm and pondered the mysteries of its lines and crevices, a crowd gathered around and hundreds of others watched from their tables.

Sensing the building drama, Bobby took his time and seemed to peer even more deeply at the hand. Then, with a look on his face that promised he was going to reveal the meaning of life, he said in stentorian tones: "I can see in your palm, Mr. Tal, that the next World Champion will be . . ."

At that point Bobby and Tal spoke simultaneously. Fischer said, "Bobby Fischer!" And Tal, never at a loss for a quip, said, "William Lombardy!" (who happened to be standing to his immediate left). Everyone assembled screamed with laughter.

A short while later, *Chess Life,* in describing the incident, chose to find in it an augury of things to come. Said the magazine: "By the look of confidence and self-assuredness on Fischer's face, we wonder if in fact, he did 'see' himself as the next World Champion."

7

Einstein's Theory

BOBBY LEFT THE BALLROOM of the Empire Hotel, just steps away from the construction site of the Lincoln Center for the Performing Arts cultural complex. He'd just clinched the 1960–61 United States Championship, and he walked briskly through the snow-covered streets with his mother and Jack and Ethel Collins. Jack found it tough going with his wheelchair, so he and his sister took a taxi to a victory dinner for Bobby at Vorst's, a German restaurant a few blocks from the tournament site. If there was any question of his accomplishment, *Chess Life* set the record straight:

> By winning the United States Championship for the fourth time in succession, Bobby Fischer, 17-year-old International Grandmaster from Brooklyn, has carved an indelible impression in the historic cycle of American chess and has proven without a doubt that he is both the greatest player that this country ever produced and one of the strongest players in the world. Fischer has not lost a game in an American tournament since 1957.

There was only one problem with *Chess Life*'s semi-hagiography: Reshevsky didn't agree with it, nor did many of his supporters.

Some chess players felt that it was an insult to proclaim Fischer the greatest American player at seventeen, and thereby diminish the reputation of Reshevsky at fifty. It didn't help that a study had been published that year in *American Statistician* magazine, "The Age Factor in Master Chess," in which the author posited that chess masters go downhill after a certain age, "perhaps forty." Reshevsky wanted to prove the study wrong.

For many years Reshevsky had enjoyed a reign as America's "greatest," and now all the spoils and baubles seemed to be going to Bobby, whom many thought of as simply a young, irreverent upstart from Brooklyn. That said, at least an equal number of observers couldn't get enough of "the upstart." They believed that he signaled the possibility of a chess boom in America.

The officers of the American Chess Foundation maintained that Reshevsky was the better player, and they arranged to have him prove it. During the summer of 1961 a sixteen-game match between the two players was negotiated and a prize fund of $8,000 was promised, with $1,000 awarded to each player in advance. Of the balance, 65 percent would go to the winner and 35 percent to the loser. Such a match evoked the drama of some of history's great rivalries—clashes such as Mozart vs. Salieri, Napoleon vs. Wellington, and Dempsey vs. Tunney. When four world-class chess players—Svetozar Gligoric, Bent Larsen, Paul Keres, and Tigran Petrosian—were asked their opinion of who would prevail, *all* predicted that Reshevsky would be the winner, and by a substantial margin.

Reshevsky, a small, bald man who dressed conservatively, had a solemn and resolute personality. He was an ice king who was courteous but curt. Bobby couldn't have been more different. He was a tall, gangly, intense, quarrelsome teenager, a quixotic chess prince who exhibited occasional flashes of charm and grace. And their styles on the board were just as divergent. Reshevsky's games were rarely poetic—they displayed no passion. The longtime champion often lapsed into time pressure, barely making the control. Fischer's games, though, were crystalline—transparent but ingenious. Bobby had taught himself, after years of practice, to budget his time and he hardly ever drifted into time pressure. (The regimen Jack Collins had imposed when he imported a German clock for Bobby had proved its worth.)

The other differences? Fischer was thoroughly prepared—"booked up," as it was called—with opening innovations. Reshevsky, though, tended to be underprepared and often had to determine the most effective moves during play, wasting valuable time. Fischer was more of a tactical player, with flames of brilliance, while Reshevsky was a positional player. He maneuvered for tiny advantages and exhibited an obdurate patience. He was methodically capable of eking out a win from a seemingly hopeless and delicate position.

Ultimately, though, the match wouldn't be rendering a judgment on which player's *style* was the best. Its agenda was more basic—that is, to determine who was the best American player *period*.

Hardly a pas de deux, there was a seesaw of results: wins for Bobby . . . draws . . . wins for Reshevsky. One day Bobby was King Kong; the next, Fay Wray. By the eleventh game, which was played in Los Angeles, the score was tied at 5½–5½. There was difficulty scheduling the twelfth round, which fell on a Saturday. Reshevsky, an Orthodox Jew, couldn't play on Saturday until after sundown. (Early in his career he *did* play before sundown, but he came to believe that this was a transgression that had caused the death of his father, and thereafter he refused to compete on the Sabbath.) The starting time was therefore changed to 8:30 p.m. When someone pointed out that the game could easily last until two in the morning, it was rescheduled to begin at 1:30 p.m. the next day, Sunday afternoon.

Complications set in. Jacqueline Piatigorsky (née Rothchild, a member of one of the richest families in Europe) was one of the sponsors of the match and was paying for all of the players' expenses. She was married to the cellist Gregor Piatigorsky, who happened to be giving a concert in Los Angeles that Sunday afternoon. So that she could attend her husband's concert, Jacqueline asked that the game begin at 11:00 a.m. When Bobby, a classically late sleeper, heard of yet another change of schedule, he protested immediately. He simply couldn't play at that time, he said. "It's ridiculous." Bobby also didn't see why he had to cater to Mrs. Piatigorsky. She could always come to the game after the concert, he argued. They'd probably still be playing.

At the tournament site—the Beverly Hilton Hotel—Bobby's chess clock was started promptly at eleven a.m. Reshevsky paced up and down, a few spectators waited patiently, and when the little red flag fell precisely at noon, the tournament director declared the game a forfeit. The thirteenth game had been scheduled to be played back in New York at the Empire Hotel.

Bobby said he was willing to continue the match, but the next game had to be a replay of the twelfth game. He didn't want to play burdened by such a massive disadvantage; the forfeited game could possibly decide the match's outcome.

Reshevsky nervously paced the stage, once again waiting for the absent Bobby to arrive, this time to play the disputed thirteenth game. About twenty spectators and as many journalists and photographers also waited, staring at the empty, lonely board, and at Reshevsky, who never stopped his pacing.

When an hour had elapsed on the clock, I. A. Horowitz, the referee, declared the game forfeited. Then Walter Fried, the president of the American Chess Foundation, who'd just burst into the room, noticed that Fischer was in absentia and declared Reshevsky the winner of the series. "Fischer had a gun to our heads," he later said, explaining the abrupt termination of one of the most important American chess matches ever played.

Bobby ultimately sued Reshevsky and the American Chess Foundation, seeking a court order to resume the match and asking to have Reshevsky banned from tournament play until the matter was settled. The case lingered in the courts for years and was finally dropped. Although the two men would subsequently meet over the board in other tournaments, the "Match of the Century," as it had been billed, was the unfortunate casualty of Bobby's ingrained sleep habits and the long shadow of patronage in chess.

Bobby took the elevator to the thirtieth floor of the skyscraper at 110 West Fortieth Street, on the edge of the garment district, and when he disembarked, the elevator operator pointed to a doorway. "It's up those metal stairs." Bobby started climbing the spiral staircase, up and up, four flights. "Is that you, Bobby?" came a disembodied voice from above. It was Ralph Ginzburg, the journalist who'd scheduled an interview with Bobby for *Harper's* magazine.

Bobby was guided into a strange round office, about the size of a small living room and positioned in the tower of the building, with windows on all sides. Everything was battleship gray: the floor, walls, filing cabinets, a desk, and two chairs. The tower room swayed ever so slightly as the wind whistled through the spires outside.

Ginzburg, thirty-two, wore horn-rimmed glasses and was going prematurely bald. A risk-taking journalist, he'd previously worked for *Look* magazine and *Esquire,* and was the author of two books, including a history of lynching in America. Clever, extremely industrious, he talked loudly and rapidly with a Bronx accent and was proud of his bent for sensationalism. Later he went to prison on an obscenity conviction for publishing a magazine called *Eros*.

It's important to know this background about Ginzburg, not just because his article about Bobby has been used for more than forty years as a source for other writers and biographers, but also because of the negative effect it had on Bobby's life and the consequent role it had in making him forever suspicious of journalists.

In preparation for the interview, Ginzburg had read Elias Canetti's classic work *Auto-da-Fé*, written eight years before Bobby was born. The story, which helped Canetti earn the Nobel Prize in literature, includes a character named Fischerele who aspires to become chess champion of the world. When he wins the title, he plans to change his name to Fischer, and after becoming rich and famous, he will own "new suits made at the best possible tailor" and live in a "gigantic palace with real castles, knights, pawns."

Ginzburg quoted Fischer as saying that he bought his suits, shirts, and shoes from the best tailors all over the world and was "going to hire the best architect and have him build it [my house] in the shape of a rook . . . spiral staircases, parapets, everything. I want to live the rest of my life in a house built exactly like a rook."

The article, which also included provocative material, caused a sensation, coloring many of the interview questions that would be fired at Bobby for years after. When, on the heels of *Harper's*, widely read British magazine *Chess* published the article in full, Bobby turned livid and screamed: "Those bastards!"

Bobby insisted that most of the article had twisted what he said and used his quotes out of context. For example, he never told Ginzburg that he had to "get rid of his mother." It's true that Regina Fischer left the apartment to go on a long peace march, met a man, got married, and settled in England. She did say that Bobby, a highly independent adolescent, was probably better off without her living with him; like many mothers, she was doting and continually trying to help her son, sometimes to the point of exasperating him. She and Bobby both realized that living alone gave him more time to study according to his own time and pace, but Ginzburg's negative interpretation of their relationship was totally incorrect. Bobby and his mother loved each other.

Listening to the tapes or reading the transcripts of Ginzburg's interview with Bobby would have proven what the teenager did or didn't say, but Ginzburg said he destroyed all of the research materials that backed up the article. If so, this was unusual: Most professional journalists retain interview transcripts lest what they've written generate a charge of libel or invasion of privacy. One can never know the full truth, of course, but even if Ginzburg merely reported verbatim what Bobby had said, it was a cruel piece of journalism, a penned mugging, in that it made a vulnerable teenager appear uneducated, homophobic, and misogynistic, none of which was a true portrait.

Previous to this, Bobby had already been wary of journalists. The Ginzburg article, though, sent him into a permanent fury and created a distrust of reporters that lasted the rest of his life. When anyone asked about the article, he would scream: "I don't want to talk about it! Don't ever mention Ginzburg's name to me!"

♜

To exorcise the disgruntled feeling he still had from *l'affaire* Reshevsky, and to shake off the *Harper's* article affront, Bobby wanted to get away from New York and just get back to doing what made him happy: He wanted to play chess—without lawyers, without publicity, without threats and counterthreats. He accepted an invitation to play in Yugoslavia in a month-long, twenty-player event in Bled that promised to be one of the strongest international tournaments conducted in years. But first he had to prepare, and he had only three weeks to do so.

Normally, Bobby's schedule consisted of five hours per day of study: games, openings, variations, endings. And then, of course, he'd play speed games for an additional five or more hours with the Collins cluster or at one of the clubs. He loved to play fast chess, since it gave him the opportunity to try out dubious or experimental lines through an instant gaze of the board. It honed his instinct and forced him to trust himself.

But to play in an international tournament of the caliber announced, he had to spend much more time at careful, precise study, analysis, and memorization. He stopped answering his phone, because he didn't want to be interrupted or tempted to socialize—even for a chess party—and at one point, to be alone with the chessboard, he just threw some clothes in a suitcase, didn't tell anyone where he was going, and checked into the Brooklyn YMCA. During his stay there, he sometimes studied more than sixteen hours per day.

Malcolm Gladwell, in his book *Outliers,* describes how people in all fields reach success. He quotes neurologist Daniel Levitin: "In study after study, of composers, basketball players, fiction writers, ice skaters, concert pianists, chessplayers, criminals and what have you, the number comes up again and again [the magic number for true expertise: ten thousand hours of practice]." Gladwell then refers to Bobby: "To become a chess grandmaster also seems to take about ten years. (Only the legendary Bobby Fischer got to that elite level in less than that amount of time: it took him nine years.) Practice isn't the thing you do once you're good. It's the thing you do that makes you good." A fair estimate is that Bobby played one thousand games a year between the ages of nine and eleven, and twelve thousand a year from the ages of eleven to thirteen, most of them speed games. Although all of these games could be considered "practice," not all were particularly instructive. Specific moves or positions reached, however, could be highly enlightening and might even remain locked in his unconscious mind—in the same way, for example, that one remembered chord or even a single note can be of value to a musician. Bobby's study of the nuances of *others'* games had the same effect: He paid careful attention to the accumulation of fine detail.

Bobby loved Yugoslavia because of the superstar status accorded him by its chess adherents, and, on a delightful autumnal day, he entered the tournament hall at Lake Bled primed to play. Now eighteen and dressed in an impeccably tailored suit with a white handkerchief deftly positioned in his breast pocket, he looked somewhat older and carried himself with an athletic swagger. He looked a little like a budding movie star. Many of the Yugoslavs didn't recognize him at first.

Walking in the streets, he'd be besieged by autograph seekers. From his experience at the Interzonal and the Candidates tournament in 1958–59, both held in Yugoslavia, he'd grasped enough of the language to at least autograph his name in Serbo-Croat. Fans went wild when he inscribed their scorecards in their own language. When a spectator from Moscow asked for an autograph, Bobby signed it using the Russian Cyrillic alphabet, needing to change only a few letters.

For Bobby, the highlight of the tournament was his game against Tal in the second round. Tal, who was much better behaved than the last time he played Bobby—doing less staring and snickering—seemed to suffer a lapse of chess logic on the sixth move, and he blundered again on the ninth move, becoming enmeshed in the opening that Bobby had prepared against him. Tal's spotty play was blamed on the fact that he wasn't feeling well. Bobby's own play was not at its sharpest, but he exploited the weak moves of his opponent and pressed home the advantage until Tal lapsed into a hopeless endgame and resigned. The applause was tumultuous. "A charmer," piped *Chess Review.* Bobby was almost giddy with delight at notching his first win against one of the strongest players in the world, a former World Champion, the man he'd fantasized about murdering during the 1959 Candidates.

As Tal and Fischer left the stage, journalists rushed to them begging for a comment. The two combatants, both a little playful, performed for the crowd:

Tal [Sighing]: It is difficult to play against Einstein's theory.

Fischer [Exulting]: Finally, he has not escaped from me!

Bobby was not happy with his eventual second-place showing in the tournament, and like Tal, he blamed some of his draws on illness. By the end of the competition, he was feeling mild discomfort in the lower right part of his abdomen, and he was also having difficulty keeping food down. When the pain worsened, and he mentioned it to some of the players, they insisted he see a physician.

Suspicious as always of doctors, Bobby was also concerned about communicating in Serbo-Croat. Would he be able to understand what was being said to him? A doctor was summoned to the Hotel Toplice, and one of the Yugoslavian players served as translator. As soon as the doctor touched his abdomen, Bobby flinched in pain. "It seems like appendicitis," the doctor warned. "You'll have to go to a hospital. If the appendix ruptures, you may get peritonitis, and the infection will spread." Bobby asked if there was anything that could be done without going to a hospital. "No," the doctor answered emphatically. Bobby reluctantly agreed, and he was driven from Bled in Slovenia to Banja Luka in Bosnia for treatment at a large university hospital. He begged the doctors not to operate, even though they told him that it was a relatively simple procedure and cautioned him of the dangers involved in not operating. They assured him he'd be up and walking around in a few days, but he was still resistant. Not only was he philosophically opposed to surgery, he was frightened of anesthesia. He didn't even want to take medicine to stop the pain. The doctors prevailed on that point and also insisted that he take a regimen of antibiotics. Eventually, the pain lessened and within two or three days he was feeling himself again. He was effusively thankful to the doctors for not insisting he be put under the knife.

After the appendicitis scare, the British Broadcasting Corporation invited him to London to appear on a show called *Chess Treasury of the Air*, and he spent about ten days in England. Christmas in London was a charming experience for Bobby. It seemed to be what he imagined New York City might have been like around 1890 or 1900. He admired the gentility of the city's citizens and the cleanliness of its streets. Pal Benko was there for a while with him and noticed that though he himself had a thick Hungarian accent, he could be more easily understood by the Londoners than Bobby with his pronounced Brooklyn dialect. Bobby spent a British Christmas with his mother and her new husband, Cyril Pustan, who'd heard him on the BBC show.

As he continued to prepare for upcoming tournaments, Bobby was also being drawn closer to the Worldwide Church of God, and he began to face a time conflict between his two commitments: religion and chess. "I split my life into two pieces," he told an interviewer later. "One was where my chess career lies. There I kept my sanity, so to speak. And the other was my religious life. I tried to apply what I learned in the church to my chess career, too. But I was still studying chess. I wasn't just 'trusting in God' to give me the moves." Bobby's pragmatic philosophy was similar to the old Arabic saying "Trust in Allah but tie up your camel."

In addition to his Bible correspondence course, listening to Reverend Armstrong's sermons, and his in-depth study of the Old and New Testaments,

Bobby was reading the *Plain Truth,* the Church's bimonthly magazine, which claimed to have a circulation of more than 2,500,000. Articles in the magazine were, as the title implies, written plainly and seemed as much political as religious. Bobby read every issue cover to cover, though, and much of what he ingested made sense to him. Forty years later he'd still be espousing ideas put forth by Armstrong and the *Plain Truth.*

One issue outlined horrific prophecies, graphically illustrated, of what Armstrong predicted would be World War III, when the United States and Great Britain would be destroyed by a United States of Europe. Armstrong said that before the war began, he'd lead his church members to Jordan, where they'd be saved because they were "God's People." Bobby, too.

Bobby wrote a preachy letter to his mother, enthusiastically discussing Armstrong's teachings and his intense biblical studies, which had "changed my whole outlook on life." He'd become convinced that only by following Armstrong's interpretation of the Bible could he find health and happiness, become successful, and gain eternal life, and he urged her to read the Bible and Armstrong's writings. Regina wasn't buying his sales pitch and wrote back that Armstrong and his church were feeding Bobby a line of mumbo jumbo and engaging in fear mongering. A good and tolerant life was the best life, she said; call it a religion if you like. After that, they both agreed not to discuss his religious views or hers. Neither mother nor son was willing to try to make a convert of the other.

Bobby tried to live and practice his beliefs; he felt truly *born again,* and he was applying the same sense of discipline and reverence to the Bible that he had all his life to chess. He began making donations to worthy causes; he wouldn't have sex, because he wasn't married; he scorned profanity and pornography; and he attempted to follow the Ten Commandments in every detail. "If anyone tried to live by the letter of the law, it was me," he said later, in an interview published by the *Ambassador Report.*

But eventually his religious commitments began tearing him apart. He couldn't spend ten or twelve hours a day studying chess and another six to eight hours on Bible studies; and the constant surfacing of impure thoughts and other minor sins was plaguing him. "The more I tried [to be obedient] the more crazy I became," he noted. "I was half out of my head—almost stoned." Without giving up on Armstrong, he realized that Caissa (the patron goddess of chess) had more meaning for him than the Worldwide Church of God. *Focus, focus, focus!* Chess *had* to become paramount again; it *had* to be his first priority, or his dream of achieving the World Championship would be just that: a dream.

January 1962

Spending two months in Sweden in the middle of winter, Bobby found the weather less cold than he'd thought it would be. Temperatures remained close to fifty degrees Fahrenheit. He wasn't in Stockholm, though, to stalk the cobblestoned streets of Old Town, or walk through the underground tunnels, or ready himself for a cruise on the Baltic Sea. Rather, he was there to, once again, try to become the player the whole chess world should pay homage to. Aside from the accolades that would flow to the winner of the Stockholm tournament, the *real* prize for Bobby was to qualify for the Candidates tournament, which, in turn, could give him a chance at the World Championship.

Chess Life, on its front page, wrapped up the eventual Stockholm results this way:

> Stockholm, 1962, may come to be recognized as the event which marked the beginning of a decisive shift of power in world chess. For the first time since the Interzonal and Candidates' tournaments began as eliminating contests for the World's Championship in 1948, the Soviet grandmasters failed to capture first prize. Bobby Fischer's margin of 2 ½ points reflects his complete domination of the event. It owed nothing to luck: he never had a clearly lost position.

What Bobby achieved in going undefeated in both Bled and Stockholm was the chess equivalent of pitching two successive no-hitters in baseball's World Series. Most would have thought the feat impossible. Less than a week shy of his nineteenth birthday, Bobby Fischer had just established himself as one of the most extraordinary chess players in the world. But this wasn't the time to gloat or preen, or even to relax. Bobby's goal was the World Championship, and the next step toward that objective was almost upon him.

The economics of chess enforced a certain humility anyway. Before Bobby left Sweden, he was given a small white envelope containing his earnings from the tour-de-force playing he'd just demonstrated. The envelope contained the cash equivalent of $750 in Swedish krona. Bobby could only shake his head ruefully.

He now had barely six weeks to prepare for the Candidates tournament to be held on the island of Curaçao, thirty-eight miles off the coast of Venezuela. The winner of the Curaçao tournament would earn the right to play the current World Champion, Mikhail Botvinnik, in the next world title match.

Home in his apartment in Brooklyn, Bobby went through what was becoming his routine: elimination of social engagements, long periods of solitary study, analysis of games, and a search for innovations in openings. He classified the lines he studied into stratifications of importance, always eliminating the not-quite-perfect continuation and seeking what he called the "true move," that which could not be refuted. A Socratic dialogue raged within him: How unusual was the resulting position if he followed that particular line? Would his opponent feel at sea? Would *he* (Bobby) feel comfortable playing it? How would he ground himself if he had to continue to play that variation until the endgame?

Grandmaster Pal Benko, a former Hungarian freedom fighter who became a U.S. citizen and, like many other chess players, an investment broker, entered Bobby's room at the Hotel Intercontinental in Curaçao shortly after Arthur Bisguier, Bobby's second, had arrived.

"We're going to work now," Bobby said dismissively to Benko, as he was eating a large late-night room service dinner. He and Bisguier had planned to go over some games. "You can't come in."

"Yes I can. Bisguier also my second," said Benko.

"Bisguier also my second," parroted Bobby, trying to duplicate Benko's Magyar accent.

"Why you make fun at me?" Benko asked.

"Why you make fun at me?" Bobby parroted again.

"Stop it!"

"Stop it!"

All the while Bisguier stood by and, with body language and a few words of attempted peacemaking, tried to calm things down.

"Get out of my room!" Bobby commanded.

"No, you get out!" Benko replied, somewhat illogically.

It isn't clear who hit first, but since Bobby was sitting, he was at a disadvantage. Blows and slaps were exchanged as both grandmasters screamed at each other. Bisguier jumped in and separated the two men. Benko had achieved the "better" of it and years later would confess: "I am sorry that I beat up Bobby. He was a sick man, even then." In the annals of chess, this was the first fistfight ever recorded by two grandmasters, both prospective World Champions.

The day after the fight, Bobby penned a letter to the Tournament Committee, asking them to expel Benko. The committee chose to do nothing about the protest.

Before May and June of 1962 Bobby seemed to be gaining strength with every contest. "Fischer grows from one tournament to the next," Mikhail Tal had said. He'd surpassed his great achievement at Bled in 1961 with an even more dazzling triumph at Stockholm. He'd defeated at least once all of the five Soviet grandmasters he was to meet at Curaçao, and he seemed to be reaching the peak of his powers sooner than anyone (but himself) had expected.

Pundits' predictions were proven totally wrong when the first news issued from Curaçao that May. Fischer and Tal had both lost in the first and second rounds, and Bobby was soon lagging in fourth place. All in all, Eliot Hearst observed in *Chess Life,* the Candidates tournament had furnished "a series of early-round surprises that are probably without parallel in chess history."

Some have speculated that Bobby might have been spending too much of his off time gambling, but Bisguier said that all Bobby would do was, on occasion, wander into the casino in the evenings and play the slot machines—the "one-armed bandits" as they were called—until he got bored. He didn't watch television or go to the local movie house, because he said such activity was bad for his eyes and he didn't want to hurt his play. He did attend a prizefight one night and went to a local nightclub a few times, but his heart and interest weren't in it.

Henry Stockhold, a chess player who was covering the match for the Associated Press, brought Bobby to a brothel one night and waited for him. When Bobby exited an hour later, Stockhold asked him how he enjoyed it, and Bobby's comment, which he repeated at other times, has often been quoted: "Chess is better."

Tigran Petrosian won the 1962 Candidates tournament with a score of eight wins, nineteen draws, and no losses, for 17½ points. Soviets Efim Geller and Paul Keres tied for second, a half point behind, and Bobby's fourth-place score was three full points below the three leaders and a half point ahead of Korchnoi.

Bobby wanted the world to know what really happened at Curaçao. He wrote: "There was open collusion between the Russian [Soviet] players. They agreed ahead of time to draw the games that they played against each other. . . . They consulted during the games. If I was playing a Russian [Soviet] opponent, the other Russians watched my games, and commented on my moves in my hearing."

Korchnoi, in his memoir *Chess Is My Life,* backed Bobby's accusations: "Everything was arranged by Petrosian. He agreed with his friend Geller to play draws in all their games together. They also persuaded Keres to join their coalition . . . this gave them a great advantage over the remaining competitors."

When asked why Fischer hadn't won, Pal Benko, still smarting over his fight with Bobby, replied: "He simply wasn't the best player."

Bobby's self-image was shattered as a result of Curaçao. His dream—his obsession—of becoming the youngest World Champion in history had eluded him. It had seemed inevitable to him that he'd win the title, but that was not enough. His ascendancy to international chess prominence at such a young age had made him certain that he'd become champion, but the Russians—through what he considered their chicanery—had proven that they could hold him back, and this both enraged and saddened him.

Bobby *now* realized that there was nothing about his destiny that was inevitable, and yet he would not go quietly into the chess night. He despised the Soviets for what they'd done to him. He was convinced they'd stolen the championship, and he insisted that the world know it.

♖

In its August 20, 1962, issue, *Sports Illustrated* published Bobby's *j'accuse:* "The Russians Have Fixed World Chess." The article was reprinted in German, Dutch, Spanish, Swedish, Icelandic, and even the Russian chess journalists made mention of it. Bobby announced that he'd never again participate in a Candidates tournament, because the FIDE system made it impossible for any but a Soviet player to win. He wrote, "The system set up by the *Fédération Internationale des Échecs* . . . insures that there will always be a Russian world champion. . . . The Russians arranged it that way." At Portorož he confirmed that he'd grown in strength sufficiently to have defeated all the Soviet grandmasters competing with him for the title. He believed that Russian manipulation of tournaments had become a great deal more "open," or apparent, presumably in response to his threat of domination.

Chess watchers seem to agree that it was likely the Soviets had colluded, on *some* level, at Curaçao. And yet Bobby failed to mention that neither he nor anyone else ever proved a threat to the three leading Russians throughout this tournament, so the question of why the Russians would have colluded as flagrantly as Bobby maintained remains unanswered. Economics professors Charles C. Moul and John V. C. Nye wrote a scholarly analysis, "Did the Soviets Collude? A Statistical Analysis of Championship Chess, 1940–64," examining hundreds of tournament results involving Soviet and non-Soviet players, and concluded that there was a 75 percent probability, in general, that Soviet players *did* collude. The authors were quick to point out, however, that "Fischer was not a strong enough favorite to be severely harmed by the draw collusion in the notorious Candidates Tournament in Curaçao, 1962."

Curaçao aside, the *real* reason the Soviets always seemed to be among the finalists in tournaments was, of course, that they were overrepresented in the field of players, due to the game's popularity in their home country and the level of government support. The Soviet Union had more first-rate players than any other three nations combined. So long as that imbalance remained—and with the superb Soviet "farm system," it continued to reinforce itself—two to three Russians would always survive the Interzonal to enter the Candidates, with one or two more seeded over. That created the possibility of the Russians "teaming up" if they so chose, and led to charges such as Bobby's that no Westerner could hope to win the world title under the existing FIDE system.

Perhaps because of Fischer's intransigent article in *Sports Illustrated,* the Soviets and the rest of the chess world were shocked into accepting a new FIDE dictum: A radical reform of the Candidates was instituted. From that point forward, the old setup would be replaced with a series of matches of ten or twelve games each between the eight individual contestants, with the loser of each match being eliminated.

Still unanswered was the question of whether Bobby Fischer would really drop out of the World Championship cycle and never realize his dream. Some wondered: Might he even drop out of chess altogether?

The answer came quickly.

8

Legends Clash

ABOARD THE *New Amsterdam* ocean liner nineteen-year-old Bobby Fischer didn't wear a tuxedo to dinner in the first-class lounge, but he dressed as conservatively as he could, with a blue serge suit, white shirt, and dark tie. Forgetting that he'd ever been way behind the fashion curve, he was appalled, in some priggish, nouveau riche kind of way, that certain passengers appeared in the dining room in slacks and sneakers.

During the nine-day voyage from New York to Rotterdam in September 1962 he slept as much as could, played over some games, and sat on the promenade deck to take in the bracing sea air. The trip was paid for from the $5,000 appearance fee he was getting to compete for the United States in the Olympiad in Varna, Bulgaria. He had a triple motive in sailing, instead of flying, across the Atlantic: He wanted to see and experience how the "aristocrats" traveled, he needed some rest and time alone, and he was also beginning to become afraid—in a way that many might consider paranoid—that the Soviets, to protect their national chess honor and remove him as a threat to their hegemony, might sabotage a plane that he was in.

Bobby's diatribe about cheating by the Soviets was being discussed all over the world, and the chess hierarchy in Russia was incensed. Consequently, he believed the Soviets might be furious enough to, as he put it, murder him by "tinkering with the engine of a plane."

The anticipation of playing against World Champion Mikhail Botvinnik for the first time was exhilarating, though, and worth the discomfort of participating at what was rumored to be a not-so-exemplary tournament site—the Black Sea resort called Golden Sands.

Mikhail Moisevich Botvinnik of Leningrad was fifty-one years old and arguably one of the best chess players who ever lived. Winner three times of the World Championship, he'd defeated Alexander Alekhine, José Capablanca, Max Euwe, and Emanuel Lasker, among other renowned players, and was a living legend. Ironically, despite his much-deserved reputation, he was apprehensive about playing Bobby Fischer for the first time. The Russian had, of course, heard of Bobby's "Game of the Century," his near-perfect performance at Bled, and his astounding win at Stockholm. But there was another factor putting Botvinnik on edge: He considered Bobby an enemy of the Soviet state, owing to the nineteen-year-old's post-Curaçao accusations.

What loomed was a mini Cold War—one played across sixty-four squares.

Fischer and Botvinnik had met once—but not to play—at the Leipzig Olympiad in 1960, and when introduced, Bobby shook hands and said succinctly, "Fischer." No other words of greeting were exchanged. Although he spoke passable English, Botvinnik was not known for his cordiality.

Botvinnik surmised that someday Bobby might be his or someone else's challenger for the World Championship—and perhaps even hold the title—but even if that did not occur, the whole world would be studying and analyzing his game with Fischer at this Olympiad perhaps for hundreds of years. Thinking of the embarrassment if he lost, Botvinnik suggested to the organizers that the game be played in a private room: At least then he wouldn't have to face spectators and the other players in the hour of his possible defeat. But no such room was available, and anyway the organizers wanted the game to be in public view for the publicity it would generate. Of the thousands of games to be played at this Olympiad, Fischer-Botvinnik promised to be the tournament's one marquee event, and the organizers didn't want chess fans to be robbed of the excitement.

Botvinnik, who wore steel-rimmed glasses and a gray suit, exhibited a serious, businesslike demeanor. He was buttoned up, both literally and figuratively, projecting the look of a scientist—which, in addition to being a grandmaster, was exactly what he was. He knew he was a major representative of the Soviet Union, and he chose his words as if his every conversation might end up as a part of a court transcript somewhere. His pupil, Anatoly Karpov, said of him that he had an "Olympian inaccessibility."

Bobby had already played fifteen games over four weeks in the Olympiad by the time he sat down to play Botvinnik, so long before their matchup he'd shaken off any rust. As they met at the board, they shook hands and then slightly banged heads when they went to be seated. "Sorry," said Bobby, uttering the second word he'd ever spoken to Botvinnik, again without a reply.

When the game was adjourned, it appeared that Fischer's position was clearly superior.

Fischer dined alone that night, took a cursory look at the game, was confident he had it won, and went to sleep early. Not so, the Soviets. Mikhail Tal, Boris Spassky, Paul Keres, Efim Geller, team coach Semyon Furman, and Botvinnik worked on the position until five-thirty the next morning. They also called Moscow and spoke to Yuri Averbach—an endgame authority—and asked for his opinion. It was Geller who suggested that although Fischer was ahead materially, there was a subtle way that the game might be drawn.

The next morning at breakfast, someone approached Botvinnik and asked him what he thought about the position. He answered in Russian with one word: *"Nichia."* Draw.

When play resumed, Botvinnik was in shirtsleeves, a look so unusual for him that the other players knew he was worried and prepared for serious work. Bobby, meanwhile, was unaware that he was about to play against the analysis of no less than seven Soviet grandmasters, not just the ingenuity of his opponent. Slowly, he saw what Botvinnik was up to, and his face became ashen. Botvinnik, who rarely rose from the board until the game was over, was so exuberant about having changed the game's momentum that he could not sit still. He stood, walked over to the Soviet team captain, Lev Abramov, and, once again, whispered, *"Nichia."* Bobby, still remembering the argument he'd had with Abramov in Moscow in 1958—the men hadn't spoken since—immediately complained to the arbiter. "Look," he said. "Botvinnik is getting assistance!"

Abramov, though he was far less skilled than Botvinnik, was nevertheless an international master and might have, at that moment, relayed to Botvinnik information from the other Soviet grandmasters. At least, that's what Bobby was *thinking.* No official protest was put before the tournament committee, however, because Bobby's own teammates believed he was being extreme and wrongheaded.

Eventually, Bobby could make no headway in this game that he should have won. He looked up at Botvinnik and said the third word he'd ever spoken to him: "Draw." Botvinnik simply offered his hand. Later, he recalled that Bobby, his face pallid, shook hands and left the tournament hall in tears. The United States team wound up finishing a disappointing fourth, mainly as a result of Bobby's disappointing results. Mysteriously, the nineteen-year-old wrote a letter of apology to Dr. Eliot Hearst, the United States team captain, saying he'd been under great stress that had nothing to do with the Olympiad or chess.

Aboard the *New Amsterdam* once again, heading back to New York, Bobby wrote a note to his friend Bernard Zuckerman explaining how he felt about his draw against Botvinnik. The message was cabled to Brooklyn. Bobby felt that he had fallen into a "cheapo"—that he'd been tricked by one of his opponent's ruses and had made an unsound move—and that, prior to Bobby's committing this error, Botvinnik, because of Bobby's superior position, seemed so upset that he looked like he was going to collapse.

In an estimation filled with sour grapes, Bobby also wrote that Botvinnik, the well-respected former World Champion, was never really a great player, never "first among equals" as Botvinnik had once described himself. Instead, Bobby claimed that Botvinnik's superiority lay in the field of politics. He suggested that Botvinnik might have been able to become Premier of the Soviet Union because of his [political] ability "off the chessboard."

Curaçao was a watershed for Bobby in his vow to never again play in the World Championship cycle. The Varna match, with the assistance of Botvinnik's teammates to eke out a draw, was also a turning point. It would be two years before Bobby accepted an invitation to play in another international tournament. The Russians claimed that his retreat from the world stage was because of his "pathological" fear of the "hand of Moscow." But back in Brooklyn, Bobby said he just no longer wanted to be involved with those "commie cheaters," as he called them.

Then—a little more than a year later, in December 1963—came the 1963–64 United States Championship, held in the unpretentious Henry Hudson Hotel in New York. Bobby's opponents fell as if they were tenpins, Bobby scoring a strike—game after game they toppled—with not a hint of a draw. The audience sensed that something unusual was about to happen. It did.

Bobby defeated the powerful champion Arthur Bisguier and the aging Samuel Reshevsky, and speculation surged through the hotel ballroom: Was it possible Bobby could make a clean sweep—pull off a win against every foe, with not even a single draw? The audience increased every round as word of Fischer's incredible run spread throughout the chess community.

Tension, always high in a major tournament, was escalating. Bobby's immaculate timing and apparently infallible play was creating a psychological handicap for players who hadn't yet faced him. He vanquished every player he met. It was December 30, 1963, and Bobby had played all but one game of the championship without losing or drawing a game. There was only one more to go.

The combatants rested on New Year's Day and returned to the contest on January 2. Bobby's score made him the winner already, but how the tournament would end was not inevitable. His final game was against Anthony Saidy, a friend. In his mid-twenties, six years older than Fischer, Saidy was then a medical doctor with the Peace Corps and had been given a leave to play in the championship. He'd been playing very well, and this round gave him a chance at second place. He could also be the "spoiler," the person to ruin Fischer's chance for a perfect score in the championship. If that happened, it would go into the chess history books. And Saidy might, in fact, *win,* especially since he had the advantage of the white pieces.

By now there were hundreds of spectators at the hotel, tensely watching the big demonstration board. Most of them were clearly, but very quietly, rooting for Bobby, in part because his win that day would give him a clean sweep. But as the game grew longer, a win seemed very unlikely. Saidy's position was powerful, and Bobby's was precarious. The two-and-a-half-hour time limit ended, and there was no winner as yet. It was Saidy's turn to move. The young doctor thought for about forty minutes, wrote down his intended move on his score sheet, sealed it in an envelope according to the rules, and handed it to the tournament director. The game was then adjourned until the next day. Everyone left the hotel ballroom assuming that when the game resumed it would be a draw, at best. It was not. It took Saidy about thirty minutes to realize that he'd sealed a blunder. The next day when the envelope was opened by the director, and the move made on the board, Bobby realized immediately that Saidy hadn't chosen wisely. He looked up at Saidy and a slight smile appeared on his face. Saidy's blunder gave Fischer an opportunity to develop a winning endgame, and half an hour after the adjourned game was resumed, Saidy was forced to resign.

The incredible final score was picked up by the wire services and sent by radio, newspapers, and television throughout the world: eleven championship games, eleven wins. At this level of competition, such a streak wasn't suppose to happen, no matter how adept a given player might be. Fischer's first prize for his two weeks of intensity and brilliance was just $2,000.

The non-chess media gave the tournament far more attention than usual, though they'd never been sure whether chess was a sport or an art. *Life* and the *Saturday Evening Post* arranged to interview Bobby. *Sports Illustrated* headlined its story THE AMAZING VICTORY STREAK OF BOBBY FISCHER. Chess publications around the world wrote of the unparalleled achievement. Only Bent Larsen, always a Fischer detractor, was unimpressed: "Fischer was playing against children," he said.

Reshevsky a child? Robert Byrne? Larry Evans? Pal Benko?

On March 9, 1964, Bobby Fischer was twenty-one. His birthday gave him something in common with many young American males during that time of military escalation: participation in the military draft. President John F. Kennedy had been assassinated the previous November, and his successor, Lyndon Baines Johnson, had escalated the war in Vietnam. To be drafted at that time meant a strong likelihood of serving in Southeast Asia.

As a "1-A" candidate, Bobby was scheduled to take his physical examination at the U.S. Army Recruiting Station on Whitehall Street in New York City. If selected, he'd spend the next two years in the army. Fischer was patriotic at that time, but his focus was chess, and the chess community was counting on him to play in the Interzonal at Amsterdam. True, he'd said that he would never play in the FIDE cycle again because it was stacked in favor of the Soviets. But might he somehow get back on the road to the championship? The world wanted it, and in his heart Bobby wanted it—but he said he wouldn't change his mind. Nevertheless, several people began researching whether there might be a way to get Fischer a deferment until after the Interzonal was completed . . . just in case he played in it.

On Bobby's behalf, an official of the United States Chess Federation contacted General George B. Hershey, head of the Selective Service bureau. Hershey explained that "a *temporary* deferment, on almost any grounds, is usually an easy matter to secure from a local board, but eventually Fischer will probably be drafted."

A somewhat longer deferment was available, and totally legal, for college students. Bobby had dropped out of high school, but the New School for Social Research, a progressive college in New York City, was willing to accept his extraordinary chess accomplishments in lieu of traditional schoolwork. Alfred Landa, then assistant to the president, said that Fischer would not only be allowed to matriculate into the college, but be given a full scholarship. Bobby thought long and hard about the offer. One afternoon he started to walk to the New School to put in his application—and then stopped. His experience with schools had been distasteful, and perhaps that caused forebodings. Without giving an explanation, he refused to enter the school building, and he refused to apply for a student deferment.

He was rescheduled to take his physical examination and went to the recruiting station by himself. Afterward, it was announced that Bobby had been rejected—for reasons that have never been made public. Bobby Fischer was classified 4F—the military rating that meant you had one or more medical conditions that totally disqualified you from serving in uniform. He *seemed* and appeared fine, physically.

Whatever the reason, Bobby Fischer never served in the military.

Bobby sat confined in a small wood-paneled room at the Marshall Chess Club, with only the chessboard and a referee. There was no player facing him. After deciding on his move, he wrote it down on his score sheet, which was then carried by the referee to a "runner," who brought it quickly to a nearby room where a Teletype machine had been set up. Bobby then waited, still alone, as the move was transmitted to Havana, Cuba, where his opponent sat facing his own chessboard. When the opponent made his answering move, it was transmitted by wire from Havana back to the Marshall, the

Teletype operator turned the reply over to the runner, and the move was carried back to the silent room where Bobby tensely awaited it.

It was 1965 and Bobby had accepted an invitation to play in the Capablanca Memorial Tournament in Havana. It was exactly the type of tournament he'd been seeking for his return to international competition. There would be thirteen grandmasters and eight international masters, not quite as strong a field as at Bobby's last international tournament, but incredibly powerful. The $3,000 appearance fee sealed it for him. Bobby was back.

But not quite. Diplomatic relations between the United States and Cuba were still severely strained. The State Department had begun to permit journalists access to Cuba, although it denied entry to ordinary citizens. Fischer had applied for a visa, since he was a regular contributor to *Chess Life* and had made special arrangements to do an article on this tournament for the *Saturday Review,* which sent a letter to the United States Department of State—as did the U.S. Chess Federation—confirming the legitimacy of his trip and petitioning permission for him to go to Cuba. There's no question that his primary motivation in wanting to go was to play in the tournament, but he also intended to write about it. Nonetheless, the State Department flatly refused to recognize him as a legitimate columnist, and therefore denied him the opportunity to travel to Havana.

What no one knew was that the FBI was investigating Bobby, and had been for years. Their interest in him may have been triggered by their belief that his mother was a Communist, in part because she'd spent six years in Moscow attending medical school; they'd been investigating Regina since Bobby was a child. When Bobby went to Moscow in 1958, when he was fifteen, the FBI presumed that Regina had sent him there to be indoctrinated.

The Bureau obviously had trouble believing that someone would travel so much simply for the purpose of playing chess, especially to countries that were restricted for political reasons. A notice in Bobby's FBI file states that his passport was "not valid for travel to Albania, Cuba, and those portions of China, Korea and Vietnam under communist control," and it contains a 1965 memorandum from the Office of the Coordinator of Cuban Affairs which advises that "Cuban travel criteria make no provision for validation for the purpose of participating in chess competitions."

FBI target or not, Bobby was primed to play in the tournament, and he wouldn't be denied. Helping him out were officials in the United States Chess Federation who came up with a highly unorthodox idea: Bobby would stay in New York and play the tournament from a room in the Marshall Chess Club. There were no cell phones in 1965, and there was certainly no Internet. But Fischer could play the tournament by Teletype. Cuban chess officials were delighted, offering to pay some $10,000 in expenses for the open telephone line and Teletype machine that were required. As for the other participants in the tournament, they agreed, some reluctantly, to the novel arrangement. Che Guevara, a strong chess player, was the principal force behind organizing the tournament.

Then Fidel Castro intervened, calling the situation a "great propaganda victory for Cuba." It made headlines. Furious, Bobby cabled Castro, threatening to withdraw from the tournament unless the premier promised to stop using him as a political ploy. Bobby continued:

```
I WOULD ONLY BE ABLE TO TAKE PART IN THE TOURNAMENT IN
THE EVENT THAT YOU IMMEDIATELY SENT ME A TELEGRAM
DECLARING THAT NEITHER YOU, NOR YOUR GOVERNMENT WILL
ATTEMPT TO MAKE POLITICAL CAPITAL OUT OF MY
PARTICIPATION IN THE TOURNEY, AND THAT IN THE FUTURE NO
POLITICAL COMMENTARIES ON THIS SCORE WILL BE MADE.
                                        BOBBY FISCHER
```

Castro cabled back, denying making the statement and questioning Bobby's courage:

```
OUR LAND NEEDS NO SUCH "PROPAGANDA VICTORIES." IT IS
YOUR PERSONAL AFFAIR WHETHER YOU WILL TAKE PART IN THE
TOURNAMENT OR NOT. HENCE YOUR WORDS ARE UNJUST. IF YOU
ARE FRIGHTENED AND REPENT YOUR PREVIOUS DECISION, THEN
IT WOULD BE BETTER TO FIND ANOTHER EXCUSE OR TO HAVE THE
COURAGE TO REMAIN HONEST.
                                        FIDEL CASTRO
```

Upon receiving word from Castro, Bobby confirmed his participation in the tournament without any further sparring. He wanted to play the game of chess, not be a party to sensationalism.

The arrangement was certainly awkward for Bobby, however. To avoid any hint of cheating, he had to be isolated from everyone except the referee. It was a sterile, feedback-barren experience with no chance to read his opponent's body language. As Bobby sat with the referee, not a word was spoken; the afternoons crept slowly into summer twilight. Occasionally, while waiting for his opponent's move to come back from Havana, Bobby would gaze out into the club's garden. A bust of Philidor, the eighteenth-century French chess player and composer who was considered the best player of his day, was perched atop an étagère of chess sets, almost as if he were at the game. The tick of the chess clock was the only sound heard.

A typical four-hour game was transformed by the Teletype process into an eight- or nine-hour affair. Some games stretched to twelve hours. The tournament became a test of endurance and stamina. Bobby grew exhausted. His opponents had the same problem, but each only had to submit to the process once—when playing Fischer. Bobby had to play this strange, isolated form of chess every single game. In the midst of the tournament, someone asked how well he thought he'd do and he answered, "It's a question of when I'll crack up."

Bobby won his first two games but as the tournament wore on he lost to some players and drew with several others well below his caliber. While he exhibited flashes of brilliance, this wasn't the same Bobby Fischer who'd swept through the United States Championship eighteen months earlier. Still, he tied for second, a half point behind Russia's Vasily Smyslov, the former World Champion.

Had Fischer not done as well as he did, his story might have ended right there, surrealistically, in the quiet back room of a chess club. Havana was his comeback in the world spotlight, and a poor showing would only have deepened Bobby's disillusionment with himself, probably permanently. Two setbacks in international tournaments would have been intolerable to him. True, for Bobby there was only one place in a tournament and that was first. But after the long international layoff, and playing every game under grueling conditions, he likely considered his second-place showing somewhat acceptable.

Openly, Bobby disparaged how he'd performed, but the Soviet chess establishment was dazzled by how he managed to place so high under such arduous conditions. They were convinced that he was continuing to grow as a player, and that unless something were done quickly, he'd smash the Soviets' hegemony.

Worry about Fischer led the All-Union Scientific Research Institute of Sports, which studied the psychology of sports, to appoint a Soviet grandmaster and theoretician, Vladimir Alatortsev, to create a secret laboratory (located near the Moscow Central Chess Club). Its mission was to analyze Fischer's games. Alatortsev and a small group of other masters and psychologists worked tirelessly for ten years attempting to "solve" the mystery of Fischer's prowess, in addition to analyzing his personality and behavior. They rigorously studied his opening, middle game, and endings—and filtered classified analyses of their findings to the top Soviet players.

Though he didn't realize it, if Fischer hadn't accepted the invitation to the 1966 Piatigorsky Cup in Santa Monica, California, there wouldn't have been such a tournament at all. "We *must* get Bobby Fischer," Gregor Piatigorsky told his wife. A few years prior, Mrs. Piatigorsky had been criticized in some quarters for not acceding to Fischer's demands for the 1963 tournament, which had led to his not playing. Her solution this time was to pay everyone the same amount—$2,000—therefore saving face and securing the greatest American player.

The story of how Fischer went into a swoon in the tournament's first half, tying for last, yet ended up in the penultimate round tying for first with Spassky, has been told many times. At the beginning of the competition, Fischer looked Abraham Lincoln–thin; his cheeks were hollow, and he had deep, dark circles under his eyes, all indicating that he might be ill.

As Fischer's losses and draws mounted, it became clear that he was having the most disastrous tournament of his adult career, perhaps even worse than his Buenos Aires debacle. Bobby was at an existential precipice. He somehow had to find a better method of play, a better understanding of what he was doing wrong; he had to find lessons in his failures, or else his chess career would be, if not over, forever tarnished. Skirting or briefly inhabiting the bottom of the scoreboard does not make one a failure, but remaining there, refusing to fight, does.

Fortunately, drawing deep from his inner reserves, Bobby *did* climb. His ability and character enabled him to emerge from the depths. He came back in the second half of the tournament and ended just a half point below Spassky. His reaction was a study in ambivalence. He was overjoyed that he'd pulled himself out of the abyss in which he'd found himself in the tournament's first half, but devastated that he hadn't won first prize.

At the closing ceremony, Mr. and Mrs. Piatigorsky posed for a photograph with Spassky on one side and Fischer on the other. Fischer, with a weak smile, looked somewhat embarrassed, as if to say, "I really should have won this tournament, and I can't blame the Russians this time. It was me . . . all alone."

As the players left the Miramar Hotel to go home to their respective countries or states, Bobby simply refused to check out. Other players have been known to do the same thing. It's like an actor remaining in character and refusing to leave his dressing room, or a writer refusing to leave his garret after finishing a book. The challenge is tearing oneself away from a venue that has been one's creative home for so many hours, days, weeks, or months.

Three weeks after everyone else had left, Bobby was still at the Miramar, just steps from the ocean, surrounded by gardens and palm trees, breathing in the pungent smell of eucalyptus. He swam and walked, and then often spent the rest of the day—and a good portion of the night—playing over all the games of the tournament, torturing himself over the mistakes he'd made. Someone finally pointed out to him that the Piatigorskys would no longer continue to pick up his hotel costs, so, reluctantly, he flew back home to Brooklyn.

9

The Candidate

D URING THE 1960s, Bobby Fischer continued his often brilliant
and sometimes self-sabotaging career: He won the Monte Carlo
International and ungallantly refused to pose for a photograph with
His Royal Highness Prince Rainier, the tournament's sponsor, and at a public
ceremony when Princess Grace awarded him his cash prize, he rudely tore
open the envelope and counted the money first before he thanked her; he led
the American Olympiad team to Cuba, where he won the silver medal for his
play on top board, and was more cordial to Fidel Castro, whom he presented
with an autographed copy of his book *Bobby Fischer Teaches Chess;* and
he summarily dropped out of the 1967 Interzonal in Tunisia—even though
he was leading and was almost assured of first place—because of the refusal
of the organizers to agree to his scheduling demands. When tracked down
by a journalist at his hotel in Tunisia, he wouldn't open the door: "Leave
me in peace!" he yelled, "I have nothing to say." He realized that by not
participating in the tournament he was allowing yet another chance for the
World Championship to slip from his grasp, but he was resolved no matter
what the consequences: *He,* not the organizers, would decide when he'd play
and when he wouldn't.

Fischer's most significant accomplishment of 1969 was actually publishing-
related. His long-promised games collection, *My 60 Memorable Games,* was
published by Simon & Schuster, and it made an immediate and indelible impression on the chess public. Ten years previously, Bobby's slender volume
Bobby Fischer's Games of Chess was seen as a revealing glimpse into the
teenager's mind, but it was criticized for its sparse annotations. In this new

book, his first—and, ultimately, only—serious work as an adult, Fischer was anything but sparse. In fact, what he produced was one of the most painstakingly precise and delightful chess books ever written, rivaling the works of Tarrasch, Alekhine, and Reti. Fischer, like his predecessor Morphy, the nineteenth-century American prodigy, wasn't especially prolific when it came to writing about chess, so the public greedily awaited each word he produced. In the 1969 book, he omitted his 1956 "Game of the Century" with Donald Byrne, instead including nine of his draws and three of his losses—a humble gesture unheard of in the annals of grandmaster literature. Fischer actually devoted fourteen pages of exhaustive analysis to his draw against Botvinnik at Varna.

Bobby was at first going to title his book *My Life in Chess,* but he changed his mind, possibly deciding to reserve that title for his future autobiography. His original plan for the volume was to include only fifty-two games, but as he continued to make corrections and also to play in more events, he eventually added eight more games. It took more than three years to complete.

Simon & Schuster was in a constant state of anxiety over the book since the changes over the years seemed almost endless, and at one point Fischer deleted *all* of the annotations, returning the book to the publisher and requesting a release from his contract. He may not have wanted to reveal all of his ideas to his competitors. The company reached a financial accommodation with him and publishing plans were dropped. Two years later, however, he changed his mind. Larry Evans, who wrote the introductions to the games, suggested that Bobby's decision to go ahead was a pragmatic one: "He was feeling depressed about the world and thought there was an excellent chance that there would be a nuclear holocaust soon. He felt he should enjoy whatever money he could get before it was too late."

My 60 Memorable Games was an immediate success. If Fischer had never played another game of chess, his reputation, certainly as an analyst, would have been preserved through its publication.

Bobby withdrew from playing competitive chess in late 1968, and with the exception of one widely praised game played as part of the New York Metropolitan League in 1969, he took an eighteen-month hiatus, to the consternation and curiosity of the chess world. He wouldn't explain his reasons, later telling one interviewer that he'd refused to play because of undefined "hang-ups." To another, he was quoted as saying that he avoided competition "to plot my revenge. I wanted to come back and put all those people in their place," but the venue, prize fund, and roster of competitors all had to be right. And so he refused offer after offer, opportunity after opportunity.

Then, unpredictably, he made an exception: He'd play in the "USSR vs. the Rest of the World" match. On March 26, 1970, Bobby flew to Belgrade and lunched at the Hotel Metropol with chess columnist George Koltanowski and Larry Evans, who was reporting on the match instead of playing in it and would act as Fischer's second. Optimistic and uncharacteristically friendly, Bobby autographed cards for most of the hotel waiters. When a female chess columnist asked him for an interview after lunch, he agreed; she shrieked joyfully, hugged Bobby, and kissed him on the cheek. Bobby accepted it fairly calmly, then Evans remarked: "This is not surprising, but if you see Bobby kiss the girl, *then* you have a news item!" Even Bobby laughed. Afterward, Bobby went to inspect the lighting and playing conditions at the theater inside the Dom Sindikata, on Marx-Engels Square. Often used for trade union meetings, the huge domed theater had been modified for the match. It met with Bobby's approval.

Bobby walked into the enormous theater, ready to play his first game, and looked up. Hanging on the wall was his photograph, three stories high. Looking around, he saw equally huge pictures of the twenty competing grandmasters. There was the brooding Mikhail Tal, he of the disconcerting stare; Bent Larsen, his blond hair brushed straight back; Mikhail Botvinnik, who looked like a conservative businessman; the Czechoslovakian Vlastimil Hort, just a few months younger than Fischer; Bobby's friend Svetozar Gligoric, the handsome, mustached Serbian whose personality made him one of the most popular players; and the swarthy Tigran Petrosian, whom Bobby was about to play.

Bobby initiated an unexpected variation in response to Petrosian's opening. He revealed later that he'd manipulated the Russian into a variation that Fischer had studied years before, and for which he had originated a favorable response. The two dueled for the first half of the game, but Bobby clearly had the advantage after that and he won on the thirty-ninth move. After all the first-round games were over, a jury chose Fischer to receive the best-game award. The audience applauded for three minutes, despite attempts by the ushers to keep them quiet. Bobby had triggered similar reactions at other tournaments and matches; fans often wrote him admiring letters. He'd even received some marriage proposals. Commenting on his win afterward, Bobby said: "I could have played better."

For the third round, excitement in Belgrade was so great that fans filled the large hall to capacity in less than half an hour. Black market vendors left their normal posts in front of theaters and cinemas, and stationed themselves in front of the Dom Sindikata to peddle entrance tickets to the match, which were in great demand. President Ribicic of Yugoslavia, who'd attended the first two rounds, came back to see the third.

Fischer drew the game, then relaxed and looked at the rest of the games. Samuel Reshevsky's game vs. Vasily Smyslov had been adjourned. Back at the Metropol Hotel, Bobby sat down with Reshevsky to analyze the position and consider possible strategies the older grandmaster might play when the game resumed. After ten years of bitterness and competition, this was the first time Fischer had had a friendly interchange with his American rival. (The next day, Reshevsky won his game.) In Bobby's fourth and final game he managed to hold on to a draw.

The Soviet Union won by one point over the Rest of the World: 20½–19½, and the Russians were shaken by their near defeat. "It's a catastrophe," said one team member. "At home they don't understand. They think it means there's something wrong with our culture." On the top four boards, the Soviets managed to win only one game out of a possible sixteen. Bobby Fischer was the high scorer for his team, with a 3–1 score against Petrosian (two wins and two draws). As the winner of the second board he also won a Russian car, the Moskvich.

He wanted to *win* the car, not to *keep* the car. Once he had it, he chose to sell it immediately. He said: "Last year in the United States, we had 56,000 deaths as a result of car accidents, and I decided I'd rather use buses."

All of the players gathered together after the match to pose for the official photographs. As was typical, Bobby was not there. Argentina's Miguel Najdorf, who knew Bobby fairly well, said: "He prefers to enter chess history alone."

♖

If Bobby Fischer was ever going to become the World Chess Champion, he would first need to finish near the top at an Interzonal, and he did this quite easily at Palma de Majorca in 1970. After eleven rounds, nearing the tournament's midpoint, Fischer was in second place, one-half point behind the leader, Efim Geller of the USSR. Fischer and Geller were to meet in the twelfth round in a pivotal matchup.

Geller had not yet lost a game in the tournament. Perhaps more important, he'd beaten Fischer in their last three meetings and had more wins against Fischer than any living player. Here was a definite challenge for Bobby, and he attempted to stay focused and confident by carefully studying Geller's other games in the tournament. Geller, who talked like a sailor and who had the look and build of a wrestler, arrived with his tie loosened, and wearing rumpled clothing.

Within the first few minutes of the game, Geller insulted Bobby by offering him a draw after his seventh move. Fischer sat back and initially laughed, and Geller chimed in. Bobby then responded with a statement that no one but Geller heard clearly. A bystander reported that Fischer had said, "Too early," but Geller's face turned red, suggesting that Fischer's reply had been more caustic. Speculation was that Fischer's response had been along the lines that early draws were solely the property of the Soviet state. When the official book of the tournament was published, the editors wrote of Geller's seventh-move affront: "But why would Geller expect Fischer to take a quick draw? Fischer's entire record as a player shows his abhorrence of quick draws and his wish at every reasonable (and sometimes unreasonable) occasion to play until there is absolutely no chance of winning. No draws in under 40 moves is an essential part of his philosophy."

In subsequent moves Geller blundered badly, and Fischer won the game, beating a man who'd become a personal nemesis.

Bobby seemed to have come of age at Palma. Despite besting twenty-three of the world's most eminent chess players, though, he remained relatively unimpressed with his performance: "I am satisfied with the result, but not with my play." When reminded of his disastrous performance at the 1962 Candidates, he said: "Maybe this was a good thing. I didn't have the maturity to handle it then." He certainly had it at Palma.

♜

Bobby's success at Palma had brought him to the next level in his quest for the world title. After he'd failed to win the Candidates tournaments in Yugoslavia in 1959 and in Curaçao in 1962, he'd protested that he was gang raped by the Soviets who, with their short premeditated draws stole the championship from him. Now FIDE had finally acceded to Fischer's repeated urgings and changed its system of choosing an opponent to vie for the World Championship. The federation eliminated the Candidates *tournament,* an event that had multiple players competing against one another, which Fischer charged led to the opportunity for collusion among the Soviets. In its stead, FIDE instituted Candidates *matches.* Fischer would now play games against each of the three contenders: two Soviets—Mark Taimanov and Tigran Petrosian—and the Dane Bent Larsen.

Analysts and players alike predicted that Fischer would win the Candidates, but not without a struggle. Even the Soviets were concerned. Tal predicted that Fischer would win 5 ½–4 ½ against Taimanov. Fischer himself seemed uncharacteristically self-doubting. Although he'd played seventy-four tournament games in the past nine months, with straight wins in his last seven games at Palma, he felt he was not in the best shape, and that he needed to play in more tournaments. Candidates matches require thorough preparations. Taking nothing for granted was one of the keys to Fischer's success. As usual, he prepared arduously for his encounter with each opponent in the series of tension-filled matches that would eventually spread over six tiring months.

Mark Taimanov was his first opponent, a powerful competitor who, at forty-five, was playing some of the best chess of his life, and who'd played exceedingly well at Palma. Fischer was twenty-eight and in excellent physical shape. Their match was to begin in May 1971 in Vancouver, Canada, on the beautiful campus of the University of British Columbia.

Taimanov arrived with a full Russian entourage: a second, an assistant, and a match manager, but even with all the help, he was, nevertheless, help-less. Bobby defeated him in six straight games, the first shutout of a grand-master in chess history.

The crushing loss virtually ended Taimanov's chess career. The Soviet gov-ernment considered it a national embarrassment and punished him for not drawing at least one game. Officials canceled his salary and forbade him to travel overseas. At the conclusion of the match, Taimanov had sadly told Fischer: "Well, I still have my music."

Bobby's match against Bent Larsen began in Denver on July 6 at four p.m., in the midst of an uncomfortable one-hundred-degree heat wave. Fischer was as dominant against Larsen as he'd been against Taimanov: He annihilated the Dane, shutting him out and winning every game.

It was nine p.m. on July 20, 1971, and Bobby Fischer had achieved what no one else had ever accomplished in chess: winning two grandmaster matches without drawing or losing a single game. He'd now won an unprec-edented nineteen straight games against the strongest players in the world.

Fischer-doubters, especially the Soviets, had suggested that his total de-struction of Taimanov was an aberration. His equally absolute defeat of the younger, highly respected Larsen proved that Fischer was in a class by him-self. Robert Byrne, watching the match in astonishment, said he couldn't explain how Bobby, how anyone, could win six games in a row from such a genius of the game as Bent Larsen.

The Soviets were relieved at first, since Larsen's loss lessened Taimanov's stigma. Television and radio networks throughout the Soviet Union inter-rupted regular broadcasts to announce the result. Millions of Soviets were avidly following the progress of the match, fascinated by Fischer's mastery. *Sovietsky Sport* declared, "A miracle has occurred."

Fischer arrived in Buenos Aires a few days before the start of the first round against Petrosian. This time he was not alone. Larry Evans came along as Bobby's second, and the ever-present Edmund B. Edmondson of the U.S. Chess Federation was there as Bobby's manager-representative. Petrosian had an entourage too: his manager, two seconds, his wife Rona, and *two* bodyguards.

Argentina treated the match as though it were an event of global signifi-cance. The president, Lieutenant General Alejandro Lanusse, received the

two players, official photographs were taken, and Lanusse presented each
with a beautiful marble board and a set of onyx chessmen. A single chess
table was placed in the center of the vast stage in the Teatro General San
Martín. Behind it hung a blue-and-gold circle, some fifteen feet in diameter,
bearing the emblem of FIDE, its motto *Gens Una Sumus* ("We Are One
People"), and the name of the Argentine chess federation. Slightly off center
stood a demonstration board, about five feet by five feet, on which a man
duplicated each move as the contestants manevered their pieces on the central chessboard, so that the audience of twelve hundred attentive people
could follow the game. If they made a sound, red signs flashed SILENCIO.

Reporters asked Petrosian whether the match would last the full twelve
games, the maximum that would be required if every game were drawn, with
no wins or losses. "It might be possible that I win it earlier," Petrosian replied, and confidently went on to explain that he wasn't impressed with
Fischer.

Bobby's prediction was calm and direct, and reveals his belief in himself
and his abilities. "I am the best player in the world, and I am here to prove it.
I have waited ten years for this moment, but I was hindered by Russian ma-
neuvers. I shall depart from Buenos Aires before the twelfth game is
scheduled."

Both players surprised everyone, and probably each other, by virtually re-
versing their normal playing behavior during the first game. Petrosian's style
was closed and defensive, like a motionless but watchful snake, ready to strike
the moment his opponent made the slightest mistake. Bobby's style was one
of relentless aggression—usually. Experts expected that Petrosian would follow his conservative style and try to achieve a draw, to break Fischer's winning streak. Instead, he was startlingly aggressive, forcing Bobby into the
defensive position he hated. Petrosian introduced an innovative move not
normally used, and probably provided by Soviet theorists working behind
the scenes. He was clearly forcing a draw when the lights went out. Literally.
The theater was plunged into darkness. Alarmed, Fischer asked, "What happened? What happened?" The players were told that a fuse had blown and
would take a few minutes to replace. Petrosian left the board; Fischer and the
audience of twelve hundred continued to sit in darkened silence. Eventually,
Petrosian complained that Fischer was still studying the board—in total

darkness—and that therefore his clock should be started. Fischer agreed, and Lothar Schmid, the German referee, who was himself a grandmaster, started the clock. For eleven minutes, Fischer continued to visualize the position in his head, evaluating it without seeing it. Then the lights came back on.

The interruption seemed to have hurt Petrosian's concentration, because he made some mistakes and resigned on the fortieth move. It was Bobby Fischer's twentieth straight win. The army of assembled reporters and photographers flocked around both players as they left the stage, but both hurried out of the theater, declining to give any statements.

Bobby was obviously sick with a bad head cold during the second round. Once again, the players seemed to switch personalities as they played, with Petrosian as the aggressor. Not able to focus clearly on the game, Bobby realized that he wouldn't be able to play well enough: He offered a handshake and his resignation. The crowd went wild. Petrosian's wife rushed to her husband to embrace him. Some members of the audience began to chant *"Tigran un tigre! Tigran un tigre!"* and the victory cheer spread to the outer lobby and street. Some players rushed onto the stage and tried to lift the joyful Petrosian to their shoulders, but they were stopped by officials. He didn't care: He'd just accomplished what the finest players in the world had been unable to do on twenty occasions during the previous nine months. He'd won a game from Bobby Fischer.

Fischer screamed at Edmundson that he had been seeing too many people, and for the next ten days as he and Petrosian battled, Bobby agreed to see only the young Argentine player Miguel Quinteros.

Now supremely confident of his chances of winning both the eighth and the ninth games, which would give him the match, Bobby rather formally declared that he would dethrone Spassky. When the eighth round finally began, the lights went out again, but this time only for eight minutes. It had no effect on the results. Both players used attacking moves, but Petrosian resigned, giving Fischer his fourth victory of the match. Gone was the speculation that Bobby Fischer had played his best chess too soon. Rather, it seemed obvious that he couldn't be stopped.

At the start of the ninth game, more than ten thousand fans packed the playing hall, the lobby, and the surrounding streets. Even in Russia, chess crowds this enormous had never been seen. Petrosian resigned on the forty-sixth move, and Bobby Fischer was the new challenger for the World Championship. Against a former World Champion who was known to be one of the most difficult to defeat, Bobby had won five games, drawn three, and lost one, for a total score of 6 ½–2 ½.

Fischer would now be the first non-Soviet or non-Russian in more than three decades to play for the title against the reigning World Champion. For years Soviet grandmasters had competed only against one another, ensuring that the championship would remain in the hands of the Soviet Union. For his labors, Bobby was awarded a $7,500 prize plus an honorarium of $3,000 from the U.S. Chess Federation. More significant, he ignited a phenomenon in the United States not seen before: Almost overnight, a chess boom arose. Sales of chess sets shot up over 20 percent. Virtually every major magazine and newspaper in the country ran a story about Fischer, often with pictures of him and a diagram of his final position against Petrosian. The *New York Daily News* reprinted the score of every game, and *The New York Times* ran an article on the cover of its Sunday Magazine section, and then a news story on its front page the following day. The last time chess had made the *Times* front page was in 1954, when the Soviet team visited the United States and Carmine Nigro had brought the eleven-year-old Bobby to witness the international match.

Bobby Fischer had become a national hero. After returning home, he appeared on television constantly and his face became so familiar that people on the streets of New York City asked him for his autograph. But he became more than a household name, more than the equivalent of a pop star. He was the American who had a fighting chance of defeating a Soviet champion. The Cold War—or at least a version of it—was about to be decided not on a battlefield or in a diplomatic meeting, but in a contest of intellect and will involving thirty-two enigmatic pieces.

10

The Champion

TO KEEP BOBBY FISCHER HAPPY, the American Chess Foundation provided him with a room at the Henry Hudson Hotel in early 1972. *As Fischer goes, so goes the chess nation,* organizers believed. Also, since he was preparing to play Boris Spassky for the World Championship, his lawyers and U.S. Chess Federation officials needed to know where he was at all times. Questions arose almost daily about such details as the prize money, the schedule, and the venue. Decisions had to be made.

Up to that point, much of Bobby's life had been nomadic because he spent so much time traveling from one competition to another. Whenever he returned to Brooklyn to prepare for the next tournament or match, he tended to sequester himself in his apartment. He'd often disconnect the telephone and render himself incommunicado—sometimes for weeks. This modus operandi wouldn't have been workable as officials scurried to arrange a host of details for the World Championship match. So the Henry Hudson Hotel made sense, and it had the right atmospherics. It was where Bobby had won several United States Championships, and should he grow lonely in his room or want to play or talk chess, all he need do was take the elevator down a few floors and enter the Manhattan Chess Club. As its most eminent member, he was always given the red carpet treatment whenever he entered.

So it was that one night, shortly after taking up residence at the hotel, Bobby found himself stretched out on his bed, his heels locked over the edge, unself-consciously talking with two of his closest friends. The 1970s were the years of Nixon's visit to China, the advent of Transcendental Meditation, cigarette advertising being banned from the airwaves, and fast-food chains

172

multiplying. But none of those topics interested the three men in the room that evening. They were there to talk about chess and the anxiety Bobby was feeling.

Sam Sloan was a reed-thin stockbroker, with a slight Virginian drawl. A year younger than Bobby, his notable accomplishment wasn't in chess—he was a tournament player but not of championship caliber—but in law. Aided by an eidetic memory, he was the last non-lawyer to argue a case before the United States Supreme Court—a case he won. Bobby trusted him.

The other man in the room that night was Bernard Zuckerman, only twenty-two days younger than Bobby, a fellow Brooklynite, and an international master. He was called "Zuck the Book" because he was considered by many—including Fischer—to have studied the literature on chess so thoroughly ("booked up," as it is known in chess circles) that he was the most up-to-date opening theoretician in the country. However, he claimed that Fischer knew more. Zuckerman had soulful eyes, immensely long lashes, and shoulder-length hair, a residue of the '60s. At tournaments he often arrived a half hour late for games, played rapidly, and usually offered a draw, which was invariably accepted. Bobby respected him. Both Sloan and Zuckerman were intensely interested in chess, Bobby, and women—interests that Bobby resoundingly shared in the first two cases and peripherally in the third.

That night the two men were being true friends and trying to calm down Bobby about his impending match. Although he'd just accomplished one of the greatest feats in the annals of chess by defeating Taimanov, Larsen, and Petrosian with a combined score of 18 ½–2 ½, Fischer was concerned about the strength of Spassky, who, he believed, had a "dynamic, individual style." Bobby had never beaten him, and he revealed to his friends that he thought he might have trouble. "Why don't you think you can beat him easily?" asked Zuckerman gently, pointing out that Spassky was no better than Petrosian, for example. "Spassky *is* better," said Bobby somewhat woefully. "Not much better, but better." Little did he know that Spassky, comparing his own performance to Bobby's in 1971, judged Bobby the stronger player.

So much was at stake in the upcoming match that conflict was almost bound to result. Eventually, internecine warfare erupted between the United States and Soviet Chess federations and FIDE. The Soviets spared no energy in maneuvering for every advantage they could. They'd held the World Championship title for thirty-four years and had no intention of handing it to an American, especially an "uneducated" American. There were financial considerations as well. The six-figure purse that was being discussed would be the richest prize ever for a head-to-head confrontation in any sport other than boxing.

When Iceland submitted a bid to host the match, Bobby flew to its capital city, Reykjavik, to inspect the site. He was encouraged to play there by Freysteinn Thorbergsson, an Icelandic player in his early forties who'd drawn with Bobby in a tournament in Reykjavik in 1960. But the president of the Icelandic Chess Federation, thirty-two-year-old Gudmundur Thorarinsson, a soft-spoken engineer and Shakespearean scholar, was wary of Bobby. A man who carried a big stick and had political ambitions (eventually, he became a member of parliament), Thorarinsson wanted the match in his country but had a low tolerance for Fischer's shenanigans.

While negotiations as to the venue and the prize fund continued, both players went to the mountains to train. Spassky ensconced himself in the Caucasus while Fischer settled in the Catskills, more than seven thousand miles away. Grossinger's, a mammoth hotel complex in Ferndale, New York, the heart of the "Borscht Belt" where much of the New York City Jewish population had been vacationing for more than half a century, served as Fischer's training camp for the four months preceding the match. Since Fischer's Worldwide Church of God faith observed the same dietary and many of the Sabbath laws as the Judaic tradition, Grossinger's was an ideal selection. There was no pork served in the dining room, and from Friday sundown to Saturday sundown, the devout observed a sabbatical decorum.

Grossinger's removed Bobby from the pressures of New York City, where he was just a ten-cent telephone call away from anyone who wanted to reach him, and it prevented people from dropping in for a casual visit and disturbing his concentration and study. The hotel was also renowned for catering to famous guests. Bobby loved being there and was in a perpetually good mood, with thoughts of growing rich from the impending match. He was saving money from his book royalties, tournament winnings, and exhibitions, and he informed his mother that he was doing "real well financially."

At that time it looked as though the match with Spassky would have a total prize fund of $138,000, the highest amount ever for a chess match. Bobby was trying to not get too excited about the money that would be coming his way. In spite of all the money and acclaim, he wrote with a certain humility that he was doing his best "not to forget who I really am, and to keep my mind on the eternal values."

He was also happy to learn that Regina had passed the examination that would allow her to practice medicine in the United States, and he was hoping that she would consider moving back from Europe.

To prepare for the strenuousness of the World Championship match, Fischer trained his body as well as his mind, with workouts in the hotel gym, fast laps in the pool, and a few games of tennis each day. He seemed to dominate the tennis court while he was at Grossinger's, and other than his games with the resident pro, Fischer usually won all of his matches. His serve was graceful and forcibly delivered, as were his return volleys. While waiting for his opponent to serve, he rapidly twisted the racket, bounced from foot to foot, and swayed his body, always ready to move to either side of the court. Walking back to his cottage or off to the swimming pool, he often swung the racket at an invisible tennis ball, just as he did as a boy when he'd swing an imaginary baseball bat while gamboling along Flatbush Avenue. All this physical activity kept him in great shape. He wrote to his mother that he was feeling "real fine" and that everyone was saying that he looked good because of his daily training.

Only after hours of exercise would he sit down at his chessboard. In the evenings, in a state of quiet contemplation, he began his exhaustive inspection of Spassky's games. This microscopic analysis often continued until the early hours of the morning. The reference text he consulted most frequently was what journalists were quick to describe as the "Big Red Book"— number 27 of the excellent *Weltgeschichte des Schachs* series—the games of champions—containing 355 games of Spassky's, conveniently typeset with a diagram at every fifth move. Bobby never let the book out of his sight and carried it everywhere. It contained his own notes on Spassky's games, jotted in pencil, with comments and question marks designating poor moves, exclamation marks designating good ones. Almost as a parlor trick, he would often ask someone to pick a game at random from the book, tell him who played it against Spassky and where the game was played, and he would then recite the game move by move. He had memorized more than 14,000 moves!

Although Bobby said in his letter to his mother that he was "studying a bit" for the match, in reality he was spending as much as twelve hours a day, seven days a week, going over such issues as what openings he would or wouldn't play against Spassky and what kinds of games he felt Spassky was most uncomfortable playing. He was buoyed when he played over Spassky's games in the recently concluded Alekhine Memorial tournament in Moscow. Bobby told an interviewer: "They were atrocious games. He was really lost in half the games in that tournament; really bad games on his part."

While Spassky was supported by a small army of helpers, Fischer basically toiled alone. A British player, Robert Wade, supplied Bobby with a detailed analysis of Spassky's openings in two loose-leaf books, one marked "Spassky: White" and the other "Spassky: Black." Other than that, Bobby relied on his own efforts. To the press, however, he displayed nothing but confidence. "I'm not worried," he said. And in a Muhammad Ali–type quote, destined to be picked up by the press, he added: "The odds should be twenty to one [that I will win]."

During the months Fischer spent in training at Grossinger's, he was visited by several other players, but while chess was the topic du jour, no one really contributed to Fischer's preparatory efforts. Larry Evans and then Bernard Zuckerman visited, helping Bobby in any way they could, but even though he respected them, he sometimes asked them to sit away from the board so he could think things through himself.

Later, Lombardy fought the notion of Fischer as a player who was totally self-sufficient, an island unto himself. "It's true that he works alone, but he is learning from the games of other players all the time," he said. "To say that Bobby Fischer developed his talent all by himself is like saying that Beethoven or Mozart developed without the benefit of the music . . . that came before them. If other chess players had never existed for Bobby Fischer to learn from, then there would *be* no Bobby Fischer today."

Since Bobby's suite had two bedrooms, he liked to have guests from time to time. Jackie Beers was his most frequent visitor. Bobby had known Jackie since childhood and they were an odd pair. Jackie was a rated expert, an excellent speed player, but he was always finding himself in trouble at chess clubs, usually because of his ferocious temper. Once, a fight at the Manhattan Chess Club resulted in a lawsuit against him that was eventually settled out of court, and there were stories of his chasing people in the street or their chasing him because of altercations. With Bobby, Jackie acted meekly and respectfully. He often stayed overnight in the Fischer apartment in Brooklyn and later was Bobby's houseguest when Fischer lived in California. Jackie was no sycophant or whipping boy, as he's been described by other writers. He recognized that Bobby was the "chief" of their friendship, but he wasn't afraid to speak up and disagree. While Bobby knew of Jackie's reputation for truculence and tolerated him nevertheless, he was careful not to include him in all areas of his life, knowing instinctively when Beers wouldn't be welcomed by others.

At the beginning of May, Bobby's Iceland acquaintance Freysteinn Thorbergsson made the journey from Iceland to America and checked in at Grossinger's. At first, Bobby was a little reserved with him, but as they talked—for about seven hours—he warmed up. Though Bobby had always pushed for Belgrade as the site of the championship match, a tentative understanding seemed to have been worked out to at least split the match between Belgrade and Reykjavik. Thorbergsson clearly favored the idea of all the games being staged in Iceland. Going back to Bobby's chalet, the two analyzed some games, and Thorbergsson continued his volley of subtle arguments for why Bobby should play exclusively in Iceland.

A gentle man, Thorbergsson had lived in Russia and was a rabid anti-Communist. He saw Bobby's playing for the World Championship as a political act as much as a cultural one; and he used that line of reasoning with Bobby, maintaining that it would be morally wrong to allow the championship to be played within the Soviets' sphere of influence. In an essay, he'd later write: "The Russians have for decades enslaved other nations and their own nationals. They use their victories in various sports, chess and in other fields to fool people and make them believe their system is the best." He added that a Fischer victory would "strike at the uplifted propaganda fists of the Communists."

By the time the Icelander left Grossinger's the next morning, he felt that Bobby was on the verge of agreeing to play exclusively in Reykjavik.

As the date of the championship match grew closer, Bobby quit Grossinger's and, assisted by one of his lawyers, Andrew Davis, a Yale University alumnus, checked into the Yale Club in midtown Manhattan, where he stayed for a few weeks.

As summer approached, the reality of the match caused such heightened curiosity that it seemed like Fischer's every remark, his every action, was recorded around the globe. Even at Grossinger's, far removed from the business of Manhattan, he'd been besieged by calls, cables, and visits suggesting schemes to make him—and their originators—rich. A "Bobby Fischer Chess Set" was suggested. Endorsements were sought. One Wall Street broker even tried convincing Bobby to become a "corporation," like the Beatles, so that shares of "Bobby Fischer" could be traded on the New York Stock Exchange. Fischer went his own way, agreeing to little and signing nothing.

Chess players were beginning to regard the forthcoming Fischer-Spassky duel as the most important match ever played by an American. *Time* magazine was just one of many media outlets beating the geopolitical drum. It dubbed the contest "The Russian Bear vs. the Brooklyn Wolf." Spassky's defense of his title became, symbolically, a defense of the Soviet Union, and the Russian's millstone was a heavy weight to bear. Fischer, completely aware of the encounter's political and cultural implications, accepted the extra layer of significance as his own responsibility. "I now feel a sense of mission to win the championship," he declared. Asked if the bout would be a grudge match, he replied: "In a sense. But not personally between me and Spassky . . . it's against the Russians."

The challenger in any contest often has a special advantage in that he's forced to play "up" in order to win; he's motivated to compete harder because he must prove that he's better than the champion. The title holder, secure in the knowledge of his superiority, frequently plays on his own "normal" level, falsely assuming that because he *is* the champion, the proven quality of his past play is sufficient for current victory. One advantage Spassky enjoyed, though, was a rule stipulation called "draw odds." If he could draw every game, giving him 12 points, Spassky would retain his title without winning a game. Fischer needed 12 ½ points to dethrone Spassky.

♜

Earliest known photograph of Bobby Fischer, sitting on his mother's lap in 1944, when he was one year old. Regina Fischer was homeless when she gave birth to Bobby, and they first lived in a shelter for indigent mothers.
MCF photo

Bobby's mother, Regina, and her husband, Gerhardt Fischer, while in France during the 1930s. Though Gerhardt's name is on Bobby's birth certificate, it is not certain that he was Bobby's father.
MCF photo

Chess can be studied virtually anywhere, and Bobby was seldom without a chess board. One night, exasperated, Regina lightly tapped her nine-year-old son on his head with her bare foot: "Get out of the bathtub!"
MCF photo

The ebullient Carmine Nigro, Bobby's first chess teacher, visited New York's Washington Square Park in 1955, where Bobby was playing in an outdoor tournament.
MCF photo

Before he became obsessed with chess, Bobby dreamed of becoming a professional baseball player. Here he is wielding a bat for his grade school's team during a game in Brooklyn, in 1955.
dailynewspix

Bobby engaged in a systematic regimen of reading every chess book in the Brooklyn Public Library and memorizing what was most helpful in each. Here he is, at age fourteen, reading a volume of Alexander Alekhine's best games.
FB Photo

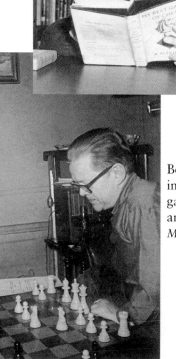

Bobby at fourteen, interrupted while playing a game with his friend, teacher, and mentor, Jack Collins.
MCF photo

Regina picked up her son at the Manhattan Chess Club many a late evening and escorted him home on the subway. Here he's fallen asleep with his head on his mother's shoulder. This snapshot was taken by Bobby's sister, Joan.
MCF photo

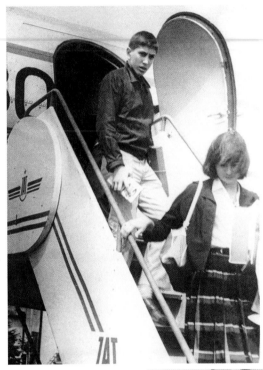

In 1958, after being refused an extension of his visa in Russia because of his rude behavior, Bobby arrived in Yugoslavia with his sister, Joan.
JAT, the Yugoslavian airline

Although Bobby had played some speed games against Tigran Petrosian in Moscow, this game at the Portoroz International, in 1958, was their first formal encounter. They drew.
Yugoslavian Chess Federation

David Bronstein was one of the strongest players in the world in 1958, but was only able to draw his game with Bobby, which created a sensation, proving that Bobby was of World Championship caliber.
Yugoslavian Chess Federation

Regina Fischer, a frequent protester, at the head of a peace march in Moscow, 1960. She went from there to East Germany, where she completed her medical degree.
Planet News, Ltd.

Bobby played three games against Mikhail Tal in Curaçao, in 1962, just before the flamboyant Russian became ill and was hospitalized.
Brooklyn Public Library, Brooklyn Collection

Banned from traveling to Havana in 1965, Bobby sat in a closed room in New York's Marshall Chess Club and played his opponents by teletype. After he defeated Vassily Smyslov, the two analyzed their game by phone.
The Queens Borough Public Library, Long Island Div., New York Herald-Tribune Photo Morgue

William Lombardy (left) and the bearded Miguel Quinteros, both grandmasters, served as Bobby's seconds at the 1972 match.
Icelandic Chess Federation

Regina Fischer, wearing a blond wig as a disguise, secretly visited Bobby in his hotel room during his match in Iceland. Bobby was preparing for his next game against Boris Spassky.
MCF photo

In 1972 Fischer finally reached the summit of chess, playing in Iceland for the World Championship against Boris Spassky of the Soviet Union. *Icelandic Chess Federation*

At the banquet after he had won the match, Bobby, who often seemed uninterested in women, surprised the assembled dignitaries by dancing with an Icelandic beauty. *Icelandic Chess Federation*

Back in the United States, Bobby had become America's hero by defeating the Soviet Union. In New York, on the steps of City Hall, Mayor John Lindsay awarded Bobby a gold medal and a Proclamation of Acclaim. *dailynewspix*

After winning the championship, Bobby appeared on a number of television shows and received unprecedented media coverage. Here he is in late 1972 on *The Merv Griffin Show*, thinking about a move.
Courtesy of The Merv Griffin Show

In 2004, Bobby was imprisoned in Japan for traveling without a valid passport, and was threatened with extradition back to the United States. Icelandic friends worked to free him, but after ten months in jail, bearded and haggard, Bobby appeared to be a broken man.
Einar Einarsson

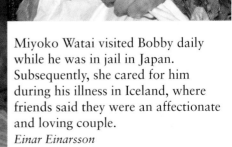

Miyoko Watai visited Bobby daily while he was in jail in Japan. Subsequently, she cared for him during his illness in Iceland, where friends said they were an affectionate and loving couple.
Einar Einarsson

Bobby, nearing the end of his life, walking down a country road near Álþingi, the site of Iceland's original parliament. Founded in AD 930 during the Viking era, Iceland's national parliament is the oldest in the world and still in existence.
Einar Einarsson

The last known photographic portrait of Bobby Fischer, who had become an Icelandic citizen, taken at 3 Frakkar (3 Coats), his favorite restaurant in Reykjavik.
Einar Einarsson

Iceland, the westernmost and one of the smallest countries in Europe, sitting remotely in the North Atlantic just below the Arctic Circle, may have seemed a curious venue for a World Chess Championship. Largely uninhabited except around the coast, the island is a physical contradiction, partly covered with vast ice fields yet home to several active volcanoes that rise in flames from both the land and the sea around it. Virtually treeless, it features frosted picture-book mountains that are interspersed with rugged, lava-strewn terrain, giving the landscape an unnatural, almost lunar appearance: American astronauts trained there before their voyages to the moon. In 1972 the average income for an Icelander was barely $2,000 a year. But it is a spirited country, is pollution-free, and has no urban slums and virtually no crime.

So what made Iceland the ideal country to stage the Fischer-Spassky match? Undoubtedly it was the resoluteness, pride, and enthusiasm of its people, and their love of the game as an intellectual and cultural pursuit. Icelanders are among the most literate in the world and the Icelandic sagas rate among the greatest in literature. Icelanders read more books per capita than any other people on the globe, and—like the Russians—they almost all play chess. In the winter months when there is almost twenty-four hours of darkness, what better way to spend an evening or a weekend than to stay at home or visit a comfortably heated club, play chess for hours, and avoid the chill of the Atlantic winter with its gales, thunderstorms, and biting rain.

Over the years, Icelanders have sponsored many international tournaments and matches, and the possibility of holding what was being billed as the Match of the Century was more than exhilarating to chess players throughout the country. As it developed, the 1972 Fischer-Spassky match was one of the most expertly organized World Championship matches ever conducted, intoxicating for Icelanders as well as the tourists and members of the international press who descended on the capital city of Reykjavik. Photographic blowups of Fischer and Spassky adorned the windows of almost every shop, with black-and-white checkered displays serving as backdrops for huge papier-mâché chess pieces.

Most of the residents started out wishing for Fischer's victory, but after the numerous false starts, threats, and general difficulties Bobby caused, sympathy began to swing to the gentlemanly Spassky. Fischer wasn't satisfied with the financial arrangements. The winner was to receive $78,125 and the loser

$46,875. Beyond that, each was to be given 30 percent of all television and film rights. Fischer, though, demanded 30 percent of the gate receipts *in addition,* arguing that paid admissions might amount to $250,000 and that he and Spassky should receive a share.

The Icelandic chess officials—who weren't at all sure how they were going to fill the three-thousand-seat Laugardalshöll, the site of the match, game after game for as many as twenty-four sessions, not counting adjournments—argued that gate-receipt income should go entirely to them to cover their outlay for the stakes and the arrangements.

Fischer canceled his flight to Iceland at the last minute, on the evening of June 25. The airline had reserved a full row of seats just for him and had stocked the plane's refrigerator with oranges so that Fischer could have fresh juice "squeezed in front of him," as he'd requested, during the four-hour trip across the Atlantic. Meanwhile, talks continued between Bobby's lawyers, Paul Marshall and Andrew Davis, and the Icelandic Chess Federation concerning the matter of the gate receipts. Both sides stood firm. During the ensuing week, additional flights were booked and then canceled by Fischer as headlines began to question whether he'd appear at all. Icelandic papers were asking HVENAER KEMUR HINN DULARFULLI FISCHER? ("WHEN COMETH THE MYSTERIOUS FISCHER?") A few days after Fischer's first flight was changed, Bobby and Davis drove to John F. Kennedy International Airport, apparently to board a Pan American flight. But, strangely, Fischer paused to buy an alarm clock and was seen by reporters and photographers (there were more than a hundred members of the press waiting to interview and photograph him). He fled the airline terminal and missed the flight. Later, he was observed at a nearby Howard Johnson's restaurant, having dinner. When, indeed, would Bobby goeth to Iceland?

Although money was the focal point of the controversy, it wasn't just about dollars (or kroners); rather, it was about Bobby getting his way. In this case, he was pretty confident he could receive what he demanded. As an editorial in *The New York Times* suggested: "If he plays in Reykjavik and wins—as he has an excellent chance of doing—his prospective earnings would make the amount he is arguing about now seem infinitesimal." Fischer knew that. He also knew that the world was clamoring for the match and that if he held out a little longer, more money might be forthcoming.

The world press was, to say the least, not amused. Foreign papers reflected the outrage of their readership. RUSSIANS DISDAIN FISCHER FOR CONCERN WITH MONEY, blared a headline in *The New York Times,* and Tass, the Soviet press agency, editorialized: "Whenever the matter concerns Fischer, money comes first while sports motives are relegated to the background. Characteristically, his confidants are not chessplayers, but lawyers to whom he [entrusts] all his chess affairs." The leading German Sunday newspaper, *Bild am Sonntag,* reported: "Fischer has dragged chess down to the level of a wrestling match. We've never known of such arrogance and snobbism." The London *Daily Mail* stated: "Bobby Fischer is quite certainly the most ill-mannered, temperamental and neurotic brat ever to be reared in Brooklyn. As far as the international prestige battle goes, the Soviet Union has won the opening round 10 to 0." What the press—and seemingly everyone else—failed to understand was that it was Bobby's shrewdness in protecting his financial interests, rather than temper tantrums or neuroses, that was making him hesitate. He knew instinctively that the longer he waited, the more swollen the prize fund would become.

Bobby felt that journalists weren't really interested in how or why he moved the chess pieces, but rather in the scandal, tragedy, and comedy of his life. To him, the press was a puzzle that he could never quite solve. He felt that he couldn't lie if asked a direct question, and yet if he simply refused to answer, the assumption was that he was hiding something crucial.

Whispers had been bandied about as far back as 1958, when he played at Portorož, that he was an anti-Semite, but privately, he categorically denied it when playing at Netanya, Israel, in 1968. One of Bobby's closest friends, Anthony Saidy, said that he never heard Fischer make an anti-Semitic remark until at some point after the 1972 championship.

During the match, Bobby didn't issue any statements that were either anti-Semitic or anti-American—on the contrary, he appeared deeply patriotic and included many Jews among his friends, lawyers, and colleagues. But Wilfrid Sheed, an American novelist and essayist, penned a comment just before the match ended that many would later regard as prescient. In his *The New York Times Book Review* of a work by Ezra Pound, Sheed likened Bobby to Pound, the infamous anti-Semite and anti-American who was indicted for treason by the United States for his fascist broadcasts. Sheed wrote: "Of Ezra

Pound, as of Bobby Fischer, all that can be decently said is that his colleagues admire him. There is no reason for anyone else to."

By the time the opening ceremonies took place at Iceland's National Theatre on Saturday evening, July 1, less than twenty-four hours before the beginning of the scheduled first game, reporters and spectators were making reservations to return home, in the belief that Fischer wouldn't appear. Bobby had moved from the Yale Club to the home of Anthony Saidy, who lived with his parents in a large Tudor house in Douglaston, Queens. As Saidy later related, the house was subjected to an unending media barrage. Fischer was besieged with calls and cables, and photographers and journalists staked out the grounds in hopes of just a glimpse of him. Fischer headlines dominated the front pages of newspapers all over the world, crowding off such "secondary" news items as the 1972 United States presidential nominations.

Saidy suggested that there was an actual plot to keep Fischer from becoming World Champion, and this involved the wiretapping of his parents' phone. "At one point, when Bobby was talking to Davis, who was in Iceland," Saidy said, "Bobby made a reference to one of the Icelandic Chess Federation officials as being 'stupid.' Suddenly, he heard a woman's voice cutting through the line saying: 'He said: "He's stupid."'" The line was obviously tapped." Saidy added that Fischer also believed that the line was tapped.

Anything is possible, of course. There was a theory prevalent among a number of Americans, such as Fred Cramer, who was on Bobby's team, that the Icelanders were underhandedly working with the Russians to repel Fischer's assault on Soviet chess hegemony. Aside from the personal dislike for Fischer that a number of the Icelandic chess officials, such as Thorarinsson, openly felt, though, not one instance emerged suggesting that they did anything to hinder Fischer's World Championship bid. Indeed, some of the Icelandic officials were convinced that Spassky was the better player and that he was going to defeat Fischer rather easily anyway. At the commencement of the match, they were privately expecting to see Fischer humiliated *on the board*.

The drawing for colors for the first game didn't take place during the opening ceremonies, which failed to develop strictly according to schedule. Spassky was seated in the first row, elegantly attired in a gray-checked vested suit. Meanwhile, an empty seat, also in the front row, which Fischer was to have occupied, remained conspicuously vacant. While speeches were made in

English, Russian, and Icelandic, the audience fidgeted, craning their necks to the side entrance, half expecting—hoping—that at any moment Fischer would make a grand entrance. It didn't happen.

Dr. Max Euwe, representing FIDE, allowed Fischer a two-day postponement. "But if he does not show up by Tuesday at twelve noon, at the drawing of lots, he loses all of his rights as challenger," Euwe said.

Fischer remained apparently unmoved: He wanted 30 percent of the gate receipts and was not traveling to Iceland unless his demands were met. The ICF received hundreds of cancellations of tickets and reservations. People who'd traveled from all over Iceland to see the first game, and who hadn't heard that it had been canceled, were sadly turned away from the hall. Then a rumor spread through the press corps (there were now about two hundred accredited reporters and photographers) that Fischer was already on the island, that he'd arrived in a navy submarine to avoid the press and was hiding out somewhere in the countryside. Even though it was a rumor, several newspapers and agencies—including the eminent gray lady, *The New York Times*—published it as at least a *possibility.*

The Soviet Chess Federation lodged a biting protest with FIDE against the forty-eight-hour postponement, saying that Fischer actually warranted "unconditional disqualification." Charging Dr. Euwe as the responsible agent, the federation warned him that it would consider the match "wrecked" if Fischer did not appear in Reykjavik by noon on July 4, Euwe's deadline. Finally, two unexpected phone calls were placed, one from England, the other from Washington, D.C. The calls saved the match.

Journalist Leonard Barden phoned the Icelandic organizers to tell them that British financier James Derrick Slater, a chess devotee and investment banker, was willing to donate $125,000 to double the existing prize fund—if Fischer would agree to play. Slater, a millionaire, stated: "The money is mine. I like chess and have played it for years. Many want to see this match and everything was arranged. If Fischer does not go to Iceland, many will be disappointed. I want to remove the problem of money from Fischer and see if he has any other problems."

Fischer's first reaction was immensely positive. "It's stupendous," he said. "I have to accept it." Later, he told a newsman that though he hadn't studied the offer in detail, he'd decided to play the match because "there's an awful lot of prestige of the country at stake." Yet he still needed one more nudge to propel him to the board.

The second call proved to be that needed nudge. Saidy answered the phone for what seemed to be the twentieth time that day, thinking it was yet another request for Bobby to make a statement or grant an interview. Instead, it was the personal secretary of Henry Kissinger, President Nixon's national security advisor (and later, secretary of state), wanting to set up a telephone conversation with Bobby. Bobby dragged himself to the phone, and Kissinger started off in his deep, German-accented voice, "This is the worst chess player in the world calling the best chess player in the world." Kissinger told Bobby that he should go to Iceland and beat the Russians at their own game. "The United States government wishes you well and I wish you well."

After this ten-minute conversation, Bobby said he was going to play "no matter what," and that the interests of the United States were greater than his personal interests. It was at this point that Bobby saw himself not just as a chess player, but as a Cold War warrior in defense of his country.

After months of disenchanting negotiations, the millionaire Slater, backed by the diplomat Kissinger, had accomplished the impossible. What made Bobby run—in this case, to Iceland? Three elements apparently: pride, money, and patriotism.

To avoid being spotted by either reporters or the public, Fischer was smuggled onto a Loftleidir (Icelandic Airlines) flight. He made the overnight trip with William Lombardy, whom he'd announced as his official second that same day. Lombardy, the large, pale, and intense Roman Catholic priest, was perhaps the chief supporting actor in the drama at Reykjavik. Thirty-five years old, six years older than Fischer, he was the first chess master of international importance connected with the Catholic Church since Ruy Lopez (sixteenth century) and Domenico Ponziani (eighteenth century) made their imprints on the game.

The drawing of the lots to determine who'd play what color, scheduled for noon at the Hotel Esja, attracted hundreds of journalists, officials of the ICF, and members of both the American and Russian sides. When Spassky arrived, he was told that Fischer was still sleeping and had sent Lombardy to draw for him. Unnerved, Spassky refused to draw and left the hotel in a huff. At lunch, shortly afterward, he told a newsman that he was "not abandoning the match," but Fischer had acted improperly. "I still want to play," he said, "but *I* will decide when." He then issued the following statement, possibly written for him in Moscow:

> Soviet public opinion and I, personally, are full with indignation at Fischer's behavior. According to concepts common to all people, he has completely disqualified himself.
>
> Therefore he has, in my opinion, called in doubt his moral rights to play the match.
>
> If there now is to be any hope for conducting the match, Fischer must be subjected to just penalty. Only after that I can return to the question whether it is possible to conduct the match.
>
> Boris Spassky
> World Champion

The penalty the Soviets required was a forfeit of the first game. The Soviet Delegation also said:

1. Robert Fischer must apologize.
2. The President of FIDE has to condemn the behavior of the challenger.
3. The President of FIDE has to admit that this two-day postponement violated FIDE rules.

Euwe, again rising to the occasion, said in a touching display of humility that since two of the conditions concerned him, he'd be happy to compose a statement right there, admitting that he'd broken the rules and condemning Fischer "not only in the last two days but all through the negotiations." After working on his statement for about ten minutes, while the audience— in uncomfortable sympathy—sat waiting, Euwe read his confession aloud, signed it, and handed it to Efim Geller, Spassky's second. It stated: "1. The FIDE condemns the behavior of the challenger in not arriving on time, thus leaving the entire delegation and others in doubt about the realization of the match, and causing many troubles. 2. The President of FIDE admits that we had to postpone the match for two days; we violated the FIDE rules. I think it's for special reasons, and on the basis of some presumptions which proved to be wrong afterwards. I declare that the FIDE rules and match agreements approved by FIDE shall be strictly observed in the future." Euwe's face was flushed by the chastisement and he was on the verge of tears. The Soviets claimed that, according to the rules, Fischer should have lost the match when he failed to appear on opening day; and only through their benevolence was the contest continuing. It was now up to Fischer to make the next move.

That night, Fischer composed an elegant apology to Spassky. One reporter, Brad Darrach of *Life,* contended that in the first draft of the letter, Fischer had renounced any share in the prize money and had said he was willing to play for nothing but the love of chess. Though one can imagine Bobby, on the spur of the moment, proclaiming: "I'll prove to the world that I love chess more than the Russians!" it's easy to understand that his poor Brooklyn roots ultimately spoke to him of the need for pragmatism. He still wanted a paycheck, but the desire to prove himself over the board was his strongest motivation for trying to heal the rift.

In the end, a second letter was composed, and it was this version that was finally presented to Spassky. Fischer drove to the Saga Hotel early on the morning of July 6 and accompanied the bellboy to Spassky's room to watch him slide the apology under the door. The text:

```
Dear Boris:

    Please accept my sincerest apology for my disrespectful
behavior in not attending the opening ceremony. I simply
became carried away by my petty dispute over money with
the Icelandic chess organizers. I have offended you and
your country, the Soviet Union, where chess has a
prestigious position. Also, I would like to apologize to
Dr. Max Euwe, President of FIDE, to the Match Organizers
in Iceland, to the thousands of chess fans around the
world and especially to the millions of fans and the many
friends I have in the United States.
```

After I did not show up for the first game, Dr. Euwe announced that the first game would be postponed without prejudice to me. At that time you made no protest. Now I am informed that the Russian chess federation is demanding that the first game be forfeited to you. The timing of this demand seems to place in doubt the motives for your federation's not insisting at first for a forfeit on the first game.

If this forfeit demand were respected, it would place me at a tremendous handicap. Even without this handicap, you will have an advantage to begin with of needing twelve points out of twenty four to retain your title, whereas I will need twelve and a half to win the title. If this demand were granted, you would need only eleven points out of twenty three but I would still need twelve and a half out of my twenty three. In other words I must win three! games without losses, just to obtain the position you would have at the beginning of the match and I don't believe that the world's champion desires such an advantage in order to play me.

I know you to be a sportsman and a gentleman, and I am looking forward to some exciting chess games with you.

                              Sincerely,
                              Bobby Fischer
              Reykjavik, July 6, 1972

One obstacle remained and that was the Soviet Union itself. A Russian minister, Sergei Pavlov, head of the State Sports Committee, had cabled Spassky, furiously insisting that he return home to Moscow. Pavlov said that Fischer's "tantrums" were an insult to the World Champion, who had every legal and moral right to refuse to meet Fischer. Normally, such a "recommendation" had the force of law, but Spassky refused, as politely and diplomatically as possible. He replied to Pavlov that he could not debase his own standards of sportsmanship and would see the match through despite Fischer's outrageous conduct. It was a courageous act, and one that called for much finesse and force of will on Spassky's part.

Fischer arrived twenty minutes late for the drawing of colors, and he and Spassky met backstage. After shaking hands, Spassky humorously tested Fischer's biceps, as though they were two boxers "weighing in." They then sequestered themselves for a few minutes to discuss the schedule. Spassky wanted a short postponement before the start of the match. Fischer agreed if Spassky would drop the demand for a forfeit. They came to terms, and a moment later they walked to the stage, applauded by the journalists and well-wishers who'd been waiting patiently. Fischer, spying the chess table, galumphed to the center of the stage and immediately lifted the white queen, testing its weight. Then, one hand in his pocket, he tested all the other white pieces and sat down, stretching his legs under the Scandinavian-designed mahogany table. Spassky also sat.

After introducing both challenger and champion, and their respective seconds and aides, FIDE representative Harry Golombek, an international master from the UK, announced that Geller wanted to make a statement before the drawing of the lots took place. Speaking in Russian, Geller said:

> The challenger apologized in writing and the President of FIDE has declared that the match rules of FIDE will be strictly observed in the future. Taking into consideration the efforts made by the Icelandic organizers of the match, and the desire of millions of chess admirers all over the world to see the match, the world champion has decided to play with Robert Fischer.

Though the statement was mild enough, there was growing irritation in Fischer as he listened to the translation, and by the time it was completed, he was pale with indignation at the phrase "the world champion has decided to play with Robert Fischer," as if Spassky were doing him a favor. Bobby was mortified. For one very brief second, he considered walking off the stage and out of the match forever. He felt he'd complied with the wishes of the Soviets by making the apology to Spassky, writing it by hand and personally delivering it, and he'd just agreed to go along with Spassky's postponement. For

Bobby, the Geller statement had soiled the first official ceremony of the match. The Russians were censuring his behavior in front of his friends and the world press. Somehow, Bobby maintained his composure. Fortunately, the drawing of colors quickly followed, leaving no opportunity to reflect further on the incident.

Lothar Schmid, the elegant German referee, handed each man a blank envelope, and Spassky chose the one that indicated he'd hold the pieces. Spassky concealed a black pawn and a white pawn behind his back in the time-honored fashion and then brought his closed hands forward across the board. Fischer, without hesitation, tapped Spassky's right hand—and Spassky opened it to reveal the black pawn. Fischer didn't change his expression.

Several hours later, coming home from bowling in the early hours of the morning, before returning to the hotel, Bobby sneaked into the playing hall to check out the conditions. After an eighty-minute inspection, he had a number of complaints: He thought the lighting should be brighter; the pieces of the chess set were too small for the squares of the custom-built board; the board itself was not quite right—it was made of stone, and he thought wood would be preferable. Finally, he thought that the two cameras hidden in burlap-covered towers might be distracting when he began to play, and the towers themselves, looming over the stage like medieval battering rams, were disconcerting.

The organizers started working on the problems immediately. They wanted everything perfect before the first pawn was moved on opening day.

When Fischer finally awoke on the afternoon of July 11, 1972, and it slowly began to permeate his consciousness that he was actually in Iceland about to play his first game for the championship of the world, he was nervous. After years and years of tribulation and controversy, and the brouhaha about the match, Fischer had arrived at the threshold of his lifelong goal. Laugardalshöll was to be his universe for the next two months.

All details had been checked and double-checked in the playing hall to ensure maximum comfort for the players. Laugardalshöll was a cavernous, dome-shaped stadium (someone described it as a large Icelandic mushroom), with white-covered sound baffles on the ceiling that resembled mammoth albino bats. The entire first floor was covered with carpeting to muffle the noise made by spectators, and the folding seats had been replaced with upholstered and consequently "soundless" chairs. The two film towers had been pushed back, at Fischer's request, and the lighting intensity on stage increased. A handsome Eames-designed executive swivel chair, an exact duplicate of the one Fischer had sat in while playing Petrosian in Buenos Aires, was flown in from the United States.

Fischer rushed through the backstage corridor onto the subtly flower-bedecked stage and was greeted by the polite applause of an audience of twenty-three hundred. Spassky had made his first move precisely at five, and Schmid had started Fischer's clock. Fischer, dressed in a white shirt and blue business suit, sped to the table; the two opponents shook hands while Fischer kept his eyes on the board. Then he sat down in his black leather chair, considered his move for ninety-five seconds, and played his knight to his king bishop's third square.

It was a unique moment in the life of a charismatic prodigy in that, to arrive where he was, he'd somehow overcome his objections to how he'd been treated by the Soviets over the years. Everyone knew it, not only in Laugardalshöll but all over the world. As grandmaster Isaac Kashdan said: "It was the single most important chess event [ever]." A lone American from Brooklyn, equipped with just a single stone—his brilliance—was about to fling it against the hegemony of the Soviet Union.

Fischer left the stage twice during the game (pre-adjournment), once complaining that the orange juice left in his dressing room backstage wasn't cold enough. Ice cubes were provided. He also asked for a bottle of cold water and a dish of *skyr*, an Icelandic yogurt-type dessert. This last request caused confusion in the stadium's cafeteria, as they were unable to supply the *skyr*. Fortunately, a local restaurant could, and did.

As moves were made on the board, they were simultaneously shown on forty closed-circuit television monitors, in all points of the stadium. In the cafeteria, where spectators wolfed down the local variety of lamb-based hot dogs and gurgled bottles of 2 percent Icelandic beer, the action on the stage was discussed vociferously. In the basement, Icelandic masters more quietly explained and analyzed the moves on a demonstration board, while in the press rooms, lordly grandmasters surveyed the television screens and analyzed in their heads, to the confusion and awe of most of the journalists. In the playing hall itself, decorum and quiet reigned. When it didn't, Lothar Schmid would activate a white electrical sign that commanded, in both English and Icelandic:

THÖGN!

SILENCE!

As the first game progressed, most experts began predicting a draw. And then, on the twenty-ninth move, with the position equal, Fischer engaged in one of the most dangerous gambles of his career. Without consuming much time on his clock (he'd equalized on the seventeenth move and was now ahead of Spassky on time), Fischer sacrificed his bishop for two pawns in a move that thoroughly electrified the audience and sent Spassky's eyebrows arching. The trade of pieces looked like a schoolboy's blunder. Grandmaster Edmar Mednis said in retrospect: "I couldn't believe that Fischer was capable of such an error. How is such an error possible from a top master, or from *any* master?"

At first impression, it appeared that Fischer, overly eager to gain the psychological momentum of winning the first game, had overextended himself. But on closer inspection, the game still looked as though it could possibly end in a draw. Next, Fischer complained to Schmid that one of the cameras, which was poking through a hole in the blue-and-white FIDE sign located at the back of the stage, was disturbing him. No change was made, however.

On his forty-first move Spassky decided to adjourn the game: This would enable him to take advantage of overnight analysis. Since five hours—the official adjournment time—hadn't yet been reached, he took a loss of thirty-five minutes on his clock. Spassky had a bishop and three pawns against Fischer's five pawns. He sealed his move and handed the large brown envelope to Schmid.

Fischer analyzed the position through the night and appeared at the hall looking tired and worried, just two minutes before Schmid opened the sealed-move envelope. Following FIDE tradition, Schmid made Spassky's adjourned move for him on the board, showed Fischer the score sheet so he could check that the correct move had been made, and activated Fischer's clock. Fischer responded within seconds, prepared by his night-long study of the game, and a few moves were exchanged.

Fischer then pointed to the camera aperture he'd complained about the previous day, and quickly left the stage with his clock running. Backstage, he vehemently complained about the camera and said he wanted it dismantled before he continued. ICF officials quickly conferred with Chester Fox, owner of the film and television rights, who agreed to remove the camera. All of this took time, and Fischer's clock continued running while the dismantling went on. When Fischer returned to the stage, thirty-five minutes had elapsed on his clock.

Fischer began fighting for a draw, but Spassky's moves were a study in precision and his position got stronger. Eventually, it became clear that Spassky could queen a pawn. Instead of making his fifty-sixth move, Fischer stopped the clock and offered his hand in resignation. He wasn't smiling. Spassky didn't look him in the eye as they shook hands—rather, he continued to study the position. Fischer signed his score sheet, made a helpless gesture as if to say "What am I supposed to do now?" and left the stage. It wasn't difficult to guess his emotional state.

Though there have been a number of World Championship matches in which the loser of the first game went on to win, there's no question that Fischer considered the loss of the first game almost tantamount to losing the match itself. Not only had he lost, but he'd been unable to prove to himself— and the public—that he could win a single game against Spassky. Their life-time record against each other now stood at four wins for Spassky, two draws, and no wins for Fischer. In the next several hours Bobby descended into self-doubt and uncertainty, but eventually his psyche shifted to rational-ization: Since there could be no defect in his calculation and no question of his being the lesser player, the distracting camera was to blame for the loss.

The next morning, Thursday, July 13, the American delegation announced that Fischer wouldn't play the next game unless *all* cameras were removed from the hall. Fischer insisted—and rightly so—that only he could say what disturbed him. But he refused to go to the hall to inspect the new conditions and decide whether they'd been sufficiently improved.

Schmid declared that the second game would start at five p.m., and if Fischer didn't appear after one hour of official play had elapsed, he'd be for-feited. To complicate matters, one of the Soviets leaked to the press that if Fischer failed to come for the second game, Spassky would probably return to Moscow.

Spassky appeared on stage at two minutes to five, to a round of applause. At precisely 5:00, Schmid started Fischer's clock, since Bobby was to play the white pieces. Back at the Hotel Loftleidir, Lombardy and officials of the U.S. Chess Federation futilely appealed to Fischer to go to the hall. A police car, with its motor running, was stationed outside the hotel to whisk him down Suderlans-braut Boulevard to the hall, should he change his mind. At 5:30 p.m., with Fischer's clock still running, Chester Fox's lawyer in Reykjavik agreed to the suggestion that the cameras be removed just for the one game, pending further discussion. When this solution was relayed to Fischer, he demanded that his clock be set back to its original time. Schmid wouldn't agree, claiming that there had to be some limits. Fischer, in his underwear, sat in his hotel room, the door bolted and telephone unplugged, a picture in stony resistance. His mind was made up: "If I ask for one thing and they don't give it to me, I don't play."

The spectators continued to gaze hypnotically at the two empty chairs (Spassky had retreated to his dressing room backstage) and a chessboard of thirty-two pieces, none of which had been moved. The only motion was the minute hand and the agitated red star-shaped time indicator on Fischer's clock. It was a lonely tableau.

At exactly 6:00 p.m., Schmid stopped the clock, walked to the front of the stage, and announced the first forfeiture of any game in World Champion-ship history. "Ladies and gentlemen, according to Rule 5 of the regulations, Robert Fischer has lost the game. He has not turned up within the stipulated hour of time."

Spassky was given a standing ovation. He said to Schmid, "It's a pity," while someone from the audience, angry at Fischer, yelled: "Send him back to the United States!"

Fischer lodged a formal protest less than six hours after the forfeiture. It was overruled by the match committee on the grounds that he'd failed to ap-pear at the game. The committee upheld the forfeit, but not without some trepidation and soul-searching. Everyone knew that Fischer wouldn't accept it lightly. And he didn't. His instant reaction was to make a reservation to fly home immediately. He was dissuaded by Lombardy, but it seemed likely that he'd refuse to continue the match unless the forfeit was removed. Schmid himself voiced his sincere concern regarding the danger to Fischer's career if he walked out of the match: "What will happen to Bobby? What city would ever host a match for him?"

Bobby had his supporters, though. Grandmaster Svetozar Gligoric sug-gested that the cameras, staring constantly at him, may have signified human eyes peering at Bobby and distracted his attention. Vladimir Nabokov, the

Russian-born novelist who'd written *The Defense* (about a genius who lives only for chess), also spoke up for Bobby, saying that he was "quite right" in objecting to the use of cameras in the match: "He can't be subject to the clicks and flashes of those machines [on their tall tripods] above him."

Notified of the decision and realizing its implications, Dr. Euwe, who'd returned to the Netherlands, cabled his own decision to Schmid in case Fischer refused to appear at the next game:

```
IN CASE OF NON-APPEARANCE OF FISCHER IN THIRD GAME,
PRESIDENT OF FIDE DECLARES IF FISCHER NOT IN THE FOURTH
GAME, MATCH WILL BE CONCLUDED AND SPASSKY WILL BE
PROCLAIMED WORLD CHAMPION.
```

Fischer began receiving thousands of letters and cables urging him to continue the match, and Henry Kissinger called him once again, this time from California, to appeal to his patriotism. *The New York Times* even issued an open plea urging Fischer to continue his challenge. In an editorial entitled "Bobby Fischer's Tragedy," the paper wrote:

> The possibility seems strong that his temper tantrums will turn the present world championship match into a non-event in which Spassky will retain his crown because of Fischer's refusal to play.
>
> The tragedy in all this is particularly great because for nearly a decade, there has been strong reason to suppose that Fischer could demonstrate his supremacy convincingly if only given the opportunity to do so. . . .
>
> Is it too much to hope that even at this late state he will regain his balance and fulfill his obligation to the chess world by trying to play Spassky without histrionics? Consequential as is the two-game lead the Soviet champion now enjoys, the board is still set for a duel that could rank among the most brilliant in this ancient game's annals.

Perhaps as a result of Kissinger's interest in the match and his two conversations with Bobby, President Nixon also relayed an invitation to Fischer, through *Life*'s photographer Harry Benson, to visit the White House after the match was over, win or lose. Nixon said that he liked Bobby "because he is a fighter."

In an effort to ease the situation and encourage Fischer to continue the match, Schmid announced that according to the rules, he had the right to move the match from the stage of the hall to a backstage room. Speaking privately to Spassky, Schmid appealed to him "as a sportsman" to agree to this new attempt to enable the match to continue. Spassky, ever a gentleman, was willing. By the time Fischer was notified of the new arrangement, he'd already made reservations on all three flights going back to New York on the day of the third game. He took a few hours to consider the offer, and ninety minutes before the start of play he said he'd be willing to give it a try if he was assured complete privacy and no cameras.

Why *did* Fischer continue to play? Probably a combination of genuine nationalism, faith in his ability to overcome the odds of a two-point deficit, a desire to get paid (even if he lost the match, he was to receive $91,875 in prize money, in addition to an estimated $30,000 from television and movie rights), and an overwhelming need to do what he'd always vowed to do, almost from his first official match: prove that he was the most gifted chess player on earth.

Spassky appeared on time at the backstage location; at first he sat in Fischer's chair and, perhaps unaware that he was on camera, smiled and swiveled around several times as a child might do. Then he moved to his own chair, and waited. Fischer arrived eight minutes late, looking very pale, and the two men shook hands. Spassky, playing white, made his first move and Fischer replied. Suddenly, Fischer pointed to a camera and began shouting.

Spassky was now on his feet. "I am leaving!" he announced curtly, with the bearing of a Russian count, informing Fischer and Schmid that he was going to the stage to play the game there.

Schmid recalled later that "for a second, I didn't know what to do. Then I stopped Spassky's clock, breaking the rules. But somehow I had to get that incredible situation under control."

The men continued talking, but their voices became subdued. Schmid put his arms around Spassky's shoulders, saying: "Boris, you promised me you would play this game here. Are you breaking that promise?" Then turning to Fischer, Schmid said: "Bobby, please be kind."

Spassky gaped for about ten seconds, thinking about what to do, and finally sat down. Fischer was told that it was just a closed-circuit, noiseless camera that was projecting the game onto a large screen on the stage. No copy would be kept. He somehow accepted it.

Fischer apologized for his hasty words, and both men finally got down to business. They played one of the best games of the match. After Fischer's seventh move (fifteen minutes had elapsed on his clock, to Spassky's five), he briefly left the room. As he walked past Schmid, the referee noted that he appeared intensely grave. "He looked like death," Schmid said afterward. Yes, and also incensed, indignant, and thoroughly, almost maniacally, determined.

When the game was adjourned on the forty-first move, Fischer's powerful position was irresistible. The game was resumed the next day and Bobby, feeling ebullient because he was in a winning position, agreed to play on the main stage. At the start of play Spassky took one fleeting glimpse at Fischer's sealed move, which won by force, meaning that there was no ambiguity to the position: Bobby had a clear win that was demonstrable and resolute. Spassky stopped his clock, signaling his resignation.

Tardy as usual, Fischer dashed onto the stage fifteen minutes late, out of breath. Spassky was already en route to his hotel. "What happened?" he asked, and Schmid said: "Mr. Spassky has resigned." Fischer signed his score sheet and left the stage without another word. By the time he reached the backstage exit, he could no longer resist smiling at the well-wishers waiting there.

Though it seems ludicrous to suggest that the outcome of the Fischer-Spassky match was predictable after only two games had been completed, one point going to each player, the case *can* be made. The fact is, Fischer's first win over Spassky was more than a narrowing of the gap. It was the creation of the gestalt Bobby needed to prove to himself that he was capable of dominance. A drawn game would have had no significance. He'd demonstrated in the past that he could, though admittedly infrequently, draw with Spassky. By winning, Bobby not only extracted the first drop of his opponent's blood, he ensured that the wound would not soon close up.

Even as Bobby was waging a secondary battle against cameras in Reykjavik, cameras in New York were televising his epic struggle on the board. A thirty-five-year-old sociology professor, Shelby Lyman, a master who'd been ranked high among players in the United States, conducted a five-hour program almost every day on public television, discussing the games, move by move, as information and color commentary was phoned in to him by the PBS reporter in Iceland. He showed each new move on a demonstration board and attempted to predict what Fischer's or Spassky's next move might be. In a primitive form of interactive programming, members of the television audience phoned the studio to offer their suggested next move. Grandmasters were often guests on the show, evaluating the audience's suggestions and discussing the win-loss possibilities of the contestants.

Lyman was eloquent in a homespun way, and in addition to his analysis of the match, he added explanations so that the analysis would be understandable to chess novices. For example, he once said: "It's not enough to have respect for bishops in the abstract, you gotta watch out for them!" After the first few broadcasts, there were more than a million viewers following the games, and after two months Lyman became a star himself, with people stopping him on the street and asking for his autograph. So popular was the show that it crowded out the baseball and tennis coverage normally seen in sports bars in New York, and when the channel was covering the Democratic National Convention in Washington, the station was flooded with thousands of calls asking to have the chess match put back on. Station officials gave in to their viewers' demands, dropped the convention, and went back to broadcasting the match.

Fischer's quest and charisma transformed the image and status of chess in the United States and other countries, as well. In New York, intense demand quickly made chess sets an out-of-stock item at department stores such as Bloomingdale's and Macy's. Nor could the publishers of Bobby's two books, *My 60 Memorable Games* and *Bobby Fischer Teaches Chess*, easily keep up with demand for the chess star's perspective. Chess clubs everywhere saw memberships swell; during the match, the Marshall Chess Club's roster doubled to six hundred, and the United States Chess Federation added tens of thousands to the fold. For the first time in their lives, chess masters could make a decent living giving lessons because they had so many new students. People were playing chess at work, during their lunch hour, in restaurants, on their front stoops, and in their backyards. There's no reliable statistic documenting how many people embraced the game as a result of the publicity surrounding the Fischer-Spassky match, but some estimates put the number in the millions.

Off-the-board pressures were undoubtedly placing Spassky (who was less inured than Bobby to being at the center of a storm) under great stress. And that might, in turn, have affected the sharpness of his thinking, because in the fifth game, after committing perhaps the worst blunder of his career on the twenty-seventh move, he resigned, ending one of the shortest decisive encounters in World Championship history.

Grandmaster Miguel Najdorf, seated on the sidelines, likened the next game, the sixth, to a Mozart symphony. Fischer built a crushing attack and enveloped Spassky in a mating net, forcing his capitulation. Fischer later implied that this was his favorite game of the match, and many grandmasters, such as Larry Evans, have indicated that the game was so beautifully executed that it became the match's turning point.

Fischer began telling friends that he thought the match would be over in his favor in two weeks. He was becoming convivial and even made attempts at dry, almost British humor. At the beginning of August, while gazing out the picture window of his hotel room at the northern void during a gray, raw day, he quipped: "Iceland is a nice place. I must come back here in the summertime."

Although it's never been revealed before, Regina Fischer, disguised in a blond wig and stylish clothing, flew in from England and visited Bobby at the Loftleidir to wish him good cheer and congratulate him on what appeared to be the certainty of his winning the championship. She didn't want to be recognized. Journalists' curiosity about her would simply take away, she felt, from her son's shining moment. She slept in Bobby's suite overnight but didn't go to the Laugardalshöll to see him play. Instead, she flew back to the UK the next day.

In many ways, "unlucky thirteen" was the pivotal game of the Fischer-Spassky championship encounter. It was a nine-and-a-half-hour marathon in which Fischer, even though a pawn ahead, had a difficult position right up to adjournment. He could find no improvement with overnight analysis, and upon resumption he was forced to continue seeking what looked like a draw. On the sixty-ninth move, obviously exhausted, Spassky blundered. When he realized his mistake, he could barely look at the board, turning his head away several times in humiliation and frustration. Fischer, after moving to collect Spassky's gift, sat back in his chair, grimly, staring at the Russian— studying him. For a long, long moment, he didn't take his eyes off Spassky.

There was just a bit of compassion in Fischer's eyes, which turned the episode into a true Aristotelian tragedy: Spassky's terror combined with Fischer's pity. Spassky finally moved, but resigned on the seventy-fourth move.

At that point in the match, Fischer stopped taking the chances that are often necessary to win a game. Because of his unusual caution, the following seven games, numbers fourteen to twenty, were all draws. After the match, Fischer explained that he hadn't been playing for draws but realized that his three-point lead was enough to win the title, as long as he could prevent Spassky from winning a game.

After twenty games, the score stood at 11 ½–8 ½ in favor of Fischer. He needed just two draws or one win out of the remaining four games to wrest the title from the Russian, and from Russia. Fischer's future was manifest.

Shortly before the concluding week of the match, the Soviet delegation, by way of a long and preposterous statement, made an accusation that Fischer might be "influencing" the World Champion's behavior by "chemical substances if not by electronic means." Incredibly, an investigation was launched by the Reykjavik Police Department and Icelandic scientists. They field-stripped Spassky's chair, x-rayed it, took scrapings of all the surroundings, and even examined the air on the stage. The image of a burly policeman traipsing across the stage with an empty plastic bag, attempting to "capture" the air, was the stuff of Chaplinesque comedy. One object was found in Spassky's chair that was not in Fischer's otherwise identical chair! But the secret weapon turned out to be a blob of wood filler, placed there by the manufacturer. Fischer guffawed when he heard of it and said that he'd been expecting rougher tactics from the Russians.

Donald Schultz, part of Fischer's team, was there when the wood from the chair was x-rayed, and he saw the X-ray itself. He also saw a second X-ray and noticed that the blob was no longer there. He couldn't help wondering if one of the Russians had planted something in the chair to embarrass Bobby but on second thought had somehow removed it so that the Soviets themselves wouldn't be embarrassed if it could be proven they'd put it there in the first place.

The Russians insisted that a lighting fixture above the stage be taken apart to see if there was an electronic device hidden there that might be affecting Spassky's play. As a policeman began to unscrew the globe, he yelled down from the ladder that there *was* something in there. The Russians and the Americans ran to the base of the ladder as the policeman descended with his discovery: "Two dead flies!"

The case was embarrassingly closed, it having become clear that the Soviets, stunned at the probable loss of "their" title, were searching for an alibi, one that would sully Bobby's achievement. The London *Times* summed up the chess circus in humorous, though pointed, fashion: "It started out as a farce by Beckett—*Waiting for Godot*. Then it turned into a Kafka tragedy. Now it's beyond Kafka. Perhaps Strindberg could do it justice."

The twenty-first game commenced on August 31, and Fischer, playing black, conducted the endgame in stellar fashion; at adjournment it looked as though he could win. If that were to occur, the twenty-first game would be Bobby's last. To conquer Spassky and become World Champion, he'd always needed to collect 12 ½ points, and a win would get him to that magic number.

The next day, Harry Benson, a Scotsman who was a key photographer for *Time Life,* met Spassky at the Saga Hotel. "There's a new champion," Spassky said. "I'm not sad. It's a sporting event and I lost. Bobby's the new champion. Now I must take a walk and get some fresh air."

Benson immediately drove to the Hotel Loftleidir and called Bobby on the house phone. "Are you sure it's official?" Fischer asked. Told that it was, he said: "Well, thanks."

At 2:47 p.m., Fischer appeared on stage at Laugardalshöll to sign his score sheet. Schmid made the official announcement: "Ladies and gentlemen, Mr. Spassky has resigned by telephone at 12:50. This is a traditional and legal way of resignation. Mr. Fischer has won this game, number twenty-one, and he is the winner of the match."

The spectators went wild. Fischer smiled when Schmid shook his hand, then he nodded awkwardly at the audience, appeared uncomfortable, and started to go. Just before leaving, he paused ever so briefly and looked out into the crowd, as though he might be about to say something or perhaps wave. Then he quickly disappeared backstage and left the building. A mob swarmed around his car, which was driven by Saemi Palsson, his bodyguard. Television and radio reporters poked microphones and cameras at the closed windows. Lombardy sat in the backseat, and the three men drove off. Only after they were under way did Fischer allow himself to break into a big, boyish grin. He was the World Chess Champion.

Two days after Fischer won the championship, a lavish banquet was held in his honor at Laugardalshöll. Boris Spassky attended, as did the arbiter Lothar Schmid and FIDE's president Dr. Max Euwe, who officiated. The event had been planned for weeks and was sold out long before the match was over. More than one thousand people attended (scalpers obtained $75 to $100 for a $22 ticket), and everyone feasted on lamb and suckling pig grilled over charcoal braziers, served by waiters in Viking helmets. The "Vikings" kept goblets filled with something called "Viking's Blood," a powerful concoction of red wine and cognac. On the same stage where Fischer and Spassky had fought it out for two months, an orchestra now played, but the music was a pleasant potpourri from *The Tales of Hoffmann* and *La Traviata*. The whole evening radiated an Old World ambience, as though the event were taking place in 1872, in a huge European beer garden, rather than 1972, in a covered Icelandic arena.

But where was Bobby Fischer? The clucks and whispers spread throughout the hall: "He isn't coming!" "He has to come . . . even his sister is here!" "He wouldn't do this to Spassky!" "He still has to collect his check!" "He's already back in Brooklyn!" "He won't come!"

After an hour had passed with no sign of the champion and with revelers already deep into their goblets of Viking's Blood, Dr. Euwe lumbered up onto the stage, while the orchestra played the anthem of FIDE: *"Gens Una Sumus."* Then suddenly, wearing a maroon corduroy suit that he'd had custom made in Reykjavik, Bobby appeared. Without waiting for the music to stop, he walked to the head table and sat. Spassky was two seats away, and eventually Bobby stretched his hand across and they shook. Euwe called Fischer to the stage, draped a large laurel wreath over his shoulders, and proclaimed him Champion of the World. Then he presented him with a gold medal and a certificate. The coronation was over in a blink.

Examining the medal, Bobby whispered to Euwe, "But my name is not on it." Euwe smiled and replied, "We didn't know if you were going to be the winner!" Without speaking further, Bobby returned to his table. Euwe continued to talk and mentioned that the rules would have to be changed for future World Championships, in large part because of Bobby Fischer, who'd brought so much attention to the game.

As Euwe continued with his remarks, Bobby appeared bored and lonely, perhaps because more than a thousand people were looking up regularly to stare at him. But even those who knew him well seemed afraid to approach. Two burly Icelanders, the size of restaurant refrigerators—both chess players—sat guard near his table, and whenever anyone came near Bobby to get an autograph, or a kiss, or just to offer their felicitations, they were not so gently steered away.

At his seat Bobby studied the stage from the audience's perspective, seeing it as they must have seen it for two months, when they'd watched the combatants in profile. He was lost in a reverie, and one can only guess at his thoughts. Did he mentally replay some of his games with Spassky? Did he consider lines that he should have pursued—weigh whether he could have performed better? Did he admonish himself for all of the disquiet he'd caused—all of the disputes over money and cameras and lighting?

Some yearning for the comfort of old habits must have seized him, because, finally, he pulled out his leather pocket chess set and started going over the last game of the match. Spassky had moved to the seat next to him and was listening to Bobby's analysis. The dialogue seemed natural, almost as if they were still playing. "I should have played *here* as my sealed move," said Spassky, moving a little plastic piece and trying to demonstrate how he might have held on to the game. "It wouldn't have made any difference," Bobby responded. He then showed the Russian all of the variations he'd worked out during the adjournment. Soon, grandmasters Efim Geller and Robert Byrne jumped into the fray. There was a blur of hands as the four men made moves on a chess set hardly larger than an index card. At that moment Offenbach's *"Les oiseaux dans la charmille"* filtered down from the stage. But the chess players seemed not to notice.

Eventually, Fischer was given his two prize checks, one from the Icelandic Chess Federation and the other from James Slater, the millionaire whose eleventh-hour financial offer had saved the match. Bobby's winnings came to $153,240. He was also given a collector's item, a huge leather-bound, slipcased book on the history of Iceland. Guthmundur Thorarinsson privately complained—but not to Bobby—that the Icelandic Chess Federation had lost $50,000 on the match, because there was no money from television or film rights.

When Bobby had had enough of the party, he slipped out the back door with his friend, the Argentinean player Miguel Quinteros, and went off into the night to frolic with Icelandic girls whom they hoped to pick up. So anxious was he to leave the party, he forgot to take his commemorative Icelandic book, and it was never found.

Just before Spassky left Reykjavik, Bobby had delivered to the Russian at his hotel an amiable letter and a gift-wrapped camera as a token of friendship. Spassky seemed to have no animosity for the man who'd defeated him, although he knew he was going to face difficult times when he returned home to Moscow. His last comment about Bobby was "Fischer is a man of art, but he is a rare human being in the everyday life of this century. I like Fischer and I think I understand him."

Mayor Lindsay's limousine was waiting for Bobby when he touched down in New York. Bobby's retinue included his bodyguard Saemi Palsson and Palsson's wife, as well as Quinteros. "It's great to be back in America" was Fischer's only comment to the waiting reporters. The mayor had offered Bobby a ticker-tape parade down the "Canyon of Heroes" on Broadway in lower Manhattan, a rare honor given in the past to such luminaries as Charles Lindbergh, Franklin D. Roosevelt, and the Apollo astronauts, but Bobby wasn't much excited by the idea. Friends and advisors reminded him that if he accepted, he'd be the only chess player ever to have a ticker-tape parade, and probably there'd never be another chess player receiving the distinction. He was unmoved: "No, I don't want it," he decided. He would, however, agree to a "small" ceremony on the steps of City Hall.

He received hundreds of congratulatory letters and telegrams, but the one that he was most proud of was as follows:

Dear Bobby,

Your convincing victory at Reykjavik is eloquent witness
to your complete mastery of the world's most difficult and
challenging game. The Championship you have won is a great
personal triumph for you and I am pleased to join

```
countless of your fellow-citizens in extending my
heartiest congratulations and best wishes.
```

```
                              Sincerely yours,
                              Richard Nixon
```

The "small" ceremony turned out to be "Bobby Fischer Day" in New York City. More than one thousand well-wishers gathered at the steps of City Hall as Mayor Lindsay awarded Bobby with a gold medal (and not the key to the city as has been incorrectly reported) and proclaimed him "the grandest master of them all." Many of Bobby's friends were there, such as Jack and Ethel Collins, Edmar Mednis, Paul Marshall (Bobby's lawyer) and his wife Betty, and Sam Sloan. This time Bobby gave a speech: "I want to deny a vicious rumor that's been going around. I think it was started by Moscow. It is not true that Henry Kissinger phoned me during the night to tell me the moves." The audience roared. "I never thought I'd see the day when chess would be all over the front pages here, but confined only to one paragraph in *Pravda*." That day, Bobby was not the old curmudgeonly Bobby: He was gracious, humorous, and willing to sign countless autographs. *The New York Times* in a mammoth editorial summed up what he'd managed to achieve:

> Fischer has done more, however, than simply win the world title he has so long, even obsessively, considered his right. He has transformed the image and status of chess in the minds of millions, suddenly multiplying manifold both the audience for chess as a sport and the number of people actually playing the game. . . . From a wider perspective, the Fischer-Spassky match has a unique political importance. . . . The result was an atmosphere that, for all its tenseness, contributed to improving the broader ambience of Soviet-American relations.

Fischer, the Cold War hero, traveled to New Jersey and became the temporary houseguest of his lawyer Paul Marshall. So besieged was Bobby by the media that for a while Marshall had to have a bodyguard stationed in front of his palatial home to keep the press hordes at bay.

11

The Wilderness Years

BOBBY FISCHER'S LONG, almost monastic pursuit of the World Championship, although not totally chaste, gave him little time to connect with women. "I want to meet girls," Bobby said when he moved back to Los Angeles in 1973. "Vivacious girls with big breasts." He was twenty-nine years old, and though there'd been a few brief liaisons, at no time had he experienced a meaningful romantic relationship. Now, with his earnings from Reykjavik and a new place to live—an apartment provided for him at a modest rental fee of $200 per month by the Worldwide Church of God—he felt that he was starting a new life. He wanted to read more—not just chess journals—acquire more money, continue his religious studies, and possibly meet someone with whom he could fall in love. What it all added up to was an intense need to recharge his emotional and spiritual life.

Not all was altruism and ebullience, however; certain realities still cast a pall. His alienation from the press caused ongoing problems. He'd suffered a series of fractured relationships with chess organizers in the United States (he was no longer speaking to Edmondson, the executive director of the U.S. Chess Federation) and looming in the near future were the Soviets, with what he foresaw would be a resumption of their underhanded ways of competing.

After Bobby's period of post-Reykjavik idleness had stretched to about a year, he decided that his first priority should be accumulating more money, always on his terms. So, working with Stanley Rader, the chief counsel for the Worldwide Church, he called a press conference in August of 1973 to publicly discuss his plans.

Rader was a lawyer and Armstrong's closest advisor. As chief counsel, he was becoming rich through his work with the Church, and Bobby was impressed with Rader's trappings: his Ferrari, his chauffeur-driven limousine, his palatial mansion in Beverly Hills, and his use of a private jet. Rader was in charge of the $70-million-a-year windfall that the Church was bringing in, mostly from tithing its members. Bobby himself had given the Church more than $60,000 from his Icelandic winnings, and ultimately his tithe would be close to $100,000.

For the press conference, dozens of journalists and photographers assembled in Rader's soaring living room. Aside from two television appearances right after Reykjavik, it had been almost twelve months since Bobby had made any statements or, for that matter, been seen in public. The words "secluded" and "recluse" had begun straying into newspaper stories about him. Hardly days after his win in Iceland, an article in *The New York Times* headlined NEW CHAMPION STILL MYSTERY MAN speculated as to whether he'd ever play again. The Associated Press took the same tack, publishing a story entitled BOBBY FISCHER TURNS DOWN FAME, FORTUNE; GOES INTO SECLUSION. It was an odd slant, since at that point Bobby had no intention of isolating himself or turning down money; he was just tending to personal matters that he'd neglected for years. Also, up to that time chess champions would traditionally defend their title only every three years. Although the public wanted to see Bobby back at the board, his absence from chess for less than a year was not an aberration.

Rader did most of the talking at the press conference, and he was good at it, having graduated first in his class at the University of California Law School. Bobby, dressed conservatively, stood somewhat nervously at his side. Throughout the event, photographers took photos, and Bobby looked annoyed every time a flashbulb popped. Rader said, in a voice that was both sonorous and emphatic, that Fischer would like to announce that he will soon be back at the 64 squares and 32 pieces again . . . quite soon. "We are making arrangements for a series of simultaneous exhibitions and matches for early next year. We are also considering an exhibition match where Bobby would play the entire Dutch Olympic team *simultaneously*." A reporter shot out a question: "What about a re-match for the championship?" Rader and

Bobby exchanged a flicker of a glance, and the lawyer responded: "That is a possibility." The reporter came back with an immediate follow-up: "Would that match be under the authority of the World Chess Federation?" Rader didn't hesitate: "That would not be likely but it is under discussion." Rader also mentioned that a tour of both Russia and South America was being talked about.

The reporters wanted a go at Fischer: "What have you been doing for the last year?" was one of the first questions. Bobby drawled out his response: "Well, uh, I've been reading, working out, playing over some games, that sort of thing." A few other general questions were tossed out, and Bobby answered them succinctly and with aplomb, until someone asked whether he was living in an apartment subsidized by the Church. "That's personal," he said. "I don't want to answer any more personal questions." A reporter asked him about a supposed offer of $1 million for a match against Spassky in Las Vegas. Rader jumped in with the answer: "To begin with, the Las Vegas offer was not a firm $1 million offer. They said the offer was for a million but it would have turned out less, and Bobby didn't want to agree with anything less than a firm $1 million."

Rader pointed out that aside from any non-sanctioned matches, the official match for the World Championship would be in 1975, and it would consist of Bobby against whoever qualified through the Candidates system. "When he defends his title in 1975," Rader added, "he'll be much better able to capitalize financially."

And then the conference was over. "That's all gentlemen. Thank you," said Rader, and he and Bobby scurried away. The reporters looked at one another, incredulous at the abrupt termination. As a result of the non-event event, the resulting press coverage was practically nil.

Rader had reason to be helpful to Bobby. If Bobby could make millions, and if he continued tithing large amounts to the Church, he could emerge as one of the Church's biggest benefactors. Also, the more publicity Bobby received, the more publicity the Church would receive. Before anything was completed, however, complications set in.

Attractive financial offers kept tumbling Bobby's way—almost pouring over him—but nothing was to his satisfaction:

- Warner Bros. offered him a million dollars to make a series of phonograph records on how to play chess, but Bobby wanted to voice the series himself. Scripts written by Larry Evans were translated into several languages and rendered phonetically to make it easier for Bobby to read. Unfortunately, when he voiced one of the scripts for a pilot recording, he didn't like the sound of his own voice, and he wouldn't approve a professional announcer as a substitute. Ultimately, he rejected the whole project.

- An entrepreneur, hearing of the $1 million offer from the Hilton Corporation in Las Vegas for a Fischer-Spassky match, offered to raise the amount of the prize fund to $1.5 million if the two men played in his home state of Texas. Nothing came of it.

- A publishing company offered Bobby a "small fortune," according to press reports, to write a book on his title match. He refused.

- A television producer wanted him to make a series of chess films that could be marketed throughout the world. No agreement could be reached.

- Bobby was offered $75,000 plus residual royalties plus a new car simply to say in a commercial that he drove only that car, which would have been true since it would have been the only car he owned. He declined.

- The most fabulous offer came to Fischer in 1974, right after the Muhammad Ali–George Foreman fight (known as "The Rumble in the Jungle") in Zaire. The Zaire government offered Bobby $5 million to play Anatoly Karpov in their country in what would have been a month-long championship chess match. "Too short," said Bobby. "How dare they offer me five million dollars for a month-long match? Ali received twice that much for one night!" (He didn't.) It was after that match that Ali began calling himself "The Greatest," and Bobby took issue with that, too. "Ali stole that from me," said Bobby. "I used 'The Greatest' for myself on television before he ever used it."

Bobby *did* accept one offer, but not for millions—rather, for $20,000. He was invited to be the guest of honor at the First Philippine International Chess Tournament in 1973, and in addition to the honorarium mentioned above, all of his expenses were paid. He stayed at the Tropical Palace resort

on the outskirts of Manila for a month. At the tournament he made the ceremonial first move and played a mock game with President Marcos—one
that ended in a mock draw after eight moves.

Journalists asked Fischer why he'd accepted the offer to come to the Philippines on his first "official" visit when he'd turned down similar offers from
other countries. "I was there in 1967," he said. "I was not yet World Champion but they treated me like a world champion." According to Casto
Abundo, a chess player who described himself as Bobby's "Young Man Friday" during his 1973 stay, Bobby studied chess every night, already preparing himself to face whoever emerged as the winner of the Candidates match.
After finishing his studying, he often took long walks at three in the morning
and didn't fall asleep till four. Film footage from the visit shows Bobby at the
apex of his life. Wearing the traditional crisp white *barong* shirt and often
sporting a lei of flowers, he looked fit and handsome and was always smiling.
The Filipinos loved him; Marcos entertained him at the palace and on his
yacht; Marcos's wife, Imelda, dined with him at lunch; young ladies gathered
around him constantly, as if he were a movie star. On a Bangkok stopover en
route to Manila, he'd bought a number of Thai music cassettes, which he
played over and over again at night while he was going over games. By the
time he sailed back to the United States, his fondness for the Filipino people
had intensified.

Paul Marshall, Bobby's lawyer during the Fischer-Spassky match negotiations, has said that by the time Bobby came back from Iceland he'd received
offers that could have totaled up to $10 million—but he turned down all
of them. Bobby's interest in making money was undeniable, so theories
abounded as to why he acted contrary to his own financial interests. One
friend chalked it up to Bobby's winner-take-all mentality, saying, "If someone offers him a million dollars, he thinks there is a lot more available, and
he wants it all." Grandmaster Larry Evans preferred a more neutral explanation: "I think he feels that lending his name to something is beneath his dig-
nity." International master George Koltanowski conjectured that Bobby just
didn't trust people and didn't want to be cheated: "There's a word for it in
German: *Verfolgungswahnsinn,*" he said. "It means 'persecution mania.' "
But perhaps the best explanation of why Bobby cast aside all financial offers
came from Bobby himself: "People are trying to exploit me. Nobody is going

to make a nickel off of me!" Nor, as it developed, would he make a dime off of them—in the short term, at least.

As all of these financial shenanigans were happening—offers, discussions, negotiations, acceptances, and then rejections—Bobby was going his own way but under the influence and guidance of the Church. Church officials set him up with young, amply endowed women—all Church members—but since no physical intimacy was permitted, Bobby soon grew disillusioned. After dates with eight different "candidates," each of whom adhered to the same sexless script, he abandoned Church relationships as the avenue to an amorous life.

His connection to the Church was always somewhat ambiguous. He was not a registered member, since he hadn't agreed to be baptized by full immersion in water by Armstrong or one of his ministers. And since he wasn't considered a duly recognized convert, he was sometimes referred to as a "co-worker" or, less politely, as a "fringer"—someone on the fringes or edges of the Church but not totally committed to its mission. The Church imposed a number of rules that Bobby thought were ridiculous and refused to adhere to, such as a ban on listening to hard rock or soul music (even though he preferred rhythm and blues) and prohibitions against seeing movies not rated G or PG, dating or fraternizing with non–Church members, and having premarital sex.

Ironically, despite Bobby's unwillingness to follow principles espoused by the Church, his life still revolved around it. He sat in on a demanding Bible course, even though it was open only to members (the Church made an exception for him); he discussed personal and financial matters with both Rader and Armstrong; and he prayed at least an hour a day, in addition to spending time on a careful study of Church teachings. On a visit back to New York, while driving around Manhattan with his friend Bernard Zuckerman, Bobby made a reference to Satan. Zuckerman, ever sarcastic, said, "Satan? Why don't you introduce me?" Bobby was appalled. "What? Don't you believe in Satan?"

As he continued to tithe more and more money to the Church, he enjoyed perks only available to high-ranking members, such as occasional use of a private jet and a chauffeur-driven limousine; invitations to exclusive events such as parties, concerts, and dinners; and a continuous parade of bright and pretty women whom he couldn't touch. He was also given access to the Church's personal trainer, Harry Sneider, a former weight-lifting champion who took a special interest in Bobby. Sneider trained Bobby in swimming, weight lifting, tennis, and soccer, and they became friends.

With the same diligence he'd brought to the task of soaking up chess knowledge, Bobby around this time started a relentless search for general knowledge. The library at the Worldwide Church's Ambassador College, to which he had access, was highly limited. It contained books on religion and theology, but he wanted other points of view and to explore other topics, and he never set foot back in the library after he heard it was sprayed with insecticide for termites.

Botvinnik may have been right when he suggested that Bobby suffered from a lack of culture and a thinness of education. But he was determined to catch up. He started by going to bookstores in Pasadena, and when he'd depleted their shelves, he took the bus into downtown Los Angeles and scoured the shelves of every bookstore he could find. He became a voracious reader.

There have been many theories offered over the years as to why Fischer eventually turned against Jews, including speculation that Bobby's rhetoric was triggered by distaste he felt as a child for his mother's Jewish friends; that he was antagonistic toward officials of the American Chess Foundation, most of whom were Jewish; that he was ultimately disillusioned with Stanley Rader, who was Jewish but had converted to the Worldwide Church of God; that he was somehow influenced by Forry Laucks's Nazism; and that he was propelled by ideas he'd read in some of the literature that fell into his hands during the time he lived in California. Perhaps all of those factors contributed.

David Mamet, the Pulitzer Prize–winning writer, described the prototypical self-hating Jew in his book *The Wicked Son,* and his description, although arguable, could conceivably be applied to Bobby: "The Jew-hater begins with a proposition that glorifies and comforts him, that there exists a force of evil that he has, to his credit, discovered and bravely proclaimed. In opposing it he is self-glorified. One triumphs over evil, thus becoming a god, at no cost other than recognition of his own divinity. Ignorant of the practices of his own tribe, he (the apostate) gravitates toward those he considers *Other* . . . thinking, as does the adolescent, that they possess some special merit. But these new groups are attractive to the apostate merely because they are foreign."

In at least one significant case, Bobby woke up to the fact that the *Other* was less appealing than he'd first thought. More and more he was becoming alienated from the Worldwide Church of God. Herbert W. Armstrong had made prophecies that there would be a worldwide catastrophe and that the Messiah would return in 1972. As 1973 wound down, Bobby didn't need much convincing to have an epiphany about the evils of the Church. In an interview that he gave to the *Ambassador Report* (an irreverent and controversial publication that criticized the Church) he said: "The real proof for me were those [false] prophecies . . . that show to me that he [Armstrong] is an outright huckster. . . . I thought, 'This doesn't seem right. I gave all my money. Everybody has been telling me this [that 1972 would be the date that the Worldwide Church of God would flee to a place of safety] for years. And now he's half-denying he ever said it, when I remember him saying it a hundred times.' . . . If you talk about fulfillment of prophecy, he [Armstrong] is a fulfillment of Elmer Gantry. If Elmer Gantry was the Elijah, Armstrong's the 'Christ' of religious hucksters. There is no way he could truly be God's prophet. Either God is a masochist and likes to be made a fool of, or else Herbert Armstrong is a false prophet."

Before he knew it, Bobby's winnings from Reykjavik were beginning to diminish, and yet he saw that Rader and Armstrong were flying all over the world, entertaining lavishly, and proffering gifts to world leaders. "The whole thing is so sick," said Bobby.

Wandering into a used bookstore in downtown Los Angeles, Bobby stumbled on a dusty old book called *The Protocols of the Elders of Zion*. Though he was introduced to the book by happenstance, he was ready for it. A work of fiction, it purported to be the actual master plan by Jewish leaders to take over the world. First published in 1905, the book, at the time Bobby found it, was still believed by some to be an authentic work of *non*fiction. Even today those who are predisposed to believe it swear by its accuracy, and over the years its publication has done its share to stoke worldwide anti-Semitism.

To fire up hatred toward Jews, the book uses reverse psychology in presenting a damning case against gentiles: "It is the bottomless rascality of the *goyim* people, who crawl on their bellies to force, but are merciless toward weakness, unsparing to faults, and indulgent to crimes, unwilling to bear the contradictions of a free social system but patient unto martyrdom under the violence of a bold despotism."

As Bobby read *The Protocols,* he thought he saw authenticity in the book's pages, and their implicit message resonated with him. Soon he began sending copies of the book to friends. To one he wrote: "I carefully studied the *Protocols.* I think anyone who casually dismisses them as a forgery, hoax, etc., is either kidding themselves, is ignorant of them or else may well be a hypocrite!" At the time, one of the most militant anti-Semites and anti-blacks in the United States, Ben Klassen, had just written his first book, *Nature's Eternal Religion,* and Bobby, who wasn't particularly anti-black, nevertheless connected with Klassen's theories concerning Jews. "The book shows," Bobby wrote, "that Christianity itself is just a Jewish hoax and one more Jewish tool for their conquest of the world." As Regina had proselytized all her life for various causes—always liberal and humanistic ones—so, too, Bobby had become a proselytizer. The pawn did not stray too far from the queen.

At one point Bobby had both *Protocols* and *Nature's Eternal Religion* mailed to Jack and Ethel Collins, without asking whether they wanted to read them. He gave their address directly to the bookseller and then wrote them a letter of apology for disclosing their address.

Bobby's evolving credo was not only anti-Semitic, but as he fell away from the Worldwide Church of God, completely anti-Christian. He discredited both the Old and New Testaments of the Bible, the very book that had been so much a part of his belief system. The idea of God in the form of a man appearing on Earth and then doing a "disappearing act," as Bobby put it, for two thousand years was both "incredible and illogical."

Despite holding what had become strongly antireligious views, Bobby liked to quote from a song written by Les Crane, a radio and television talk-show host. Based on the poem *Desiderata,* the lyrics conveyed that everyone in the universe has a right to be here. Apparently, Bobby didn't see the discrepancy between the gentle acceptance espoused by the song and poem, and his growing philosophy of exclusivity, which rejected all people who didn't believe as he did.

The Collinses didn't know what to say to Bobby about his newfound convictions, which on their face seemed contradictory: If everyone has the right to be here, why was Bobby inveighing against Jews? Following the gift of the Klassen book, Fischer sent the Collinses another hate-filled screed, *Secret World Government,* by Major General Count Cherep-Spiridovich. The count starts off his book by saying that the Jews are Satanists, and it offers the theory that there's a Jewish conspiracy to take over the world. Bobby followed up with another letter: "Did you like the books I sent you?" Jack Collins never answered, and indeed, it's possible that neither he nor Ethel ever read the books.

But Bobby was nothing but complex. Although much of his reading was confined to hate literature, he also embraced other works, such as Dag Hammarskjöld's piquant book of aphorisms and poetry, *Markings;* and Eric Hoffer's *The True Believer,* which in many ways repudiates Armstrongism and about which Bobby said: "The greatest danger to an authoritarian organization like the Worldwide Church of God is when the authority is relaxed a bit—they ease up on the people a bit. Then the true believers begin to lose their fear. Most people are sheep, and they need the support of others."

Nevertheless, despite acknowledging the validity of certain liberal ideas, Bobby seemed to be hardening toward the world and losing sensitivity to people in need. He was also reading Friedrich Nietzsche at this time and was influenced by such books as *The Anti-Christ* and *Thus Spoke Zarathustra.* Although the German philosopher possessed great animus toward Christianity (he referred to Jesus as an idiot), he was definitely not anti-Semitic, possibly creating a conflict in Bobby's beliefs.

Through telephone conversations and correspondence, Regina began to sense Bobby's drift toward racial and religious prejudice, and she was driven to write him when he refused to offer financial help to his titular father, Gerhardt Fischer, and Gerhardt's wife and children who had been briefly imprisoned in South America for their political protests and had just been released. They fled to France. Regina's words were a not-so-subtle attempt to educate her son:

I was really shocked when you refused to discuss the matter or do anything . . . to let somebody go under without the slightest interest in the matter. That is bad for the person who does it, too. It takes longer but that person is destroyed gradually, by his or her own conscience. The greater the person's mind and talent, the greater the destruction. A stupid, coarse person may not suffer; he does not believe his behavior was not worthy of himself. If you are thinking I am making this up, read Hawthorne's *The Scarlet Letter*. . . . Don't let millions of people down who regard you as a genius and an example to themselves. It's no joke to be in your position. But even if you were an unknown, just being a decent person is a job these days. It's easier to shut your eyes. But that's what people did in Nazi Germany while people were being tortured and murdered, children gassed to death like vermin. It was more convenient not to want to hear about it or talk about it because then their conscience would have made them do something about it.

So if you are now going to be mad at me, don't be. Remember, whatever you do or whatever happens I am still your mother and there is nothing I would refuse you if you wanted or needed it, and nothing would change it.

Love,

Mother

Rumors began to spread that Bobby and his mother were estranged. Though Fischer *was* alienating some people, such as Jack and Ethel Collins, who'd been virtual grandparents to him, he did remain close to his mother, as their ongoing correspondence at the time indicates. As the saying goes, they could agree to disagree.

Bobby's life during this period was not all theological, political, or philosophical, however. There were also legal battles to wage.

The old adage "Talk is cheap until you hire a lawyer" didn't apply to

Bobby since he had two high-profile lawyers working for him pro bono. Still clinging to the material support of the Church, despite his grumbling about it, Bobby was using Stanley Rader as his "on-site" attorney in California for present and future deals and Paul Marshall in New York for any business left over that concerned the Icelandic match. Three issues emerged, all in 1973, concerning publications and film rights. One was a sixty-four-page booklet, *1972 World Chess Championship, Boris Spassky vs. Bobby Fischer: Icelandic Chess Federation Official Commemorative Program,* which presented the games with notes written by Gligoric. It also gave a history of the match—before, during, and after—and was not particularly flattering to Bobby. Both Rader and Marshall considered a lawsuit since Bobby hadn't given permission for the booklet, since his name on the cover falsely implied that he'd had a role in its creation; and since neither he nor Spassky were to receive any remuneration for its publication. Marshall wrote a cease and desist letter to the prime minister of Iceland and to the president of the Icelandic Chess Federation, but it's not known how many copies of the booklets were sold from bookstores in the United States before it was withdrawn from sale.

It was then announced that a book entitled *Bobby Fischer vs. the Rest of the World* was to be published in 1974, written by Brad Darrach, the *Life* magazine writer who'd covered the match and was given exclusive access to Bobby. Marshall investigated a possible injunction to stop publication of the work since according to Bobby, Darrach had allegedly violated his contract: Supposedly, he'd agreed to write only *articles* about Bobby, not a book. Gaining such an injunction through what is called "prior restraint" was almost impossible in the courts, however, and Marshall advised Bobby to wait until the book was published. Then, if there were any other violations by Darrach, such as libel or invasion of privacy, a stronger suit could be brought. Marshall, after all, was well aware of Darrach's reputation for revealing the most intimate details of the lives of his subjects. Bobby ultimately did go to court but lost, the judge throwing the case out because it was so poorly presented and without sufficient evidence.

The third legal problem was that Bobby was being sued by Chester Fox because he'd interfered with the filming of the Icelandic match. Although Bobby had received numerous requests to give a deposition, he continued to refuse, so the case was dragging on.

While he was waiting to see how these entanglements would work out, Bobby began to prepare for his defense of the World Championship, almost a year away.

Anatoly Karpov, a pale, short, slight twenty-three-year-old economics student from Leningrad University, who always looked as though he could use a haircut, seemed an unlikely contender for the title against Bobby Fischer, the thirty-two-year-old ex-wunderkind from Brooklyn, the World Champion with the physique of an athlete and the confidence of a king. But Karpov had qualified to play Bobby by winning his three Candidates matches, during which he'd played forty-six grueling games and only lost three. Contrasted with Bobby at the same age, he was further along in his chess ability by several years, and many chess players—not only Soviets—were saying that he could be even greater than Bobby as he matured. Bobby's former nemesis Botvinnik had become Karpov's teacher.

Hoping the match would be another Reykjavik—in explosive media attention if not financial outcome—cities around the world submitted bids to host the competition. Topping them all was Manila, which came up with a staggering $5 million offer—a sum that, were the match to happen, would make it one of the most lucrative sporting events (if, indeed, chess is a sport) ever. There was only one problem: Bobby Fischer.

He petitioned FIDE for a rules change that would scrap the old Reykjavik-style method of determining the winner of a twenty-four-game match. The old method dictated that in the event all the games were played and there was a tie, the reigning champion would retain the title. Bobby proposed a new approach whereby a match would consist of an *unlimited* number of games, and the first player who scored ten wins would be named the winner. Draws wouldn't count, and in case of a 9–9 tie, the reigning champion would retain his title.

FIDE agreed to the ten-game-win idea but voted against the 9–9 rule. Also, instead of approving the idea of an unlimited number of games, it narrowed the number to thirty-six—which struck Bobby as an outrageously small number if draws weren't going to count. This was hardly a compromise. Bobby claimed that his system would actually reduce the number of draws, that it would produce games in which the players would take more chances, trying to achieve wins rather than half points.

Fischer cabled the FIDE Extraordinary Council in the Netherlands that his match condition proposals were "non-negotiable." He also pointed out in *Chess Life & Review* that his demands weren't unprecedented and had been used in many great championship matches: "Steinitz, Tchigorin, Lasker (too), Gunsberg, Zukertort . . . all played under the ten-win system (and some matches with the 9–9 clause). The whole idea is to make the players draw blood and give the spectators their money's worth."

Colonel Edmund B. Edmondson, the executive director of the U.S. Chess Federation, attempted in vain to get FIDE to change its vote, or get Bobby to change his mind. The story of the machinations employed to enable the Fischer-Karpov World Championship match to take place are enough to fill a separate book—and have!—but the details are hardly dramatic in retrospect.

Fischer continued his intransigence: FIDE *must* change the rules to meet his demands or he simply wouldn't play. He began making God-like pronouncements about the match to his friends: "I will *punish* them and not play," as if retribution was his sovereign right to dispense. The deadline for moving ahead or abandoning the match was looming, and then it came . . . and went, with no further word from the champion. FIDE gave Bobby one more day to change his mind. Euwe finally cabled him:

YOUR PROFESSIONALISM, COMPETITIVE SPIRIT, AND
OUTSTANDING SKILL HAVE THRILLED ALL DURING THE YEAR YOU
FOUGHT TO ATTAIN THE WORLD CHAMPIONSHIP. FIDE GENERAL
ASSEMBLY ASKS THAT YOU RECONSIDER POSSIBLITY OF
DEFENDING TITLE.

When Bobby didn't answer and the press interviewed Euwe about it, he issued an apt reply: "At the moment we are in a complete stalemate." Bobby was about to checkmate himself, however.

The next day he sent the following cable (in part) to Euwe:

FIDE HAS DECIDED AGAINST MY PARTICIPATION IN THE 1975
WORLD CHESS CHAMPIONSHIP. THEREFORE, I RESIGN MY FIDE

WORLD CHESS CHAMPIONSHIP TITLE. SINCERELY, BOBBY
FISCHER.

His echo of resolve was heard around the world.

The New York Times ran a story by international grandmaster Robert Byrne, "Bobby Fischer's Fear of Failing," which opined that Bobby's fears had always kept him out of certain tournaments because he thought if he lost a game or two at the beginning of an event, he was practically eliminated as a prizewinner. The main fear of every top notch chess player, the story went on, "is the inexplicable error from which no one is immune," the chance blunder. Even Paul Marshall, Bobby's lawyer, addressed Bobby's "dread": "Bobby fears the unknown, whatever lies beyond his control. He tries to eliminate any element of chance from his life and his chess." What everyone seemed to overlook was that at the board Bobby feared no one. He did show nervousness before a game, as certain great actors show stage fright before a demanding performance, but this state of anxiety shouldn't be confused with fear. This anxiety was the mother of Bobby's foresight, it kept him on edge and gave him an advantage. Ultimately, it was his supreme confidence in himself that made him a great player.

A psychoanalyst, M. Barrie Richmond, M.D., wrote a dissertation titled "The Meaning of Bobby Fischer's Decision" that took issue with Robert Byrne and held that Fischer should be thought of as a profound artist, a phenomenon on the order of a Picasso. Richmond maintained that Bobby's failure to defend his title bespoke a responsibility he felt to himself as the World Champion: His attempt to shape, create, and alter his own universe of rules addressed that burden and had nothing to do with fear.

Without moving a pawn, on April 3, 1975, Anatoly Karpov was declared the twelfth World Champion by Dr. Max Euwe, president of FIDE. And on that day, Bobby Fischer became the first-ever champion to willingly relinquish the title and along with it the chance to compete for the winner's share of a $5 million purse . . . *five million dollars!* It was the largest refusal of a prize fund in sports history. The winner would have received $3.5 million, and the loser would have walked away with $1.5 million, guaranteed. It was all declined, and over a mere rules dispute.

"I had no idea why Fischer refused to defend his title," Karpov later said, somewhat coldly. Although he was champion, he was without a convincing portfolio, his right to wear the crown left in doubt by Bobby's shadow. He was also bereft of the millions of dollars he would have received had the two men played. He huffed: "It is an unprecedented instance in chess history."

Just to get away from it all—the World Championship imbroglio and the constant stalking of him by reporters and photographers—Bobby took a two-month cruise by himself around the world. His boat trips in the past—to and from Europe, and from the Philippines to the United States via Hong Kong—had been thoroughly relaxing: no telephone contact, no mail, no people bothering him, and magnificent meals served all day long. It was heaven. Now that he'd grown a beard, most people didn't recognize him, and he recaptured the peace and incognito of his earlier trips. It eased him into a placid mood, at least for the trip's duration. He was still prone to ruminate on race and religion, however, and at one point he wrote to Ethel Collins that he liked Indonesia, where he stayed on a farm for a few days while the boat docked at Bali. Noting that most of the people were Muslims, Bobby seemed pleased that they'd retained their "cultural purity." At New Delhi, he bought for $15 a peg-in travel chess set with a beautifully detailed design that was made of fragrant sandalwood—but he felt guilty about paying so little for it. He realized that the artisan who carved it probably received only a fraction of the sale price for his labor.

Bobby was content in his basement apartment on Mockingbird Lane in South Pasadena, a small, quiet place out of sight from the world, and he lived there for several years. His friends from the Church, Arthur and Claudia Mokarow, owned the house, and Claudia became a kind of buffer for Bobby, answering queries, shooing away reporters, and serving as his majordomo and resident Gorgon, even to the point of considering offers (and rejecting them) without even discussing them with Bobby.

Bobby's support came from unexpected sources. New York City's mayor Edward I. Koch wrote him a letter trying to convince him to come back to the chessboard. "Your extraordinary skill and genius at the most difficult of games is a source of pride to me and to all who stand in the light of your remarkable accomplishments."

Often, photographers or reporters staked out the front of the house, attempting to get Bobby's photograph or interview him. He once said that the only thing he feared was a journalist, and slipping in and out of the house without being confronted by the press took the ingenuity of a Houdini and the dexterity of a gymnast. Sometimes it sent Bobby into a panic.

If a friend wanted to reach him, he or she would call Claudia first, and she'd run downstairs and either give Bobby the message or leave it for him, and then Bobby would call back if he so chose. Bobby never accepted calls directly unless he'd initiated them. Claudia would also drive him to and from certain out-of-the-way Los Angeles destinations; otherwise he was quite adept at traveling by bus to wherever he wanted to go. He became a man of routine: up and out by four p.m., and into Los Angeles or downtown Pasadena for his first meal of the day, followed by his hunt through the bookstores, searching, searching, searching. He loved Indian and Chinese food and consumed what seemed like barrelsful of salads whenever they were available.

When he was finished with that day's pursuit of books, he returned to South Pasadena in the early evening for a workout at the gym, forty-five minutes of swimming, and then a sauna; by nightfall he was back at Mockingbird Lane, settling into his world of reading, and studying chess: *peace*. Unless a friend was visiting, he rarely went out at night, enjoying the comfort and safety of his home.

The apartment was strewn with books, magazines, and piles of clothing and had the smell of fresh oranges: Bobby would buy them and other fruits and vegetables by the bagful. Every day, he'd drink one or two pint glasses of carrot juice, one right after the other. Dozens of bottles of vitamin pills, Indian herbal medicines, Mexican rattlesnake pills, lotions, and exotic teas were piled on tables and ledges everywhere, all to help keep him on what he believed was a strict, healthful diet—and to treat some ailments he had from time to time. Often he'd take his hand-cranked juicer to a restaurant with him, order breakfast, ask for an empty glass, and break out a half dozen oranges, cut them in half, and squeeze them at his table while customers and waiters looked on in either puzzlement or amusement. He began to put on bulk and muscle and he seemed to be in perfect physical shape.

He'd collected hundreds of chess magazines in five or six languages, and all genres of chess books, the majority of which were sent to him by his mother. Now living in Jena, East Germany, behind the Iron Curtain, where she was completing her medical degree, Regina could purchase the latest Soviet chess literature quite inexpensively, and she regularly made shipments to her son, either at random or by request. At one point Bobby had to tell her to stop sending chess books because he was running out of room.

Far into the night he'd play over the latest games by himself—from tournaments in places ranging from England to Latvia to Yugoslavia to Bulgaria—and he'd hiss and scream as he followed the moves. So loudly did he exclaim "Yes!", "Absurd!", "It's the knight!", or "Always the rook on that rank!" that his pronouncements could be heard on the quiet lane where he lived. Bobby's outbursts would startle the infrequent passersby and sometimes produce complaints from neighbors.

By the late 1970s, Fischer hadn't played a single game of chess in public since Iceland. He was continuing to study the game, but he spent more time exploring his theories on religion. At one point, he was spotted in a parking lot with an armful of anti-Semitic flyers that promulgated the superiority of the Aryan race. In between handing out the flyers to those who walked by, he placed his declarations on windshields. Gradually, his savings were evaporating, and other than biannual royalty checks from his books, *Bobby Fischer Teaches Chess* and *My 60 Memorable Games*—which netted him roughly $6,000 a year in total—he had no other source of income.

Either by choice or necessity, Bobby moved out of the Mokarow house and settled in Los Angeles, in a small, dingy, dark, and inexpensive furnished room on Orange Avenue, one block off Wilshire Boulevard. Within a short while, though, the rent for the room became too much of a financial burden to carry. So he wrote to his mother, who was living in Nicaragua doing pro bono medical work for the poor, to see if she could help out. She immediately instructed his sister, Joan, to send the entire amount of her monthly Social Security check to Bobby to assist him with his rent. Joan had been collecting Regina's checks and then banking them for her so that she'd have a small nest egg when she returned to the United States. Bobby continued to accept the proceeds of his mother's Social Security checks for years.

His settlement on Orange Avenue wasn't permanent, however, and he eventually began renting in the skid row section of L.A. near MacArthur

Park, taking rooms in what might be called flophouses, sometimes just for the night or by the week.

In time, judging from his uncombed and disheveled physical appearance, it was difficult to differentiate Bobby from the down-and-outers of the area. His ten $400 suits were in storage somewhere, but he just didn't seem to care to dress well anymore. He stopped regularly working out, started developing a paunch, began dressing in whatever clothes he happened to have handy, rarely had his hair or beard cut professionally, and even had the fillings of his teeth removed.

This last piece of physical business has been so distorted by the press over the years that it has entered the "Bobby Fischer Urban Legend Storybook" as *proof* of his "insanity." Somewhere he was quoted as saying that he'd had his fillings removed because he feared that the Soviets could affect his mind by sending harmful radio signals through the metal in his teeth—and virtually every profile and book written about Bobby since has mentioned it. Either the quote was spurious or misremembered, or Bobby was joshing the re- porter who recorded it, because the truth is that he had the fillings removed for what he believed was a legitimate health reason. He was solicitous to- ward Ethel Collins about this, since she'd been suffering with a chronic gum problem for years.

Bobby believed that false teeth and metal fillings (especially silver) were detrimental to periodontal health because they irritated the gums. He was also convinced that mercury in most fillings has a toxic effect on the body.

Consequently, Bobby had all of his fillings removed by a dentist in a quick procedure (it only took a few minutes), and he recommended that Ethel do so too. He admitted that eating without fillings was "uncomfortable," but it was better than the alternative of losing all of one's teeth, which he predicted would happen if the fillings remained.

Years later in Iceland, he told his closest friend Gardar Sverrisson that the "radio signal" story about the fillings was bogus: The reason he'd had them removed was because he felt that fillings caused more problems than they cured.

The problem for Bobby became that, since his teeth no longer had fillings, they also no longer had any support and became more fragile. They were also open to decay, and therefore began to chip away. The result: over time he lost a number of teeth. Since he no longer believed in going to a dentist (nor could he afford it) for crowns, implants, or replacements, his broken and missing teeth added to his vagrant look.

Despite his cordial exchanges with the Collinses, and his attempt at proselytizing them into accepting his conspiracy theories, he hurt Jack Collins deeply when he refused to write the introduction to Jack's book *My Seven Chess Prodigies* (1974). Jack had told him that if he would just write a short introduction, it would mean a sizable advance from the publisher. Collins needed the extra money; although not indigent, he was always short of income since he was living off Ethel's salary as a part-time nurse. His request of Bobby was couched in cordial, nonpleading terms, but Bobby heartlessly never answered him, and Lombardy stepped in to do the job.

When Bobby became unbearably lonely for companionship, he would often head up north to Palo Alto and stay with his sister and her husband, Russell Targ, a Stanford University scientist who was an authority on extrasensory perception. Joan was Jewish, as were Russell and their three children, and after hearing Bobby's rants time and again against Jews, the family asked their houseguest to leave.

Living not too far from his sister was Bobby's friend, grandmaster Peter Biyiasas and his wife Ruth, so Bobby stayed there for weeks on end. Over a period of four months Fischer and Biyiasas played seventeen five-minute games and Bobby won them all, with Biyiasis claiming that he never got into an endgame once: Bobby would just wipe him off the board in short order every time.

On three occasions, Bobby went to Berkeley in the San Francisco Bay Area to visit Walter Browne, an Australian-American grandmaster. They went over some of the games from Browne's recent tournaments, although they didn't play chess, and once took a long walk at sunset to enjoy the spectacular views of the city across the Bay. During the walk, Bobby kept up a continuous spiel about the Jewish World Conspiracy and made various anti-Semitic remarks, but when they returned to the house and sat down for dinner with Browne's family he ceased his outré comments. On his third visit with Browne, Bobby was to stay overnight. After dinner he asked to use the phone and talked long distance for the rest of the evening—"perhaps for four hours," Browne later recalled. Finally Browne said, "You know, Bobby, you'll really have to get off the phone. I can't afford this." Bobby hung up and immediately said he had to leave and couldn't spend the night with the Brownes. They never talked again.

Back in Los Angeles, Bobby wrote to his mother, asking her when she could visit him, hoping it would be "soon," and advising her to sail from England instead of flying, telling her that his boat trips in the past had been "a real experience." At the end of the letter he included instructions: "Write to me at the Post Office box and do not put my name on the address. It's not necessary."

He simply did not want contact from anyone he didn't know, and he made it quite clear, peremptorily, to Jack Collins that *no mail*—even important, flattering, or personal messages—should be forwarded to him. Possibly, he was worried that that a letter might contain poison or that a package could contain an explosive.

Chess colleagues of Bobby's—including grandmaster Robert Byrne—have said that the real reason he was so private, and didn't want anyone to know where he was at any given time, was that he feared a KGB assassination plot. Bobby believed, they said, that the Soviets were so enraged by his winning the crown from Spassky and thereby diminishing their greatest cultural achievement that they wanted him murdered. Of course, Bobby's fears were thought by some to be incipient paranoia, and although it was highly unlikely that the KGB was plotting against him, even paranoids can have real enemies. At restaurants Bobby always carried with him a virtual pharmacy of remedies and potions to immediately counteract any poisons that the Soviets might slip into his food or drink. Hans Ree, a Dutch grandmaster and an accomplished journalist, summed it up this way: "It is undeniable that Fischer had real enemies and that they were extremely powerful ones." He then went on to indicate that Mikhail Suslov, one of the most influential Soviet leaders, became involved in issuing instructions on how to subvert (not murder) Bobby, by creating a situation "unfavorable to R. Fischer." Ree concludes: "There is nothing in the [KGB] documents that there ever were any plans to kill him. But that doesn't mean there weren't any." The important point is that Bobby was convinced it was so and acted accordingly.

Part of his desire for privacy may have been attributable to his readings. Nietzsche said that solitude makes us tougher toward ourselves and more tender toward others. He held that in both ways it improves one's character. It's possible that since Bobby was influenced by Nietzsche to some extent, he was following this course to the extreme. By refusing to read letters that might have been laudatory or complimentary, or those that would have been for his own good, such as a letter from an old friend or an invitation to be a guest of honor at West Point, he was deliberately maintaining his isolation.

It was clear, though, that Bobby had a very difficult time considering anything that wasn't on his own agenda. He was so focused on his path of righteousness and giving free rein to his different-drummer sensibilities that he refused to be distracted by trivia—as he saw it—entering his mailbox from a possibly unknown or unwelcome source.

Because Jack Collins was known as Bobby's teacher, and he was readily available for contact—his telephone number was listed in the Manhattan telephone directory—he received calls and messages on a daily basis from people who for various reasons wanted to reach Bobby. Unfortunately for them, and even sadder for Bobby, after Collins received the letter warning him against forwarding anything, that conduit was cut off and the requests for contact drifted down into wastebasket oblivion.

Generally, Bobby was depressed, but he still managed to get up and out every day. He was attentive to his surroundings and hardly limited in his physical activity. But in retrospect, he was upset at having passed on the chance to acquire a portion of that $5 million purse in 1975. Who knew, after all, when the next opportunity to earn significant money would come along? The truth was, having to make ends meet was wearing on him. Also preying on his mind were his failure to find romantic love, and his constant religious doubts. This cumulative sadness contributed to his not wanting to be with people . . . unless he felt highly secure and comfortable with them. So he walked and walked for miles every day, lost in his dreams, or dwelling in a meditative state.

A sportswriter once wrote that Fischer was the fastest walker he ever saw outside of an Olympian. He took great strides, creating a slight wind in his wake, his left arm swinging high with his left leg, his right with his right, in an unusual cadence. Another journalist, Brad Darrach—who Fischer was suing—said that when he walked with Fischer, he felt as if he were Dopey, one of the Seven Dwarfs, trying to keep up with the big folks. Fischer's erstwhile friend Walter Browne talked about walking with Bobby—very fast—from the Manhattan Chess Club all the way down to Greenwich Village on the West Side of Manhattan—over three miles—having dinner at a Mediterranean restaurant, and then walking all the way back uptown on the East Side, another three miles. Walking gave Bobby time to think—or to lose himself—and it kept him trim. He listed it, along with sports and reading, among his favorite pastimes.

After visiting Harry Sneider at the gym one day—he'd continued his friendship with the trainer even after severing his relationship with the Worldwide Church of God—Bobby chose to take one of his mammoth treks around the city of Pasadena. He walked alongside the Foothill Freeway and then walked back and turned at Lake Avenue, passing the Kaiser Permanente medical facility. A police cruiser stopped him. Apparently there had been a bank robbery in the area, and Bobby fit the description of the robber. He was asked for his name, address, age, type of work, etc., and although Bobby claimed that he answered the questions dutifully, there was something suspicious about him, according to the police interrogator. His appearance didn't help, untidy as he was and carrying a soiled shopping bag containing a juicer and a number of hate books. The more questions that were asked, the more Bobby became belligerent. Perhaps because he was nervous, or perhaps because he kept moving from one flophouse to another, he couldn't remember his address. Eventually, he was brought to the station and booked for vagrancy (since the bank robber had already been caught), although he did have $9 and some change on him at the time. He was stripped of his clothing, put in a cell, and not allowed a phone call to enlist help. Moreover, he later claimed that the guards brutalized him and deprived him of food.

Just so the world would know what he'd gone through those two days, when Bobby was finally released he wrote a punch-by-punch description of his ordeal, an eighty-five-hundred-word essay titled "I Was *Tortured* in the Pasadena Jailhouse!" Although not reaching the virtuosic literary heights of incarceration essays penned by writers such as Thoreau or Martin Luther King Jr., the document was an oddly compelling account of the execrable details of his experience. Described by some as incoherent ranting and too melodramatic, Bobby's story, if it could be trusted on the basics, *was* truly horrifying. He was innocent, he claimed, and yet he was made to parade through the halls naked and threatened with being put in a mental institution.

Bobby self-published the essay in a fourteen-page booklet, with red-and-white stripes on the front to resemble cell bars, and signed it "Robert D. James (professionally known as Robert J. Fischer or Bobby Fischer, The World Chess Champion)." He had ten thousand copies printed, which cost him $3,257. How in his near destitute state he was able to obtain the needed money is not known. He sold his essay for $1 a copy, and Claudia Mokarow handled the distribution and sales. Breaking his own privacy rules, Bobby even included a PO box number that he could be written to in care of so that the reader could order "additional copies." Ironically, he ended up making money from the project—after the printing, shipping, and advertising costs were deducted. Twenty-five years later, an original copy of *I Was Tortured . . .* was selling as a collector's item for upward of $500. A collector asked Pal Benko to see if Bobby would autograph a copy of his *j'accuse*. Benko requested and Bobby refused: "Yes, I wrote it, but I had a terrible time in that jail. I want to forget about it. No, I don't want to sign it."

The pamphlet is important in offering a glimpse of Bobby's state of mind at that time (May 1981): It shows his utter outrage in being manhandled and falsely accused; his refusal to bend to authority; his use of a pseudonym (even Regina had begun to address her letters to him as "Robert D. James," the "D" standing for "Dallas") for self-protection; and his designation of himself as "The World Chess Champion." Regarding this self-description, Bobby explained to a friend that he had never been defeated. He resigned the FIDE World Championship, but he believed the true World Champion's title was still rightfully his. Further, he claimed that he had not won the World Championship in Iceland in 1972; he already *was* the World Champion: His title was stolen, he said, by the Russians.

Bobby's life, post-Reykjavik, has been referred to by the press as his "Wilderness Years," as indeed they were: living in the seamy underside of Los Angeles for the most part, twenty years out of view, refusing offers of money, on the edge of vagrancy, attempting to evaporate into anonymity so as to be shielded from perceived threats.

Money, however, was still available if he chose to avail himself of it. But the complications in getting it to him, or having him accept it, were enormous. First, those who had offers had to *find* him, not an easy task because he kept changing his address, gave his telephone number to virtually no one, and didn't have an answering machine. His use of an alias also increased the difficulty of tracking him down. The mailbox at one of his apartments read "R. D. James." Second, if contact *was* made, he'd never accept the first offer, and he usually named an amount that was double or triple—or more—pricing himself out of the market. Third, he refused to sign any contracts, making it impossible for most corporations or individuals to proceed with any kind of legally binding arrangement. Stories were told, unconfirmed by this writer, that when he was flat broke, he'd accept short telephone calls from chess players at a charge of $2,500 each, and would also give lessons over the phone for $10,000. If the stories were true, how these calls were arranged, how long they lasted, and who made them aren't known.

It *is* known that the Canadian Broadcasting Corporation wanted to interview Bobby for a documentary: He demanded $5,000 just to discuss it over the phone, with no promises of anything else. The network refused. A reporter from *Newsday*, which had one of the largest circulations of any daily tabloid in the United States, sought an interview with Bobby and was told by Claudia Mokarow to "go back to your publisher and ask for a million dollars, and then we'll talk about whether Bobby will grant you an interview." Carol J. Williams, a reporter for the *Los Angeles Times*, approached Bobby for an interview and was told his required fee was $200,000. His request was refused "on principle." Freelance photographers were willing to pay $5,000 to anyone who could arrange just to locate Bobby so they could take a single photograph, and perhaps pay $10,000 to Bobby if he'd *allow* the picture to be taken. It never happened. Edward Fox, a freelance journalist for the British *Independent* newspaper, wrote of Bobby: "The years passed, and the last extant photographs were growing more and more out of date. No one knew what Bobby Fischer looked like any more. Into the vacuum of his non-presence rushed a fog of rumors and fragmentary information. He existed as a vortex of recycled facts and second-hand quotes. Every now and then there would be a 'sighting' of a forlorn, bearded figure."

A sensationalistic television show, *Now It Can Be Told*, spent weeks in the early 1990s trying to capture the reclusive Bobby for their broadcast, and managed to film him for a few seconds in a parking lot, getting out of an automobile, en route to a restaurant with Claudia Mokarow and her husband.

Bobby Fischer! It was the first time he'd been seen by the public in almost two decades. His pants and jacket were wrinkled, but he didn't look as derelict as some of the press accounts had indicated. Aside from the fact that his hair was thinning and he'd put on weight and grown a beard, he was the unmistakable, broad-shouldered, swaggering Bobby Fischer.

12

Fischer-Spassky Redux

BOBBY'S CHESS DRAGON was not only stirring in the cave, it was lashing its tail. Perhaps because he could no longer tolerate his downtrodden life, living off his mother's checks and receiving just an occasional trickle of cash from here or there, Bobby wanted to get back to the game . . . desperately. But his urge to rejoin the fray wasn't all about remuneration—it was the call to battle, the game itself, that he missed: the prestige; the silence (hopefully) of the tournament room; the sibilant buzz of the kibitzers (damn them); the *life* of chess. Jonathan Swift defined war as "that mad game the world loves to play." Fischer felt exactly the same way about chess. But could he find his way, existentially, back to the board? Hermann Hesse, in his masterful novel *Magister Ludi (The Glass Bead Game)*, told of someone whose knowledge of "the game" was Fischer-like: "One who had experienced the ultimate meaning of the game within himself would no longer be a player; he would no longer dwell in the world of multiplicity and would no longer delight in invention, construction, and combination, since he would know altogether different joys and raptures." The difference is that the joys and raptures away from the board weren't really there for Bobby.

Spassky provided a way back to the board. He contacted Bobby in 1990 and informed him that Bessel Kok, the man who was running for the presidency of FIDE that year (1990), was interested in organizing a Fischer-Spassky rematch, and there might be millions—although not the $5 million he'd passed up in 1975 for a match with Karpov—available for the prize fund.

Kok, a Dutch businessman of extreme wealth, was president of a Belgium-based banking company, SWIFT, and was responsible for organizing several international tournaments. Kok had a noble agenda: He wanted Bobby to continue his career, and he wanted to be a privileged witness to his games, as did almost all chess players.

A meeting was planned to discuss the match, with Kok agreeing to pay all the expenses for Bobby to fly, first class, to Belgium and be lodged at the five-star Sheraton Brussels Hotel. To avoid journalists, Bobby checked in under the name of Brown. He mentioned to Kok that he'd need some cash for pocket money upon arrival. Twenty-five hundred dollars in cash was waiting for him at the hotel.

In addition to Bobby, Kok also invited Spassky and his wife Marina to Brussels. For four days, the trio spent mostly all of their time at Kok's suburban mansion, but it wasn't all a discussion of the possible match. At one point, Fischer and Kok joined the Spasskys in a doubles tennis match; there were elegant, candlelit dinners and postprandial conversations, and a few outings into Brussels itself. Kok's wife, Pierette Broodhaers, an attorney, said that she had a "normal and friendly" conversation with Bobby, not at all about chess. Nor, according to her, did he show any signs of the eccentricities the press kept referring to, with the exception of his speaking too loudly. "Maybe he is used to living alone so nobody listens to him," she said, sensing his loneliness. He forbade her to take a photograph of him.

One evening, the men, who were joined by Jan Timman from Holland, the number three–ranked chess player in the world, went off to what Broodhaers described as a "raunchy" nightclub in downtown Brussels. Timman recalled meeting Fischer for the first time: "The most interesting thing was that I had once dreamed of meeting Fischer in a nightclub. Funny I had never entertained the hope of [actually] meeting him. When I broke through internationally, he had just stopped [playing]." Talking about who might be considered the greatest player of all time, he said, "As far as I am concerned, Fischer is the best ever."

The amount being mentioned as the purse for the rematch was $2,500,000. Although Bobby was in want financially, this prize fund was not acceptable to him. Spassky wanted to go through with it, but no deal could be arranged. Little did either of them know, but Kok had already decided not to pursue the possible match. He found Fischer's neo-Nazi remarks about Jews to be "beyond the abhorrent" and concluded that any large-scale match involving him would spell trouble. Spassky flew back to Paris, and Bobby boarded a train for Germany.

Since he was in Europe—his first time there in almost twenty years—Bobby felt he should stay awhile. Gerhardt Fischer, the man listed on Bobby's birth certificate as his father, was living in Berlin, and at eighty-two he was not in good health. The press had learned that Gerhardt was somewhere in Germany—and that Bobby was in the country—and they were trying to track down the father so they could interview his famous son. Reporters believed that it was possible Bobby visited him, but there's no proof he did.

In the late 1980s, during the Chess Bundesliga competition in Germany, Boris Spassky had met a young woman named Petra Stadler. He felt paternal toward her and thought Bobby might be interested in meeting her, so he gave her Fischer's address in Los Angeles and suggested she write to him and send him her photograph. In 1988 she did just that, and to her surprise Fischer phoned her from California. Near the beginning of their conversation, he asked her if she was an Aryan. Recollecting the incident years later, she claims she replied: "I think so."

Fischer invited her to visit him in Los Angeles, where she stayed in a hotel, and the two spent the next few weeks getting to know each other. Then Petra returned to her home in Seeheim, Germany. At that time, Fischer was impoverished, so it was impossible for him to fly to Germany with her. Now that he was in Europe in 1990, courtesy of Bessel Kok, Bobby visited Petra, and with the "pocket money" Kok had given him, his mother's Social Security income, and some small royalty checks for his books, he lived for almost a year in Seeheim and in nearby towns, moving from hotel to hotel to avoid reporters, and spending time with Petra for as long as their relationship lasted.

Petra married Russian grandmaster Rustem Dautov in 1992, and in 1995 she wrote a book titled *Bobby Fischer—Wie er wirklich ist—Ein Jahr mit dem Schachgenie* (Fischer as He Really Is: A Year with a Chess Genius).

Boris Spassky saw a copy and wrote Bobby a letter of apology for having introduced him to Petra. It was dated March 23, 1995.

He told Bobby that when he introduced Petra to him he meant well, but shortly after they met "she started to talk too much about you to other people." Sensing that Petra would reveal secrets, Spassky warned Bobby to "be careful."

After Petra's revealing book was published, Spassky was very upset, primarily because he didn't want the woman or her book to come between him and Bobby and ruin their good relationship. As a result of Spassky's letter, Bobby never spoke to Petra again, but he accepted his friend's apology and maintained cordial relations with Spassky.

While he was in Germany, Bobby went to Bamberg to visit Lothar Schmid, who'd served as arbiter in the 1972 match with Spassky. Schmid's castle housed the largest known privately owned chess library in the world. Bobby wanted to scrutinize the library and view Schmid's chess art masterpieces. While there, they also analyzed a number of games together, an experience that indicated to Schmid that Bobby's command of the game hadn't waned in his years away from public competition; Schmid claimed that Bobby's analysis was still remarkably brilliant.

After having been Schmid's houseguest, Bobby moved to an inn in Pulvermühle, close to Bamberg, located in a valley between Nuremberg and Bayreuth. The inn was known to be friendly to those who played the game and was family-run by Kaspar Bezold, an amateur chess player. Petrosian was a guest there when he played in the international tournament in Bamberg in 1968, and players from throughout Europe often stayed there on holiday.

Schmid made the arrangements for Bobby to stay in Pulvermühle and, to keep journalists at bay, had him register under an assumed name. Staying at a friendly Bavarian inn in the countryside is usually a pleasant affair and can be a chance for renewal, offering long walks in the pastoral countryside, succulent German cooking, decadent desserts, and steins of *Rauchbier,* the smoked malt and hops from Bamberg that is famous throughout the Free State of Bavaria. But what Bobby liked most was that nobody at the inn, other than Bezold and his son Michael, an up-and-coming chess player, knew who he was. Bobby gave Michael lessons, and the young man went on to become an international grandmaster some eight years later, perhaps inspired by his meeting with the world's greatest player.

Bobby studied and practiced his German and was becoming semi-fluent after three months. He might have stayed in Pulvermühle much longer, or at least as long as his money held out, but he was spotted by a journalist from the German magazine *Stern,* who'd tracked him down. Bobby checked out immediately and was never seen in Pulvermühle again.

When Bobby returned from Europe and collected his months of accumulated mail from Claudia Mokarow, there was an unusual letter waiting for him. It would change his life.

I WOULD LIKE TO SELL YOU THE
WORLD'S BEST VACUUM CLEANER!

That was how the letter started off. Beneath that headline was a hand-drawn picture of a vacuum cleaner, rendered in color. Why had this been mailed to Fischer and how had the sender found his address? The odd document continued:

NOW THAT I HAVE YOUR
INTEREST, TURN THE PAGE.

It was, in fact, a letter from a seventeen-year-old girl, Zita Rajcsanyi, one of Hungary's most promising women chess players. She had sent the letter to the U.S. Chess Federation, and asked them to forward it to Bobby. "Now that I have your interest," the letter stated, "I want to tell you the real reason why I wrote to you." Why did you stop playing? Why did you disappear? she went on to ask. She wrote that she'd been intrigued by Bobby ever since she'd read about him in a book on the history of World Chess Champions. Bobby noticed that the postmark on the letter's envelope was many months past, and there was actually *another* letter from Zita in his pile of unopened mail. She was persistent and wanted an answer.

Thus it was that one morning, at about six a.m. Hungarian time, Zita's phone rang. Zita's father, an official of FIDE, answered and immediately woke her. "Hi, this is Bobby." He told her that the reason he was responding was that her letters were so "weird" and quite different from the average fan letters he received, but he thanked her for them. He told her that the reason he wasn't playing was because the Russians cheat, and over the course of future letters and phone calls he elaborated on his theory regarding how the games played by Kasparov and Karpov had all been prearranged and that he believed that Kasparov and Karpov were actually agents of the Russian regime. He asked if she was Jewish. "Everyone who is a Soviet, and everyone who is Jewish, cannot be trusted," he affirmed. When she objected to his ranting, he broke off the conversation and didn't call back for months. More phone calls eventually followed, however, often in the middle of the night, and they also started a pen pal correspondence.

Eventually, he asked Zita whether she'd like to visit him. He told her he'd send her an airline ticket and that she could stay with a friend of his, since his room was too small and it wouldn't be appropriate for her to stay with him in any event. He was right: After Regina had visited him once, she wrote to him about his cramped quarters: "You can hardly turn around."

Zita applied for a visa immediately in the summer of 1992 and after many weeks of bureaucratic processing, she arrived in Los Angeles. Bobby met her at the airport. She did not recognize him because of his beard. Although he'd paid for the round-trip ticket, when Zita met him she discovered that he was practically penniless. She lent him a few hundred dollars, virtually all of her spending money. Some of it was paid back immediately because he agreed to be interviewed by a foreign journalist for a fee of $300. Bobby's having consented to be interviewed for such a relatively small amount of money showed his financial desperation. It's not known where, or if, the intended story ever appeared.

Zita remained in Los Angeles for six weeks and stayed at the home of Robert Ellsworth, an attorney who helped Bobby with various legal matters. She was with Bobby every day. They enjoyed each other's company and, despite the May-December age gap (she was 17, he was 47), found common ground in their respective backgrounds. Both had started playing chess seriously at the age of eight and had dropped out of high school to be able to play chess full-time. Both loved the game and were highly intelligent and argumentative by nature. Bobby loved languages and, in addition to being fluent in Spanish, was becoming adept at Russian and German. Zita spoke

German and English with hardly a trace of an accent. Bobby was World Champion—or so he still claimed—and she aspired to be. In an interview later on, Zita claimed that the real reason Bobby was interested in her was "because I didn't want anything from him."

When Bobby embarrassedly showed her his room, she couldn't believe the way he lived. Barely thirty-five square feet, the living space included a small bathroom and a single bed. "He was ashamed of his poverty," she later recalled. Books, boxes, and tapes were piled high. The content of the tapes? According to to Zita, they contained Bobby's conspiracy theories. He told her he was planning to write a book that would *prove* how the Soviet players cheated in chess, and the tapes contained his thoughts on the matter.

Bobby and Zita played one game of chess: his new variation, called Fischer Random. She claims that she won and then became frightened. Perhaps he'd become violent toward her, she thought, because she was a woman and, also, not yet even a master. They never played again, but they did analyze together.

One evening when he picked her up to go out to dinner, he spotted some repairmen on the roof of a low-rise building across the street. They were probably Mossad (Israeli intelligence agents) spying on him, he said, part of his continued litany of "constant obsessions" as Zita observed.

Bobby explained that the reason he hadn't competed in almost twenty years was that he was still waiting for the right offer, though he didn't define what "right" meant. The right prize fund? Venue? Opponent? Number of games? It was probably all of those things and many more. He was also furious that although President Nixon had said he'd be invited to the White House in 1972, the invitation never arrived; Bobby had been fuming about it for two decades. In the interview Zita later gave to Tivadar Farkasházy, she claimed that Bobby was still waiting for the American government to apologize for the White House snub.

Zita couldn't figure out who was paying his rent, minimal though it was. Somehow she knew that it wasn't Claudia Mokarow. Zita thought it could be Bessel Kok; she was unaware that Kok no longer had any interest in backing Fischer for anything. In fact, Bobby's rent and other basic needs were being paid for by his mother's Social Security checks.

Regina had moved back to California from Nicaragua after having dizzy spells, a result of heart problems. She was seventy-seven and thinking of having an operation, and she wanted it performed in the United States. When Bobby heard about his mother's impending surgery, he and Zita, both out of money, used the cheapest transportation they could find—an uncomfortable Greyhound bus—to travel north along the Pacific coast for three hundred miles, to Palo Alto. Besides offering Regina support, Bobby wanted to introduce her to Zita.

Regina was about to have a pacemaker implanted. Bobby, distrustful of doctors, tried to talk her out of the procedure, and they argued about it for hours. As a medical doctor, Regina knew more about the risks than he did, but Bobby was afraid of a foreign object being implanted in his mother's body and what it might do to her. Regina remained adamant and had the operation anyway. She lived until the age of eighty-four.

In going to the United States and meeting Bobby, Zita had accomplished at least part of what she'd set out to do. She'd found out why Bobby Fischer wouldn't play: It had to be the right offer, and it had to be (echoes of the Philippines and the Karpov match) $5 million.

Although Zita denied that there was any sexual intimacy with Bobby in the six weeks she stayed in Los Angeles—"I wasn't thinking of that," she said—he was falling in love. He referred to Zita as his girlfriend, and at another point he called her his fiancée. He knew that to proceed further—for example, to get married once she was no longer a minor—he'd have to have some money, which gave him further impetus to seek a chess match that would make him financially secure.

Zita's father was a diplomat and an official of FIDE, and Zita had other contacts in the chess world who might help her find a sponsor for a Fischer-Spassky rematch. If Bobby would give her a letter saying that he was interested in playing a match, she told him she'd see whether she could secure backing. Bobby wrote out such a letter by hand. Remarkably, the man who rarely signed a letter of financial importance gave this seventeen-year-old the right, in this case, to speak for him. In mid-May Zita flew home.

It took almost a year, but she finally located someone—Janos Kubat, an internationally known chess organizer—who knew people who could raise the money for a $5 million match. When she first visited Kubat at his office, she couldn't get past his secretary to see him. Then, at an airport, she heard his name being announced over the loudspeaker, and she tracked him down. He was at first skeptical of the teenager's assertions, but when she showed him Bobby's letter and gave him Bobby's top secret telephone number, Kubat recognized that she was an authentic representative. He agreed to help.

About a month later, in July 1992, Kubat, Zita, and two officials of Jugoskandic Bank were in Los Angeles to talk to Bobby about a possible "revenge" match between Fischer and Spassky. The president of the bank, Jezdimir Vasiljevic, had given his executives the authority to offer a purse of $5 million with one stipulation: The match had to commence in three weeks in Yugoslavia. Bobby had no idea, really, who Vasiljevic was. He'd later learn that the banker was one of the most powerful men in Serbia, was involved in currency speculation, was suspected of illegally trafficking arms, and was also supposedly promoting a Ponzi scheme. He was six years younger than Bobby but acted in a fatherly way toward him.

The negotiations went back and forth, but Fischer's current demands were minor compared to the 132 conditions he'd stipulated in 1975 in order for him to play Karpov. In this proposed Fischer-Spassky match, he asked for the winner to receive $3.35 million, the loser $1.65 million. The match would continue, indefinitely, until one player achieved ten wins, draws not counting. If each player acquired nine wins, the match would be considered a draw, and the prize money would be shared equally, but Fischer would retain his title as undisputed Chess Champion of the World. He insisted that in all publicity and advertising the match be called The World Chess Championship. And last of all, he wanted the new clock that he'd invented to be used in all games.

Bobby also wanted $500,000 to be brought to him in advance—*before* he ventured from California to Yugoslavia. It was a delicate time. Kubat was afraid that Vasiljevic wouldn't release the advance payment unless Bobby first signed the contract, which had been translated into English by Zita. In the past, Bobby had often backed out of projects before they began. For the match to become a reality, he had to overcome the impulses of his nature. Just before Kubat was to leave for Belgrade to try to collect the down payment, Bobby amazed everyone: He signed the contract without complaint. In a matter of days, Kubat was back in California with the money, and Bobby made arrangements to abandon his tiny room. Because he would be entering a controversial war zone, there was a possibility he might not soon be coming back to California.

Most of his belongings—some fifty-two stuffed cartons gathered from several venues—were put into storage, and Fischer flew off to Belgrade and, ultimately, Montenegro so that he could inspect the playing site and get himself into shape before the match began. Spassky agreed to everything in the contract, and said from his home outside of Paris: "Fischer pulls me out of oblivion. It is a miracle and I am grateful."

Sveti Stefan, Yugoslavia, September 1992

Depending on the wind, a faint echo of massive artillery could be heard occasionally across the mountains near Sarajevo seventy miles to the north. The Balkan war was then at its height, during what was called the Yugoslav Era of Disintegration. Eight thousand people had been killed in just two weeks in August in Bosnia and Herzegovina, where the fighting was raging, and millions had fled their homes in the months before. Heavy fighting between forces loyal to the Bosnian government and Serbian irregulars was taking place in Eastern Herzogovina, about fifty miles from the playing site.

However, in Montenegro, on the Adriatic, one of the most beautiful spots in Europe, all was peace, joy, and entertainment on the night of September 1. Torchbearers, dressed in traditional Montenegrin costume—loose-fitting white pants and shirt and a colorful green vest—lined the isthmus leading out to a well-appointed hotel called the Maestral, which had once been a thirteenth-century medieval fort. In the past it had been one of Marshal Tito's retreats.

The forty-nine-year-old Bobby Fischer was described by a reporter who was covering the match for *The New York Times* as "an overweight, balding, bearded figure, unmistakably middle-aged, whose expression sometimes seems strikingly vacant." But Bobby's untenanted look owed itself not to vapidity but to a certain lack of interest in the world around him. Few things fired his passion. There were his political and religious theories, his vigilant search for dark conspiracies, his joy in languages, his affection for Zita, and of course, his abiding commitment to chess.

He'd just had a haircut and a beard trim, and he was neatly dressed, wearing a tan suit that he'd had custom-made in Belgrade. Surrounded by four sunglassed bodyguards—two in front and two in the rear—he slowly paraded down the rocky path with Zita, as if he were Caesar and she Cleopatra making an entrance into Rome, smiling and nodding benevolently at their subjects. They were en route to the opening party for the celebrated rematch, and also Zita's nineteenth birthday—and since they were in medieval surroundings, the entertainment took on a fourteenth-century ambience, with musicians, folk dancers, and acrobats, and fireworks ignited from a boat offshore.

All the while Zita wore a smile on her open face, which was framed by straight light brown hair and dominated by thick, pink-rimmed glasses. Small in stature, she appeared childlike beside Bobby, who, at six feet, two inches, was more than a foot taller.

During the festivities, Bobby sat on a literal throne, next to the sponsor of the match, the shadowy Jezdimir Vasiljevic, who was perched on a duplicate throne: They were two co-kings, one of chess and the other of finance. Vasiljevic had bought the hotel for $500 million, so the $5 million that he fronted for the prize fund was not a particular burden for him. After Bobby signed the contract to play, and it was returned to Vasiljevic, the Serbian screamed: "I just *made* $5 million!" since he'd been ready to negotiate with Fischer and raise the purse to $10 million if necessary. But he was careful to make sure that Bobby never knew how much more he might have won.

Before play began, there were mixed emotions, conflicting speculations, and assorted reactions throughout the chess world concerning the match. In an editorial in *The New York Times*, grandmaster Robert Byrne summarized the theories and conjectures: "At one pole, there is elation over Mr. Fischer's return from two decades of obscurity. He is, after all, the giant of American chess, and few grandmasters can say they haven't been influenced by his ideas, or awed by the brilliance of his games. If he can still play at top form, if he goes on to play further matches, if he challenges for the championship—if, if, if—then some of them [the chess public] look for a new chess craze to sweep the country, perhaps the world, as it did when Mr. Fischer defeated Mr. Spassky for the championship two decades ago." But more important than the question of whether Bobby would inspire another "Fischer boom" was the question of whether his immense and innate talent could find its release on the chessboard. There was no telling what his strength would be after such a long hiatus; even Bobby couldn't be sure that he'd held on to his former insight and brilliance. Playing—and winning—a rematch with Spassky would, to some extent, prove that Bobby's prowess was intact. However, Spassky, at age fifty-five, had sunk to about one hundredth on the FIDE rating list, so many chess players doubted that the match would be a true gauge of whether Bobby deserved to still be called the strongest player in the world. Bobby asked Gligoric ("Gliga") to play a secret ten-game training match to get into shape. Bobby won the match, but only three games have been made public: Bobby won one, and there were two draws.

Garry Kasparov, the reigning champion, was one who discounted the match's significance. When asked at the time whether he'd like to engage Fischer in a match for the official championship, Kasparov snapped, "Absolutely not. I don't believe Fischer is strong enough now. Boris and Bobby are retirees, not threats to me." The *Daily Telegraph* of London offered an atypical reaction to the impending match: "Imagine that you can hear the end of Schubert's 'Unfinished Symphony' or Beethoven's 10th, or see the missing arm of Michelangelo's *Venus*. These are the feelings that Fischer's return brings to the world's chessplayers."

Before the clock was set in motion for the first game, Bobby was receiving criticism for even *considering* playing in a war-ravaged country. The United States and some other countries, as well as the United Nations, were attempting to isolate Serbia because of its sponsorship of violence against Muslims and other minorities. On August 7, Kubat gave an interview to the *Deutsche-Presse Agentur* in which he claimed that the U.S. government had given Fischer permission to play in Serbia. Either Kubat was engaging in wishful thinking or the statement was just a public relations smoke screen to give the match more credibility.

Ten days before the match began, Bobby received the following letter from the Department of the Treasury:

ORDER TO PROVIDE INFORMATION AND
CEASE AND DESIST ACTIVITIES
FAC NO. 129405

Dear Mr. Fischer:

It has come to our attention that you are planning to
play a chess match for a cash prize in the Federal
Republic of Yugoslavia (Serbia and Montenegro)
(hereinafter "Yugoslavia") against Boris Spassky on or
about September 1, 1992. As a U.S. citizen, you are
subject to the prohibitions under Executive Order 12810,
dated June 5, 1992, imposing sanctions against Serbia and
Montenegro. The United States Department of the Treasury,
Office of Foreign Assets Control ("FAC"), is charged with
enforcement of the Executive Order.

The Executive Order prohibits U.S. persons from
performing any contract in support of a commercial project
in Yugoslavia, as well as from exporting services to
Yugoslavia. The purpose of this letter is to inform you
that the performance of your agreement with a corporate
sponsor in Yugoslavia to play chess is deemed to be in
support of that sponsor's commercial activity. Any
transactions engaged in for this purpose are outside the
scope of General License no. 6 which authorizes only
transactions to travel, not to business or commercial
activities. In addition, we consider your presence in
Yugoslavia for this purpose to be an exportation of services
to Yugoslavia in the sense that the Yugoslav sponsor is
benefiting from the use of your name and reputation.

Violations of the Executive Order are punishable by
civil penalties not to exceed $10,000 per violation, and
by criminal penalties not to exceed $250,000 per

individual, 10 years in prison, or both. You are hereby
directed to refrain from engaging in any of the activities
described above. You are further requested to file a report
with this office with[in] 10 days of your receipt of this
letter, outlining the facts and circumstances surrounding
any and all transactions relating to your scheduled chess
match in Yugoslavia against Boris Spassky. The report
should be addressed to:

  The U. S. Department of the Treasury, Office of Foreign
Assets Control, Enforcement Division, 1500 Pennsylvania
Avenue, N.W., Annex—2nd floor, Washington D.C. 20220. If
you have any questions regarding this matter, please
contact Merete M. Evans at (202) 622-2430.

Sincerely, (signed)

R. Richard Newcomb

Director

Office of Foreign Assets Control

Mr. Bobby Fischer

c/o Hotels Sten Stefan (Room. 118)

85 315 Sten Stefan

Montenegro, Yugoslavia

cc:

Charles P. Pashayan, Jr., Esq.	The Pacific Mutual Building
1418 33rd St., N.W.	523 West Sixth Street
Washington, DC 20007	Suite 541
	Los Angeles, CA 90014
Choate & Choate	
Attorneys at Law	U.S. Embassy
	Belgrade, Yugoslavia

    Bobby, who had an almost anarchistic disdain for the U.S. government
and had refused to pay taxes since 1977, was totally blasé about the receipt

of the letter and the threat of a $250,000 fine and ten-year imprisonment for violating the sanctions. As for the public, the sentiment among most people was: "What are they going to do, throw him in jail for ten years for moving wooden pieces across a chessboard?" Well, according to Charles "Chip" Pashayan, Bobby's pro bono lawyer, the Treasury Department could and would fine and imprison him. He sent Bobby a letter on August 28, 1992, practically begging him to postpone the match, and pointing out that Vasiljevic, to show his good intentions to the world, had promised to donate $500,000 to the International Red Cross for those suffering in the Balkans. Pashayan believed that the Treasury Department might appreciate the humanitarian gesture and eventually might allow the match to go forward by giving Bobby a special license to play. If Bobby returned home immediately, the match could still take place at a later date once the sanctions were lifted. "It is absolutely imperative that you comply with the attached order," he warned. Bobby was supremely obstinate, and although he could not really justify his decision to play, under the circumstances his tenacity, heart, and pocketbook prevailed. His response was to kill the messenger: He ultimately fired Pashayan.

The Yugoslav prime minister, Milan Panic, whose reasons for wanting the embargo lifted went way beyond chess, backed Bobby and said of the impending match: "Just think how it would be if the sanctions forbade a potential Mozart to write music. What if these games were to be the greatest in chess?" When the match's venue was moved to Belgrade, Slobodan Milosevic, the president of Serbia, met Bobby and Spassky and asked to be photographed with the two. He used the occasion to trumpet his propaganda to the international press: "The match is important because it is played while Yugoslavia is under unjustified blockade. That, in its best way, proves that chess and sports cannot be limited by politics." Milosevic was later charged with crimes against humanity by the International Criminal Tribunal in The Hague, and died in prison.

Despite the missing years, Bobby was being Bobby again. His list of demands continued to grow. Vasiljevic's strategy of appeasement was to give him whatever he wanted, even though the item might not have been mentioned in the contract. Bobby rejected six tables as inadequate, before asking for one from the 1950 Chess Olympics in Dubrovnik. Even that one had to be slightly altered by a carpenter to satisfy his demand. The pieces had to have the right heft and color, and he chose the same set that had been used at the Dubrovnik Olympics; he particularly liked the small color-contrasted dome on the bishops' heads, which prevented their being confused with pawns. It's difficult to believe, but Bobby rejected one set because the length of the knight's nose was too long; the anti-Semitic symbolism was hardly lost on those who heard the complaint. As a test of the size of the pieces and pawns in relation to the area of the squares, he placed four pawns inside a square to see if they overlapped the edges of the square. They didn't, so he accepted the size of the pieces as well. He asked for the lighting to be adjusted so that it wouldn't cast a shadow on the board. And oh yes, spectators were to be kept back sixty-five feet from the stage.

Bobby's invention of a new chess clock that operated differently from those traditionally used in tournaments had to be specially manufactured for the match, and Vasiljevic had it made. Bobby insisted that it be used in the match. The game would start with each player having ninety minutes, and upon his making a move, two minutes would be added to each player's time. Bobby's theory was that in this new system, players would never be left to scramble to make their moves at the end of the time allotment with only seconds to spare, thereby reducing the number of blunders under time pressure. The pride of the game was the depth of its conceptions, Fischer contended, not triumph by mechanical means.

Not all of Fischer's demands concerned the playing conditions. He also wanted the lavatory seat in his villa to be raised one inch.

According to the tale told by Washington Irving, when Rip Van Winkle awoke and returned to his village, twenty years had passed, and many things had changed. When Bobby Fischer, chess's version of Van Winkle, emerged after twenty years, the thing that had changed the most was *him*. The smiling, handsome Bobby Fischer who immediately after the 1972 championship charmed audiences on television shows and crowds on the steps of New York's City Hall, had been replaced with a swaggering Bobby Fischer filled with angst, irritation, and pique.

The very idea of Bobby Fischer wanting to talk to the press was astonishing, but this new Fischer called for a press conference the night before the match was to begin. He'd been interviewed throughout his chess career, sometimes by assembled groups of journalists, but this was his first formal press conference in more than twenty years, and he was coiled, ready to pounce on any question. Most of the members of the press were ready to see a ghostlike Bobby Fischer appear, someone totally apart from the hero of Reykjavik; many of the journalists who were assembled had never seen him in the flesh before—nor had the public had a glimpse of him during the two decades of his Wilderness Years. Bobby strode in, looking larger and healthier than imagined, and swiftly took his seat on the dais. He appeared not quite as physically impressive as a football linebacker, but certainly looked like a broad-shouldered athlete, perhaps a retired Olympic swimmer.

He'd insisted that all questions be submitted to him in advance, and he sifted through the cards searching for those he chose to answer. Spassky, looking uncomfortable, sat on Bobby's right, and Vasiljevic, smoking a meerschaum pipe and appearing relaxed, was on his left. After a few minutes of awkward suspense, Bobby looked up and read aloud a reporter's name, his affiliation, and the first question. "Let's start with some impudent questions from *The New York Times*," Bobby said impudently:

> **Roger Cohen:** Why, after turning down so many offers to make a comeback, did you accept this one?

> **Bobby Fischer:** That's not quite true. As I recall, for example, Karpov in 1975 was the one who refused to play *me* under *my* conditions, which were basically the same conditions that we are going to play now.

> **Roger Cohen:** If you beat Spassky, will you go on to challenge Kasparov for the World Championship?

> **Bobby Fischer:** This is a typical question from Mr. Roger Cohen from *The New York Times*. Can he read what it says here?

(Fischer then turned and pointed to the banner behind the dais
that said "World Championship Match." The audience
applauded.)

Traditionally, with rare exceptions, members of the media don't applaud
at press conferences, since it would be considered an endorsement of what
the speaker is saying, rather than just reporting the information being given.
Although a large number of reporters had been interested in attending Bobby
Fischer's controversial press conference, journalists were forced to pay
$1,000 for accreditation at Sveti Stefan. As a result, many chose not to cover
the match—at least, not from the "inside." There were only about thirty
journalists present in the room that day, although there were more than a
hundred people in attendance. The applause very likely came from the non-
journalists in the crowd, who may have been handpicked claques for their
anti-American and pro-Bobby leanings.

Bobby kept reading Cohen's follow-up questions and not directly answering them, just making comments such as "We'll see" or "Pass on," until he
read Cohen's final question: "Are you worried by U.S. government threats
over your defiance of the sanctions?"

> **Bobby Fischer:** One second here. [He then removed a letter from
> his briefcase and held it up.] This is the order to provide
> information of illegal activities, from the Department of the
> Treasury in Washington, D.C., August 21, 1992. So this is my
> reply to their order not to defend my title here. [He then spat on
> the letter, and applause broke out.] That is my answer.

Vasiljevic, also applauding, looked at him approvingly and smiled; Bobby
leaned back in his chair, swiveled back and forth, and smugly basked,
Mussolini-like, in his courtiers' adulation.

Bobby Fischer's spit was sprayed around the world. His anti-Americanism
was lambasted on the editorial pages of the *Daily News* ("Fischer Pawns His
Honor") and *The New York Times* ("Bosnia's Tragedy and Bobby's") and
reported in newspapers, magazines, and television broadcasts on almost

every continent. The consensus reaction was that Bobby's expectoration reeked of callousness regarding the carnage taking place in Bosnia, and was a clear flouting of, if not international law, then at least moral norms. Bobby's bizarre act was likened to such other symbols of anti-American defiance as Ezra Pound's "Heil Hitler" salute, Jane Fonda's pose on a North Vietnamese tank, and even Tokyo Rose's propaganda broadcasts during World War II.

One of the most surprising criticisms of Bobby's statements came from Bobby's close friend and former teacher Jack Collins, the Yoda of American chess. "I am bored and disgusted with him," said Collins. And then, mentioning the adulation that Bobby was receiving in Yugoslavia, Collins added, "They make so much out of a goof like him." Another close friend, William Lombardy, disagreed, however: "Yes, Fischer betrayed chess and everybody. But he's still magic, and can do a lot for the game. Bobby and Boris are finally cashing in. I don't begrudge them that."

Bobby continued making outrageous—or at least controversial—statements as he answered more of the reporters' questions. When asked about his views on Communism, he said, "Soviet Communism is basically a mask for Bolshevism which is a mask for Judaism." Denying that he was an anti-Semite, Fischer pointed out with a smirk that Arabs were Semites, too: "And I am definitely not anti-Arab, okay?" Calling Kasparov and Karpov "crooks" for what he considered their unethical collaboration, he also included Korchnoi on his hate list: "They have absolutely destroyed chess by their immoral, unethical pre-arranged games. These guys are the lowest dogs around."

Although she sat in the audience at the press conference, Zita didn't answer any questions, at least publicly. Later, in a semi-off-the-record interview she gave to a Yugoslavian journalist, she claimed that she was not planning to marry Bobby, but that she was attracted to his honesty. She added, "I like geniuses or crazy people," not saying which category, if either, Bobby fit into.

Bobby walked rapidly to the board, sat in his chair at precisely 3:30 p.m. on September 2, 1992, stretched his right arm across, and shook Spassky's hand.

He was dressed in a blue suit and wore a red-and-white tie, giving him a certain patriotic look. And if there was any doubt about his nationality, a small American flag could be seen on his side of the table, facing the audience; Spassky, who'd become a French citizen, had the tricolors of France next to him. Lothar Schmid, the arbiter who'd directed the 1972 match between the two grandmasters, was once again present, and he started the clock. And as Schmid depressed the button, a wave of nostalgia rolled over everyone watching. Twenty years had passed since the last Fischer-Spassky showdown, but each of the three main players seemed approximately the same—excepting some gray hairs, additional furrows, and extra girth around the middle. Laugardalshöll had morphed into the Hotel Maestral. Iceland had become Yugoslavia. Bobby was still Fischer. Boris was still Spassky. The game was still chess.

Within a few minutes, Bobby donned a wide-brimmed brown leather visor, the rationale for which was so that his opponent couldn't see what he was looking at. When it was his move, he pulled the visor way down and often rested his chin on his chest, almost as if he were a poker player secreting his cards.

Twenty years of rust aside, Bobby played as masterfully as he had in 1972: aggressive, relentless, brilliant, attacking on one side of the board and then the other. There were sacrifices of pieces on both players' parts.

Chess players the world over were following the game through faxes and telephone contact, and their collective question was answered at Fischer's fiftieth move. Spassky resigned. Grandmaster Yasser Seirawan wrote: "Yes, indeed, Bobby is back! A flawlessly handled game. Precise to the last moment." News outlets that, just the day prior, had criticized Fischer for his political incorrectness now had to admit that he was more than correct on the board: "Playing forcefully, the American chess genius seems to be in top form." But to paraphrase Aristotle, one chess game does not a champion make.

During the second game, Bobby seemed as if he was feeling his strength . . . until he again made his fiftieth move and this time made an atrocious error, converting the game, which he might have won, into a drawn position. In some respects he repeated the error of his ways in the third game as well: letting a potential—or at least a *possible*—win slip through his grasp and drift into a draw. Bobby's comment at the end of the game was revealing in its honesty. "This was maybe an off-day for me. I *hope* it was an off-day for me. I was in trouble." A scintilla of doubt had begun to insinuate itself. If the third game proved not to be just an "off-day" for him, it might be an indication that his long time away from the board was punishing him and hampering his ability to emerge as the old Bobby Fischer. The fourth and fifth games almost proved to him that he *was* experiencing some decline, or an accumulation of rust: He lost both.

One of the spectators at the match was the venerable Andrei Lilienthal, the eighty-one-year-old Russian grandmaster who'd lived most of his life in Hungary. He and his wife drove from Budapest to Sveti Stefan to follow the games. Lilienthal had never met Fischer, and at the conclusion of the fourth game, they were introduced at the hotel's restaurant. "Grandmaster Lilienthal, this is Bobby Fischer," said the person handling the introductions. The two chess giants shook hands, and Bobby boomed out, "Hastings, 1934/35: the queen sacrifice against Capablanca. Brilliant!"

The comment was so like Bobby in that he tended to remember and categorize people through their chess games, not necessarily anything else. Years later, Lilienthal was still shaking his head over Bobby's recollection of his famous win over Capablanca more than a half century before.

After the match, Spassky wrote:

My general approach was not to think about the result of the match but how to help Bobby to restore his best form. The sixth game was critical. I was playing for a draw with white, but Bobby played so badly that I achieved a winning position. This would, of course, give me a real chance to lead with three wins and two draws!

Could Bobby withstand such a situation? I did not know and this created a difficult psychological situation for me. I wanted to win the match but I was *afraid* to win: Bobby could simply leave the match and abandon chess forever. This uncertainty prevented me from winning [the sixth game]. Bobby saved the game with his fighting spirit, and his creative capacity was restored. His self confidence returned and [from that point on] he began to play much better.

Over the next two months, the match's momentum ebbed and flowed, but from the ninth game on, Bobby, scraping his way back, took the lead and held on to it. The stakes were huge: Whoever won ten games first would capture the lion's share of the prize money and secure the "championship." There were few Fischer tirades while playing, but Bobby continued to lose friends and make enemies as a result of his press conferences. He gave nine before the match ended, not counting brief comments that were made jointly with Spassky after each game. Some of Bobby's controversial statements to the press:

- "I think I am doing quite well, considering that I've been blacklisted for the last twenty years by world Jewry."
- "No, I have no regrets about spitting at that letter."
- "That man [Kasparov] is a pathological liar, so I wouldn't pay much attention to whatever he says."
- "I sued a company called Time Incorporated. . . . I sued them for many tens of millions of dollars, or maybe even many hundreds of millions of dollars on many different causes of action—defamation of character, breach of contract, etc. I spent two years in court, a lot of money, a lot of my time. This was in Federal Court, by the way. Then the judge just said: 'You have no case. I'm throwing it out without going to trial.' [The case was not only against Time, Inc., but also Brad Darrach, the author of *Bobby Fischer vs. the Rest of the World;* the contract that Bobby signed was to give Darrach access to write articles, not a book. The U.S. Chess Federation was also sued because they advertised the book.]

   "So I consider that the United States government and Time Incorporated went into a criminal conspiracy to cheat me out of hundreds of millions of dollars, which is the reason I have not filed and paid my Federal and California State income tax since about 1976 . . . since 1977, rather."

By the time they reached the thirtieth game, Bobby had won nine games and Spassky four. Games 26, 27, 28, and 29 were all draws; it was very hard for either man to defeat the other by that time. Both men were tired. In the final game, Spassky played his twenty-seventh move—it was hopeless at that point—and then resigned. Fischer had played resolutely and won what might be described as a comfortable game.

By his own standards, Bobby was Champion of the World once again, and $3.5 million richer. He'd made what Charles Krauthammer described in *Time* magazine, somewhat facetiously, as the greatest comeback since Napoleon Bonaparte sailed a single-masted fleet from the island of Elba in 1815. Grandmaster Yasser Seirawan said of Fischer's performance that it put him "somewhere in the top ten in the world." And a few months later, on the occasion of Bobby's fiftieth birthday, grandmaster Arnold Denker said, concerning his old friend and competitor: "True, the match with Spassky was not all that great, but after such a long lay-off, wasn't that to be expected? Yet, he did win convincingly. A match between him and the present world champion [Kasparov] would outdraw anything yet seen, and create a publicity explosion for world chess."

Bobby revealed that he'd be willing to play a match for the championship with Kasparov, but that he'd like to play a few training matches with younger players as a warm-up and then face Kasparov in 1994. But before Bobby could consider his next chess opponent, he had to, first, face a formidable *non*-chess opponent: the U.S. government. At issue were his violation of the sanctions, the fifteen years of back taxes he owed, and the taxes he potentially owed on the millions he'd just won.

At the closing banquet, Bobby was coaxed onto the dance floor for a few spins with some young Serbian women and then said some gracious words of thanks in Serbo-Croatian to his host and to the people of Yugoslavia.

After receiving the entire payment due him (within forty-eight hours of the conclusion of the match, disproving rumors that Vasiljevic would renege on the amount) Bobby by prearrangement met up with his sister, Joan, at the Belgrade Intercontinental Hotel. There *was* still a question concerning money due Bobby from the company that had purchased the television rights to the match—some $1 million. (Ultimately, Bobby never received any of it.) Joan took most of the match money, however, and traveled via train to Zurich, where she opened an account in Bobby's name at the Union Bank of Switzerland. This was done because it wasn't clear whether Bobby would be stopped at the Yugoslav border due to his violation of the sanctions and, if that were to occur, whether U.S. government officials might try to impound some, if not all, of the money.

At this time Vasiljevic was making an arrangement for another match for Bobby, this one to be played both in Belgrade and in Spain with Ljubomir Ljubojevic, the leading Yugoslavian player and one of the world's strongest tacticians. Bobby had met Ljubojevic. They liked each other, and both were eager to play.

Vasiljevic's plans concerning Bobby always contained ulterior motives. Certainly, he never made anywhere near a profit from the Fischer-Spassky match, despite the revenue from admissions fees, the sale of souvenirs, posters, television rights, etc. He promoted the match to bring global publicity to the Yugoslavian embargo and to make it appear as though the United States and other nations were attempting to suppress an important artistic endeavor. Within a few months after the match ended, Vasiljevic's financial house of cards began to collapse. Five hundred thousand depositors had funneled $2 billion into his sixteen banks and had been promised 15 percent interest on their money. Eventually, he found himself unable to meet the interest payments. He fled to Hungary and then to Israel, supposedly with bags of money—to avoid prosecution and with hope of setting up a government-in-exile. Years later he was extradited to Serbia and put into Belgrade Central Prison to face charges of embezzlement. Bobby grew to hate Vasiljevic, claiming that he was a Zionist agent. Further, he felt that the $3.5 million he had won in his match against Spassky was money garnered illegally by Vasiljevic. He made no move to return the money, however.

There were press reports that Bobby might be indicted and extradited back to the United States. Although he wanted to return to California, he didn't want to take the chance of entering the United States just yet. In mid-December, he received a telephone call from his attorney that a federal grand jury was about to meet and consider his case, and there was an almost certain chance that they'd vote for an indictment. The spitting incident, symbolically equivalent to burning the American flag, had apparently earned the government's wrath. Bobby immediately left Belgrade—taking with him his second, Eugene Torre, and two bodyguards provided by Vasiljevic—and secretly traveled to the small town of Magyarkanizsa, in the northernmost reaches of

Serbia, on the border with Hungary. Vasiljevic had selected this location for Bobby for a few reasons: Its population consisted of about 90 percent Hungarian nationals, so people from Budapest and its environs could cross the border with impunity, meaning that Zita could visit him easily. Also, should Bobby have to quickly cross from Serbia into Hungary, it was probable that he could do so without being stopped, since the checkpoint was undermanned and the guards wouldn't likely be on the lookout for him. The fact that Magyarkanizsa was known as "The City of Silence" also made it attractive to Bobby . . . at least at first.

On December 15, 1992, a single-count indictment in federal court in Washington, D.C., was handed down by a grand jury against Bobby Fischer for violating economic sanctions, through an executive order issued by President George Bush. A letter to that effect was sent to Bobby in Belgrade, and upon announcement of the indictment, federal officials issued a warrant for his arrest. It wasn't clear how rapidly—or aggressively—the government would pursue him.

In the middle of winter, there was little to do in Magyarkanizsa. Bobby didn't want to write letters or receive them, for fear of being tracked by the U.S. government, which was attempting to arrest him. When he communicated by telephone, he did so by having one of his bodyguards call the intended person and then hand over the phone. No call-back number was ever left. Trying to outwit any government pursuers, he at first stayed at a small hotel and then at an inn on the outskirts of town. And when the weather became warm, he moved into a health and rehabilitation center, not because he was ailing but because the facility had a swimming pool and a gym where he could work out. After a while, he moved to another hotel. Occasionally, Svetozar Gligoric, his old friend, would visit him and stay for a week or so.

In late May of 1993, the Polgars, the royal chess family of Hungary, visited Bobby—Laszlo, the father, and his two precocious daughters, Judit, sixteen, and Sofia, nineteen. Both girls were chess prodigies. (The oldest daughter, Zsuzsa, twenty-three—a grandmaster—was in Peru at a tournament.) Bobby welcomed their arrival since he was starved for companionship.

Soon after they left, though, he began to feel very hemmed in by circumstances. His funds were getting a bit crimped since he was fearful of traveling to Switzerland to draw money from his account—and if he tried to have the Swiss bank wire money to a bank in Magyarkanizsa, he'd once again be violating the sanctions. Not having many people to interact with or much to do was making him feel lonely and bored. ("I have no friends here; only Gliga and the bodyguards," he wrote to Zita.) Somehow, he had to extricate himself from Yugoslavia.

Without naming the country he wanted to go to, he sought legal advice from an attorney in Los Angeles and without mentioning names, should the phones be tapped, he had an English-speaking attorney in Magyarkanizsa take down the information. The country that Bobby had in mind to go to was the Philippines, although other than Torre he told no one of his intended destination. Getting there would be complicated.

If Bobby managed to get to Hungary without being arrested, he could fly directly to the Philippines. If traveling there *directly* appeared too risky, he could rent a small private plane somewhere in Hungary, or even Yugoslavia, and fly to Greece or Egypt and then to Manila. Another possibility was taking a boat or a tramp steamer, but that might be too prolonged. Bobby worried that his funds in the Union Bank of Switzerland might be sequestered, so he wanted to get the money out of there as soon as possible.

Ultimately, Bobby felt that traveling to the Philippines—as much as he *wanted* to go—was a risk he wasn't prepared to take at that particular time, and in any event, he learned that his UBS funds couldn't be sequestered. While he was still pondering what to do, he received some shocking news.

Zita had taken the bus from Budapest to visit him, and she had an announcement to make: She was pregnant, and not by Bobby. One can only imagine Bobby's shock, anger, and sadness at hearing this. He couldn't understand or accept that the passion he felt for Zita wasn't reciprocal. His proposal of marriage was categorically refused. A bitter argument raged through the night. "He was rough," Zita said. "His behavior was very, very bad. . . . he hurt those that I love." Finally, as dawn approached, Bobby went to sleep and Zita awoke a few hours later. She left a good-bye note indicating that her affair had nothing to do with why she didn't want to marry him. The fact was, she just didn't love him.

When Bobby awoke, he wrote a letter of apology to her, but she didn't answer.

When Zsuzsa Polgar returned to Budapest, her family made a second visit to Magyarkanizsa, specifically so that she could meet Bobby. Accompanying the family in Zsuzsa's VW Passat was Janos Kubat. Describing her first impressions of Bobby Fischer, Zsuzsa recalled: "I was surprised to see how tall and big he was. He was slightly overweight, though I wouldn't call him fat, and he seemed to have enormous hands and feet. He was very friendly and open with me right away, and had a lot of questions including about my recent trip to Peru."

Zsuzsa questioned Bobby about why he was staying in Magyarkanizsa—an ancient town, small and colorless—when he could be living in Budapest, the Paris of Eastern Europe, a city with many restaurants (including ones that featured his favorite Japanese cuisine), movie theaters, bookshops, thermal baths, concerts, and libraries. She added that there he could socialize with some of the great Hungarian players he knew—men such as Benko, Lilienthal, Portisch, and Szabo.

Bobby listened closely to what Zsuzsa was saying. He realized that if he was in Budapest he could continue to pursue Zita much more easily. He saw his quest for her in chess terms: "I have been in lost positions before . . . worse than this, and I won!" Laszlo Polgar invited Bobby to stay with his family anytime at his country home. That left only one question to ponder: Would he be stopped at the crossing into Hungary and turned over to the U.S. authorities?

The Polgars, thinking of everything, had taken a chance on their way across the border and asked the guards that very question. They were assured that Bobby wouldn't have any trouble entering Hungary. He was somewhat skeptical, however, and wrote apprehensively to his friend Miyoko Watai in Japan: "I think the Hungarians may arrest me as soon as I cross the border."

Realizing that his next move might ruin his life, Bobby, whose life on the chessboard had always been about preparation and calculation, decided that people in desperate positions must take desperate chances. Two weeks later, Bobby, Eugene Torre, and the two bodyguards drove in a rented car to the border of Hungary, were asked for their passports, and without further delay were allowed to pass. If the guards recognized Bobby and knew he was a wanted fugitive, they gave no evidence of it.

Entering the sparkling city of Budapest, Fischer checked into one of the most romantic and elegant hotels in the city, the Gellért, right on the Danube, and had lunch on the terrace. Bobby couldn't wait to slip into the Gellért's thermal bath; he felt he was in paradise. Even the bell captain made him feel at home. When the man carried Bobby's luggage to his room, he suddenly recognized the reclusive champion and challenged him to a game.

13

Crossing Borders

YOU DON'T NEED BODYGUARDS in Budapest," Benko told Bobby. "Only the Russian Mafia have bodyguards here." Benko was concerned that Bobby's two barrel-chested Serbian bodyguards, both with necks like wrestlers and carrying automatic pistols, would bring even more attention to Bobby than if he made his way through the city by himself. Bobby wasn't quite ready to give them up, however. Not only did they protect him, but he used them to run errands, serve as chauffeurs and occasional dinner companions, and be available to do whatever else he wanted at any hour. Primarily, of course, their job was to keep him *safe*. He thought he needed protection from the U.S. government, which just might have him assassinated instead of extraditing him and bringing him home for a costly and unpopular trial. He was worried about Israel as well. Because of his statements finding fault with Jews, he believed that either the Mossad or an inflamed pro-Israeli patriot might also try to kill him. And he'd always thought that the Soviets wanted him dead, because of the international embarrassment over the 1972 match, and his accusations of Russian cheating. To protect himself, he bought a heavy coat made of horse leather that weighed more than thirty pounds; he hoped it would be thick enough to deflect a knife attack. It's also likely that he wore a bulletproof vest.

All of these fears, tinged with paranoia, seemed to Bobby to justify constant concern for his life. Though some thought his fears were imaginary, he responded to physical threats just as he did threats on the board. He wanted to be prepared for any eventuality—an attack from *any* direction—so that it could be thwarted. His continual fear of being arrested, killed, accosted, or insulted fatigued him, and that may be one of the reasons he slept ten or twelve hours every night. He was ever fearful of what lay in the shadows, and that ever-present dread, combined with his constant tilting at windmills, exhausted him.

As soon as he was settled at the Hotel Gellért, Bobby was invited to spend part of the summer with the Polgars at their country compound at Nagymaros, about thirty-five miles north of Budapest, in the verdant Danube Bend section of the Slavic Hills of Hungary. As he and his two bodyguards drove along the banks of the Danube, Bobby noticed that the river wasn't the color he'd thought it would be. Unlike "The Blue Danube" of Strauss's waltz, this deep water was mud brown.

Bobby and his guards were given a small cottage at Nagymaros, but he ate all of his meals and spent most of his time at the large family house. All of the sisters played chess with him, but acceding to his preference, they played Fischer Random. Invented by Bobby, this was a variation on the standard game. The pawns are placed in their normal positions at the beginning of the game. The pieces remain in the back row and are placed randomly, on squares that are different from where they normally reside. Thus players who've spent years studying chess openings don't have much advantage: Memory and book learning (except as they concern endings) aren't as important. Imagination and ingenuity become more essential. As it happened, eighteen-year-old Sofia, the middle of the Polgar daughters, beat Bobby three straight. Zsuzsa played him "countless games" and never revealed the results other than to say she did "all right." She observed that Bobby's ability as an analyst was awesome.

Laszlo Polgar was a man who didn't mince words. When Bobby denied the very existence of Auschwitz, refusing to acknowledge that more than one million people had been murdered there, Laszlo told him about relatives who'd been exterminated in concentration camps. "Bobby," he said, frowning, "do you really think my family disappeared by some magic trick?" Bobby had nothing to back up his claim and could only refer to various Holocaust denial books.

It seems in keeping with Bobby's beliefs and personality that even though he was a guest, he had the audacity to voice his anti-Semitic views in the Jewish household of the Polgars'. Zsuzsa recalled: "I tried to convince him in the beginning about the realities, telling him the facts, but soon I realized that it was impossible to convince him, and I tried to change the topic." Judit was more outspoken: "He was an extremely great player, but crazy: a sick-psycho." And her father agreed: "He was schizophrenic."

Despite Bobby's insensitivity and bullheadedness, the Polgars were gracious hosts and continued to entertain and care for him. Eventually, Bobby shifted his monologues from hatred of the Jews to chess. He became angry, however, when Laszlo showed him a book published in 1910 by the Croatian writer Izidor Gross. The book described a variation of chess that seemed to be the forerunner of Fischer Random, with the exact same rules. Muttering something about Gross being Jewish, Bobby went on to change the rules of his variation to make it different from Gross's.

One day that summer the family went on an outing to the Visegrád water park. They invited Bobby to join them, along with his bodyguards. After taking the ferry across the river to reach the park, Bobby was soon in his element: swimming, and lounging in the hot tubs. He even went on the giant water slide, and wound up trying it over and over again. "He was like a big kid," Zsuzsa fondly remembered.

Laszlo kept a watchful eye on Bobby's behavior toward the three sisters. Bobby favored Zsuzsa, but she stated afterward that she wasn't aware of his growing affection. Laszlo was, and he didn't like it.

After three and a half weeks, Magyar Television somehow learned that Bobby was staying at Nagymaros and sent a camera crew to film him. Crew members hid in the woods at a distance of about fifty yards and filmed him using a telescopic lens. When someone became aware of their presence, there was panic. Bobby was a fugitive, and he obviously didn't want the world to know where he was hiding. He sent his bodyguards after the cameramen, and they wrenched the cassettes out of the cameras: No one was going to argue with the two bruisers. Bobby then asked Polgar for a hammer, sat on the stone floor of the living room, and ceremoniously and with increasing anger smashed the cassettes to pieces.

The Polgars had offered Bobby friendship and a respite, but it was now clear that the press was aware of his specific whereabouts. He departed from Nagymaros immediately, returned to Budapest, packed his bags, and left the Gellért in short order. Accompanied by his bodyguards, who were now doubling as porters, he checked into the Hotel Rege, at the foot of the Buda Hills, across the street from Benko's apartment and about fifteen minutes by bus from the city's center. Then, taking his friend's advice, he permanently dismissed his bodyguards as being too obvious and therefore potentially dangerous.

The Budapest that Bobby roamed through in 1993 was a rapidly changing city. No longer under the thumb of the Soviets, the city (and all of Hungary) had rid itself of the Iron Curtain in 1989 and had opened its border to Austria. Many businesses had been privatized, and only a small percentage were still connected to Russia. Among the people, there was a sense of vibrancy and freedom. It could be felt just walking down the Váci Utca, the city's principal mall street, with shops of all kinds selling wares. People were smiling, and staying out late enjoying themselves.

When Bobby determined, or at least believed, that he was no longer being followed or pursued, he began to freely wander the city, taking trams and buses to various destinations. Though many people undoubtedly recognized him, they almost never approached. Indeed, he always felt he was an alien and never a true resident of Budapest. Even after living there for years, he referred to himself as a "tourist."

He continued to visit the Polgars in Budapest, and on days that he wasn't playing chess or Ping-Pong with them, he'd be at the home of eighty-two-year-old Andrei Lilienthal and his wife, Olga, who was thirty years younger. The Lilienthals were genial hosts and they adored Bobby, and he greatly respected Lilienthal, a man who had once defeated former World Champion Mikhail Botvinnik. The old grandmaster had many tales to tell, and listening to him was like reading a book of chess history.

Although Olga was almost the same age as Bobby, she treated him in a motherly way—for example, by preparing the foods she knew he preferred. He spoke to Olga in Russian, and she'd later tell people that his command of the language was "pretty good." All throughout the years that he lived in Budapest, Bobby studied Russian almost every day, and he used Olga to correct his grammar and pronunciation. In his library, he collected various

Russian-English dictionaries and, also, books on Russian grammar and conversation. Lilienthal and Bobby talked in German.

When Bobby aired his views regarding the Jews, Lilienthal stopped him: "Bobby," he said, "did you know that I, in fact, am a Jew?" Bobby smiled and replied, "You are a good man, a good person, so you are not a Jew." It was becoming apparent that, although Bobby's rhetoric was clearly anti-Semitic, he tended to use the word "Jew" as a general pejorative. Anyone—whether Jewish or not—who was "bad," in Bobby's opinion, *was* a Jew. Anyone who was "good"—such as Lilienthal—whether Jewish or not, was *not* a Jew. "I reserve the right to generalize," Bobby wrote about his penchant for stereotyping.

After dinner almost every night, when he was at the Lilienthals' home, Bobby would watch a wide range of Russian television broadcasting—concerts, news, films—which he preferred to the Hungarian and American programming that was available. Such viewing also helped increase his understanding of the language. And then Bobby and Lilienthal would repair to the study and analyze games far into the night. They never played.

Since the Lilienthals were supportive of Bobby, he reciprocated with gifts: a television satellite dish, a vacuum cleaner, leather goods that he'd buy on trips to Vienna, and special gifts for birthdays and other holidays. His relationship with the Lilienthals wasn't unlike the one he'd had with Jack and Ethel Collins: Together, the three created a family atmosphere that was consistently supportive, involved chess, and hopefully would last for years.

After four years of interacting affectionately with the Lilienthals, however, two incidents severed the bond. Andrei had surreptitiously taken a photograph of Bobby at a New Year's Eve dinner party and sent it to *Shakhmatny Bulletin,* the Russian chess magazine. They published the picture and as an honorarium sent Lilienthal $200. Bobby was furious when he saw the issue and became more incensed when he learned that Lilienthal had been paid for the photo.

Bobby continually talked about the royalties he was owed for the Russian-language edition of *My 60 Memorable Games,* and Lilienthal sent a letter to Kirsan Ilyumzhinov, the current president of FIDE, and signed Bobby's name to it (without his knowledge), asking for a meeting. At one of his press conferences in Yugoslavia, Bobby had said, just to open discussions about how much was owed him, that the Russian publishers would have to pay $100,000, but that it was possible he really was owed "millions." Ilyumzhinov was also the president of the Russian Republic of Kalmykia, on the northwest shores of the Caspian Sea. An extraordinarily wealthy man with a passion for chess, he wanted to pay Bobby some of the royalties that were due him. He relayed a message to Lilienthal that he'd deliver the $100,000 in American cash to Bobby personally.

A meeting was arranged—a dinner at the Lilienthals'. It had been eighteen years since Bobby had broken off relations with FIDE, when he forfeited his match with Karpov, and therefore Bobby was not prone to be friendly, although Ilyumzhinov had had nothing to do with the organization at the time of the Karpov debacle. Speaking excellent English, Ilyumzhinov greeted Bobby and handed him a suitcase of money. Bobby sat there and resolutely counted every dollar. The dinner that followed was lively and cordial: Bobby showed Ilyumzhinov how Fischer Random was played, and he plied the president with questions about Russian politics. Ilyumzhinov recalled: "I was struck by how Fischer was up on everything that was happening in our country. He named our politicians and members of the government, and asked who I thought would win the elections."

Offers of possible reconciliation between Bobby and FIDE were made that evening, and Ilyumzhinov suggested that Bobby move to Kalmykia, where he'd be given free land and a new house could be built to his specifications. The federation president gave Bobby a deed for more than an acre of land in Elista, his capital city. Bobby thanked the president and asked about Kalmykia's medical care program but did not accept Ilyumzhinov's offer to live in Elista. Ilyumzhinov also offered to put up millions for another Fischer-Spassky match, but all Bobby would say was "I am only interested in Fischer Random." Somehow, in the course of the conversation, Bobby learned that the letter that had been sent to Ilyumzhinov had his forged name on it. The evening was getting late, and Ilyumzhinov began to make motions to go, but before doing so, he asked Bobby to pose with him for a photograph. "No," said Bobby ungraciously, silently fuming over what he regarded as two betrayals by Lilienthal (the photo and the forgery), "the $100,000 that you gave me doesn't include a photograph." Ilyumzhinov, the spurned suitor, left in a huff, and Bobby, the resentful friend, exited just behind him—with the money. Bobby always held that it was easier to forgive an enemy than a friend. He never saw the Lilienthals again.

When Bobby finally started writing a book on how he'd been cheated by various publishers, he dedicated it to: "The old Jewish scoundrel Andrei Lilienthal whose forgery of my name on his letter to FIDE was the straw that broke the camel's back [to write an anti-Semitic tract]."

Eventually, Bobby lost as friends not only the Lilienthals, but also the Polgars. Sofia Polgar was invited to give a simultaneous exhibition at the American embassy of Budapest, and Bobby was furious that she'd even consider it, claiming that his enemies—that is, the U.S. government and, therefore, the American embassy—must be considered the Polgars' enemies as well. Bobby quarreled not only with Sofia but with the entire Polgar family about the exhibition. Incredulous, Bobby asked Sofia: "How can you even talk to those people?" She went ahead anyway and performed well. The Polgars stopped all contact with Bobby after that, and he with them.

All while he was attempting to establish a life in Budapest, and yet alienating everyone around him, Bobby was also trying to win over Zita. It was a campaign fated to end badly. In the nearly eight years that he lived in Hungary, he only managed to convince her to see him a few times—once when she attended his fiftieth birthday party in Bulgaria. That time, he again proposed marriage, even though she was happily ensconced with her boyfriend and had a child. "It's out of the question," she told him. "Then what about your sister Lilla?" he asked. When Zita told her mother what he'd said, that Bobby was looking for a breeder, Mrs. Rajcsanyi was horrified.

Zita's theory about Bobby was that he was dominated by an idée fixe of reproducing himself, much as Henry VIII quested after a son. She felt that the obsession driving Bobby was *I must get married, I must have a child, I cannot die without an offspring, or else my genius will vanish forever.* Fischer began collecting photos of other Hungarian girls he'd like to meet, and he recruited his new friend and assistant Janos Rigo—an international master and chess organizer—to serve as a matchmaker. The girls had to have certain characteristics or else he didn't even want to meet them. They must be: (1) blond and blue-eyed, (2) young, (3) beautiful, and (4) a serious chess-player. When Rigo would bring photos to him, Bobby almost always rejected the women as not having all or enough of those qualities. Finally, Bobby placed the following advertisement in several Hungarian newspapers (his description of himself is revealing, as is the fact that he didn't risk narrowing the pool of candidates by sticking with all four of his requirements):

> Single, tall, rich, handsome, middle-aged American man with good personality desires to meet beautiful young Hungarian girl for serious relationship. One or more photos please.

He gave Rigo's address for replies, and there were some responses, but none met his perfectionist standards, and ultimately, he nixed them all.

Bobby continued reading anti-Semitic literature as well as neo-Nazi tracts and getting into heated arguments about the evilness of the Jews with virtually everyone he met. Once, when coming home late at night from an event, with Rigo serving as his driver, he refused to allow a Jewish chess player to enter the car until the man was willing to proclaim that the Holocaust didn't happen.

Some of the many hate books Bobby read while in Budapest were *The Myth of the Six Million* by David Hoggan; *On the Jews and Their Lies* by Martin Luther, written in 1543; and *Jewish Ritual Murder* by Arnold S. Leese. He also read an account of Nazi general Ernst Kaltenbrunner, a leader of the SS who ended up being found guilty at the Nuremberg trials and executed. While in prison and awaiting judgment, Kaltenbrunner wrote a letter to his family and Bobby was affected by it. Here are excerpts of what Kaltenbrunner wrote:

> My own destiny lies in the hands of God. I am glad that I never separated from Him. I cannot believe that I shall be held responsible for the mistakes of our leaders, for in the short time of my activity I have striven hard for a reasonable attitude, both internal and external. . . . They ought to have paid more attention to my words. . . . We have no property worth mentioning. Perhaps the only resource for you will be my small stamp collection. . . . Was it not my duty to open the door to socialism and freedom as we imagined and desired

them? . . . I have not given up hope that the truth will be found out and for a just legal decision.

When Bobby discovered that Kaltenbrunner's son was still alive, living in Vienna, he visited him to discuss whether the concentration camps did or didn't exist. If they *did* exist, he wanted to know whether the entire Holocaust story was blown out of proportion, and the account of millions being exterminated a myth. Bobby was disappointed when he met the executed SS leader's son. The younger Kaltenbrunner was an avowed liberal and had no interest in discussing his father, the camps, or anything else concerning Nazism or anti-Semitism. But he *was* a chess player! To Kaltenbrunner the fact that the great Bobby Fischer was gracing his home—for whatever reason— was equivalent to having the president of a country stop in to pay a visit. When Bobby left, Kaltenbrunner affixed an engraved plaque to the chair in which Bobby sat: IN THIS CHAIR SAT THE WORLD'S CHESS CHAMPION, ROBERT J. FISCHER.

In the summer of 1993, an American feature film called *Searching for Bobby Fischer* was released to stellar reviews. Originally titled *Innocent Moves,* the film was retitled before final release, with producers deciding to mimic the title of the book on which the film was based. Using Bobby's name, they thought, would have more promotional power. *Searching for Bobby Fischer* was the true story of a young boy, Josh Waitzkin, who showed incredible talent for the game, and how he became successful at the board, at first despite his parents' doubts and then with the encouragement of his parents and his extraordinary chess teacher, Bruce Pandolfini, played in the film by Ben Kingsley. It was one of the most respectful and sensitive films ever made about chess. The character of Bobby is not in the film, but he is seen in documentary footage. What he accomplished in Iceland inspired the film, which discusses the so-called Fischer Boom of increased chess activity, post-1972. The film grossed more than $7 million and was nominated for an Academy Award. Bobby was indignant and then irate when he heard about it, proclaiming the film a misappropriation of his name and, therefore, an invasion of his privacy. When the final box office receipts were tallied, the producers were disappointed, citing the ambiguous title of the film as the cause for relatively low attendance, and on hindsight they wished that they hadn't used Bobby's name.

He was never asked by the filmmakers to give his approval of the project, nor did he receive any compensation from it. He claimed that the film made more than "a hundred million dollars," which was highly exaggerated. It's "a monumental swindle," he wrote. After checking with his attorney, he discovered that because he was a public figure, the producers—Paramount Pictures—had the right to use his name. Even though Bobby felt Paramount's behavior was unethical and unfair, he took no legal action. Even so, after that he continually complained and wrote negatively about the film, even though he'd never seen it and had been told that it was an excellent depiction of how a child enters the chess world.

Bobby felt safe enough to travel and eventually went to many countries: often to Germany as a companion to Benko, who was playing chess for a team there . . . to Austria to go shopping with Rigo . . . to Switzerland to meet his bankers . . . to Argentina to promote his Fischer Random variation . . . and to the Philippines, China, and Japan for social and business reasons. Mysteriously, he also journeyed to Italy to meet a member of the Mafia; he wanted to meet a mafioso because he admired the Mafia's family structure and code of conduct and wanted to know more about it. Whether this was the *real* reason he flew to Italy is not known.

At the beginning of 1997 Fischer's passport was expiring. Though it could have been renewed at the U.S. embassy in Budapest, Bobby was worried: What if his passport was confiscated and he was trapped in Hungary, unable to travel anywhere and possibly unable to access his bank account? Or, even worse, what if they arrested him? He considered all possibilities as if he were analyzing a chess problem, and decided that he didn't want to be confined in Hungary. Bobby asked Rigo to drive him to Bern, Switzerland. When they arrived, he entered the U.S. embassy, trying to look calm, though he was feeling intense trepidation. His reason for attempting a passport renewal in Switzerland rather than Hungary was that even if he were stymied and had to stay put in Switzerland, he would still be able to access the money he had on deposit in the Union Bank of Switzerland. Rigo waited for him in the car outside of the embassy, equipped with a list of emergency telephone numbers to call should Bobby be detained or arrested; he also had a set of keys to

Bobby's safe deposit boxes and other locked cases. Within forty minutes, Bobby exited the building with a big smile on his face: He had a new U.S. passport, valid until 2007. It was now safe for him to return to Budapest.

Of course, there was one country Bobby still couldn't travel to, since if he did it would mean almost certain arrest: the United States. This presented an emotional dilemma in July of 1997. Regina had died and Bobby wanted to attend her funeral. Some chess players in the state of Washington conjectured that he surreptitiously entered the United States wearing a disguise, first flying to Vancouver, Canada, and then crossing the border to Seattle and traveling south to California by car, where he attended the service incognito. According to the story, he didn't talk to his sister, nephews, or anyone else. He just stood on the sidelines, unrecognized.

Not a year later, Bobby's sister, Joan, then age sixty, died suddenly of a stroke, and Bobby once again felt the pangs of not being able to show his respects at a family member's graveside. This enforced separation from his family aggravated the hatred for America that he'd felt since 1976, when he lost his case in federal court and refused thereafter to pay taxes. It's not clear why, during Bobby's years eluding American authorities, his sister and her family didn't visit him in Europe; his mother, however, had visited him once in Budapest.

After the schism with the Polgars and the Lilienthals, Bobby's life in Budapest became less social, but since he'd lived an isolated life for so long, he didn't appear outwardly affected by the two families' lack of warmth. Still, the absence of these supportive relationships must have hurt, despite his role in the schism.

His daily routine consisted of rising in the afternoon and having breakfast at his hotel—usually in his room, but occasionally in the dining room—swimming in the indoor pool or taking a trip to one of the city's many thermal baths, then making a visit to a library or bookstore. Sometimes he'd vary his routine and go on long walks, wandering with his memories near the caves in the Buda Hills—or he'd have an espresso on the terrace of the Hilton on Castle Hill. Rigo usually picked him up at his hotel at about seven p.m. for dinner. Bobby deliberately varied the kinds of food he ate: Japanese, Chinese, Indian, Hungarian, even Kosher, alternating restaurants every night. Occasionally he was joined by Pal Benko or Lajos Portisch or Peter Leko—a young Hungarian grandmaster—or one or two others. Bobby would only sit with his back against the wall, preferably in a corner and away from the windows—all tactics to escape notice by other diners or passersby. He always picked up the check for everyone at his table.

He carried his own bottle of water and only occasionally would have alcohol. Once he drank a little too much *palinka,* a plum brandy made in Hungary and Transylvania that is supposed to aid digestion after a meal, and he got drunk. He was so unused to such a quantity of alcohol that his hangover lasted for three days.

Many have wondered how much of the Hungarian language Bobby mastered during his almost eight years in Budapest. Zsuzsa Polgar believed that he spoke almost no Hungarian; Zita claimed he only knew about seven words, *gymulcsriz,* his favorite desert, being one of them; and Rigo thought he knew about two hundred words, enough to order from a menu, ask for directions, and make himself understood to shop owners and others. The fact that most older Hungarians knew Russian, and that many also had a command of German, while most of the younger generation could speak English, helped Bobby in communicating.

Once or twice a week in the late afternoon Bobby went to the movies and saw mostly popular American films. He said that he identified with the character played by Jim Carrey in *The Truman Show,* that he sometimes felt as though he lived in a Kafkaesque world where he—Bobby—like Truman, was the only honest person in the world and everyone else was an actor.

Back in his hotel room at around eleven p.m., Bobby would read and listen to music and the news on BBC radio. He had decided to write an anti-America book in which he'd present his arguments against the country, tying that in somehow with his distrust of and animosity toward Jews (and his personal enemies, whom he called "Jews" regardless of their religion). He connected all this with the rage he still felt for the loss of personal effects he'd kept for years in a storeroom in California, which had been sold at auction when the storage rent wasn't paid. As preparation for the book, Bobby spent part of his nighttime hours recording on cassette tapes his anti-Semitic and anti-American screeds.

As the hours faded into dawn, he'd play over games from the latest tournaments, impeccably dissecting each move using his mental microscope, looking for errors, misinterpretations, and fallacious conclusions—especially ones that might prove conspiracies among those he believed were the chess world's thieves and embezzlers. Each game became a mystery novel. The goal was never to find a murderer—rather, it was to discover how the "cheating" had occurred.

He began to limp noticeably, and several of his colleagues urged him to see a doctor, a dreaded experience that Bobby would only agree to if he were in enormous pain. Finally, after the suffering became intolerable, he relented, was examined, and was told that he was suffering from orchitis, an inflammation of the testicle. As he walked, he was "guarding" the gland and therefore limping. Usually, a ten-day antibiotic treatment alleviates the symptoms, or a fast in-office medical procedure can release the pressure. Bobby availed himself of neither. Instead, he told everyone that his limp was caused by an old leg injury (he'd broken his leg many years before), and he just suffered through the pain of orchitis until the swelling subsided on its own. He continued to walk with a slight limp for the rest of his life.

"As Adolf Hitler wrote in *Mein Kampf*, the Jews are not the victims, they are the victimizers!" blared Bobby Fischer during a live broadcast on Calypso Radio in Budapest on January 13, 1999. How many of the 1.5 million citizens of Budapest, or the ten million people who lived in all of Hungary, were listening to Bobby when he offered his hate-filled comments is not known, but the interviewer, Thomas Monath, was dumbfounded as to what to do. Turn off his microphone? Shout him down? Bobby's rant could be heard for years all over the world because the show went online.

It was Bobby, through Pal Benko, who'd approached the station to say that he wanted to give an interview, his first since he'd won the match against Spassky in 1992. At first, the interview was fairly benign, and questions such as why Bobby preferred to live in Budapest were answered politely ("I like the mineral baths, the people; you have a fabulous city here"), but soon he became impatient, saying he wanted to discuss much more substantive things. If the world, at least the Hungarians, had missed his anti-Semitic remarks during his press conferences in 1992, they certainly couldn't have missed his near hysterical posturing on Calypso Radio seven years later.

The rationale that Bobby offered for his blather was that all of his personal belongings and memorabilia—admittedly valuable to him, and some of interest to collectors—that he'd stored at the Bekins warehouse in Pasadena, California, had been auctioned off because of the failure of his agent Robert Ellsworth to pay the storage bill of $480. "It was worth tens of millions, or even hundreds of millions of dollars, and it was stolen!" Bobby complained. Then in some incredible leap of illogic, he equated the loss of his property to a conspiracy hatched by the Jewish people, and his argument was delivered with such venom and vulgarity that the broadcasting station considered ending his time on the show. Monath appealed to him, "Will you please allow me to ask you some friendly questions about chess?" Raising his voice and bullying his way forward, Bobby replied: "No, I won't let you!" He continued his rant, talking about how he was being "persecuted by the Jews," and claiming that "the Holocaust never happened," and using four-letter words to describe "the Jew Ellsworth." It was almost as though he felt that this opportunity of being on the air live might be his one and only chance to set the record straight—to inform both the station's listeners and the world of the injustices done to him. His hatred continued to spill out into the broadcasting ether until Monath could stand it no longer: "Mr. Fischer, you are destroyed in your mind," he said, and Fischer's microphone was rendered mute.

The facts of Fischer's loss of belongings are fairly straightforward: He'd been paying for storage costs for about ten years, and his bin contained a large safe with such things as his letter from President Nixon congratulating him for his win in Iceland, his World Championship medal presented to him by FIDE, letters, score sheets, paintings, trophies, statues, scrapbooks, photos, books, and hundreds of other items. One great loss for the chess world was the original scores of games that Bobby played in a series of simultaneous exhibitions throughout South America and about which he planned to write a book, since he had played a number of interesting games during that time. If sold individually—there were *thousands* of games, according to Bobby—or as one large cache to a collector, the value of these score sheets alone would have totaled somewhere around $100,000.

Bobby had been giving Ellsworth, his agent, about $5,000 a year to pay the storage cost and some minimal taxes on property—five lots—that he owned in Clearwater and Tarpon Springs, Florida, which were originally owned by his grandfather (Bobby bought them from his mother in 1992). Those various expenses came to about $4,000 a year; the $1,000 left over was for Ellsworth's management. The storage room was registered under the names of "Claudia Mokarow and Robert D. James," and since Ellsworth was paying the charges year after year, it is possible that the storage company had no idea that the material in the bin belonged to Bobby Fischer. Somehow Ellsworth had blundered—either through carelessness or a clerical error—and didn't pay $480 that was owed, and as contractually agreed upon, the company had the right to dispose of the storage room's contents. As soon as Ellsworth discovered his mistake, he felt guilty about it, and one can understand how heartbreaking it was to Bobby: "My whole life!" he said, outraged.

Ellsworth actually realized his error in time to attend the auction and buy back $8,000 worth of the material, not bidding on comic books and other memorabilia that he believed—wrongfully, as it developed—would no longer be of any interest to Fischer. Harry Sneider, Fischer's former physical trainer, accompanied Ellsworth to the auction and Sneider's son subsequently traveled to Budapest with twelve boxes of material. When he handed them over, Bobby said, "Where's the rest?" He claimed to have had at least one hundred boxes in his storage unit and maintained that what had been brought to him was only one percent of his belongings.

He just wouldn't let it rest. Before he was done, he gave thirty-five radio broadcast interviews—they all found their way online—most of them through a small public radio station in the Philippines and some lasting almost two hours, expounding on his theory that he was a victim of a conspiracy that involved a Jewish cabal, the U.S. government, the Russians, Robert Ellsworth, and the Bekins Storage company.

It seemed that Bobby had lapsed over the years into a state of increasingly frequent paranoia, believing as he did that people and organizations, bonded in a conspiracy, were out to persecute him. It was as if he had a form of Tourette's syndrome where, plagued by a temporary storm in his mind, he couldn't stop himself from denigrating Jews in the vilest terms: His hate rhetoric just spewed out and he couldn't—nor did he want to—control it. He was not delusional nor did he have hallucinations—that anyone knows of—so he could not be labeled psychotic. (One psychiatrist, Dr. Magnus Skulasson, who knew Bobby well toward the end of his life, insisted that the term "psychotic" definitely didn't apply to him.) Indeed, removed from stressful situations (such as the loss of his possessions at Bekins), he was completely in touch with reality and could be charming, friendly, and even rational (if limited to certain topics) at times. Dr. Anthony Saidy, one of Bobby's oldest and closet friends, wrote a letter to *Chess Life* about Bobby's broadcasts in which he stated: "His paranoia has worsened through the years, and he is more isolated than ever in an alien culture." Saidy added that the media were exploitative in publishing the most hideous of Bobby's statements, that the press should leave him alone.

When Bobby read Saidy's comments he was furious. He lambasted Saidy for living in the United States, a truly alien culture by his definition, and called Saidy a Jew (he is not).

The smell of camphor trees in Kamata, a suburban section of Tokyo, intrigued Bobby. Many of the Japanese would scoop up or pluck the aromatic leaves and boil them and inhale the steam, claiming that it was good for colds; others felt that camphor steam could be harmful. Regardless of who was correct, the trees drew people's attention, including Bobby's. If you picked up just a few of the fallen leaves and crushed them in your hands, you could smell their pungent scent. Bobby increasingly relied on homeopathic remedies as an alternative to prescription drugs for his aches or pains, and he was always looking for natural cures; this quest for medicinal herbs may have plunged him into trouble.

He'd arrived in Tokyo on January 28, 2000, after first announcing to his friends that he'd be gone from Budapest "for a few months" and storing everything in Benko's apartment. He never returned. In Japan, he had a standing invitation to stay with Miyoko Watai, the president of the Japanese Chess Association, a woman he'd known since 1973, when he first visited the country, seeking a venue for his upcoming yet never-played match with Karpov. Over the years they'd corresponded, and she'd visited him both in Los Angeles and in Budapest. Miyoko, one of the strongest women players in Japan, admitted that as a chess player Bobby was her idol and that before meeting him she'd read everything about him she could find and had played over every one of his games. She was in love with him.

To his friends, though, Bobby denied that there was a romantic relationship with Miyoko, who was two years younger than him.

Bobby was still looking for a woman who could bear him a child, and hoped he would meet a number of young Filipina women, among whom he might find a candidate. So Bobby began a routine of flying back and forth between Tokyo and the Philippines, staying in Japan just shy of three months (for immigration purposes) and then doing the same in the Philippines, and living—to some extent—a life similar to the one in the film *The Captain's Paradise,* where the protagonist has a wife in two separate ports and rotates visits to each. In Bobby's case, he wasn't married, but he was intimate with Miyoko in Tokyo and with other women in the Philippines, and this back-and-forth philandering went on for several years.

Bobby and Miyoko, both in their late fifties, lived a quiet life in the quiet suburb of Tokyo called Ikegami, traveling to various *onsen*—hot springs—going to movies, taking long walks, sitting in the park, where no one seemed to recognize Bobby, and just living what could be called an unremarkable but romantic middle-class life. A rare false note was struck when Bobby and Miyoko attended a screening of the American film *Pearl Harbor.* When the Japanese Zeroes began bombing the ships in Battleship Row and destroyed the USS *Arizona,* Bobby began clapping loudly. He was the only one in the theater to do so—much to the embarrassment of the Japanese. He said that he was shocked that no one else joined in.

But then the three months were up, and just before the flag fell on the immigration clock, Bobby would scoot off to the Philippines.

Life in Baguio City, about 130 miles from Manila, was somewhat more exotic than Tokyo. Half of the city's population consisted of university students (some 150,000 of them), so the opportunity to meet the type of girls Bobby preferred (young and beautiful) was greater than in Japan. Curiously, though, during those periods when Bobby was in Japan he didn't stray from Miyoko.

In the Philippines Fischer was hosted by an admirer at the Baguio Country Club for his first three months, played tennis every day, and met and dined with Torre and occasionally with the dignified Florencio Campomanes, the former president of the International Chess Federation (FIDE). Eventually, Bobby leased a home in the same compound where Torre lived and, as a constant dinner guest, often enjoying the cooking of Torre's wife.

At a party hosted by Torre at the country club in early 2000, Bobby met an attractive young woman named Justine Ong, who changed her name to Marilyn Young, a Filipina of Chinese extraction, and they began dating. Several months later, she announced that she was pregnant. The idea of abortion was abhorrent to Bobby and he refused to even discuss it. At the birth of the child, named Jinky, Marilyn had Bobby's name recorded on the birth certificate as the father. He promised to support mother and child, as he did, buying them a home in the Philippines, sending occasional gifts to the child, and money to Marilyn. His friends have said that he wasn't certain that the child was his, but just as he was supported by Paul Nemenyi, not knowing whether Nemenyi was his father, he would do the same for Jinky, and even stand in as the child's titular father. This arrangement went on for seven years, with Bobby sending greeting cards to the young girl signed "Daddy," and having mother and child visit him later on. One of his friends who observed them together said that Bobby treated little Jinky with affection, but he didn't seem as close to her as one would expect if he thought she was truly his daughter.

In one of Bobby's broadcasts (August 9, 2000) from Tokyo to Radio Baguio, he made mention of having been arrested in Japan around that time on a "trumped-up drug charge" but gave very little other information about it except to say that he was in jail for eighteen days before being released and how absurd it was because he took no drugs, not even aspirin. The arrest took place in the spring or summer of 2000, and it received no publicity that this writer could find; it's possible that the Japanese authorities, not knowing who Fischer was, simply saw a foreigner coming frequently in and out of the country with a backpack of herbs—the profile of a drug dealer—and interrogated him. Knowing Bobby's penchant for noncooperation with authority figures, he might well have been incarcerated more for his attitude than anything else.

Perhaps the most horrendous of Bobby's broadcasts came on September

11, 2001. He was called by Radio Baguio in the Philippines (he was living in Tokyo at the time) to comment on the attacks in the United States on the World Trade Center and the Pentagon. The interview was his shortest, only twelve minutes, but it created an international fury since it was picked up in its entirety online. Bobby's polemic was a full-frontal attack on a suffering nation.

In speaking his mind, Bobby had no idea—or if he did, maybe he didn't care—that he was sealing his fate with the U.S. government, Jews around the world, and the vast majority of the American people who felt wounded and outraged over the carnage of the 9/11 attacks and Bobby's blasphemy concerning them. To say that Bobby's broadcast was one of the most hateful by an American in the history of radio would not be an exaggeration. Following is a transcribed version of some of his comments:

Fischer: Yes, well, this is all wonderful news. It's time for the fucking U.S. to get their heads kicked in. It's time to finish off the U.S. once and for all.

Interviewer: You are happy at what happened?

Fischer: Yes, I applaud the act. . . . Fuck the U.S. I want to see the U.S. wiped out.

Fischer: The United States is based on lies. It's based on theft. Look at all I have done for the U.S. Nobody has single-handedly done more for the U.S. than me. I really believe this. You know, when I won the World Championship in 1972, the United States had an image of a football country, a baseball country, but nobody thought of it as an intellectual country. I turned that all around single-handedly, right?

Fischer: But I'm hoping for a *Seven Days in May* scenario, where sane people will take over the U.S. . . .

Interviewer: "Sane people"?

Fischer: Sane people, military people. Yes. They will imprison the Jews; they will execute several hundred thousand of them at least. . . .

Fischer: I say death to President Bush! I say death to the United States. Fuck the United States! Fuck the Jews! The Jews are a criminal people. They mutilate [circumcise] their children. They're murderous, criminal, thieving, lying bastards. They made up the Holocaust. There's not a word of truth to it. . . . This is a wonderful day. Fuck the United States. Cry, you crybabies! Whine, you bastards! Now your time is coming.

14

Arrest and Rescue

OBBY FISCHER WAS a non-convicted felon-at-large with a ten-year prison sentence hanging over his head. After nine years of the government's apparent lack of interest in pursuing him, however, he really didn't feel like a fugitive. He traveled almost anywhere and did virtually anything he wanted to do, was a multimillionaire, had a woman who loved him, and although he was a man without a country, a modern-day Flying Dutchman hauntingly roaming the seas, he felt relatively secure. Then everything went amiss when he discovered that his memorabilia had been auctioned off; it was as if he'd lost not just old letters and score sheets, but a part of his inner being.

In a real sense, he'd lost himself—his grip was slipping.

It was a conspiracy, he conjectured, and the United States government and the Jews were responsible. He wanted the world to know about his devastating loss. That was when the radio broadcasts started. Most were aired over a small station in Baguio City, and if he'd gone on the air at that same station ten years earlier, he probably could have continued to live as he had since 1992, since so few listeners were normally tuned in. In 2001, though, with the Internet rapidly expanding, his rants were heard all over the world, and what he said brought renewed scrutiny by the United States government.

Following Bobby's 9/11 remarks, editorials were written denouncing him; the U.S. Chess Federation made a motion to ban him from its organization; and players—and even some of his closest friends—who'd forgiven his 1992 hate mongering in Yugoslavia, were now totally incensed. Scores of letters were sent to the White House and the Justice Department demanding his arrest; many of them stated it was long overdue. The government's engine of bureaucracy accelerated slowly, however, and although the Justice Department decided to make its move against him, it took time and approvals to decide when and where an arrest could be made.

Bobby was astute enough to know that by making more and more broadcasts calling the United States a "shit country of criminals," demanding a new Holocaust for Jews, and chanting "death to the President," he was increasing his chances of eventual arrest. When nothing happened, however, he felt invulnerable and continued to travel without hiding. Since he was never questioned or stopped at any airport or customs entry point to any country, he felt free to persist with his broadcast vitriol.

Nevertheless, he did exhibit a certain wariness in dealing with the U.S. government. His passport (which he'd renewed for ten years in 1997) was running out of space on the pages that are normally stamped when one leaves or enters a country. From 1997 to 2000, while living in Hungary, he'd traveled to many European countries, and from 2000 to 2003 he'd made fifteen trips from Tokyo to Manila and back again. Finally, he was told by a customs agent that he had to have additional pages added to his passport. It would have been more convenient to go to the American embassy in either Tokyo or Manila, but he chose to have it done in Switzerland, for the same reason he chose that country when he'd had his passport renewed in 1997: In case they confiscated the passport, he could remain in Switzerland, where his money was safe and he could have physical access to it (unless he was arrested). He was also considering the possibility of settling in Switzerland permanently, so he looked for any excuse to visit that beautiful country.

Bobby arrived in Bern at the end of October 2003, checked into an inexpensive hotel, and the next afternoon went to the U.S. embassy on Sulgeneckstrasse. Although he didn't know the Bernese dialect, his German was fluent enough to be understood easily, and since it was the U.S. embassy, everybody spoke English anyway. He was told that his passport would be taken apart and then new pages would be inserted. The process would take about ten days. Bobby gave the authorities the address of his hotel and his cell phone number and asked if they could call him when the reconstructed passport was ready.

When he returned to the hotel, he checked out immediately. A short time later, he took the train to Zurich about one hour away and registered at an upscale hotel there, using an assumed name. All of this cloak-and-dagger movement was a way of hiding his whereabouts should the embassy at Bern be informed by Washington that a warrant had been issued for his arrest and his passport should be confiscated. It's true that the embassy had his cell phone number, but he'd left no forwarding address at the Bern hotel. If the authorities came after him in Zurich, he could probably make an escape before they arrived. As it developed, after about a week he called the embassy himself and discovered that all was well: His passport was waiting for him.

Back at Bern he wondered if it was a trap, if the moment he entered the embassy he'd be arrested. He took the chance and walked into the building as nonchalantly as he could. *Voilà!* The documents clerk handed him his passport, and he remarked to her how nice it looked with the twenty-four new pages perfectly sewn in. With the knowledge that his old passport was good until 2007, he then flew "home" to Tokyo.

Barely six weeks later the Department of Justice sent him a letter revoking his passport, stating that the revocation was issued because he was "the subject of an outstanding federal warrant of arrest for a felony," which didn't refer by name to the Fischer-Spassky match of 1992, but made reference to the U.S. Code under which Fischer was accused: the International Emergency Economic Powers Act, Title 50, Sections 1701, 1702, and 1705, signed by President George H. W. Bush.

There were problems with the revocation of the passport, however. Fischer never received the notice and therefore couldn't appeal it, which according to law he had the right to do. The Justice Department claimed that the letter had been sent to the hotel in Bern (the location Bobby had given to the embassy) and was returned to them with no forwarding address appended. It was dated December 11, 2003, and when a faxed copy of the letter was ultimately examined, it didn't have an address for Fischer on it, the implication being that the embassy had never sent the letter to Bern. According to law, Bobby would have had sixty days for a hearing and perhaps another sixty days to confront the appeal if it didn't go his way. Such a hearing would only determine whether he was the subject of the warrant for arrest and whether the proper procedures for his application had been in effect when he applied for the passport renewal in 1997. The law stated that a passport "shall not be issued to an applicant subject to a federal arrest warrant or subpoena for any matter involving a felony." One of two things had to be operative in Bern in 1997: Either the State Department made a clerical mistake in issuing him a renewed passport at that time, or else Fischer didn't indicate on his application that he was a wanted felon. If he'd lied by omission, he would have been guilty of fraud, a charge that could have been added to his sanction violation and his income tax evasion.

Had he received the notice, his appeal—had he attempted it—would probably have been denied, but it might have given him some time to travel to another country, or to some hideout—perhaps somewhere in Switzerland, such as the Alps—to avoid arrest.

Not knowing that his arrest was imminent, and believing that his passport was legal, on July 13, 2004, he went to Narita Airport in Tokyo to board a plane bound for Manila. He was arrested and shackled in chains.

One of the first things Fischer tried to do while he was behind bars was to ask permission to call someone—perhaps an attorney who could assist with setting bail. The authorities wouldn't permit him access to a telephone, however. People who violate Japanese law, even unknowingly, may be arrested, imprisoned, and deported. They may also be held in detention for a minor offense, without bail, for months or more during investigation and legal proceedings. Bobby's claim that he was an American citizen and had a right to make a phone call was ignored.

Twenty-four hours later, an immigration official at the airport called Miyoko to tell her what had happened, and she immediately contacted an attorney and headed for the airport detention facility to see Bobby—but when she arrived there, visiting hours were over. She did see him the next day, for thirty minutes. "He was so upset, and I didn't know what to say to console him," she told a journalist.

Fischer was kept in the Narita Airport Detention Center for illegal immigrants for almost a month on the initial charge that he was attempting to travel on an invalid passport, but the more serious charge echoed back to 1992, for defying the American trade embargo and participating in the match with Spassky in the former Yugoslavia. It's possible that Fischer's broadcasts were the fuel that sparked the U.S. government to activate the decade-old charge against him. Certainly, the Department of Justice wanted him deported back to the United States to stand trial for his violations, possibly in concert with the Department of the Treasury, for income tax evasion. Miyoko, for her part, thought that U.S. authorities could have arrested Bobby anytime post-1992, but they didn't and only went after him when "suddenly he started to attack America and it made the government very angry."

Bobby was like a caged panther, pacing up and down, continually complaining about everything, from the food, to the temperature, to the disrespect his captors showed him, and screaming at the guards. He wasn't the ideal prisoner; he was the type of person who couldn't be incarcerated indefinitely without doing harm to himself or others. As it was, he sparked fights with the jailers and eventually was transferred to the East Japan Immigration Detention Center in Ushiku, forty miles northeast of Tokyo. The center had all of the trappings of a high-security prison, and its inmates were incarcerated there for relatively long periods. Fischer claimed that at sixty-one he was the oldest prisoner in the center and therefore deserved more deference. But his seniority and chess credentials counted little with the guards. Once, when he told the guard who brought him his breakfast that his soft-boiled eggs were really hard-boiled and that he wanted an additional egg, they got into a scuffle. He ended up in solitary confinement for several days and wasn't permitted visits or even allowed to leave his cell. Another time, he purposely stepped on the glasses of a guard he didn't like and was given solitary again.

Miyoko visited him a few times each week—a two-hour trip each way from Tokyo—and she brought him newspapers and some money so he could buy extra food (usually *natto*, which was fermented soybeans) from the jailers. Several people immediately tried to assist Bobby in securing his release, most prominently Masako Suzuki, a brilliant young lawyer who became his chief counsel and most determined advocate, and John Bosnitch, a forty-three-year-old Canadian journalist of Bosnian origin who was stationed in Tokyo. They formed a committee called "Free Bobby Fischer" and worked with others trying to extricate Fischer from his cell. Suzuki filed proceedings to address what she claimed was an illegal arrest. Fischer called it a "kidnapping."

It isn't known how much Fischer paid for his legal defense, but it probably wasn't all that much since Suzuki was receiving pro bono advice and assistance from those who felt Bobby was being persecuted. His plight had become a cause. And although Bosnitch was not a lawyer, he seemed to know the intricacies of the Japanese legal system and was both pleasantly aggressive and courteous, which impressed the lawmakers and officials he had to deal with. He was subsequently named an amicus curiae in Fischer's case and sat in on and participated in all of the legal proceedings. One of the first orders of business was to prevent Fischer's deportation to the United States. Bobby believed that if he were brought back and forced to stand trial, he'd be convicted. But that was the least of it. He was convinced that he was so hated by the government that he'd be murdered while serving time. One of the ways he thought the deportation might be prevented, or at least delayed, was for him to become stateless by legally renouncing his citizenship. Then the United States would have less jurisdiction over him. He wanted to stay in Japan.

Renunciation of United States citizenship requires three things: (1) an appearance before a U.S. consular or diplomatic officer, (2) the renunciation must be done in a foreign country (normally at a U.S. embassy or consulate), and (3) an oath of renunciation must be signed in person before a U.S. official.

Bobby wrote to the U.S. embassy in Tokyo asking them to send a member of the diplomatic staff to the detention center so that an official could accept his citizenship renunciation. No one came. He also wrote to Secretary of State Colin Powell to enlist his help in allowing him to renounce his citizenship. No answer. Finally, Bobby wrote another letter to the U.S. embassy in Tokyo *insisting* that they send someone, and in case they didn't comply, he appended his renunciation. If Bobby had any trepidation about permanently severing his relationship with the United States, there was no evidence of it in the renunciation he wrote. He *had* to get out of his imprisonment, and so he attempted to surgically remove himself—quickly and precisely, slicing away at his homeland, aware that it would be a permanent farewell, never to be undone. The text:

> I am Robert James Fischer. I am a U.S. citizen. I was born on March 9, 1943 in Chicago, Ill. U.S.A. My U.S. passport no. is or was Z7792702. It was issued at the U.S. Embassy in Bern, Switzerland. The issue date is January 24, 1997 and the expiry date is January 23,

2007. I Robert James Fischer do hereby irrevocably and permanently renounce my U.S. citizenship and all the supposed rights and privileges of United States citizenship.

Bobby Fischer's renunciation of his citizenship was never accepted by the United States. He remained a citizen. Meanwhile, Suzuki and Bosnitch appealed to the courts on Bobby's behalf for him to become a political refugee from the United States and be allowed to live in Japan. Their argument was that when he competed in Yugoslavia, he violated the trade sanctions purely as a political act against the United States, and he was now being punished for it. This request was denied. Bobby's team also pleaded to the court that it strike down the deportation order requested by the United States and brought by the Japanese Immigration Bureau. That request was denied too. Bobby had been locked up for over a month at this point and was becoming desperate. Finally able to make outgoing calls, he, along with his team, started contacting a number of countries to determine if they would offer him asylum:

Germany—Bobby's plea was based on his paternity, in that his father, Gerhardt Fischer, was German, and under the blood citizenship law of the country, Bobby claimed to be a German citizen. The problem was that Bobby was a Holocaust denier, which is a crime in Germany. If the country offered him asylum, his past remarks would get him arrested as soon as he entered.

Cuba—Since Castro was so anti-American, and Fischer knew the premier, he thought Cuba might accept him. Nada.

North Korea—Possibly the most anti-American country in the world. The problem was that Miyoko thought it was the *worst* country in the world and could not see herself living there or even visiting.

Libya—Mu'ammar Gadhafi was attempting to ingratiate himself with the United States and couldn't take the chance of antagonizing President Bush.

Iran—To the Iranians' way of thinking, Bobby was Jewish, and they had no interest.

Venezuela—No reason given for rejection.

Switzerland—Although the country was politically neutral, Bobby's anti-Semitic views were not acceptable there.

Montenegro—Fischer's connection with Vasiljevic, who had scammed so much money from the citizens, left them unenthused.

The Philippines—Although Bobby was adored by the Philippine chess community and had established ties there, he was unhappy with the ouster of president Joseph Estrada, whom he believed was "pushed out illegally." He also felt that crime and corruption was rising in Manila and even in Baguio, and although he enjoyed living there, he was uncertain about gaining, or even wanting, asylum.

Iceland—Yes, Iceland! As a result of the 1972 match, Fischer had more to do with promoting Iceland than anyone in modern times. In effect, as a hero who'd come to the island and performed great deeds, he'd become part of the Icelandic sagas. The Icelanders were also known for their strength, fairness, and stubbornness. They had the ability as a people not only to offer him asylum, but to secure it and extricate him from prison.

♖

Saemi Palsson, Fischer's old bodyguard, was tracked down at his winter home in the north of Spain. "Saemi, this is Bobby. I need your help. I'm a prisoner in Japan and I want to get asylum in Iceland. Can you help me?"

A former policeman and carpenter who in his youth had gained unlikely fame as a "rock dancer," who delighted people with his "twist" performances, Saemi would do anything for a friend. He also had an innate sense of self-publicity. Although he hadn't seen Bobby in thirty-two years, Saemi phoned some political and business leaders and several from the chess community who he thought might be able to help Bobby. He was on a plane to the East in short order.

While Palsson was en route to Japan, a group of stalwart Icelanders met in Reykjavik to discuss whether there was any way asylum could be offered to Fischer. A committee was formed using Bobby's initials: "RJF." Perhaps as an afterthought someone came up with another meaning for the acronym: "Rights, Justice, Freedom."

Though the rest of the world, including his own country, was vilifying Bobby for his outrageous positions and statements, the Icelanders felt sorry for him. They deplored what he'd said, but felt he had a right to express himself. The Icelanders also felt a sense of obligation. Fischer, in effect, had honored the country of Iceland by playing there in 1972, and now he was in trouble. To not help him, they believed, would be a greater moral offense and act of ingratitude than even his verbal attacks of hostility and hatred.

All of the members of the committee were eminent Icelanders and ardent chess enthusiasts: Gudmundur Thorarinsson, former member of parliament and the principal organizer of the 1972 Fischer-Spassky match; Magnus Sku-lasson, a psychiatrist; Gardar Sverrisson, a political scientist; Helgi Olafsson, a grandmaster; and Einar Einarsson, a bank executive. The group met for over five months in formal meetings, and there was much correspondence and phone exchanges between them as they began lobbying the Icelandic government to consider Fischer's case. In the midst of this, they contacted both the United States and Japanese embassies in Reykjavik to protest Fi-scher's incarceration. In a letter to Fumiko Saiga, the Japanese ambassador to Iceland, the RJF Committee stated, in part:

> We feel obliged to express our deepest dismay and sorrow of the Japanese authorities' grotesque violation of his [Fischer's] human rights and of international law. . . . As we protest in the strongest possible terms against your handling of this matter, we request immediate release of Mr. Robert J. Fischer.

Palsson began visiting Bobby at the jail and met with some of the Japanese officials to see what he could do. Having a representative there from Iceland, although Saemi wasn't an official, helped Bobby somewhat to make a credible case that the country was considering asylum. The problem was that he wasn't helping his own case.

Bobby continued making broadcasts, this time directly from the detention center's pay telephone, and they went immediately on the World Wide Web. Most of his vitriol was directed toward the Jews ("absolute pigs"), with a slight softening of his invective against the United States. Although still unkind ("the whole country has no culture, no taste, it's filled with pollution"), his anti-American remarks were tempered somewhat—though hardly enough to win points with the U.S. Justice Department.

Fischer then announced that he was going to marry Miyoko Watai, his long-time companion. "I could be a sacrifice pawn," she said to the press. "But in chess there is such a thing as pawn promotion, where a pawn can become a queen. Bobby-san is my king and I will become his queen." Shortly after that the couple was married in a private ceremony in the prison. John Bosnitch was a witness. But was the marriage ceremony legal? More than a year later, when asked by a reporter whether she ever "tied the knot" with Fischer, Miyoko replied, "I'd rather not say," and then added, "I prefer not to talk about private things." Immediately, the media began implying that the alleged marriage was just a ploy to help Fischer obtain his release and live in Japan, but Suzuki disagreed: "It was already a de-facto marriage," she said. "Now it is a legal marriage. I have never seen a case where there is so much passion and devotion." Miyoko was more forthright when she stated: "We had been satisfied with our life before he was detained. Marrying him legally may be helpful to avoid the possible deportation and enable him to get a permanent visa in Japan."

Fischer, on the advice of the RJF Committee, wrote to Iceland's foreign minister, David Oddsson, and requested a residence permit, which was forwarded to him immediately. The Japanese court didn't accept it, though. If a country offered Fischer *citizenship*, they specified, they'd consider deporting him to that country. In the meantime, the Tokyo District Court issued an injunction to stay the deportation order on the grounds that a passport violation was not an extraditable offense. The final lawsuit against the deportation could take as long as a year. After months behind bars, it didn't look as though Bobby could emotionally survive for much longer.

Almost every day Fischer's team attempted a new strategy. He was encouraged to write a letter to the Althingi, the Icelandic parliament, and he composed a five-hundred-word plea, extracts of which follow:

```
                                  Ushiku, Japan January 19, 2005


    Althingi, The Icelandic Parliament
    150 Reykjavik
    Iceland


        Honorable Members of Althingi:


        I, the undersigned, Robert James Fischer sincerely thank
    the Icelandic nation for the friendship it has shown to me
```

ever since I came to your country many years ago and
competed for the title of World Champion in chess—and even
before that. . . .

For the past six months I have been forcibly and
illegally imprisoned in Japan on the completely false and
ludicrous grounds that I entered Japan on April 15, 2004
and that I "departed" or attempted to depart Japan on July
13, 2004 with an invalid passport. During this period my
health has steadily deteriorated, I've been dizzy for
about the past two months now. . . .

When the Narita Airport Immigration Security authorities
brutally and violently "arrested" me . . . I was seriously
injured and very nearly killed. Furthermore it is surely
not beneficial to my health either physically or
psychologically that they've dragged me here to Ushiku
which is only about 66 kilometers from the leaking
Tokaimura Nuclear Power Plant (Japan's Chernobyl!!) in
Tokai City. They just had another accident there on
October 14, 2004! . . .

Neither the Japanese nor the American authorities have
ever bothered to offer any explanation whatsoever for this
outrageously criminal act [his arrest]. Apparently,
they're strictly heeding Disraeli's advice which was to
"Never apologize, never explain!"

Because of all of the foregoing I would therefore like to
formally request that Althingi grant me Icelandic
citizenship so that I may actually enjoy the offer of
residence in Iceland that your Minister of Foreign Affairs,
Mr. David Oddsson has so graciously extended to me.

                                Most Respectfully,
                                BOBBY FISCHER

During his incarceration in Japan, the only respites Bobby had from bore-
dom and emotional turmoil were the visits from his lawyers and Miyoko,

and his use of the telephone. He was allowed out of his cell to make collect calls, and the jailers seemed to put no time limit on them. He talked with Palsson, and later he had long, wide-ranging conversations with Gardar Sverrisson, the Icelandic political scientist on the RJF Committee. These calls to Gardar were important to Bobby because they went beyond the complicated aspects of his imprisonment and touched on other matters, such as politics, religion, and philosophy. Bobby asked Gardar in what religion, if any, he'd been raised, and when he was told it was Catholicism, Bobby pressed for more insight, wanting to know the nuances of that theology. The two men created a tele-pal relationship, forming a bond that would last for years.

Bobby also discussed Catholicism with a second person during this time. Richard Vattuone of San Diego, California, was another attorney who was helping out with the case. He visited Bobby in the jail and gave him a copy of *The Apostle of Common Sense,* a book about the writer G. K. Chesterton, which covered various matters of religion and culture. Bobby read some of the book and had conversations with Vattuone about religion. Chesterton was a convert to Catholicism.

When Miyoko came to visit, often she'd have to wait to see Bobby if he had another visitor—such as Suzuki or Bosnitch—since the detention center only allowed one visitor at a time, and visiting hours were limited. Fischer would have to pass through sixteen locked doors before reaching the visitors' room, and could only talk through a plate-glass wall, as if he were not just in an immigration detention center but a maximum security prison.

Three members of the RJF Committee—Einarsson, Thorarinsson, and Sverrisson—traveled to Japan at their own expense to see if they could find a way to expedite Fischer's release. No matter what logic they offered to the authorities, such as the fact that Iceland's foreign minister David Oddsson had issued Bobby a foreigner's passport—similar to what is called a green card in the United States—the rules-conscious, bureaucratic Japanese were not persuaded. They continued to maintain that Bobby would be deported back to the United States once the legal proceedings were concluded.

The RJF members were about to leave Japan, depressed that they'd made little headway, when a call came in from Suzuki that bore potentially good news. A member of the Japanese parliament was willing to meet with the committee to see whether there was a way he could help. He'd studied the issues and sided with Bobby.

The meeting was held in secret, and the parliamentarian, who spoke perfect English, having been educated at Oxford, asked for anonymity, which he believed would enable him to better work behind the scenes. After he heard all of the arguments as to why Bobby should be released, and judged that the RJF members were committed to their cause, he went into action. Somehow he ignited the interest of Miszuko Fukushima, chairman of the Japanese Social Democratic Party. The goal was to get Fukushima to petition for Bobby's right to be deported to—and accepted by—Iceland. Fukushima criticized Chieko Nohno, Japan's minister of justice, for the arrest and detention, and asked him to reconsider the case. Although it was not a watershed moment, the current was beginning to shift, and as Bobby saw the accumulation of small advantages—a concept in chess described by Wilhelm Steinitz—he became optimistic, although not exhilarated.

When the RJF Committee members returned to Iceland, they worked full-time arousing their parliament's interest in the case, warning that if action weren't taken quickly, it would be too late for Fischer to receive justice. He would be extradited to the United States and probably imprisoned for ten years. Many of them believed, as did Fischer, that he could be murdered while in prison.

The Icelandic Chess Federation took a calculated risk in attempting to add strength to the argument for releasing Bobby. They issued a strong critique condemning Bobby's statements, while hoping that an appeal to the United States' sense of humanitarianism might alleviate the tension in Japan:

> The Icelandic Chess Federation is, of course, aware of the obscene anti-Semitic and anti-American remarks that Bobby Fischer has made over the last year on different occasions. The Federation is appalled by these remarks, as any civilized body would be, and sees them as signs of a deranged and devastated psyche. In 1992, in Yugoslavia, however, Bobby Fischer's only crime was to play chess again, after years of isolation. The Icelandic Chess Federation urges the President of the United States to pardon Bobby Fischer and let him go free.

The letter was sent to President George W. Bush and received no reply.

Twelve years prior, months after the 1992 indictment had been issued, Bill Clinton had been elected President of the United States. David Oddsson, then the prime minister of Iceland, had visited the White House at the time and made a personal appeal to one of Clinton's senior aides, asking that the president drop the charges against Fischer. Word came back that Clinton would prefer not to make a ruling on the matter, "an unusual decision," according to Oddsson. "When the leader of a country makes a personal plea about a relatively small matter (in the scheme of things) to another leader, it is usually granted."

Back at the time of the sanctions controversy, Spassky wasn't indicted by the French, and Lothar Schmid wasn't indicted by the Germans. Bobby Fischer was the only person in the world ever known to have faced charges under President Bush's bill.

Trying to prevent Fischer's escape to Iceland, various agencies in the United States accelerated their pursuit of Bobby, putting more pressure on Japan to extradite him. A federal grand jury in Washington began what turned out to be a smoke-screen investigation accusing Fischer of money laundering after his match with Spassky in 1992. Since there was no evidence of such laundering, it was Fischer's lawyers' belief that the government was attempting to propagandize Fischer's sanctions case by further tarnishing his public image. Nothing came of the investigation and no additional indictment was handed down.

At this time James Gadsen, the U.S. ambassador to Iceland, got involved, suggesting that Iceland drop the offer of sanctuary to Bobby Fischer. David Oddsson, in his foreign minister role, invited Gadsen to his office and then categorically refused to back down, adding that Fischer's alleged crime of a violation of trade sanctions in Yugoslavia had exceeded Iceland's statute of limitations.

Perhaps because of the political pressure exerted on him, Japanese justice minister Chieko Nohno told reporters after a cabinet meeting, "If he [Fischer] has Icelandic citizenship it would be legally possible to deport him to that country. The Immigration Bureau must think about the most appropriate place for him to be deported to."

The situation remained unresolved, however, and as Bobby reached his sixty-second birthday in his cell, he was morose. He'd served nine months in prison, and the few people who visited him said he looked wretched. Thorarinsson said that Fischer, locked behind bars, reminded him of Hamlet, and then he quoted a line from Shakespeare's play:

> *I could be bound in a nutshell*
> *And count myself a king of infinite space*
> *Were it not that I had bad dreams.*

The RJF members called virtually every member of parliament to lobby for citizenship: full, *permanent* citizenship, not just a temporary permit to live in Iceland. They then met with the General Committee of Althingi. A bill was written asking for approval of citizenship for Bobby Fischer, and an Extraordinary Session of Parliament was called for Saturday, March 21, 2005. Three rounds of discussion took place in the space of twelve minutes, and questions were posed regarding the extent of the emergency. The answers were succinct and forthcoming: Bobby Fischer's improper incarceration was a violation of his rights; all he was really guilty of was moving some wooden pieces across a chessboard; he'd been a friend of Iceland, and had a historical connection to it, and now he needed the country's help.

Once the issues had been dealt with, each member of the Althingi was polled on whether to grant Fischer permanent citizenship. "*Já,*" said forty members, one by one. "*Forõast,*" said two members who abstained. No one voted "*Nei.*"

Bobby smiled for the first time in months when he heard that the Icelandic bill had been enacted, and on March 23, 2005, he was released from his cell. He was picked up by a limousine supplied by the Icelandic embassy, given his new Icelandic passport, and he and Miyoko, hand in hand, sped to Narita Airport.

When Bobby emerged from the limousine at Narita, the scene resembled that moment in *A Tale of Two Cities* when Dr. Manette is released from the Bastille, "recalled to life" as it were: white-haired, battered, with a grizzly beard and old clothes. The difference between Bobby and Dickens's good doctor was the voice: Manette's was faint, "dreadful and pitiable"; Bobby's was booming, ferocious and vengeful. "This was nothing but a kidnapping, pure and simple!" he said to the dozens of reporters and photographers who were following him into the terminal. "Bush and Koizumi [the American and Japanese presidents] are criminals. They deserve to be hung!" said bad old Bobby, showing that prison had done nothing to tamp down his denunciatory fervor. But something in him *had* changed. When Zita, then thirty years old, saw the footage of him on television, she said: "It is not his beard. There is something bothering about his eyes. He is a hopeless, broken man."

When Bobby's plane touched down at Keflavik Airport, and he stepped on the tarmac, he didn't kneel down and kiss the ground—at least, not literally. Metaphorically, however, he genuflected to the land of the Vikings. He was now in a country that really wanted him, and for the first time in thirteen years he felt truly safe. His first order of business was to settle into the Presidential Suite at the Hotel Loftleidir and order one of his Rabelaisian meals, with bowls and bowls of *skyr*.

15

Living and Dying in Iceland

IRST THERE WERE the familiar hazel eyes. They stared at everything furtively, judgmentally, not wanting or permitting eye contact with others. Bobby Fischer's gaze ricocheted from the partially cobble-stoned road of Klappirstigur Street, where he lived, to the slight rise up to the busy thoroughfare of Laugavegur, with its little shops, then back to the BMWs and Volvos parked at meters and the blue-eyed and cherry-cheeked Icelanders heading back to work after lunch. The passersby recognized Bobby: He'd become the most famous man in Iceland and was remembered not for his public venom toward America but for putting Iceland on the map in 1972. His frozen glance denied them access, however, and they walked with their heads down, trying to lessen the slight of his disregard as they bent against the bitterly cold wind sweeping down from Mount Esja and off the bay. A crunch of snow seeped slowly into the sides of Bobby's black Birkenstock clogs.

Then there was his ineffective signature disguise: blue denim work shirt and pants, a black leather fingertip coat with a leather baseball cap to match, and the obligatory blue fleece sweater, all carefully selected so that he'd appear to fit in, to be seen as just one of the Norse folk who were his new countrymen.

Gone were the elegant handmade suits and carefully knotted ties. The man who'd proudly owned eighteen suits as a teenager, and who'd aspired to own a hundred more, now dressed the same way every day. People, even his friends, thought Bobby only owned one outfit, because his appearance was unvarying, but he owned several copies of the same denim pants and shirt, and he laundered and ironed them himself, often daily, usually late at night, singing as he pressed for perfect creases. As for what people thought about his dress, he was cynical and terse: "That's their problem."

Downtown Reykjavik, a charming city of almost 120,000 people, has the atmosphere of a typical Scandinavian village, although it's somewhat larger. A visitor sees twisting streets, tidy clapboard houses with colored roofs, shops for tourists and locals, and people dressed in boots, parkas, scarves, and woolen hats pulled over their ears. It's not quite Gstaad or Aspen, but the weather is cold enough to ski on the snow-covered mountains looming to the north.

Often, Bobby walked barely two blocks from his apartment to one of his favorite restaurants, Anestu Grösum—"The First Vegetarian"—and climbed the stairway to the pumpkin-painted second-floor eatery. The food was spread out behind a counter, cafeteria style, and he simply pointed to what he wanted. The server behind the counter, who looked something like the actress Shelley Duvall, smiled and handed him a tray with his selected food. The portions were huge.

When Bobby, as was typical, arrived past two o'clock, the restaurant would be sparsely filled: perhaps a Danish hippie, two American tourists, and three young local girls preoccupied with what they thought was important gossip. Ever a creature of habit, Bobby moved to his favorite table—one by the window looking out onto a side street, with a few birch and juniper trees not yet in bloom. Before he sat, he'd go to the cooler and help himself to a bottle of organic beer, Oxford Gold, and as he confronted his food, he'd open his latest reading matter. He was particularly taken with a book entitled *The Myth of Progress,* by Georg Henrik von Wright, a Finnish philosopher and successor to Ludwig Wittgenstein at the University of Cambridge. A moral pessimist, von Wright questioned whether the material and technological advances of modern society could really be considered "progress" at all. Bobby had found an English-language copy of the book at the local bookstore, Bókin ("Book"), and it seemed to mesh with his own philosophy. He was so taken by von Wright's ideas that when he discovered an Icelandic edition of the book at Bókin, he gave it as a gift to his new friend Gardar Sverrisson.

Was this the same Bobby Fischer who supposedly knew only chess, the sullen high school dropout from Brooklyn? He looked something like the Bobby Fischer of decades past, the intelligent eyes, the slight bumpish imperfection on the right side of the nose, the broad shoulders, the loping gait, but this Bobby Fischer was harder, a balding man with a slight paunch, a man at the far end of middle age who looked as if he'd known if not tragedy then at least major reversals. Something about his aura reminded an observer of an ill-treated dog just escaped from his captors. There was a lump the size of a large fingertip above his right eyebrow. He rarely smiled, perhaps because of embarrassment over his broken and missing teeth; he never looked at himself in a mirror because he disapproved of what his appearance had become. The real inconsistency, however, was that this Bobby Fischer—the great chess player who some thought was a cultural dolt, a man who supposedly knew nothing of life except a *game* ("Fischer came close to being a moron," Martin Gardner, a writer for *Scientific American,* seriously opined)—was reading a philosophical treatise!

Many people who haven't been formally educated awaken later in life with a desire to progress and deepen their view of the world, to go back to school or self-educate themselves. Bobby joined their ranks out of an essential self-awareness. "Larry Evans once said," Bobby commented, "that I didn't know anything about life; all I knew was chess, and he was right!" In a somewhat different mood, Bobby also said at one point that he felt like giving up chess from time to time, "but what else would I do?"

Bobby's lack of traditional institutional education was well known and continually reported in the press, but what wasn't common knowledge was that after he won the World Championship at age twenty-nine, he began a systemized regimen of study outside chess. History, government, religion, politics, and current events became his greatest interests, and during the thirty-three-year interval from his first Reykjavik stay to his second he spent most of his spare time reading and amassing knowledge.

Several Icelanders indicated that there was nothing he couldn't discuss in depth. He could talk about such subjects as the French Revolution and the Siberian gulags, the philosophy of Nietzsche, and the discourses of Disraeli.

After spending close to two hours eating and reading at Anestu Grösum, and finishing off two helpings of *skyr* with redundant whipped cream, Bobby would invariably walk to Bókin. It was a book lover's dream and delightfully eccentric: A stuffed monkey doll with spectacles sat outside the store with a book in its lap; there were thousands of used books, mainly in Icelandic but a great portion in English, German, and Danish, some on subjects so arcane that only a few could understand or appreciate them, such as the mating habits of the puffin—the national bird—or an analysis of the inscriptions on the churches of Heidelberg. The aisles of bookshelves meandered all over the store, and in the center of the room there was a huge hillock of books more than five feet tall, haphazardly thrown there and cascading to the floor because there was simply no room to put them anywhere else. There were fewer than a dozen chess books for sale.

Each day Bobby collected his mail at the store, kept for him behind the counter. He'd say a few words to the store's owner, Bragi Kristjonsson, and head to *his* spot at the store's farthest reaches, at the end of one of the not quite three-foot-wide corridors, with low stacks of books and old copies of *National Geographic* lining the edges of the aisle. Perhaps as a gesture of respect toward his famous customer, Bragi placed a battered chair at the end of the corridor, and Bobby sat there next to a small window that looked out at a tattoo parlor (which he disapproved of) across the street, reading and dreaming—and sometimes even falling asleep—often to closing time. It was his home. "It's good to be free," he wrote to a friend.

The greatest portion of Bobby's reading was devoted to history, everything from *The Rise and Fall of the Roman Empire* to *The Rise and Fall of the Third Reich;* he pored over books on battles from ancient Greece to World War II and conspiracy theories such as *Hitler's Secret Bankers: How Switzerland Profited from Nazi Germany,* as well as anti-Semitic tracts such as *Jewish Ritual Murder.* It's possible that he was trying to find his own place in history through his voracious reading, but it was more likely a search for understanding, an attempt to comprehend his complicated gestalt—"the whole catastrophe," as the fictional Zorba the Greek perceptively described himself.

Just as Fischer was becoming settled in Iceland, hardly before he had a chance to unpack his bags (which held few possessions: only what clothes and books he owned in Japan), an impending match with his friend Pal Benko was suddenly announced by Janos Kubat, the man who'd helped arrange the Fischer-Spassky match in 1992. Kubat issued the announcement to

RIA, the Russian News Agency, and said the match would take place in the town of Magyarkanizsa on the border of Hungary and Serbia, where Bobby had lived for several months in 1992. Kubat claimed that a financial sponsor had been found and that the venue was already chosen. There was only one problem: Bobby knew nothing of the match. He'd had a falling-out with Kubat in August of 1993 over a moral issue, according to Bobby, and they weren't on speaking terms. Most important, he had no intention of leaving Iceland, because of the threat of extradition to the United States.

Two weeks after being greeted as a hero in Iceland, and after stating that he just wanted to live in peace, Bobby found that his troubles weren't over. He received a letter dated April 7, 2005, from the Union Bank of Switzerland to the effect that the institution was closing his account. UBS was holding some $3 million of his assets, originally deposited there in 1992, and wanted to know to which bank in Iceland Bobby wished his investments transferred.

Bobby had no intention of placing his money in an Icelandic bank (despite being able to receive a potentially higher interest rate there) and demanded to know what was going on. While he and the bank were exchanging intransigent letters, he gave an interview to *Morgunbladid* in which he said: "Possibly a third party has had something to do with this as a part of further attacks against me. In fact, I don't know what the directors of UBS are thinking but it seems quite clear that the bank is afraid to keep me as a customer. This is absolutely vicious, illegal and unfair of the UBS." He threatened a lawsuit. The third party he presumed responsible was the United States government.

Bobby turned to Einar Einarsson for advice. Not only was Einarsson a member of the Icelandic committee that had helped secure Bobby's release from imprisonment, he'd also been a leading banker before introducing the Visa credit card to Iceland. Careful and methodical, Einarsson began to coach Bobby through an exchange of long, technical e-mails with UBS. Bobby was impatient. He didn't have a chess tournament to discharge his competitive energy, so he vented his anger at the Swiss bank, which he insisted was run by Jews. This was a different kind of opponent, though, and Bobby hadn't mastered the techniques of dueling with international financial institutions. So he lost. Eventually, UBS liquidated all of his assets and transferred them to Landsbanki in Reykjavik. Bobby claimed that he lost a sizable amount in the transaction.

In retrospect, it seems quite clear what UBS was doing. Many of its fifty-two thousand accounts were offshore holdings, secretly deposited—many without names, just numbers—as tax havens for American citizens. In Bobby's case, he was broadcasting, some might say *boasting*—without cover—that he had $3 million at UBS (he may have even given his account number over the air), and since he'd paid no income tax on it, or on any of his other income since 1977, the U.S. Internal Revenue Service was making its displeasure known to UBS.

Within a few years after Bobby's dispute with the UBS, thousands of American tax evaders, most millionaires like Bobby, came forth to avoid prosecution, and others who continued to hide their money at UBS were being pursued and arrested for income tax evasion. UBS wasn't conspiring against Bobby: They just wanted to get rid of one of their most public and foolish clients.

Since Iceland's interest rate at that time was higher than Switzerland's, it's curious why Bobby didn't want the transfer. Some have speculated that he was somehow prescient or had insider or special knowledge that the Icelandic banks would fail (as they did in 2008, in the country's economic collapse). A more likely explanation is that he really didn't see himself staying in Iceland forever. Perhaps he was hoping to gain citizenship in yet another country when the time was right.

The bank battle was an unpleasant interlude, but it didn't interrupt what was becoming the key portion of most of Bobby's days: reading. As the study of chess had been compulsive when he was a boy, so now his mind was captivated by deep, serious study of history, philosophy, and other topics. Prowling the aisles at Bókin, he was sometimes brought up short by the absence of a book he wanted, in which case he'd have the store order it for him. He was continually buying books, usually two or three a day, keeping most, discarding a few, and giving others to friends.

In ambience, although not in content, Bókin reminded him of Dr. Albrecht Buschke's chess bookstore in Greenwich Village, the one he'd visited as a child and as a young man. The books at Buschke's were slapdashedly scattered, but the disarray was nothing compared to the confusion of Bókin. Bobby seriously asked Bragi to hire him to confront and organize "the pile," because he thought there had to be books there, hidden deep within, that would be of interest to him, and also because he just couldn't stand the mess. Finally, he said he'd work for nothing. "But where would we put them?" was Bragi's refusal.

Bobby's aisle was a totally secure spot. With his back to the wall, gangster style, he could see anyone coming down the long, narrow corridor, and if he sensed that the person was an autograph seeker—or worse, a reporter—he would either scowl or feign total absorption in what he was reading and not respond if spoken to. Those ploys proved as effective as hanging a Do Not Disturb sign around his neck.

Often, if he noticed that the time was nearing six o'clock, he'd dash off to Yggdrasil, a health food store—the name refers to the mythological Tree of Life—deliberately arriving there just one minute before closing time. He'd then shop at his leisure, much to the discontent of the shop workers who wanted to quit for the day. By arriving as late as he did, he avoided the stares of other shoppers.

Checking out at the counter one day, he noticed a brand of candy bars called Rapunzel; there were two types available, chocolate-covered halvah and coconut. "Does this come from Israel?" he asked suspiciously. When told that the candy came from Germany—"You know, the fairy tale and the Brothers Grimm," the clerk said—Bobby was reassured and bought a few bars, his anti-Semitic sensibilities appeased.

Although he was often recognized in the street, few Icelanders intruded on his privacy. Foreigners weren't always so considerate, though, and he usually lashed out at anyone audacious enough to address him. There was *one* exception, noteworthy because it was so abnormal for him. An American tourist—a chess player—approached Bobby one day and invited him to dinner. After checking the man's passport to make sure he was who he said, and informally interrogating him to make sure he wasn't a reporter, Bobby atypically agreed to dine with the stranger. They went to one of Reykjavik's most expensive and elegant restaurants and were said to have a long conversation, mainly about politics.

Months passed placidly until Bobby had been living in Iceland for about a year. When Helgi Olafsson, a grandmaster, asked him how he liked living in the country, Bobby answered in his typical Calvin Coolidge style: "Good." But his sanctuary at Bókin began to become known, and stories appeared in the press about his going there, together with interviews of the store's proprietor, Bragi. A Russian television crew showed up to try to interview Fischer, and he fled. Eventually he tired of the reporters waiting to ambush him outside the bookstore, and he changed his routine. He began to frequent the Reykjavik Public Library, only a few blocks farther from where he lived. The library became the focal point of his life.

On the building's fifth floor, within a few feet of the tall cases of books on history and politics, he'd tuck himself away for hours at a table beside a window. In contrast to the unattractive side street outside the window of Bókin, the library's window provided a view of the fishing trawlers docked in the bay, and the mountains just beyond the water. For all of the days and months that Bobby went to the library, his new routine never leaked to the press. All of the librarians knew who Bobby was, but they never revealed his presence.

Right down the block from the library was an inexpensive Thai restaurant, Krua Thai, where Bobby began dining at least two or three times a week. Not on the normal tourist route, it was clean and cozy, with dark-painted walls, a giant silver-sequined elephant and other decorations from Thailand, and dim lighting, which his eyes preferred. Bobby liked the fish dishes with vegetables and rice. He also liked the owner, an intelligent, vivacious Thai woman named Sonja, and insisted that only she wait on him. "Where's the lady?" he'd demand as soon as he entered, knowing that she'd bring his favorite food and drink without his needing to order. There was only one item he absolutely refused to partake of: Icelandic bottled water. He said it made him sick. He drank only beer or tea. After he'd been going to Krua Thai for about a year, Sonja gently asked if he'd pose for a photo with her. He refused.

Bobby told no one, not even his closest friends, about Krua Thai, since, although he was lonely, he often preferred to dine alone; like Thomas Jefferson in the White House, he enjoyed his own company, the opportunity to read or to contemplate books, ideas, and memories. Paradoxically, it was when he was with others that he felt an uncomfortable solitude.

Bobby was conflicted about his intense desire for privacy, and his need—from his earliest days of childhood—for attention. He demanded constant reassurances of adoration, or at least notice. One day in downtown Reykjavik, he was asked for directions by some American tourists. "Gee, they didn't know who I was," he said disappointedly to Einarsson. "And they were *Americans*!" Another time, just to give himself a change from the city, he took a bus alone to a small fishing village named Grindavík near the famous Blue Lagoon, an outdoor thermal pool that he liked to bathe in. He stayed at an inn there for a few days. The waitress in the restaurant was friendly, especially since he was one of the only customers. "Are you famous?" she asked, possibly sensing Bobby's fame, or maybe because she'd seen his photo in *Morgunbladid* or some other periodical. "Perhaps," Bobby answered coyly. "What are you famous for?" she asked. More coyness: "A board game." The girl thought for a moment and then it came to her: "You're Mr. Bingo!" Bobby was mortified that she couldn't identify him.

Bobby still ate at Anestu Grösum, but he established a new regimen of taking a long walk around the City Pond, watching children feed ducks, geese, and the lovely whooping swans entwining their necks, and finally working his way to the library. Typically, his walks had no destination: To him they were akin to meditation—a chance to think without thinking—and he rambled about even during the bitterly cold winters. Most of the parks had benches, and if the weather was pleasant, he'd sit, read, think, and just *be,* an activity not atypical of many men entering late life.

Some Icelanders said that they spotted Bobby late at night, walking ghostlike down the deserted and windswept streets near the Old Harbor—like Charles Dickens prowling the docks of London—lost in thought, slightly limping but walking rapidly, as alone as if he'd been roaming the desolate, lava-strewn fields of Iceland's interior. Bobby's nocturnal perambulations were an echo of the late night walks he used to take when he lived in New York or Pasadena, and a continuation of the pattern he'd begun in childhood, staying up until the early morning studying chess, and then sleeping until noon or later.

It's possible that, at this point in his life, a year and a half after landing at Keflavik as a freed man, Bobby began feeling that Iceland was his personal Devil's Island: once there, never to leave. David Oddsson believed that

Fischer felt "trapped" in Iceland in general, and Reykjavik in particular. "I'm a city person," Oddsson said of himself. "I spend most of my time in Reykjavik. But if I could never go out to the country, that's precisely where I'd want to go. I would feel trapped in Reykjavik, as Fischer probably feels trapped in Iceland." Gardar Sverrisson said that, to Bobby, Iceland was a "prison."

By the time Fischer was completing his second year as an Icelandic citizen, he'd begun to grumble about the country and its people. He missed Europe and friends there, but he didn't dare leave his ocean-bound haven for fear that he might be captured and extradited. Interpol, the international police organization, had him flagged to be arrested at any one of 368 airports throughout the world.

Finding a permanent place to live in Reykjavik was difficult. Bobby's first apartment, a furnished sublet he rented for six months, had been ideal: It was downtown, had a bit of a view and a terrace, and he could walk quickly to stores and restaurants. Since Bobby ate every meal out—he never cooked—it was important that he live within minutes of a variety of dining establishments. "Eating was very important to him," Zsuzsa Polgar said in describing his life in Hungary. It *always* was, wherever he lived, and quiet meals with foods he enjoyed seemed to be even more important in Iceland.

When the owner of Bobby's apartment returned from her work abroad, as planned, she notified Bobby that he needed to vacate. Although he realized that he had to move, he didn't want to give up his comfortable residence. Einarsson managed to convince the owner to let Bobby stay an additional six months, but it was obvious that he'd need to arrange a permanent home after that. Einarsson and Sverrisson began escorting Bobby to various condominium apartments, looking for a place for him to buy. As was typical of him, he approached the purchase of his first apartment as he would a chess game: Before he made a move, *everything* had to be perfect. It was no surprise then that, initially, there was something wrong with every place he saw: One apartment was too close to the church and he was afraid that the morning bells would wake him; another had too many windows facing the street and he feared for his privacy; a third was too "high"—it was on the ninth floor—and he didn't want to rely on an elevator. A fourth apartment at first looked ideal, but Bobby detected something "wrong with the air." He claimed that it hurt his lungs to breathe there. While inspecting a fifth apartment, a plane flew overhead, and he immediately vetoed it as being "too noisy." Finally, he thought that one apartment had "possibilities," but his two friends quickly tried to talk him out of buying it because it was right below a tawdry sex shop. That didn't seem to bother Bobby, since the shop opened late in the afternoon, and therefore it would be quiet in the mornings. Einarsson and Sverrisson pointed out, though, that the apartment was in extremely poor condition and would need repairs amounting to tens of thousands of dollars. Bobby grimaced and agreed not to buy it.

He finally settled on an apartment in Gardar Sverrisson's building on Espergerdi Street, in a residential section on the east side of Reykjavik, too far to walk downtown, but accessible by two buses. The apartment had two minuses: It was on the ninth floor (which Bobby had previously said was too high), and he'd already rejected this very building because of its "bad air." *Voilà!* Magically, heights and air quality suddenly didn't bother him anymore—for no explicable reason. He just changed his mind.

Even though he was continents away from his wife, Bobby and Miyoko were in constant touch through e-mail and the telephone. She came to Reykjavik as much as her job in a pharmaceutical company—and her editorship of a chess journal in Tokyo—would allow. Most of her visits lasted two weeks and according to Gardar were idyllic for both Bobby and her. The Sverissons and the Fischers would go on weekend outings to the countryside, staying at friendly inns and basking in the majestic lunarlike countryside of Iceland. Family dinners were joyous occasions. "They were an affectionate couple, and acted as any husband and wife might: They were in love and showed it in many small ways," said Gardar. Although one can't know what exactly was in Bobby's mind relative to his marriage, it is altogether possible that he hoped to somehow leave Iceland one day and convince Miyoko to live with him permanently in another country.

His chosen apartment was decidedly not luxurious. Bobby could have afforded a place much larger, but this one was sufficient for his needs. It was a small one-bedroom, had an adequate-sized living room with an open kitchen, and a Juliet balcony that faced the sea. He furnished it comfortably but simply. Prints of Matisse graced the walls.

Bobby's purchasing the condominium at a price of 14 million kroner (about $200,000 at that time) may have been unconsciously motivated by the desire to be near a friend. According to Einarsson, Bobby had begun to feel ill, although he denied it not only to others but to himself. Having friends nearby would, as it developed, prove beneficial, especially since Gardar's wife was a nurse.

Once he'd moved into his new apartment, Bobby's daily pattern changed. He still woke up between noon and two p.m., drank his carrot juice, and went out for his first meal of the day. While he was well, he often took a very long walk to Anestu Grösum, the vegetarian restaurant. Bobby didn't drive, and if he had the need to go someplace beyond walking distance, he took a bus. A friend observed: "Despite the fact that he was a millionaire, he thought it idiotic to pay for taxis. He had no [misgivings about] standing and waiting for buses in all kinds of weather. Icelanders, for the most part, wouldn't do it. But he also liked to study people while he was riding." He was skittish about being driven, whether it was in a taxi—when he was forced to use one—or by a friend, and he'd insist that the driver keep both hands on the steering wheel at all times, never drive too fast, and obey every traffic law and signal. He always sat in the middle section of a bus, which he believed was much safer than the front or back.

Bobby couldn't escape chess, although he desperately wanted to. "I hate the old chess and the old chess scene," he wrote to a friend, making reference to his invention of Fischer Random. Nevertheless, there were entrepreneurs flying to Iceland or contacting him from Russia, France, the United States, and elsewhere, who were trying to entice him to play—any kind of chess was acceptable, just to encourage and ease him back into the game. It had been more than thirteen years since the second Fischer-Spassky match, and people were saying, fearing, he might never play again. They didn't want another twenty-year disappearance.

Another match against Spassky was discussed (and Spassky was agreeable to playing Fischer Random), but these talks ended in a matter of days. The potential match organizer, Dr. Alex Titomirov, a Russian scientist who was an expert in DNA transfer technology and CEO of a company called ATEO

Holdings Ltd., invited Spassky to meet him in Reykjavik to help with his negotiations with Bobby. Canadian-born Joel Lautier, the top player in France, was also a part of the group that met Bobby. It became clear, however, that Titomirov had no interest in yet another Fischer-Spassky contest, but wanted a Fischer-Kramnik match instead. Spassky was just being used to convince Fischer to "come back to chess." Fischer was open to discussions, but nothing was signed or agreed upon. Spassky was angered when he learned that he was not being considered for the match with Fischer, and he used insulting language when referring to Titomirov. Bobby chimed in with an equally vicious slur, again using what had happened as typical of Russian machinations.

Other offers proved to be too small or, in a few cases, even spurious. Some of Bobby's Icelandic friends thought certain "match organizers" weren't seriously negotiating, but rather just wanted to meet the mysterious Fischer, an event akin to meeting J. D. Salinger or Greta Garbo—something to boast about for the rest of their lives.

One offer, to play a twelve-game match with Karpov in a variation called Gothic Chess (with an expanded board of eighty squares, three extra pawns, and two new pieces—one that would combine the moves of the rook and the knight, and another that would combine the moves of the bishop and the knight), seemed like it had a chance to result in a match of historic significance, especially since the announced prize fund was $14 million: $10 million for the winner and $4 million for the loser. Karpov signed the contract, but when the promoters showed up in Reykjavik, Bobby wanted to be paid in three installments, one per meeting—in amounts of $10,000, $50,000, and $100,000 respectively—*just to discuss it*. Bobby also wanted proof that the prize fund was actually in a bank, and when that information, or proof of equity, wasn't forthcoming, the entire venture dribbled away.

Next came a proposal for a $2 million "Bobby Fischer Museum," to be housed in Iceland—or maybe it should be Brooklyn, the promoters mused. It appeared and dissolved like a dream almost before anyone had a chance to wake up.

Bobby peered over the chessboard, scanning and evaluating—attempting not just to suggest a Russian conspiracy, but to *prove* it unequivocally. Despite his promotion of Fischer Random and his rejection of and scorn for the "old chess," he still played over games, tempted by the action of contemporary tournaments and matches. A board and set, with pieces in their traditional positions, sat on the coffee table in his apartment, always ready for a session of analysis. On this particular day, Bobby was going over once again, perhaps for the hundredth time, the fourth game of the 1985 World Championship match between the two Russian grandmasters Garry Kasparov and Anatoly Karpov. Bobby's belief in a Russian cabal involving the two Ks had become his crusade, and he'd been airing his views all over the world for several years. He never wavered from claiming that all of the games in the 1985 match were fixed and prearranged move-by-move. "Even Polgar and Spassky, both World Champions, understand what I'm talking about," he said to no one in particular, becoming more strident as he went on. "These games are fake! Kasparov should answer my charges! He should be put through a lie detector test, and then the whole world will see what a liar he is!"

The cheating in that 1985 match was *obvious,* he insisted. In the fourth game Karpov moved his knight on his twenty-first move, which Bobby insisted was the "proof" of the beginning of the staged sequence. He pointed out to anyone who'd listen that Karpov "makes no less than eighteen consecutive moves on the light squares. Incredible!" This was statistically unusual, but not totally improbable, and was certainly not incontrovertible evidence of a plot.

Despite that, no one could talk Bobby out of his belief that Kasparov and Karpov were "crooks." Bobby remained resolute in his views, even though almost all grandmasters and many other members of the chess fraternity insisted that his accusations had no credible foundation. A scientist at the Center for Bioformatics and Molecular Biostatistics of the University of California, Mark Segal, proved mathematically that such a charge was specious and that the moves in the 1985 contest were more statistically likely to have occurred than Fischer's own shutouts of Taimanov and Larsen, and his near total defeat of Petrosian. Segal concluded his scholarly paper by facetiously musing, "Perhaps Fischer's ascent to world champion was part of some conspiracy."

Some people believed that Bobby was still stewing over the fact that he'd refused to play Karpov in 1975, and therefore was trying to belittle Karpov's resulting match with Kasparov. Others held that his accusations were a ploy to promote his new Fischer Random chess. Still others chalked them up to simple paranoia. For his part, Bobby never explained what either Karpov or Kasparov had to gain from prearranging match results, except to keep the title in the Russian family. But since both men were Russian that made no sense.

If gratitude is the heart's memory, Bobby's call to remembrance was weak or sometimes nonexistent. Not only did the stouthearted Icelanders on the RJF Committee manage to extricate him from a Japanese jail and a looming ten-year prison term, they did everything they could for him once he arrived in their country: finding him a place to live, protecting him from exploiters and prying journalists, advising him on his finances, driving him to the thermal baths, inviting him to dinners and holiday celebrations, taking him fishing and on tours throughout the country, trying to make him feel at home.

Indeed, they created a cultlike following around Bobby, treating him almost as seventeenth-century royalty. Each functionary had his own role to play in granting whatever wishes the king requested. What they didn't expect was that the king would respond to even the smallest failure with an "off with his head!" attitude. Bobby had behaved this way in his teen years, displaying unforgiving impatience toward any of his young followers who chanced, inadvertently, to displease him. Now, in Reykjavik, despite being the recipient of numerous acts of kindness and generosity, Bobby began finding fault, negatively overgeneralizing, and snapping at those who'd shown him the most loyalty.

His first break was with his obsequious bodyguard Saemi Palsson. Palsson had never been paid anything ("not a cent," he complained, although there was a report that Bobby gave him a check for $300 before he went back to Iceland) for the months of bodyguard work he'd provided for Bobby in

Reykjavik in 1972 and in the United States after the match. And Palsson had been the initial Icelander to join forces with Bobby in his attempt to get out of jail. Palsson had traveled to Japan at his own expense, and he continued to help when Bobby became an Icelandic citizen. Palsson had ample reason to expect goodwill from Bobby. The seeds of their ultimate break were sown, though, when, even prior to Bobby's departure from Japan, Palsson was approached by an Icelandic filmmaker, Fridrik Gudmundsson, to do a documentary for Icelandic television about Bobby's incarceration, the fight to release him, and his escape to freedom. Palsson and Bobby *might* see some money, it was suggested, if the film made a profit, although it was highly unlikely for a documentary to realize even a slight windfall.

Bobby initially agreed to cooperate, but with the explicit caveat that the film was to be a dissertation on the evils of the United States, not about his personal life or about chess. As Bobby envisioned it, it would be mainly about his "kidnapping" (as he referred to his arrest and detention) and escape.

Filming began the moment Bobby touched down in Copenhagen, with a camera in the sports vehicle that drove him, Miyoko, and Saemi to Sweden, en route to Iceland. Shot using various cinema verité techniques, with low production values, the film was poorly edited and thematically scattered. It was produced for 30 million kronur (about $500,000 dollars). The initial footage was intriguing, however, since it provided the first real glimpse of Bobby since his match with Spassky in 1992. Bobby was clear-eyed and focused as he forcefully held forth: "I hate America: it's an illegitimate state. It was robbed from the Native Americans and built by black African slaves. It has no right to exist." As he delivered his poison against the Jews, the Japanese government, and the United States, he was oddly frisky, as if he'd just become aware that he was free. He and Saemi began to sing "That's Amore" and other familiar old songs, almost as if they were long-lost friends—as they were at that time—taking a ride in the country and singing to pass the time. There was even laughter on occasion. Miyoko sat quietly, her Mona Lisa smile emerging as she looked with reverence at Bobby.

Continuing to shoot the film in Reykjavik over the next months, Gudmundsson kept trying to pin down Bobby for further interviews and increase his involvement in the project. "What's the title of the film going to be?"

Bobby asked. When he was told it was *My Friend Bobby* (it was eventually changed to *Me and Bobby Fischer*), he immediately began to question the whole endeavor. "This is a film that is supposed to be about my kidnapping, not about Saemi," he complained. Then money became an obstacle. Bobby was angry that he was not being given any "up front" money. Gudmundsson offered Bobby 15 percent of the profits, with Saemi, the producer Steinthor Birgisson, and Gudmundsson also getting 15 percent each, the remaining 40 percent to be paid to the coproduction partners. Fischer was furious. Why was Saemi being paid *anything*? And since the film was about Bobby, why shouldn't he receive more money than the others? "I should be paid at least 30 percent," he argued vehemently, "more than anyone else because I am Bobby Fischer." He repeated this refrain over and over again: "*I* am Bobby Fischer! *I* am Bobby Fischer! *I* am Bobby Fischer!"

Gudmundsson tried to explain what he was doing. He told Bobby that the film had the potential to become a masterpiece: "This will be a postmodernist documentary with feature elements."

"Never mind about that," Bobby shouted. "Tell me what the film is going to be *about*."

Gudmundsson mapped it out in writing in an all-inclusive public relations proposal:

This film is about the atom bomb.
This film is about a retired policeman.
This film is about unconditional love.
This film is about a world champion of chess.
This film is about unconditional hate.
This film is about an icon.
This film is about victory.
This film is about the war on terror.
This film is about an international fugitive.
This film is about insanity.
This film is about rockdancing.

The more of the description Bobby read, the more disgusted he became with the film, with Gudmundsson, and with Saemi. Bobby appealed to the members of the RJF Committee to see if they could help stop the film or get an injunction issued before it was completed. Sympathetic to Bobby's plight, the committee circulated to its members a letter of protest that was ultimately sent to Icelandic Television, other media, and to the financial backers and distributors of the film. Bobby changed some of the wording of the protest before it was mailed, making it much stronger and less diplomatic. It read, in part:

> Mr. Fischer wishes the group to draw attention to the fact the manuscript and structure of the aforementioned "documentary," of which he is the main subject, are grossly inconsistent with further discussions and that the material was obtained by fraud.
>
> The primary theme of the film now, which working title is *"My Friend Bobby,"* is in his opinion, quite contrary to the ideas that were proposed in the year 2005 concerning a possible news program for Icelandic television of the U.S. organized kidnapping and imprisonment of Mr. Fischer in Japan, his being granted Icelandic citizenship and release from prison.
>
> For this reason, it is absolutely against his wishes that parties in Iceland and elsewhere should provide financial subsidy for the production of this film or should show it once completed.

Bobby had already stopped talking to Saemi and taking calls from Gudmundsson, and he began referring to his ex-bodyguard as a "Judas" for trying to make a film that was more about Saemi than about Bobby's travails. Bobby wanted the film to be a polemic, not a biography—and he *certainly* didn't want it to be about his bodyguard. Almost to a man, members of the RJF Committee broke off any further contact with Saemi Palsson. As it turned out, the film was a box office dud, bringing in only $40,000; it did make additional revenue from DVD sales and television licensing.

Then Bobby's royal displeasure was directed at another Icelander, Gudmundur Thorarinsson. "I never received the full amount from the gate receipts from 1972," Bobby suddenly accused Thorarinsson at a party at his house. "I want to see the books. Where are the books?" Bobby demanded.

Thorarinsson gasped quietly and explained that Bobby had received his full share of the gate receipts in 1972, that he didn't have the account books at home, but that he'd look for them at the offices of the Icelandic Chess Federation, where he'd been president in 1972 and had been instrumental in initiating the World Championship match. After more than thirty years there was little hope that the records still existed. Bobby was unsatisfied with the answer. The books were never found and Bobby never talked to Thorarinsson again.

Bobby had been using different forms of fallacious logic to accuse and attack whole classes of people, such as the Jews. Now he used his spurious logic against benevolent Icelanders. His illogical syllogism went something like this:

Saemi cheated and betrayed me.
Saemi is an Icelander.
Therefore all Icelanders are cheaters and betrayers.

A litany of attacks, suspicions, and far-fetched offenses began erupting in the RJFers' direction after the Saemi incident, and few from the group escaped Bobby's wrath. Even key stalwarts felt his sting: Helgi Olaffson for not tolerating Bobby's anti-Semitic enmity, and for asking too many questions about the "old chess" ("He must be writing a book"); David Oddsson for reasons unknown, even to Oddsson himself; and, surprisingly, Gardar Sverrisson, his closest friend, spokesman, and neighbor, because Gardar didn't inform him about a silly and harmless photograph of Bobby's shoes that appeared in *Morgunbladid*. Gardar got off relatively unscathed—Bobby's snit against him lasted only twenty-four hours. The rest of the group became persona non grata.

By the fall of 2007, Bobby's disillusionment with Iceland was fixed. He called it a "God-forsaken country" and referred to Icelanders as "special but only in the negative sense." If his Icelandic benefactors knew of his expressions of ingratitude ("I don't owe these [people] anything!" he spitefully proclaimed), they didn't discuss them publicly, a characteristic of many Scandinavians. Those who directly experienced his thanklessness were saddened but stoic. "Well, that's Bobby," one Icelander observed. "We have to take him as he is." It was as if he were a changeling, a troubled child not so secretly adopted by the Icelanders, but with love and without foreboding.

"You are truth. You are love. You are bliss. You are freedom."

Bobby was reading *The Rajneesh Bible,* a work by the charismatic and controversial guru Bhagwan Shree Rajneesh. Like Bobby, Bhagwan had also had trouble with the United States Immigration Department, and was arrested and made to leave the country. Bobby identified with him in that respect and especially valued one of his dicta: "Never obey anyone's command unless it is coming from within you."

Bhagwan's philosophy had attracted Bobby ever since he began exploring it during his eight years in Hungary. Although Bobby never practiced meditation, an essential part of Bhagwan's belief system, he became deeply interested in the qualities of the ideal—or "realized"— self being described by Bhagwan. Bobby didn't appear to much consider Bhagwan's endorsement of such qualities as love, celebration, and humor. Rather, what seemed to appeal was the idea of the individual rising to a higher plateau. Fischer thought of himself as a warrior in all things, not just chess—and living in Iceland, free of incarceration, he made no exceptions. "I am always on the attack," he proudly divulged while he was there—and he wasn't talking about a board game. There was little time for humor or celebration in a time of war. He was poised for battle against the chess establishment, the Union Bank of Switzerland, the Jews, the United States, Japan, Icelanders in general, the media, processed foods, Coca-Cola, noise, pollution, nuclear energy, and circumcision.

Bobby thought of himself as being totally aware and equated himself with Bhagwan's concept of the Nietzschean "Superman" who transcends the constraints of society. "I am a genius," he said shortly after arriving back in Iceland, not pontifically but sincerely. "Not just a chess genius but a genius in other things as well."

Bobby's attempt to find some deeper, perhaps religious meaning to his life took a wide and twisted path. At first, as a child, there was Judaism, of which he never really felt a part; then Fundamentalism, until he became disillusioned with the leaders of the Worldwide Church of God. Anti-Semitism also became a quasi religion—or certainly a profound belief—for him, and one that he never really abandoned. At one point of his life he embraced atheism, although not for long. He was intrigued with the cult of Rajneesh himself, rather than the guru's practices. Finally, near the end of his life, he began to explore Catholicism.

A contradiction in terms, an oxymoron? A Catholic Bobby Fischer?

Something was missing in the life of Bobby Fischer, a chasm that needed to be filled. Delving through books, he discovered the writings of Catholic theologians, and he became intrigued with the religion. Gardar Sverrisson, his closest friend in Reykjavik, was Catholic (one of the few: 95 percent of Icelanders are Lutheran), and Bobby began to ask him questions about the liturgy, the adoration of saints, the theological mysteries, and other aspects of the religion. Gardar answered what he could, but he was no theologian. Eventually, Bobby brought *him* a copy of *Basic Catechism: Creed, Sacraments, Morality, Prayer,* so that Gardar could be more informed when they had discussions.

It's not certain whether Bobby was baptized in the Roman Catholic religion in the traditional manner, which entails the pouring of—or immersion in—water, the anointing of sacred chrism (special oil), and a solemn blessing by a priest performing the sacrament, but it's unlikely. Einarsson and Skulasson both concluded that Bobby, despite his late-life deliberations on the topic, was *not* a strong believer in the Catholic Church and that he *hadn't* converted to the faith. But there are three forms of baptism: by water (the usual way), by fire (as in martyrdom), and by spirit (in that the recipient *desires* to be baptized). If Bobby did *wish* to become Catholic, it's possible that aspiration was sufficient for him to have been accepted into the Church, at least by less conservative clergy. According to Gardar Sverrisson, Bobby talked with him about the transformation of society by creating harmony with one another, and then professed that he thought "the only hope for the world is through Catholicism."

Bobby's attraction to Catholicism, a religion that is defined by its emphasis on charity, humility, and repentance for sins, seems hard to reconcile with his writings such as: "Unfortunately we're not strong enough just to wipe out all the Jews at this time. So what I believe we should do is engage in vigilante random killing of Jews. What I want to do is to arouse people against the Jews to the point of violence! Because the Jews are criminal people. They deserve to have their heads cracked open."

"I am not now that which I have been," Byron wrote in *Childe Harold's Pilgrimage,* and that could have been Bobby's answer to his spiritual change near the end of his life. Or, as cynical as it may sound, his possible acceptance of Catholicism may have been merely a theological chess game, a tactic and long-term strategy that he calculated might lead to eternal salvation. Men often believe that they've converted as soon as they decide to do so, although they haven't yet achieved—and often aren't even aware that they must enter—a state of inner worship. Only Bobby Fischer knew what was in his heart.

A photograph of Bobby taken by Einar Einarsson in the summer of 2005, just a few months after he arrived in Iceland, clearly shows an encroaching illness. Fischer usually would never sit for a photograph, but when dining with Einarsson at 3 Frakkar ("Three Coats"), Bobby was greeted by an old chef whom he knew from 1972, who asked if he could pose with Bobby. Einarsson took a picture of the two men and then moved the camera slightly to the left and took a single shot of Bobby. The result was a revealing portrait of a man in pain: psychic and perhaps physical. David Surratt, a chess editor, observed: "The expressiveness of the eyes, my goodness, you can practically feel his sadness, and perhaps a sense of regret, too. Perhaps regret over what might have been, or what he lost over the latter half of his life."

Bobby started to have urinary problems and thought it might simply be caused by an enlarged prostate gland, at first denying that anything might be seriously wrong with him. His lungs were also bothering him and he was having difficulty breathing. Since he had a lifelong distrust of doctors, he tolerated the discomfort until October 2007, when his pain and inability to urinate became excruciating. He went to a doctor and requested a cursory, nonintrusive examination, but it was explained that only a blood test would enable the doctor to evaluate his kidney function. Reluctantly, he acquiesced;

the test showed that he suffered from elevated levels of serum creatinine with a value way above 1.4, the highest parameter in the normal range. The finding indicated that he had a blocked urinary tract. This abnormality could be checked, although possibly not cured, by taking certain drugs. But there were also problems with his kidneys, which were not functioning properly. On principle, harking back to his Worldwide Church of God teachings, Bobby refused to take any medicine, and the idea of being hooked up to a dialysis machine to cleanse his blood every few days for the rest of his life was out of the question. When the dialysis treatment was proposed he said it was absurd. He was warned that unless treated, he could experience total kidney failure, seizures, and even dementia. When he asked for more information about his prognosis, the doctor told him that unless dialysis treatment began immediately, he probably didn't have more than three months to live. Despite these dire warnings, he still refused to be treated, and he even rejected taking pain medicine to ease his agony. It's possible that Bobby was just giving up, letting go of his life, beginning a slow form of suicide. His friend Pal Benko believed that to be the case.

Bobby allowed himself to be checked into Landspitali Hospital by Dr. Erikur Jónsson, who supervised the limited amount of treatment and nursing his patient would permit, for seven weeks. It was a difficult time not only for Bobby but for the nursing staff as well. He wouldn't allow a fixed catheter and insisted that they help him urinate each and every time he had to go. He placed restrictions on what he would eat, created a list of potential visitors who'd be allowed to see him and another list of those who'd be summarily barred from entering his room.

Grandmaster Fridrik Olafsson visited him once a week. Bobby asked him to bring bottles of fresh-squeezed carrot juice from Yggdrasil; if the health food store didn't have it available, Olafsson was to buy juice imported from Germany. Under no circumstances, Bobby instructed sternly, was Olafsson to buy anything from Israel. Not surprisingly, during some of their visits the two grandmasters discussed chess. Bobby wanted Fridrik to bring a copy of the Kasparov-Karpov game that he'd claimed for years was prearranged, so they could discuss it and play it over on Bobby's pocket set. But instead of bringing the whole book in which the game was published, Fridrik simply brought a copy of the few relevant pages so that he'd have less to carry. Bobby was deeply disappointed. "Why didn't you bring the whole book!?"

Bobby asked if a photograph of his mother could be sent to him, and Russell Targ, his brother-in-law, complied. Bobby looked at it from time to time, but contrary to reports that he had it perched on his bedside table, he kept it in the drawer, knowing that it was there, symbolically protective.

Of all of the people who visited him in the hospital, in many ways the man who was the most comforting to Bobby was Dr. Magnus Skulasson, a member of the RJF Committee who'd had a fairly low profile with the group and had hardly been in Bobby's presence during the three years he'd lived in Iceland. Skulasson was a psychiatrist and the head doctor of Sogn Mental Asylum for the Criminally Insane. He was also a chess player who had a great reverence for the accomplishments of Bobby Fischer and an affection for him as a man.

It should be stressed that Skulasson was not "Bobby's psychiatrist," as has been implied in the general press, nor did he offer Bobby any analysis or psychotherapy. He was at Bobby's bedside as a friend, to try to do anything he could for him. Because of his training, however, he couldn't fail to take note of Bobby's mental condition. "He definitely was not schizophrenic," Skulasson said. "He had problems, possibly certain childhood traumas that had affected him. He was misunderstood. Underneath I think he was a caring and sensitive person."

Skulasson is a gentle and intense man with a gravitas that is arresting. In his conversations, he appears to be more a philosopher than someone with a medical and psychological background, quoting Hegel as much as Freud, Plato as much as Jung. Bobby asked him to bring foods and juices to the hospital, which he did, and often Skulasson just sat at the bedside, both men not speaking. When Bobby was experiencing severe pain in his legs, Skulasson began to massage them, using the back of his hand. Bobby looked at him and said, "Nothing soothes as much as the human touch." Once Bobby woke and said: "Why are you so kind to me?" Of course, Skulasson had no answer.

Dr. Jónsson began to get pressure from the hospital to release Bobby because of his refusal of proper treatment. Jónsson realized that releasing him would be a death sentence, so he kept making excuses to keep Bobby in the hospital, trying to keep him comfortable as long as he could. Without Bobby's knowledge, the nurses applied morphine patches to his body to ease his pain. Eventually, terminally ill, still stubborn about refusing proper treatment, he was discharged and returned to his apartment on Espergerdi in December 2007, where Sverrisson, his wife Kristin, and their two children, who lived two floors below Bobby, became his attendants and guardians. In particular, Kristin used her nursing skills to help care for him.

Being out of the hospital perked up Bobby's spirits for a while, and he began to feel better, even going to a movie with Sverrisson's twenty-year-old son, a professional soccer player. At Christmastime, when all of Reykjavik is festooned with lights and takes on the ambience of a Currier and Ives painting and there are days and days of celebrations, Miyoko came and stayed with Bobby at the apartment for two weeks. On January 10, 2008, she flew back to Tokyo, losing a day with the time difference. Soon, she received a call from Sverrisson that Bobby had grown substantially more ill. By the time a new reservation could be arranged and she could make her way back to Iceland, Bobby had been taken to the hospital by Sverrisson in the car. He died there, peacefully, on January 17. Like the number of squares on a chessboard—an irony that nevertheless cannot be pressed too far—he was sixty-four.

Epilogue

BORIS SPASSKY WAS STUNNED. Long concerned about Bobby's illness, he'd kept in close contact. Then, shockingly, he learned that Bobby had died. Momentarily unable to express his sense of loss, Spassky e-mailed Einar Einarsson: "My brother is dead."

In those four words he showed how deeply he felt about Bobby, although the world already knew. He'd told people that he "loved" Bobby Fischer . . . as a brother. At the 1992 match he publicly stated that he was ready to fight "and I want to fight, but on the other hand I would like Bobby to win because I believe that Bobby must come back to chess." When Bobby was incarcerated in Japan, Spassky had been serious when he announced that he was willing to be imprisoned with him (and a chessboard). Spassky's respect for his nemesis bordered on adulation and possibly even fear. He once said: "It's not if you win or lose against Bobby Fischer; it's if you survive." But there was true camaraderie between them that went beyond just chess and that Spassky was always quick to express. He felt they sensed each other's frayed loneliness as past champions, a nostalgia to which few could relate.

Only three weeks before Bobby's death Spassky had sent his old friend a lighthearted message, telling him to obey his doctors, and that when he "escaped" from the hospital, he should get in touch.

Spassky had been informed that Bobby's condition was serious, but he wasn't aware that it was grave. Icelandic tradition discourages a person's illness from being discussed outside of family or intimate friends, but because of Spassky's solicitous comments about his longtime opponent, Einarsson considered him a part of Bobby's "family" and had let him know his friend's condition was worsening. Spassky wrote: "I have a brother's feeling toward Bobby. He is a good friend."

♖

In the last days of Bobby's life he was becoming more frail and could hardly speak, nor could he keep down any food. His lips were always dry. Either the forty-eight-year-old Gardar Sverrisson—who wasn't well himself—or his wife Kristin, a nurse, would stay with Bobby at his apartment all through the night, watching out for him when he slept and attending to his needs when he woke.

Bobby had told Sverrisson that he would like to be buried in the small country graveyard close to the town of Selfoss, about an hour's drive from Reykjavik, in a rural farmland community called Laugardaelir. The cemetery was reported to be at least a thousand years old, established about the time that Eric the Red left for Greenland and the Althingi—Iceland's parliament (the first in Europe)—was formed; ironically this is the same governmental body that gave Bobby his citizenship in 2005.

An unpretentious Lutheran church—a chapel, really—that looks like a set for an Ingmar Bergman drama and can seat only about fifty parishioners, guards the site of the cemetery. Bobby had felt the peaceful atmosphere of the surroundings when he'd visited Sverrisson's wife's parents, who live in Selfoss, and Bobby and his friend Gardar took long walks among the ancient rocks and paths in the area. In a memorial article in the *Iceland Review,* writer Sara Blask summed up Bobby's feelings about what he wanted after his death: "Fischer just wanted to be buried like a normal human being—not a chessplayer, just as a *person.*"

It took a long time for Bobby to admit to himself that he was dying, but when he came to accept it, he made it clear to Sverrisson that he wanted no fanfare, no media circus, no lavish funeral, and he wanted it to be *private.* Desiring control until the end, he was particularly emphatic that none of his "enemies" attend his funeral: those who he felt exploited him or with whom he'd established feuds. Above all, he stressed that there were to be no reporters, television cameras, or gaping tourists.

Sverrisson arranged the funeral and carried it out with strict observance of Bobby's last directives. He knew that the other members of the RJF Committee, who'd worked so tirelessly for Bobby, would be deeply hurt if they couldn't pay their last respects by attending a ceremonial funeral, but he was nothing if not a loyal friend to Bobby, and he'd spent years protecting him and carrying out his wishes. This last service performed for his friend would cause Sverrisson years of enmity from certain members of the RJF Committee and others who felt close to Bobby during his Icelandic years. Russell Targ, Bobby's brother-in-law, was particularly irritated since he'd flown from California to attend the funeral, only to find that he'd missed it by hours. The U.S. Chess Federation sent a communiqué to the Icelandic Chess Federation asking about the disposition of Bobby's body, presumably wanting to bring him back to the United States, a move that Bobby would have detested. Especially at his death, Sverrisson believed it was his duty to fully comply with Bobby's requests. His friend would be buried where, when, and how he wanted.

It took several days to arrange the details: The grave had to be dug—not an easy task in the frozen volcanic earth of Iceland's winter; a priest had to be secured; documents had to be approved before the morgue released the body; yet everything had to wait for Miyoko to arrive from Japan. Four days after his death, at eight p.m. a hearse carrying Bobby's body took the hour's drive to Selfoss and then to the graveyard. The funeral procession was without pomp and circumstance, exactly as Bobby had wished, and as the hearse drove into Laugadaelir, the long and biting winds of winter awaited the remains of the world's greatest chess player. It had snowed all morning, and now it was dark and raining. Sverrisson, his wife and two children, and Miyoko had traveled to Selfoss the night before to ensure that the arrangements were in order.

Father Jacob Rolland, a diminutive Catholic priest, originally from France, who also had the distinction of overseeing the burial of Haldor Laxness (Iceland's only Nobel Prize winner—for literature—and a convert to Catholicism), said a few words of blessing, reportedly likening Bobby's burial to that of Mozart's, before the coffin was lowered into the grave. "Like him, he was buried with few present, and he had an intelligence like him that could see what others could not begin to understand." There was no dirge, no incense, no requiem. Even the wide expanse of stars normally visible in the unpolluted sky was hidden behind rain clouds on that gloomy night. The ceremony took just twelve minutes, and then the freezing mourners departed. A white wooden cross was hastily erected on the grave mound with a placard that read:

Robert James Fischer
F. 9 mars 1943
D. 17 januar 2008
Hvil i friði

"Rest in Peace" it said in Old Norse Icelandic.

Within a few weeks daily buses began to arrive from Reykjavik—sometimes two or three a day—filled with the gaping tourists that Bobby had so desperately wanted to avoid. The grave, now with a two-foot-high plain marble stone, had become one of Iceland's sightseeing attractions.

At the time of his death, Bobby Fischer's estate was worth more than $2 million, primarily the prize money left over from the $3.5 million that he'd won in his 1992 match with Spassky. Yet Fischer, the man who'd tried so hard to control things on and off the chessboard, never wrote a will. Perhaps he thought he could control his illness and didn't believe that he was dying until he was too ill to think about legal documents. Or perhaps, in some odd way, it amused him to realize that his money would become a major cause of contention, that it would initiate a baroque chess match in which each of the estate's possible recipients took a turn at the board to gain a stronger position.

There were four people claiming to be Bobby's true heir: Miyoko Watai, who lived with Bobby and contended that she was his wife; Nicholas and Alexander Targ, Bobby's nephews (the two sons of Bobby's late sister, Joan); and Jinky Young, who claimed to be Bobby's daughter. All filed papers in Iceland, and were waiting for the court to sort out their respective petitions. The U.S. government also entered the fray in the hopes of gaining twenty years of back taxes owed by Bobby.

According to Icelandic law, a wife receives 100 percent of her husband's estate if there are no children and only one-third if there is one child or more. However, the Icelandic court questioned the Japanese marriage certificate that Miyoko presented because it was only a photocopy, and she had difficulty proving that she was in fact Bobby's legal wife.

The claim of the Targ brothers was clear: They are indeed his nephews. Now grown men—one a doctor and the other an attorney—both live in California. They were fully aware that they could only inherit their uncle's fortune if "closer" relatives—such as a wife or child—are proven not to be rightful heirs. It behooved them, therefore, to try to determine the legitimacy of the other claims.

Finally, there was Jinky. Eight years old at the time of Bobby's death, the girl was supported financially by Bobby all of her life. Icelandic friends said that Fischer was kind to the little girl, played with her, and bought her presents while she was in Iceland. Surprisingly, though, during the three years that Bobby lived in Iceland, Jinky and Marilyn visited him in Reykjavik only once, remaining there for about a month, in a separate apartment.

Then, a year and a half after Bobby's death, Marilyn and Jinky traveled to Iceland again, this time to file a claim to his estate. With Eugene Torre's assistance, an Icelandic lawyer—Thordur Bogason—was hired to represent the child, and soon after the attorney petitioned the court for a DNA test in an attempt to prove Bobby's paternity. Getting a sample of Jinky's DNA was simple: Doctors just took a small vial of blood. Retrieving a sample from Bobby, however, was decidedly more problematic. The National Hospital of Iceland, where Bobby died of renal failure, hadn't saved any of his blood. His belongings were still in his apartment in Reykjavik, but who could prove whether a hair taken from a hairbrush really came from Bobby? The only foolproof way to secure Bobby's DNA was to take a sample from Bobby's body. That would settle the matter, everyone believed. In the United States the FBI, which often has to extract DNA in criminal cases, considers the DNA test, when done with the latest technology, infallible.

Exhuming Bobby's corpse was impractical for many months: His grave was covered with snow, and it was difficult to dig through Iceland's frozen soil until late spring. Until that time, arguments for and against exhumation were debated through the lower courts, and were finally settled by the Icelandic Supreme Court: It ruled that Jinky had the right to know whether Bobby was or was not her father.

At about three a.m. on July 5, 2010, the grave of Bobby Fischer was opened by a team of experts from the Reykjavik Official Cemeteries Department. The unusual time of morning to perform the exhumation was selected to thwart possible newsmen and curiosity-seekers from ogling the corpse and possibly taking photographs. After removing the dirt down to the level of the coffin lid, a section was dug around the base of the coffin so several people could stand next to it. Looking like mourners, a solemn group stood staring down at the coffin or in the dug-out space around it: The Rev. Kristinn A. Fridfinnsson, the pastor of the church; some of the Church's elders; forensic experts; government officials; the attorneys for all the claimants of the estate; Dr. Oskar Reykdalsson, who officiated; and Ólafur Kjartansson, the sheriff of Selfoss—the town near the cemetery. All were there to make sure that the process was done in a respectful and professional manner and that the exhumation would not be compromised.

At four a.m., just before the DNA samples were collected, a large white tent was erected around the gravesite to ensure even further privacy. It was a calm, beautiful summer morning with a peaceful wind.

The coffin was never moved or raised, but the lid was opened. Some newspapers around the world reported that the body wasn't actually dug up but that a drill was inserted through the earth, then through the coffin and into Bobby's body. Sheriff Kjartansson corrected that report the next day. No drill was inserted, he said, and the samples were taken directly from Bobby's body.

Normally, a DNA exhumation consists of gathering *several* specimens in the event that one might not be suitable. Forensic scientists recommend a fingernail, a tooth, a tissue sample, and a piece of the femur. In Bobby's exhumation, a fragment of bone from his left small toe was extracted, in addition to seven tissue samples—enough for a binding test. As soon as the procedure was completed, the coffin was covered with the lava-infiltrated earth and a dusting of some residual ash that had drifted to Selfoss from the recently erupted volcano. Grass turf that had been removed when the digging had begun was then placed back on top of the grave. The samples were packaged and shipped to a forensics laboratory in Germany for testing; the Icelandic

DNA laboratory was ruled out to avoid any possibility of compromise or conflict.

The idea of disturbing a dead body would be horrible for anyone—some religions such as Judaism and Islam forbid it except for highly exceptional circumstances—but Bobby, before his death one of the world's most private beings, would no doubt have considered this final invasion of his privacy the ultimate act of disrespect. Even in death, he wasn't being allowed to rest in peace.

In a way, however, he was the final arbiter. According to Article 17, act 76/2003 of Icelandic Parliament, "a man shall be deemed the father of a child if the outcome of DNA-research points decisively [to the fact that he is the father]. Otherwise he is not the father." Six weeks after the exhumation, the results of the DNA test were released by the Reykjavik District Court: the DNA did not match. Bobby Fischer was *not* Jinky's father.

With Jinky no longer being a putative heir, the remaining contenders for the estate were Miyoko Watai, the Targ nephews, and the U.S. Internal Revenue Service.

Like a chess game between equally matched competitors, however, the battle continued. Samuel Estimo, a chess master and Jinky's attorney in the Philippines, wrote to Bogason, his Icelandic counterpart, and protested that Jinky's claim had been relinquished too soon. Implying that there may have been skullduggery afoot, Estimo wrote a letter to *The New York Times* and sent it to other media as well:

```
The exhumation of Bobby Fischer was not done the normal
way. His coffin should have been brought up and opened so
that it would have been sure that the seven tissue samples
that were taken from the alleged remains in that coffin
were that of Bobby Fischer. Indeed, the procedure
undertaken borders on the doubtful. The lot where Fischer
was buried belongs to the family of Gardar Sverisson, a
close friend of Miyoko Watai, one of the claimants to the
estate of Bobby. He had complete access without the church
pastor knowing it. Fischer was buried in front of the
church in an early January morning without the church
```

```
pastor knowing it. Who knows what could have taken place
there between the date of burial and on the days before
the exhumation.
```

Although Bogason warned Estimo that his statements could be considered slanderous and that he should accept that the case was closed for their client Jinky, Estimo would *not* resign. He requested DNA samples of Bobby's nephews to determine, through their familial heredity, whether the samples taken from the gravesite actually matched Bobby's DNA. Estimo's implication—that another body might have been substituted for Bobby's and somehow placed in the grave—tested the credulity of many. And the idea of deception brought off at the exhumation itself seemed even more far-fetched. With all the government officials, doctors, scientists, and church people present, all seeking the truth as to whether Bobby was Jinky's father, it seemed impossible that the exhumation was performed improperly. Nevertheless, the Icelandic court reopened the case to allow Jinky's attorney to present more evidence in support of her claim that she is Bobby's daughter. Bogason, in disagreement with Estimo, withdrew from the case. Estimo then renewed his request that the Targ brothers submit *their* DNA, so it could be compared with the samples taken from the body in the coffin. If there's no match, Estimo can press his claim that the samples purportedly taken from Fischer's body are fraudulent.

Even if the match is positive, Estimo claims that Jinky Young is still entitled to be named an heir, because Bobby treated her as a daughter. Had the estate been negligible, one wonders whether there would have been such a fight over who is the true heir. But it is not just a question of money: The legitimacy of the girl's paternity—biological or titular—is at stake, and the Philippine nation would certainly like to know whether one of its citizens, Jinky Young, is the daughter of the greatest chess player who ever lived.

Meanwhile, the two Targ brothers now have only Miyoko standing between them and their claim to their uncle's millions. Or, at least, Miyoko *would* be the only impediment if it weren't for the U.S. government, which, ironically, may walk away from this chess match with the best score. If the U.S. Internal Revenue Service is able to collect Bobby's back taxes and fines, the multimillion-dollar "purse" the competitors are vying for will have been seriously reduced. What was once a fortune may become a pittance, a lost game for the heirs.

And what, then, will be the inheritance bequeathed by Bobby? For chess players, and for people who followed the story of Bobby Fischer's rise to become what many say is the greatest chess player who ever lived, his legacy for his heirs and the world alike may simply be the awe that his brilliance evoked.

ACKNOWLEDGMENTS

I have been studying the life of Bobby Fischer for decades. There is hardly a tournament that I attend where someone doesn't tell me a story about him, and locked away in my memory are scores of anecdotes and first-person narratives that have been given to me. The problem has been to sort through a labyrinth of fables to select what is true and what is not, what is exaggerated and what is journalistically accurate, what is biased—pro or con—and what is a credible tale. In any event, to all of those players and friends who have shared with me over the years their recollections and eyewitness accounts, their brief encounters and amusing and dramatic incidents concerning Bobby, I express my deep gratitude.

In researching this book, I have delved into just about everything that has been written about Fischer in English, listened to all of his broadcasts, read his books and other writings, and carefully examined his letters to and from his mother, Pal Benko, Jack Collins, and others. I have had translations done of other materials whose languages were unknown to me.

When I worked on previous writings about Fischer, I had discussed him with several former World Champions—Mikhail Botvinnik and Vasily Smyslov in Macedonia and Max Euwe in New York and Iceland—and dozens of players, and the reader may find a small portion of material reworked, redeployed, and integrated in *Endgame* that can be found elsewhere in other prose of mine. My attempt was to capture Bobby Fischer the man and not just offer a chronology of his tournaments and matches.

When I was in Reykjavik for two months attending every round of the first Fischer-Spassky match, I had the opportunity to talk about Bobby with such chess lights as Miguel Najdorf, Svetozar Gligoric, Robert Byrne, Bent Larsen, Max Euwe, William Lombardy, Lubomir Kavalek, Lothar Schmid, Dragoljub

Janosevic, I. A. Horowitz, and Larry Evans, as well as most of the chess community present, in addition to such literary lions as Arthur Koestler, George Steiner, and Harold Schonberg. Bobby's legal eagles, Paul Marshall and Andrew Davis, although reserved, also opened up to me. All of the above gave me the benefit of their insights into Bobby. In some cases, I have continued a dialogue with some of them in my recent preparation of *Endgame*.

Back in 1972, the Soviet players who accompanied Spassky—Efim Geller, Nikolai Krogius, and Ivo Nei—refused to speak to me, probably thinking of me as a spy for the United States side, or at least someone who would aid Bobby in some way in his pursuit of the championship, as if anyone could. Spassky, however, ever the gentleman, was not afraid to at least pass the time of day with me. We have recently corresponded, and he was kind enough to share his warm feelings about Bobby.

I am indebted to the following people who, during the past year, talked to me or helped me in other ways to grasp the essence of Bobby Fischer: Fridrik Olafsson, Walter Browne, Bernard Zuckerman, Boris Spassky, Leslie Ault, Arthur Bisguier, Lev Khariton, Renato Naranja, Kirsan Ilyumzhinov, Gabor Schnitzler, Richard Vattone, Stuart Margulies, Shelby Lyman, Joseph Smith, Aben Rudy, Eliot Hearst, David Oddsson, Mark Gerstl, William Ronalds, John Bosnitch, David Rosenblum, Tibi Vasilescu, Paul Jonsson, Arthur Feuerstein, Asa Hoffmann, Hanon Russell, Susan Polgar, Alla Baeva, Lion Calandra, Vincent Mallozzi, Bill Goichberg, Helgi Olafsson, Ralph Italie, Dr. Joseph Wagner, Gudmundur Thorarinsson, Sam Sloan, Allen Kaufman, Sal Matera, Curtis Lakdawala, James T. Sherwin, Anthony Saidy, Saemi Palsson, Russell Targ, Pal Benko, and Bragi Kristjonsson. Special thanks to International Master John Donaldson, who placed the manuscript under his microscope of chess knowledge and plucked some weeds from my prose. Edward Winter, the world's most eminent chess historian, found some rhetorical, linguistic, and factual discrepancies which were caught just a short time before publication. My deepest thanks.

Additionally, four friends, all chess players and writers, read the entire manuscript and offered truly invaluable advice, correcting whatever lacunae that had crept in: Jeffrey Tannenbaum, a relentless editor; Dr. Glenn Statile, a philosopher; Glenn Petersen, the longtime editor of *Chess Life;* and Don Schultz, who probably knows more about American chess than anyone else.

I grieve for the slaughter of some of my favorite cows that they suggested I kill, but how can I ever thank them for making this a better book?

Three Icelanders were so helpful when I traveled to Reykjavik last October that I am truly indebted to them for the deep courtesy they displayed and their concern that I accurately portray Bobby's life in their little but fascinating country: Einar Einarsson, who shared everything he knew about Bobby; Dr. Magnus Skulasson, who probably understood Bobby better than anyone I have ever met; and Gardar Sverrisson, who was closest to Bobby, and his spokesperson during his time in Iceland. Thank you, thank you, and thank you.

The following libraries offered up surprising nuggets of Fischeriana: the New York Public Library, the Brooklyn Public Library, the Long Island Collection of the Queensborough Public Library, the John G. White Collection of the Cleveland Public Library, the Columbia University Library, and the Lilly Library of the University of Indiana. The publications *New in Chess, Chess,* and *Chess Life,* as well as the websites *ChessBase, Chess Café,* and *Chessville,* were of enormous help. To each I am indebted, as I am to Mirjam Donath, a Fulbright scholar; and Taryn Westerman, my former graduate assistant; both of whom helped me research the work.

I've never had an editor before as perceptive and as hardworking as Rick Horgan. He is not only responsible for this book coming into existence, but helped shape it in every way, shoving needles into the eyes of my discursive prose from time to time and serving as a sounding board throughout the compilation of the book.

My literary agent, Jeff Schmidt, deserves special commendation for recognizing the potential of *Endgame,* and for steering the book to one of the best publishing houses in the world.

Finally, there is my wife, Maxine, to whom this book is dedicated. Like me, she also knew Bobby, spent time with him, and observed and interacted with him in our home, at parties, and at many tournaments, so her intelligence and memory—in addition to her writing and editing skills—were essential signposts for me in virtually everything that appears here. Without her contribution there would be no *Endgame.* My sincere gratitude for her constant consultation is simply not enough.

NOTES

The sources for this book come from a variety of origins: interviews of and correspondence with chess players; friends and relatives of Bobby Fischer; chess periodicals and books; the general press; Bobby Fischer's own writings; libraries and archives; and the author's own memories, conversations, and observations of Bobby Fischer spread out over a lifetime.

Abbreviations

Bobby Fischer Autobiographical Essay—BFE
John W. Collins Archive—JWC
Marshall Chess Foundation Archive—MCF
New York Times—NYT
Chess Life—CL
Chess Review—CR
Chess Life & Review—CL&R
Frank Brady Archive—FB
New In Chess—NIC
Chess Base—CB
Profile of a Prodigy—PRO
KGB Reports—KGB
Author citations refer to books in the Bibliography.

Author's Note

p. ix: "*A biography is considered complete*" Clare Colquitt, Susan Goodman, Candace Waid. *A Forward Glance: New Essays on Edith Wharton,* Associated University Presses, Inc., 1999, p. 23.

p. ix: *"a whole world of feelings"* Mack Frankfurter. *Options: A Three Dimensional Chess,* October 13, 2006. At safehaven.com. Accessed December 14, 2008.

Chapter 1: Loneliness to Passion

The sources for this chapter came, in some part, from a statement written in the third person by Bobby Fischer while he was incarcerated; examination of the FBI files on Regina Fischer; Bobby's autobiographical essay written when he was a teenager; talks of the author with Bobby's teachers, Carmine Nigro and Jack Collins, as well as Regina Fischer; observations of the author; and previously published accounts in books and periodicals.

p. 1: *"I can't breathe. I can't breathe."* Legal statement of facts written by Bobby Fischer, 6 pages, July 2004, orwelltoday.com/fischerroom202.shtml.

p. 2: *"as soon as he lands at JFK, we'll nail him."* Recollection of author, who talked with State Department official, circa late 1990s.

p. 4: *The group's destination was the Silver Moon Chinese restaurant.* This incident occurred circa 1956. Discussion with Jack Collins, circa 1956; and reported in *Newsday,* September 28, 1992.

p. 5: *he'd just returned from the U.S. Open Championship in Oklahoma City* CR, August 1956, p. 227.

p. 7: *at the first Moscow Medical Institute* Discussion of Regina and Gerhardt Fischer in Moscow. Johnson, p. 125.

p. 8: *Regina Fischer had no long-term residence* PRO, pp. 1–4.

p. 9: *One of Bobby's first memories* BFE, p. 1.

p. 9: *flung his pencil down in frustration and grabbed a brown crayon, but this time he paused* MCF

p. 10: *Later, he became enamored of Japanese interlocking puzzles* NYT, February 23, 1958, SMD 38.

p. 10: *In early 1949 Regina Fischer took the least expensive housing she could find* FBI report, 8-24-53 (SAC, New York, 100-102290).

p. 10: *on a rainy day when Bobby had just turned six* Parade, October 27, 1957, p. 22.

p. 10: *Neither Joan nor Bobby had ever seen a chess set before* BFE, p. 1.

p. 11: *"Nobody we knew ever played chess"* BFE, p. 1.

p. 11: *"At first it was just another game"* BFE, p. 1.

p. 11: *"She was too busy to take the game seriously."* BFE, p. 2

p. 11: *"My mother has an anti-talent for chess"* *Life*, February 21, 1964.

p. 12: *Instead, he sought to discover any trap or pitfall lurking in his "opponent's" position* *Life*, February 21, 1964.

p. 12: *Bobby, then seven years old, hated his new environs* BFE, p. 1.

p. 13: *The tenants downstairs complained of the banging noise* Letter from landlord to Regina Fischer, no date, MCF.

p. 13: *"Bobby could discuss concepts like infinity"* *Parade*, October 27, 1957, p. 21.

p. 14: *He then named Siegbert Tarrasch, a German player* *Chessworld*, Vol. 1, No. 1, 1964, p. 59.

p. 15: *"MOMMY I WANT TO COME HOME"* Postcard, no date, MCF.

p. 15: *In the winter of 1950, when he was seven years old* BFE, p. 1.

p. 16: *However, a distant relative of Bobby's suggested* Interview of Russell Targ by author, December 2008.

p. 16: *"my little chess miracle,"* Letter from Regina Fischer to Herman Helms, Brooklyn, New York, Nov. 14, 1951.

p. 17: *"They did not interest me too much"* BFE, p. 1.

p. 18: *One spectator at the exhibition that evening was Carmine Nigro* BFE, p. 2.

Chapter 2: Childhood Obsession

Discussions with Carmine Nigro about Bobby Fischer supplied much of the material in this chapter, as well as correspondence with Dr. Harold Sussman and Dr. Ariel Mengarini. Several notes exchanged between Bobby Fischer and his mother were also helpful in outlining this period of his life; his autobiographical essay supplied information that filled in gaps of knowledge.

p. 19: *No one had the temerity to disagree* Author's conversation with Carmine Nigro, May 1955, Brooklyn, NY.

p. 19: *Even Emanuel Lasker* Hannak, p. 17.

p. 19: *where Enrico Caruso and Geraldine Farrar had sung* CR, December 1944.

p. 20: *After coaxing from Nigro* Discussion with author, 1956.

p. 20: *"At first I used to lose all the time"* BFE, p. 2.

p. 20: *Nigro would greatly increase his son's allowance* PRO, p. 7.

p. 21: *there are 72,084 positions after two moves each* AnswerBag.com.

p. 21: *"Mr. Nigro was possibly not the best player in the world but he was a very good teacher."* BFE, p. 2.

p. 21: *"My mother was often on duty on weekends"* BFE, p. 2.

p. 21: *Dr. Sussman was also an amateur photographer* Letter from Dr. Sussman to author, circa 1972, FB.

p. 21: *one could tell by the inflection in his voice that he was affected by the experience* Author's conversation with Bobby Fischer, New York City, circa 1964.

p. 22: *Carmine Nigro was a professional musician, and taught music in a number of styles* NYT, September 2, 2001, p. 27.

p. 22: *Soon Bobby was playing "Beer Barrel Polka" and other tunes* Regina Fischer press release, circa 1956, MCF.

p. 22: *"I did fairly well on it for a while"* BFE, p. 2.

p. 22: *He played at the Brooklyn Chess Club every Friday night* BFE, p. 2.

p. 22: *Nigro would drive Bobby to Washington Square Park in Greenwich Village* BFE, p. 2.

p. 22: *Nigro felt they wouldn't tolerate Bobby's sometimes languorous tempo* Author's conversation with Carmine Nigro, May 1955, Brooklyn, NY.

p. 22: *Bobby spent hours after school at the Grand Army Plaza library* BFE, p. 3.

p. 22: *a photograph showing him studying appeared* Brooklyn Public Library News Bulletin, July 1952.

p. 23: *Years later, when a chess collector finally took possession* NIC, 2008, Issue 4, p. 6.

p. 23: *He even maintained his involvement with the game while bathing* Conversation with Regina Fischer, circa 1958.

p. 23: *"Bobby virtually inhaled chess literature"* Author's interview of Allen Kaufman, New York, March 16, 2009.

p. 24: *he was taught songs by rote for Hanukkah and Purim, in both English and Yiddish, a language he didn't know* Undated papers from Brooklyn Jewish Children's School, MCF.

p. 24: *And in the restroom he may have seen that his penis was different from the rest: He wasn't circumcised* Fischer's open letter to *Judaica Encyclopedia*, 1984.

p. 25: *and he later claimed that he'd received no training in Judaic customs or theology*   Fischer's open letter to *Judaica Encyclopedia*, 1984.

p. 25: *Bobby could concentrate on puzzles or chess for hours*   Article in *Parade*, October 27, 1957, p. 21.

p. 25: *By the time he reached the fourth grade, he'd been in and out of six schools*   Ibid.

p. 25: *In frustration, Regina registered Bobby in a school for gifted children*   Ibid.

p. 25: *In the fall of 1952, when Bobby was nine, Regina secured scholarship enrollment for him in Brooklyn Community Woodward*   Architecture 101: 321, "Clinton Avenue, The Architecture of Brooklyn."

p. 25: *The school's philosophy of education was based on the principles of Johann Heinrich Pestalozzi*   BFE, p. 9.

p. 25: *To learn early American history, for example*   *Brooklyn Eagle*, January 31, 1943.

p. 26: *"If he'd been born next to a swimming pool he would have been a swimming champion"*   Schonberg. *NYT*, February 23, 1958; P. SM 38.

p. 26: *"Dear Bobby—Finish off the soup and rice"*   Regina Fischer notebook, MCF.

p. 26: *that potential friend would have had to not only know how to play chess but*   Associated Press wire story, October 12, 1958.

p. 27: *He was happy when the glare of the winter light ceased*   Letter from Regina Fischer to Bobby Fischer, circa September 1958, MCF.

p. 27: *A young math student replied—he even knew how to play chess*   Postcard, September 24, 1951, MCF.

p. 27: *And off he'd go to his chessboard, without his mother's permission*   Author's conversation with Regina Fischer, December 1960, New York.

p. 27: *One of Bobby's few non-chess interests emerged unexpectedly during his eighth year in the summer of 1951*   BFE, p. 1.

p. 28: *Bobby would train to take various Red Cross swimming tests*   American Red Cross Swimming Cards, various dates, MCF.

pp. 28–29: *Regina insisted that he have a psychological evaluation*   Author's conversation with Regina Fischer, December 1960, New York.

p. 29: *"I just go for it."*   Author's conversation with Bobby Fischer, January 1964, New York.

p. 29: *"I told her that I could think of a lot worse things than chess that a person could devote himself to"* Letter from Dr. Ariel Mengarini to author, March 31, 1963, New York.

p. 29: *"I'd already gone through most of the books in the public library"* BFE, p. 3.

p. 30: *the money was spent on chocolate milk for lunch and a candy bar after school* Regina Fischer notebook, MCF.

p. 30: *he expected to be called in front of Senator McCarthy's House Un-American Activities Committee hearings* Author's conversation with Harold M. Phillips, New York City, June 1960.

pp. 30–31: *When Mikhail Botvinnik, who became World Chess Champion, arrived at the Bolshoi Opera House* Alexander Kotov, "Why the Russians?" *Chessworld*, 1964, No. 2.

p. 31: *One Soviet tournament registered more than seven hundred thousand players* Ibid.

p. 31: *"They are out to win for the greater glory of the Soviet Union"* NYT, June 13, 1954, p. SM19.

p. 32: *He dutifully took his seat in the auditorium, as though he were at the Academy Awards of chess* PRO, p. 9.

p. 32: *David Bronstein asked for a glass of lemon juice* NYT, June 25, 1954, p. 23.

p. 32: *there was the Soviets' recent routing of the Argentine team in Buenos Aires and the French team in Paris* NYT, June 13, 1954, p. S4.

p. 32: *Nigro noted with proud amusement that his protégé was watching carefully* Author's conversation with Carmine Nigro, May 1955, Brooklyn, NY.

p. 33: *Dr. Fine wasn't playing for the United States* CR, July 1954, p. 199.

p. 33: *the man Bobby had played in a simultaneous exhibition three years previously* Ibid.

p. 33: *"He seemed to be a nice kid, somewhat shy"* Interview of Allen Kaufman by author, March 16, 2009.

p. 33: *"Chess spectators are like Dodger fans with laryngitis"* NYT, June 23, 1954, p. 27.

p. 34: *"No matter how talented by natural heritage, the amateur lacks that sometimes brutal precision"* CL, July 5, 1954, p. 4.

p. 34: *The following year, in July 1955* NYT, July 7, 1955, p. 33.

p. 34: *There Khrushchev issued a policy statement* NYT, July 5, 1955, p. 1.

p. 35: *"Mr. Nigro introduced me around and when I got better it was easier to get a game."* BFE, p. 2.

p. 36: *Kibitzers, always free with mostly unwanted advice* BFE, p. 5.

p. 36: *"Mr. Nigro, when is the food coming?"* Author's conversation with Carmine Nigro, May 1956, New York.

p. 36: *So involved was Bobby in his games* NYT, June 20, 1955, p. 42.

p. 36: *Bobby was highly indignant* PRO, p. 10.

p. 37: *"We were glad when it was over"* BFE, p. 5.

p. 37: *He finished fifteenth, and was awarded a ballpoint pen* NYT, October 3, 1955, p. 27.

p. 37: *A few weeks later, however, while walking with his mother* BFE, p. 5.

p. 37: The New York Times *ran a small story about the results* NYT, October 3, 1955, p. 27.

p. 37: *"My grandfather had shown little interest in [me] and knew nothing about chess."* BFE, p. 5.

Chapter 3: Out of the Head of Zeus

Regina Fischer's diary entries about Bobby's trip to Cuba offered illuminating anecdotes about his interactions with his teammates. Interviews of players such as James T. Sherwin, Allen Kaufman, and Anthony Saidy, and extracts from Bobby's autobiographical essay, also elucidate aspects of his life at this time.

p. 38: *"We were looking for [a way] to get out of the heat . . ."* BFE, p. 4.

p. 39: *"I was so impressed by his play that I introduced the 12-year old to Maurice Kasper, the president of the club"* Letter from Walter Shipman, March 31, 2009, FB.

p. 40: *"perhaps half of all of the greatest players of the past hundred years have been Jews"* Saidy and Lessing, p. 179.

p. 42: *"I adored playing with Bobby"* Interview of Dr. Stuart Margulies by the author, February 19, 2009.

p. 42: *Nevertheless, the boy was impressed at being in the presence of a champion* Note by Bobby Fischer, undated, circa September 1955, FB.

p. 42: *Eighty-year-old Harold M. Phillips, a master and member of the board, wist-*

fully likened Bobby's style of play   Author's conversation with Harold M. Phillips, circa 1964, New York.

p. 43: *"You can't win every game. Just do your best every time."*   BFE, p. 5.

p. 44: *"He would just get real quiet, twist that dog tag even more and immediately set up the pieces to play again."*   Mike Franett, "The Man Who Knew Bobby Fischer," *Chess,* September 2001, pp. 8–10.

p. 44: *Regina called Bobby every day at an arranged time to see if he was all right*   Press release, undated, circa March 1956, MCF.

p. 45: *"It gave me a big thrill"*   BFE, p. 4.

p. 46: *One player, William Schneider, said he was embarrassed when he and Laucks—sporting his swastika*   Interview of William Schneider by the author, circa 2005, New York.

p. 49: *Bobby gave a twelve-board simultaneous exhibition against members of the club and won ten and drew two*   BFE, p. 8.

p. 49: *"The Cubans seem to take chess more seriously"*   BFE, p. 5.

p. 49: The New York Times *took notice of the Log Cabin tour*   NYT, March 5, 1956. p. 36.

p. 49: *the unstructured routine enabled him*   BFE, p. 5.

p. 49: *he disliked "any kind of formality and ceremony."*   BFE, p. 5.

p. 50: *"Bobby Fischer rang my doorbell one afternoon"*   Collins, pp. 34–35.

p. 51: *The short, stunted man confined to a wheelchair and the growing boy went to movies*   Peter Marks, "The Man Who Was Fischer's Chess Mentor," *Newsday,* September 28, 1992, p. 39.

p. 51: *Bobby said that he always felt Nigro was more of a friend than a teacher*   BFE, p. 2.

p. 51: *With pupils, he'd often just set up a position and say, "Let's look at this"*   Interview of Allen Kaufman by author, March 16, 2009.

p. 52: *"I think Jack helped Bobby psychologically, with chess fightingness"*   Interview of James T. Sherwin by author, February 29, 2009.

p. 52: *"geniuses like Beethoven, Leonardo da Vinci"*   Collins, pp. 48–49.

p. 54: *She persuaded Maurice Kasper of the Manhattan Chess Club to give her $125 toward Bobby's expenses*   Letter from Regina Fischer to Maurice Kasper, June 24, 1956, MCF.

p. 54: *Bobby played a twenty-one-game simultaneous exhibition* International Photo, undated, FB.

p. 55: *Some of America's youngest but strongest stars had ventured north of the border* Interview of James Sherwin by author, February 27, 2009, by telephone.

p. 56: *"I knew I should have won!"* From "Let's Play Chess," by William Oaker; clipping from unidentified newspaper, January 18, 1958. FB.

p. 57: *Freud held that dream content* Freud, pp. 350–51.

p. 57: *"I had no idea that I was talking to a future world's champion"* Interview of Larry Evans by author, January 2010, by telephone.

p. 58: *"I'll stop coming"* Author's conversation with Regina Fischer, circa 1958, New York.

p. 58: *"Industry!" Regina yelled at Bobby* Conversation between author and Regina Fischer, circa 1956, New York.

p. 59: *Bobby's remembrance of Streisand? "There was this mousey little girl"* Andersen, p. 41.

p. 59: *Indeed, he'd already begun making frequent visits to the Marshall* Recollection of author.

p. 60: *It was at this club that Cuba's brilliant José Raúl Capablanca gave his last exhibition* Archives of the Marshall Chess Club, MCF.

p. 60: *Bobby's habitual mufti of T-shirt, wrinkled pants, and sneakers was considered an outrage by Caroline Marshall* Author's conversation with Caroline Marshall, May 1964.

p. 61: *Dark-haired, elegant in speech and dress, the twenty-five-year-old Byrne invariably held a cigarette between two fingers* Observation of author, and Golombek, *Golombek's Encyclopedia*, p. 52.

p. 62: *"The onlookers were invited to sit right next to you"* BFE, p. 3.

p. 62: *Then, suddenly, he moved his knight to a square where it could be snapped off* CL, December 1956, p. 374.

p. 63: *"It was extraordinary: The game and Bobby's youth were an unbeatable combination."* Interview of Allen Kaufman by author, March 16, 2009.

p. 63: *As the game progressed, Bobby had only twenty minutes remaining on his clock to make the required forty moves* CR, December 1956, p. 374.

p. 63: *He wasn't absolutely certain he could see the full consequences of allowing Byrne to take his queen* Fischer, *My 60 Memorable Games*, p. 65.

p. 63: *"Impossible! Byrne is losing to a 13-year-old nobody."* Hammond Times, February 24, 1957, p. 15.

p. 63: *Yet, other than the rapidity with which he was responding to Byrne's moves, Bobby showed little emotion* NYT, October 18, 1956, p. 44.

p. 64: *"Bobby Fischer's [performance] sparkles with stupendous originality."* CR, December 1956, p. 374.

p. 64: *Bobby's game appeared in newspapers throughout the country and chess magazines around the world* Kasparov, p. 213.

p. 64: *The British magazine Chess relaxed its stiff upper lip, calling Bobby's effort a game of "great depth and brilliancy"* Chess, November 9, 1956.

p. 64: Chess Life *proclaimed Bobby's victory nothing short of "fantastic"* CL, November 5, 1956, p. 3.

p. 64: *"I just made the moves I thought were best."* AP wire story, February 24, 1957.

p. 64: *David Lawson, a seventy-year-old American whose accent betrayed his Scottish birth* NYT, December 28, 2008.

p. 65: *Lawson's preference for dinner was Luchow's* Author's conversation with David Lawson, December 1963, New York.

p. 68: *"Many people imagine that the chess club . . ."* BFE, p. 12.

p. 69: *"The King stands for the boy's penis"* Reuben Fine, The Psychology of the Chess Player (New York: Dover Books, 1956), p. 12.

p. 70: *"You've tricked me"* Fine, Bobby Fischer's Conquest of the World's Chess Championship, pp. 24–25.

p. 70: *"it becomes one of the ironic twists of history"* Ibid.

p. 71: *"Ask me something unusual"* NYT, February 23, 1958, p. SM 38.

p. 74: *"I went to the phone booth and called my mother . . ."* BFE, p. 12.

p. 75: *"it was the title that really mattered"* BFE, p. 13.

p. 75: *"it was, of course, ridiculous for us to consider,"* BFE, p. 13.

p. 77: *"Bobby Fischer should finish slightly over the center mark"* CR, January 1958, p. 12.

p. 79: *"Reshevsky's busted."* NYT, February 23, 1958, p. SM 38.

Chapter 4: The American Wunderkind

Letters to Bobby's teacher, Jack Collins, and to his mother, about his visit to Moscow, followed by his entry into the Interzonal, Portorož 1958, illuminated how he felt about his first international tournament. The FBI files on Regina Fischer and the KGB files as paraphrased in the book *Russians Versus Fischer* also added further evaluative information.

p. 80: *hoping to supply information to the House Un-American Activities Committee* Letter to FBI under FOI Act, sent July 24, 2009.

p. 80: *To others he proclaimed* Shakhmatny Bulletin *"the best chess magazine in the world"* Johnson, p. 131.

p. 81: *Bobby made a mental note of which openings being played around the world won more games than others* Fischer, *My 60 Memorable Games*, p. 18.

p. 81: *At the Four Continents, Bobby bought a hardcover Russian-language copy of* The Soviet School of Chess *for $2.* Kotov and Yudovich, p. 8.

p. 81: *When Bobby was 14, he gave an interview to a visiting Russian journalist* CR, January 1959, p. 8.

p. 81: *"I watch what your grandmasters do."* CR, January 1959, p. 8.

p. 82: *Bobby pored over Buschke's holdings for hours, looking for that one book* PRO, p. 11.

p. 83: *When Bobby won the U.S. Championship, Buschke gave him a $100 gift certificate* PRO, p. 27.

p. 83: *Her oft-quoted statement that she'd tried everything* Johnson, p. 127.

p. 84: *She also compiled the addresses and telephone numbers* Copies of various address books of Regina Fischer. MCF.

p. 84: *I. A. Horowitz, the editor of* Chess Review, *claimed that she was a "pain in the neck"* Author's conversation with I. A. Horowitz, July 1972, New York.

p. 84: *"I hope Bobby will become a great chess champion"* Letter from Regina Fischer to Maurice Kasper, October 1, 1957, MCF.

p. 84: *"Keep it up but don't wear yourself down at it. Swim, nap."* Letter from Regina Fischer to Bobby Fischer, August 8, 1958, MCF.

p. 85: *The $64,000* Question *was so popular that even President Eisenhower watched it every week* Metz, Robert, *CBS: Reflections in a Bloodshot Eye* (New York: NAL, 1976), p. 78.

p. 86: *"It made interesting conversation while it lasted, anyway."* Bobby reflecting on The $64,000 Question in an essay he wrote, circa 1958, MCF.

p. 86: *"I'm not afraid of anything,"* Regina answered, *"and I have nothing to hide."* FBI file, p. 139.

p. 87: *Consequently, there was a sweeping investigation taking place of her activities, past and present* FBI file.

p. 87: *The confidential FBI report on Regina* FBI.

p. 87: *Undercover agents rifled through Joan Fischer's records at Brooklyn College* FBI.

pp. 87–88: *"My mother,"* said Joan Fischer, *"is a professional protester."* Joan Fischer, undated and unsourced clipping, FB.

p. 88: *Regina had been "kicked out" of the Communist Party* FBI report to the director from SAC, NY100-102290, August 24, 1953, p. 1.

p. 88: *She sent a letter directly to Premier Nikita Khrushchev* Johnson, p. 128.

p. 88: *Agents and informers continued to spy on the Fischers* FBI report to the director from SAC, NY100-102290, August 24, 1953, p. 2.

p. 89: *As it developed, Bobby was never questioned, but the fear had been implanted* Preliminary interview of Bobby Fischer for the film *My Friend Bobby.* Interview is in "Chapters from the Film," outtakes not used in the final release copy. Reykjavik, Iceland, 2009.

p. 89: *The agent remained throughout the broadcast but did not reveal his true identity* FBI report to the director from SAC, NY100-102290, May 23, 1958, p. 1.

p. 90: *he tripped with youthful awkwardness on the microphone wire while making his exit from the stage* I've Got a Secret footage, CBS, March 26, 1958.

p. 90: *"If I have to wear a tie, I won't go,"* New York World-Telegram and Sun, June 12, 1958.

p. 90: *"The eighth wonder of the world,"* Bobby wrote to Jack Collins Postcard from Bobby Fischer to Jack Collins, June 21, 1958, JWC.

p. 90: *Nevertheless, he played some seven-minute games* Postcard, circa 1958, JWC.

p. 90: *Before boarding the plane to Russia, Bobby plugged cotton into his ears* Letter from Regina Fischer to Bobby Fischer, June 18, 1958, MCF.

p. 91: *Moscow's finest hotel, the National.* Background promotional material from the Hotel National, circa 2009.

p. 91: *"Call me," she wrote to Bobby. "It's on the house." He didn't.* Letter from Regina Fischer to Bobby Fischer, June 30, 1958, MCF.

p. 91: *His mission was to play as many masters as possible* Letter to Parkhito from Regina Fischer, June 2, 1958, MCF.

p. 92: *Everyone wanted to see the American wunderkind* Interview of Lev Khariton by author, April 17, 2009, New York.

p. 93: *Finally, Tigran Petrosian was, on a semi-official basis, summoned to the club* Golombek, *Golombek's Encyclopedia*, pp. 236–37.

p. 93: *"None. You are our guest," Abramov frostily replied, "and we don't pay fees to guests."* Abramov to Fischer, in Johnson, p. 128.

p. 93: *Many years later, Bobby indicated that* Author's conversation with Bobby Fischer, circa 1964, New York.

p. 93: *When the Soviet Union had agreed to invite Bobby to Moscow* Letter from Regina Fischer to Bobby Fischer, circa June 1958, MCF.

p. 94: *He likened himself to his hero Paul Morphy* *Chessworld*, Vol. 1, No. 1, 1964, pp. 40–46.

p. 94: *he was fed up "with these Russian pigs"* Johnson, p. 128.

p. 94: *"I don't like Russian hospitality and the people themselves. It seems they don't like me either."* Postcard from Bobby Fischer to Jack Collins, July 1958, JWC.

p. 95: *In mid-July, one hundred thousand irate Soviet citizens* NYT, July 19, 1958, p. 1.

p. 95: *The situation was serious enough that Gerhardt Fischer, Bobby's father of record, feared Joan and Bobby might be in great danger* Letter from Gerhardt Fischer to Regina Fischer, August 4, 1958, MCF.

p. 97: *The only times he left the hotel were to play the two matches* Mednis, p. 3.

p. 97: *Top players in the United States predicted that Bobby wouldn't qualify for a place in the Candidates this time* CR, October 1958, p. 315.

p. 98: *Bobby, though, seemed to feel that he'd make short work of his competitors* Plisetsky and Voronkov, p. 15.

p. 98: *Lombardy had captured the World Junior Championship by winning every game, and he was a formidable player* NYT Magazine, February 23, 1958, p. SM 38.

p. 98: *"Bobby brushes his teeth daily but has more difficulty in taking a bath."* Postcard from Lombardy to Regina Fischer, circa 1958, in DeLucia and DeLucia, 2009, p. 49.

p. 98: *Lombardy also conveyed his initial impressions of Portorož* CL, October 1958, p. 314.

p. 99: *Regina wrote to Joan that she was worried Lombardy might be damning Bobby with faint praise* Letter from Regina Fischer to Joan Fischer, circa 1958, MCF.

p. 99: *"Bobby really didn't need Lombardy"* Author's interview of James T. Sherwin, February 27, 2009, by telephone.

p. 99: *One difficulty arose when Lombardy had to leave the tournament for several days* Letter from Regina Fischer to Joan Fischer, August 1956, MCF.

p. 99: *Lombardy reported the following remarks about his friend Bobby* CR, October 1958, p. 314.

p. 100: *Bobby's managing to avoid a loss in his first European tournament "highlighted a noteworthy turn in chess history"* New York World-Telegram and Sun, August 16, 1958.

p. 100: *Fischer off form in debut abroad* NYT, August 17, 1958, p. S4.

p. 100: *he was actually the prototype of the grandmaster character Kronsteen in the James Bond film* From Russia with Love Basalla, p. 142.

p. 100: *He was a fiercely attacking player, but at the board he'd often seem as if in a trance* Golombek, *Golombek's Encyclopedia*, p. 48.

p. 101: *Fischer had publicly announced before the tournament that there might be one player who could defeat him: Bronstein* Tal, p. 105.

p. 102: *At the Marshall Chess Club, where players were analyzing the Interzonal games as they were cabled in from Portorož, there was near-delirium when word arrived of the draw* CR, October 1958, p. 291.

p. 102: *"Bronstein?!" people were saying incredulously, almost whooping, as if the Soviet player were Goliath, and Bobby as David had stood up to him* Schonberg, p. 230.

p. 102: *So great was the impact of that game that club members began planning a party for the returning hero* CR, October 1958, p. 315.

p. 103: *Years later, Fischer would judge the Larsen game one of the best he ever played* Fischer, *My 60 Memorable Games*, p. 18.

p. 103: *"Fischer won with amazing ease"* CR, November 1958, p. 342.

p. 103: *Writing to Collins, he explained: "I never should have lost"* Letter from Bobby Fischer to Jack Collins, no date, JWC.

p. 104: *"Nobody sacrifices a piece against Fischer"* Ibid.

p. 104: The New York Times *was exuberant in running a salute to Bobby on its editorial page* NYT, September 14, 1958, p. E10.

p. 105: *"Remember, next year I will have to attend the tournament of Candidates before I can think of meeting Botvinnik."* New York World-Telegram and Sun, September 12, 1958.

p. 105: *"One thing is certain—I am not going to be a professional chess player."* United Press International wire report, September 13, 1958.

p. 105: *Bobby felt manhandled in both Moscow and Portoro̎z* PRO, p. 168.

p. 106: *"That looks Continental," he said in a courtly manner* NYT, September 16, 1958, p. 29.

p. 106: *Six days after Bobby's arrival back in the United States, the Marshall Chess Club followed through on its intentions and held a reception for him* New York World-Telegram and Sun, September 29, 1958.

p. 107: *A week later Bobby was back at the Marshall to play in the weekly speed tournament* New York World-Telegram and Sun, October 4, 1958.

p. 107: *But Collins also showed Bobby a father's love* Newsday, September 23, 1992.

p. 108: *Raymond Weinstein, a strong international master and a student of Collins, wrote* Unpublished autobiographical essay by Raymond Weinstein, circa 1958, FB.

p. 108: *"If someone was willing to pay $50"* Interview of Asa Hoffmann by author, March 2008, New York.

Chapter 5: The Cold War Gladiator

Bobby Fischer's letters to his mother and to Jack Collins provided the most telling of the sources for this chapter. Information regarding his preference for radio shows and how that had an effect on his religious beliefs came from an interview with Bobby and from his conversations with the author.

p. 109: *J. H. Donner, the gigantic Dutch grandmaster, noted the contrast* Elsevier Weekend, June 13, 1959.

p. 110: *"laconic as the hero of an old cowboy movie."* NYT, September 11, 1958, p. 46.

p. 110: *Fischer was the only American, and to many he was the tournament's dark knight* Plisetsky and Voronkov, p. 21.

p. 110: *he learned the Serbo-Croatian word for "first"* Wade and O'Connell, essay in Leonard Barden, *From Portorož to Petrosian* (New York: Doubleday and Co., 1972), p. 331.

p. 110: *Bobby's second, the great Danish player Bent Larsen, who was there to help him* Letter from Bobby Fischer to Regina Fischer, October 1959, MCF.

p. 111: *One Russian master, Igor Bondarevsky, wrote that* Plisetsky and Voronkov, p. 16.

p. 111: *Bobby, for his part, was livid at the seeming collusion* Letter from Bobby Fischer to Regina Fischer, October 9, 1959, MCF.

p. 112: *Tal was an encyclopedia of kinetic movement* Letter from Bobby Fischer to Regina Fischer, 1959, MCF.

p. 112: *Tal's coach Igor Bondarevsky referred to his charge's movements as "circling around the table like a vulture"* Plisetsky and Voronkov, p. 31.

p. 112: *Since Tal's body language was so bizarre, Fischer interpreted it as an attempt to annoy him* Candidates Tournament, 1959, newsreel footage, no date, YouTube, accessed December 9, 2009.

p. 112: *and he told the organizers that Tal should be thrown out of the tournament* Letter from Bobby Fischer to Regina Fischer, October 11, 1959, MCF.

p. 112: *He wrote a complaint about the chattering* Handwritten statement of Bobby Fischer, October 1959, FB.

p. 113: *"Why did Tal say 'cuckoo' to me?"* Letter from Bobby Fischer to Regina Fischer, 1959, MCF.

p. 113: *After that, a local Bled newspaper published a group of caricatures of all eight players* DeLucia and DeLucia, p. 54.

pp. 113–114: *She hoped she could talk him back into classes somewhere* Letters from Regina Fischer to U.S. embassies in Mexico City and Buenos Aires, both December 15, 1958, MCF.

p. 114: *the assistant principal of Erasmus, Grace Corey, wrote to Bobby in Yugoslavia* Letter from Grace Corey to Bobby Fischer, June 27, 1959, FB.

p. 114: *They were unaware that Bobby had read literature in high school* Bobby Fischer conversations with author, circa 1963–64.

p. 114: *Voltaire's* Candide *was a favorite* Interview of Dr. Eliot Hearst by author, February 7, 2009.

p. 114: *Tal asked Bobby if he'd ever gone to the opera* New York Daily News, March 26, 1958.

p. 114: *He also owned a book that told the stories of all the great operas* FB.

p. 114: *"If Tal doesn't behave himself, I am going to smash out all of his front teeth."* Letter from Bobby Fischer to Regina Fischer, October 9, 1959, MCF.

p. 115: *"I am in a good mood before I win all of my games."* Letter from Bobby Fischer to Regina Fischer, October 9, 1959, MCF.

p. 115: *"If I don't win against Smyslov tomorrow, I'll cut off my ear."* Bjelica, p. 118.

p. 115: *Larsen, whom Bobby described as "sulky and unhelpful," kept discouraging him* Letter from Bobby Fischer to Regina Fischer, October 1959, MCF.

p. 116: *"He is no match for Tal"* Harry Golombek, *4th Candidates Tournament, 1959*, p. vii.

p. 116: *World Champion Mikhail Botvinnik misdiagnosed the young American's struggles* CR.

p. 116: *Bobby began to plot. Tal had to be stopped* Letter from Bobby Fischer to Regina Fischer, October 11, 1959, MCF.

p. 116: *Tal, he said, had purposely made him lose three games in a row* Letter from Bobby Fischer to Regina Fischer, October 11, 1959, MCF.

p. 116: *Bobby began to wonder and scheme* Letter from Bobby Fischer to Regina Fischer, October 11, 1959, MCF.

p. 116: *"I don't believe in psychology—I believe in good moves."* PRO, p. 230.

p. 117: *"I would very much have liked to change his decision."* Tal, p. 124.

p. 117: *"I love the dark of the night. It helps me to concentrate."* PRO, p. 174.

p. 117: *Next to each bed, resting on a chair, was a chess set.* Saturday Review, August 27, 1963; Edmonds and Eidinow, p. 10.

p. 118: *"The Bahn Frei Polka" by Eduard Strauss* NYT, March 26, 2000, WK7.

p. 118: *"It sounds like circus music," he once said in a joyful mood* Author's conversation with Bobby Fischer, circa 1964, New York.

p. 119: *Sporadically, Shepherd would mention Bobby on the air* From Jean Shepherd's radio broadcasts, circa 1964.

p. 120: *"He seems so sincere"* Ambassador Report, June 1977.

p. 120: *"We take the broken bread unworthily if"* "Does God Heal Today?" Sermon originally broadcast in 1962 and reprinted in a sixteen-page pamphlet published by the Worldwide Church of God, pp. 10-11.

p. 121: *"What is the basic cause of war and human suffering?"* *Biblical Understanding.* Correspondence course, Lesson I. MCF.

p. 121: *"The Holy Bible is the most rational"* *Ambassador Report,* June 1977.

p. 122: *Bobby became very upset.* Author's conversation with Bobby Fischer, summer 1964.

Chapter 6: The New Fischer

p. 123: *"We can eat at the Oyster Bar. You like that. C'mon."* Observation by author, circa 1959 or 1960.

p. 124: *"Anyone should be able to become a master," he said with certainty* Observation by author, circa 1960.

p. 125: Public *pairing ceremonies were the custom, he loudly pointed out, in all European and most international tournaments* Observation by author, December 1960.

p. 125: *"Simple," said Bobby in response, "just do the pairings over again"* Telephone conversation between Bobby Fischer and an official of the U.S. Chess Federation. December 1959.

p. 125: *"Note his dungarees and [plaid] shirt in contrast to his opponents' business suits and ties."* *Parade,* October 27, 1957, p. 22.

p. 125: *He introduced Bobby to his tailor in the Little Hungary section of Manhattan* PRO, p. 35.

p. 126: *She set up a trust fund with Ivan Woolworth* Agreement between Ivan Woolworth and Regina Fischer, July 15, 1960, FB.

p. 127: *Regina, ever irrepressible and somehow aware of the adverse weather* Letter from Regina Fischer to Bobby, April 4, 1960, MCF.

p. 131: *Unsurprisingly, he won all the games* NYT, August 26, 1960, p. 9.

p. 131: *He suggested that Regina undertake a hunger strike for chess* NYT, October 12, 1960, p. 43.

p. 132: *Although separated in age by almost four decades, the two players became relatively close and remained so for years* CL, December 20, 1960, p. 15.

p. 132: *The cerebral melee ended in a draw*   NYT, November 2, 1960, p. 45.

p. 133: *A short while later,* Chess Life, *in describing the incident*   CL, March 20, 1961.

Chapter 7: Einstein's Theory

Bobby Fischer's interview in a publication that was attempting to expose the Worldwide Church of God was one of the most revelatory ever published about his religious beliefs. That article and interviews of players at Curaçao in 1962 added to the sources for this chapter.

p. 134: *he and his sister took a taxi to a victory dinner for Bobby at Vorst's*   Interview of Jack Collins by author, January 1961.

p. 134: *"Fischer has not lost a game in an American tournament since 1957."*   CL, January 20, 1961, p. 1.

p. 134: *It didn't help that a study had been published that year in* American Statistician *magazine*   Ernest Rubin, "The Age Factor in Masters Chess," reprinted in *CL*, February 20, 1961, pp. 40–43.

p. 135: *During the summer of 1961 a sixteen-game match between the two players was negotiated and a prize fund of $8,000 was promised*   NYT, August 19, 1961, p. 15.

p. 135: *When four world-class chess players—Svetozar Gligoric, Bent Larsen, Paul Keres, and Tigran Petrosian—were asked*   PRO, p. 42.

p. 136: *Early in his career he* did *play before sundown*   Hooper and Whyld, p. 22.

p. 136: *He simply couldn't play at that time, he said. "It's ridiculous."*   NYT, August 15, 1961, p. 36.

p. 136: *She could always come to the game after the concert, he argued*   CL, August 1961, pp. 213–20.

p. 136: *Reshevsky paced up and down, a few spectators waited patiently*   NYT, August 14, 1961, p. 20.

p. 137: *Bobby ultimately sued Reshevsky and the American Chess Foundation*   "Chess Stars Heading for Court Battle" *The Daily Gleaner,* Kingston, Ontario, April 27, 1962.

p. 137: *"It's up those metal stairs."*   The source of the information following, pages 137–39, consisted also of interviews with Bobby Fischer, circa 1964, and with Ralph Ginzburg, circa 1962.

p. 137: *an interview with Bobby for* Harper's *magazine* Ralph Ginzburg, "Portrait of a Genius or a Young Chess Master," *Harper's*, January 1962, pp. 49–55.

p. 138: *In preparation for the interview, Ginzburg had read Elias Canetti's classic work* Auto-da-Fé See Canetti.

p. 139: *"I don't want to talk about it! Don't ever mention Ginzburg's name to me!"* PRO, p. 47.

p. 139: *It honed his instinct and forced him to trust himself* CL, February 1962, p. 25.

p. 140: *"the number comes up again and again [the magic number for true expertise: ten thousand hours of practice]"* Gladwell, p. 41.

p. 140: *"Practice isn't the thing you do once you're good. It's the thing you do that makes you good."* Gladwell, p. 41.

p. 141: *Bobby signed it using the Russian Cyrillic alphabet, needing to change only a few letters.* CL, February 1962, p. 25.

p. 141: *"A charmer"* CR, November 1961, p. 347.

p. 141: *Tal [Sighing]: "It is difficult to play against Einstein's theory."* Fischer, *My 60 Memorable Games*, p. 196; also in CL, March 1952, p. 58.

p. 141: *Bobby was not happy with his eventual second-place showing in the tournament* CR, November 1961, p. 323.

p. 141: *he was also having difficulty keeping food down* PRO, p. 50.

p. 142: *the British Broadcasting Corporation invited him to London to appear on a show called* Chess Treasury of the Air Tiller, p. 124.

p. 142: *Bobby spent a British Christmas with his mother and her new husband* Letter to Regina Pustan from Bobby Fischer, January 1963, MCF.

p. 142: *"I wasn't just 'trusting in God' to give me the moves."* "The Painful Truth," interview of Bobby Fischer in *Ambassador Report*, June 1976.

p. 143: *Bobby wrote a preachy letter to his mother* Letter to Regina Pustan from Bobby Fischer, March 9, 1964, MCF.

p. 143: *A good and tolerant life was the best life, she said* Copy of letter, perhaps unsent, to Bobby Fischer from Regina Pustan, August 1964, MCF.

p. 143: *"If anyone tried to live by the letter of the law, it was me"* *Ambassador Report*, June 1977.

p. 143: *"The more I tried [to be obedient] the more crazy I became," he noted* "The Painful Truth," interview of Bobby Fischer in *Ambassador Report,* June 1976.

p. 144: *the real prize for Bobby was to qualify for the Candidates tournament* Conversation with author, April 1962.

p. 144: *"Bobby Fischer's margin of 2½ points reflects his complete domination of the event." CL,* April 1962, p. 69.

p. 145: *entered Bobby's room at the Hotel Intercontinental in Curaçao shortly after Arthur Bisguier, Bobby's second, had arrived.* DeLucia, p. 270.

p. 146: *"No, you get out!" Benko replied, somewhat illogically.* Interview of Pal Benko by author, summer 2008.

p. 146: *"I am sorry that I beat up Bobby. He was a sick man, even then."* Ibid.

p. 146: *The day after the fight, Bobby penned a letter to the Tournament Committee, asking them to expel Benko.* Chesscafe.com/FromArchive/FromArchive.htm, "The Fischer-Benko Slapping Incident," September 1977.

p. 146: *the Candidates tournament had furnished "a series of early-round surprises that are probably without parallel in chess history" CL,* August 1962, p. 172.

p. 147: *"Chess is better."* Interview of Arthur Bisguier by author, February 21, 2009.

p. 147: *"There was open collusion between the Russian [Soviet] players" Sports Illustrated,* August 20, 1962, accessed December 10, 2009, http://sportsillustrated.cnn.com/vault.

p. 147: *Korchnoi, in his memoir* Chess Is My Life, *backed Bobby's accusations* Korchnoi, pp 44–45.

p. 147: *"He simply wasn't the best player."* Interview of Pal Benko by author, July 2000, Philadelphia, PA.

p. 148: *The article was reprinted in German, Dutch, Spanish, Swedish, Icelandic, and (with modifications) Russian.* Bobby Fischer, "The Russians Have Fixed World Chess," *Sports Illustrated,* August 20, 1962.

Chapter 8: Legends Clash

FBI files of an investigation of Bobby Fischer added facts, heretofore unknown, about his life. Interviews with players who knew him well provided additional insights. Observations by the author served as a catalyst to the research.

p. 150: *"tinkering with the engine of a plane"* Quoted in the film *Me and Bobby Fischer,* directed by Fridrik Gudmundsson, DVD, 2009.

p. 151: *Winner three times of the World Championship, he'd defeated Alexander Alekhine, José Capablanca, Max Euwe, and Emanuel Lasker* Golombek, *Golombek's Encyclopedia,* pp. 38–39.

p. 151: *Bobby shook hands and said succinctly, "Fischer"* CL, November 1962, p. 262.

p. 151: *He knew he was a major representative of the Soviet Union* Interview of M. Botvinnik by author, Skopje, Macedonia, September 1972.

p. 151: *His pupil, Anatoly Karpov, said of him that he had an "Olympian inaccessibility"* Karpov, p. 41.

p. 152: *When the game was adjourned, it appeared that Fischer's position was clearly superior.* CL, November 1962, p. 261.

p. 152: *"Look," he said. "Botvinnik is getting assistance!"* Botvinnik, pp. 170–78.

p. 152: *No official protest was put before the tournament committee* PRO, p. 66.

p. 153: *Mysteriously, the nineteen-year-old wrote a letter of apology to Dr. Eliot Hearst* Interview of Dr. Eliot Hearst by author, February 7, 2009, by telephone.

p. 153: *Aboard the* New Amsterdam *once again* DeLucia, p. 96.

p. 153: *Botvinnik might have been able to become Premier* DeLucia, p. 96.

p. 153: *But back in Brooklyn, Bobby said he just no longer wanted to be involved with those "commie cheaters," as he called them.* Conversation with author, circa December 1962, New York.

p. 154: *Saidy's position was powerful, and Bobby's was precarious.* Observation of author, 1964.

p. 155: *Saidy's blunder gave Fischer an opportunity to develop a winning endgame* Interview of Anthony Saidy by author, February 21, 2009, by telephone.

p. 155: *Fischer's first prize for his two weeks of intensity and brilliance was just $2,000* NYT, January 4, 1964.

p. 155: *"Fischer was playing against children," he said* CL, August 1964, p. 202.

p. 155: *he'd said that he would never play in the FIDE cycle again because it was stacked in favor of the Soviets.* "The Stalemate of Bobby Fischer," CL, April 1964, p. 186.

p. 156: *General George B. Hershey, head of the Selective Service bureau* Author's discussion with Harold M. Phillips, circa spring 1964.

p. 156: *Alfred Landa, then assistant to the president, said* Interview of Alfred Landa by author, circa spring 1964, New York.

p. 156: *Bobby Fischer was classified 4F* Draft deferment card, 1964, MCF.

p. 157: *Nonetheless, the State Department flatly refused to recognize him as a legitimate columnist* CL, September 1965, p. 191.

p. 157: *"Cuban travel criteria make no provision for validation for the purpose of participating in chess competitions."* FBI investigation file of Robert James Fischer, 1958–1967.

p. 158: *Furious, Bobby cabled Castro* NYT, August 25, 1965, p. 36.

p. 159: *Upon receiving word from Castro, Bobby confirmed his participation* NYT, August 25, 1965, p. 36.

p. 159: *The tick of the chess clock was the only sound heard* Observation of author, who was a referee during the Havana match, August 1965.

p. 159: *Bobby had to play this strange, isolated form of chess every single game* "Fischer Against the Odds," NYT, October 24, 1965, p. X30

p. 159: *Still, he tied for second, a half point behind Russia's Vasily Smyslov, the former World Champion* NYT, September 28, 1965, p. 10.

p. 160: *They rigorously studied his opening, middle game, and endings* Vladimir Linder and Isaac Linder, "From Morphy to Fischer, Who's Next?" ten-page unpublished essay, Moscow, 2002, p. 8.

p. 160: *"We must get Bobby Fischer," Gregor Piatigorsky told his wife.* Piatigorsky, p. 166.

p. 160: *The story of how Fischer went into a swoon* Kashdan, pp. xix–xx.

p. 161: *Fortunately, drawing deep from his inner reserves, Bobby did climb* CR, October 1966, p. 296.

Chapter 9: The Candidate

Letters and postcards to Jack Collins, and widespread media coverage that appeared in the general and chess press for Fischer's three matches leading up to the World Championship, provided most of the sources for this chapter.

p. 162: *He won the Monte Carlo International and ungallantly refused to pose for a photograph with His Royal Highness Prince Rainier* CR, May 1967, p. 131.

p. 162: *when Princess Grace awarded him his cash prize* Michael Hoffer, "Boris

Spassky Interview and Fischer-Spassky Retrospective," posted in *Chess History,* http://yes2chess.com.

p. 162: *he led the American Olympiad team to Cuba*   Andrew Soltis, *Karl Marx Plays Chess and Other Reports on the World's Oldest Game,* p. 51.

p. 162: *because of the refusal of the organizers to agree to his scheduling demands*   CR, December 1965, p. 355.

p. 162: *"Leave me in peace!"*   *Newsday,* December 1967.

p. 162: *He, not the organizers, would decide when he'd play and when he wouldn't*   Letter from William Lombardy to Anthony Saidy, November 13, 1967, FB.

p. 163: *"He felt he should enjoy whatever money he could get before it was too late."*   Evans, *The Chess Beat,* "Bobby's Dilemma," p. 5.

p. 163: *Bobby withdrew from playing competitive chess in late 1968*   Letter from Bobby Fischer to Ed Edmondson, October 29, 1969, JWC.

p. 164: *later telling one interviewer that he'd refused to play because of undefined "hang-ups"*   *Sports Illustrated,* April 20, 1970, pp. 62–63.

p. 164: *"to plot my revenge"*   NYT, November 14, 1971, pp. 32 ff.

p. 164: *Then, unpredictably, he made an exception*   NYT, April 27, 1970, p. 30.

p. 164: *Larry Evans, who was reporting on the match instead of playing in it and would act as Fischer's second*   PRO, p. 161.

p. 164: *"This is not surprising, but if you see Bobby kiss the girl,* then *you have a news item!"*   CL&R, May 1970, p. 247.

p. 165: *fans filled the large hall to capacity in less than half an hour*   "USSR vs. the Rest of the World," Glenn Giffen at Olipbase.org, 1970.

p. 165: *"At home they don't understand. They think it means there's something wrong with our culture."*   CL&R, May 1970, p. 246.

p. 165: *He wanted to* win *the car, not to* keep *the car*   Chess Digest, September 1970, p. 194.

p. 166: *"He prefers to enter chess history alone."*   CL&R, June 1970, p. 301.

p. 166: *If Bobby Fischer was ever going to become the World Chess Champion*   As published in *Courier Journal,* December 13, 1970, and NYT News Service.

p. 166: *Fischer and Geller were to meet in the twelfth round in a pivotal matchup*   PRO, p. 177.

p. 166: *"No draws in under 40 moves is an essential part of his philosophy."* Wade and Blackstock, pp 120–21.

p. 167: *"Maybe this was a good thing."* PRO, p. 181.

p. 167: *Taimanov arrived with a full Russian entourage* NYT *Magazine,* November 14, 1971, p. 130.

p. 168: *"Well, I still have my music."* PRO, p. 188.

p. 168: *Fischer-doubters, especially the Soviets, had suggested* NYT, July 21, 1971, p. 33.

p. 170: *For eleven minutes, Fischer continued to visualize the position in his head* Time, November. 8, 1971, p. 68.

p. 170: *Bobby was obviously sick with a bad head cold* NYT, November 11, 1971, p. 33.

Chapter 10: The Champion

A great amount of the facts that appear in this chapter were garnered by the author as an observer and working journalist/broadcaster during the two-month duration of the 1972 Fischer-Spassky match, and some of it has appeared in my book *Profile of a Prodigy,* 1973, 1989 editions.

p. 172: *Questions arose almost daily about such details as the prize money* Interview of Fred Cramer by the author, circa April 1972.

p. 173: *But none of those topics interested the three men in the room that evening.* Darrach, p. 6.

p. 173: *Fischer was concerned about the strength of Spassky* Chessworld, Vol. I, No. 1, January–February 1964, pp. 60-61.

p. 173: *"Spassky is better"* Darrach, p. 6.

p. 173: *Eventually, internecine warfare erupted between the United States and Soviet Chess federations and FIDE.* Official report to FIDE by Dr. Max Euwe, May 16, 1972, No. 138, pp. 1–18.

p. 174: *He was encouraged to play there by Freysteinn Thorbergsson* "Welcome to Iceland, Mr. President," a pamphlet written by Freysteinn Thorbergsson, p. 30 ff.

p. 174: *Spassky ensconced himself in the Caucasus while Fischer settled in the Catskills* PRO, p. 215.

p. 175: *This microscopic analysis often continued until the early hours of the morning.* PRO, p. 216.

p. 175: *Almost as a parlor trick*　As told to Yasser Seirawan by Allen Kaufman in *Chess Duels,* by Yasser Seirawan, (London: Gloucester Publishers plc, 2010), p. 28.

p. 176: *"The odds should be twenty to one"*　*NYT,* June 13, 1972, p. 40.

p. 176: *"It's true that he works alone"*　Interview of William Lombardy by author, July 15, 1972, Reykjavik, Iceland.

p. 177: *He often stayed overnight in the Fischer apartment in Brooklyn*　Author's conversation with Jackie Beers, circa 1974.

p. 177: *"strike at the uplifted propaganda fists of the Communists."*　Thorbergsson, p. 33.

p. 178: *"The Russian Bear vs. the Brooklyn Wolf"*　*Time,* July 31, 1972, pp. 30–35.

p. 178: *Asked if the bout would be a grudge match, he replied: "In a sense."*　Interview with Dick Cavett, 1972.

p. 179: *Photographic blowups of Fischer and Spassky adorned the windows of almost every shop*　Schultz, *Chess Don,* p. 274.

p. 180: *Fischer canceled his flight to Iceland at the last minute*　Chess Base News, ChessBase.com/NewsDateline by Prof. Christian Hesse, ABC TV, 1972.

p. 180: *But, strangely, Fischer paused to buy an alarm clock*　*NYT,* September 5, 1972.

pp. 181–82: *Sheed wrote: "Of Ezra Pound, as of Bobby Fischer, all that can be decently said is that his colleagues admire him."*　*NYT Book Review,* September 3, 1972, p. 2.

p. 182: *As Saidy later related, the house was subjected to an unending media barrage*　Interview of Anthony Saidy by author, February 21, 2009, by telephone.

p. 183: *Journalist Leonard Barden phoned the Icelandic organizers to tell them that British financier James Derrick Slater*　Roy Blount Jr., "Boris in Wonderland," *Sports Illustrated,* July 24, 1972, p. 15.

p. 184: *The second call proved to be that needed nudge*　Telegram to the U.S. Department of State from the American embassy in Reykjavik, Iceland, seeking assistance from the White House in prompting Fischer to come to Iceland, July 3, 1972, FB.

p. 184: *It was at this point that Bobby saw himself not just as a chess player*　Gligoric, *Fischer vs. Spassky,* p. 9.

p. 187: *"I know you to be a sportsman and a gentleman, and I am looking forward to some exciting chess games with you"*　*NYT,* July 7, 1972, p. 14.

p. 188: *"The challenger apologized"* Press release issued in Reykjavik, Iceland, July 6, 1972.

p. 191: *"I couldn't believe that Fischer was capable of such an error"* Edmar Mednis, *How to Beat Bobby Fischer* (New York: Dover Books, 1997), p. 274.

p. 191: *Fischer then pointed to the camera aperture he'd complained about the previous day* Steiner, p. 68.

p. 192: *Fischer began fighting for a draw* Chess world championship, 1972; "Spassky's View," excerpted from *64*, p. 258.

p. 193: *"What will happen to Bobby?"* Interview of Lothar Schmid by author, July 15, 1972, Reykjavik, Iceland.

p. 194: *"He can't be subject to the clicks and flashes of those machines [on their tall tripods] above him."* *NYT*, July 21, 1972, p. 32.

p. 194: *"In case of non-appearance of Fischer in third game"* Released press statement by Dr. Max Euwe, July 16, 1972.

p. 194: *In an editorial entitled "Bobby Fischer's Tragedy," the paper wrote* *NYT*, July 15, 1972, p. 22.

p. 194: *President Nixon also relayed an invitation to Fischer* Interview of Harry Benson by author, August 1972, Reykjavik, Iceland.

p. 194: *Spassky, ever a gentleman, was willing* *NYT*, August 16, 1972, p. 26.

p. 195: *Schmid recalled later that "for a second, I didn't know what to do"* Chessbase.com, September 28, 2009. Accessed October 15, 2009.

p. 196: *Fischer was told that it was just a closed-circuit, noiseless camera* *CL*, November 1972, p. 679.

p. 196: *A thirty-five-year-old sociology professor, Shelby Lyman* "TV's Man on the Move," *NYT*, August 10, 1972, p. 71.

p. 197: *In New York, intense demand quickly made chess sets an out-of-stock item* *NYT*, July 9, 1972, p. 30.

p. 198: *"Iceland is a nice place"* Interview of Fred Cramer by author, August 1972, Reykjavik, Iceland.

p. 199: *Shortly before the concluding week of the match, the Soviet delegation, by way of a long and preposterous statement* *NYT*, August 23, 1972, p. 1.

p. 199: *But the secret weapon turned out to be a blob of wood filler* *NYT*, September 5, 1972, p. 41.

p. 200: *"Two dead flies!"*   NYT, August 27, 1972, p. E5.

p. 200: *"It started out as a farce by Beckett"*   Interview of Harry Golombek by author, August 1972, Reykjavik, Iceland.

p. 201: *Then suddenly, wearing a maroon corduroy suit that he'd had custom made in Reykjavik, Bobby appeared*   "A Replay Precedes Fischer Crowning," NYT, September 3, 1972, p. 19.

p. 201: *"We didn't know if you were going to be the winner!"*   Interview of Dr. Max Euwe by author, September 3, 1972.

pp. 201–2: *Euwe continued to talk and mentioned that the rules would have to be changed*   Press release copy of speech by Dr. Max Euwe, September 3, 1972, FB.

p. 202: *"I should have played here as my sealed move"*   Overheard at the banquet by nearby spectators.

p. 203: *"Fischer is a man of art*   "Notes on People," NYT, CL, November 1972, p. 680.

p. 203: *The mayor had offered Bobby a ticker-tape parade*   NYT, September 2, 1972, p. 46.

p. 203: *Your convincing victory*   As reproduced in Larry Evans and Ken Smith, *Chess World Championship 1972* (New York: Simon & Schuster, 1973), p. 261.

p. 204: *"the grandest master of them all"*   New York Daily News, September 23, 1972, p. 18.

p. 204: *"I never thought I'd see the day when chess would be all over the front pages here"*   AP wire story, as appeared in *San Francisco Chronicle*, September 23, 1972, p. 23.

p. 204: *That day, Bobby was not the old curmudgeonly Bobby*   AP wire story, September 24, 1972.

p. 204: *"Fischer has done more, however, than simply win the world title"*   NYT, September 3, 1972, p. 20.

Chapter 11: The Wilderness Years

p. 205: *"I want to meet girls"*   New York, February 20, 1975, p. 38.

p. 205: *So, working with Stanley Rader, the chief counsel for the Worldwide Church*   NYT, September 23, 1973, pp. 26–34.

p. 206: *The words "secluded" and "recluse"*   NYT, September 3, 1972, p. 46.

p. 206: *The Associated Press took the same tack*   AP wire story, August 22, 1973.

p. 207: *As a result of the non-event event, the resulting press coverage was practically nil.* Reports from various news services, August 1973.

p. 207: *Attractive financial offers kept tumbling Bobby's way—almost pouring over him* NYT, September 11, 1972, p. 28.

p. 209: *"I was not yet World Champion but they treated me like a world champion."* Casto Abundo, "A Month in Manila with Bobby Fischer," March 6, 2008, HTTP://www.FIDE.com, accessed March 10, 2010.

p. 209: *by the time Bobby came back from Iceland he'd received offers that could have totaled up to $10 million* NYT, September 11, 1972, p. 28.

p. 210: *The Church imposed a number of rules that Bobby thought were ridiculous* "The W.C.G. Talmud," in *Ambassador Report,* www.hwarmstrong.com/AR/Talmud.

p. 210: *Bobby was appalled. "What? Don't you believe in Satan?"* New York Daily News, August 28, 1972.

p. 212: *"But these new groups are attractive to the apostate merely because they are foreign."* Mamet.

p. 212: *"Either God is a masochist and likes to be made a fool of, or else Herbert Armstrong is a false prophet."* "The Painful Truth," an interview of Bobby Fischer in *Ambassador Report,* www.hwarmstrong.com/ar/fischer.

p. 213: *"It is the bottomless rascality of the* goyim *people"* Protocols of the Elders of Zion; protocol no. 3, para. 16; as quoted in Eisner, p. 78.

p. 213: *"I carefully studied the protocols"* Letter from Bobby Fischer to Pal Benko, circa 1979.

p. 213: *"The book shows"* Letter from Bobby Fischer to Jack Collins, June 1976, JWC.

p. 213: *At one point Bobby had both* Protocols *and* Nature's Eternal Religion *mailed to Jack and Ethel Collins* Letter to Ethel and Jack Collins from Bobby Fischer, February 20, 1979, JWC.

p. 214: *Fischer sent the Collinses another hate-filled screed,* Secret World Government   Letter to Jack Collins from Bobby Fischer, May 14, 1978, JWC.

p. 214: *"Then the true believers begin to lose their fear."* "The Painful Truth," in *Ambassador Report,* www.hwarmstrong.com/ar/fischer.

p. 215: *"I was really shocked when you refused to discuss the matter or do anything."* Letter from Regina Fischer to Bobby Fischer, June 26, 1974.

p. 216: *Marshall investigated a possible injunction to stop publication of the work since according to Bobby, Darrach had allegedly violated his contract* Summons issued by Bobby Fischer as Plaintiff against Brad Darrach, Time Inc., U.S. Chess Federation, et al., December 22, 1975, JWC.

p. 218: *"Steinitz, Tchigorin, Lasker (too), Gunsberg, Zukertort . . . all played under the ten-win system"* CL&R, November 1974; pp. 714-15.

p. 218: *"I will* punish *them and not play"* Conversations conveyed to author, circa March 1975.

p. 218: *"Your professionalism, competitive spirit, and outstanding skill have thrilled all"* CL&R, November 1974, p. 716.

p. 218: *"At the moment we are in a complete stalemate"* Evening Standard (London), November 11, 1974, p. 6.

p. 218: *"FIDE HAS DECIDED AGAINST MY PARTICIPATION"* http://www .chessgames.com.

p. 219: The New York Times *ran a story by international grandmaster Robert Byrne,* NYT, April 13, 1975, p. 119.

p. 219: *"Bobby fears the unknown, whatever lies beyond his control"* from the film The Auld Enemy—Fischer vs. the Soviets, September 11, 1998.

p. 219: *"I had no idea why Fischer refused to defend his title"* Moscow News, April 28, 1975, p. 15.

p. 220: *"cultural purity"* Letter from Bobby Fischer to Ethel Collins, December 21, 1976, JWC.

p. 220: *His friends from the Church, Arthur and Claudia Mokarow, owned the house* Petra Dautov, Ein Jahr mit dem Schachgenie, Amazon.de, p. 41.

p. 221: *Every day, he'd drink one or two pint glasses of carrot juice,* Böhm and Jongkind, chapter called "Harry Sneider," p. 48–52.

p. 222: *Bobby's outbursts would startle the infrequent passersby* Interview with Jackie Beers, circa 1975.

p. 222: *Gradually, his savings were evaporating* Unidentified newspaper clipping, "A King Eyes His Own Crown," circa 1982, JWC.

p. 223: *He was solicitous toward*   Letter from Bobby Fischer to Ethel Collins, December 21, 1976, JWC.

p. 223: *Years later in Iceland*   Interview of Gardar Sverrisson by author, October 2009, Reykjavik, Iceland.

p. 224: *Bobby would just wipe him off the board in short order every time.*   www.BobbyFischer.net, November 23, 2009.

pp. 224–25: *Finally Browne said, "You know, Bobby, you'll really have to get off the phone."*   Telephone interview with Walter Browne by author, April 11, 2009.

p. 225: *At the end of the letter he included instructions*   Letter from Bobby Fischer to Regina Fischer, October 27, 1974, MCF.

p. 225: *He simply did not want contact*   Letter from Bobby Fischer to Jack Collins, April 30, 1979, JWC.

p. 225: *Chess colleagues of Bobby's—including grandmaster Robert Byrne—have said*   Kelly Atkins, collected anthology of Bobby Fischer quotes, Chessville.com.

p. 225: *"There is nothing in the [KGB] documents that there ever were any plans to kill him"*   Ree, p. 39.

p. 226: *A sportswriter once wrote that Fischer was the fastest walker he ever saw outside of an Olympian*   Dick Schaap, "Bobby Fischer Can Lick Muhammad Ali Any Day," *Sport*, February 1973.

p. 226: Another journalist, Brad Darrach   *Life*, November 12, 1971, p. 52.

p. 227: *Just so the world would know what he'd gone through*   Complete copy at www.anusha.com/pasadena/htm.

p. 228: *"Yes, I wrote it, but I had a terrible time in that jail"*   Interview of Pal Benko by author, summer 2008, New York City.

p. 229: *Stories were told, unconfirmed by this writer, that when he was flat broke*   Böhm and Jongkind, p. 58, states that Fischer gave chess lessons for "5,000 a shot."

p. 229: *"go back to your publisher and ask for a million dollars"*   *Los Angeles Times*, September 19, 1993.

p. 229: *His request was refused "on principle"*   DeLucia and DeLucia, p. 194.

p. 229: *Freelance photographers were willing to pay $5,000*   Ivan S. Lagaroff, "Bobby Fischer's Endgame," *Esquire*, December 1992.

p. 230: *"Every now and then there would be a 'sighting' of a forlorn, bearded figure."* *Independent,* August 29, 1992.

Chapter 12: Fischer-Spassky Redux

p. 231: *Bobby wanted to get back to the game . . . desperately* Letter from Regina Fischer to Joan Fischer Targ, March 8, 1984, MCF.

p. 231: *Spassky provided a way back to the board* *Independent,* June 25, 1990, p. 12.

p. 232: *To avoid journalists, Bobby checked in under the name of Brown* *Sports Illustrated,* May 14, 1990.

p. 232: *He forbade her to take a photograph of him* *Sports Illustrated,* May 14, 1990.

p. 232: *"When I broke through internationally, he had just stopped [playing]."* Böhm and Jongkind, p. 91.

p. 233: *He found Fischer's neo-Nazi remarks about Jews to be "beyond the abhorrent"* *CL,* March 1993, p. 28. (Kok is reported to have condemned Fischer's "Neo-Nazism.")

p. 233: *The press had learned that Gerhardt was somewhere in Germany* Interview of author by German broadcaster Stefan Loffler, spring 1991.

p. 233: *He felt paternal toward her and thought Bobby might be interested in meeting her* www.dmv.demon.nl.

p. 233: *"I think so"* www.darkdemon.nl.

p. 233: *Now that he was in Europe in 1990, courtesy of Bessel Kok, Bobby visited Petra* www.darkdemon.nl.

pp. 233–34: *Petra married Russian grandmaster Rustem Dautov in 1992, and in 1995 she wrote a book* www.darkdemon.nl.

p. 234: *"be careful"* DeLucia and DeLucia, pp. 210–11.

p. 234: *The inn was known to be friendly to those who played the game* *Chess,* July 2006, pp. 8–9.

p. 235: *It was, in fact, a letter from a seventeen-year-old girl, Zita Rajcsanyi* *Los Angeles Times,* September 19, 1993, p. 36.

p. 235: *"Now that I have your interest"* *Kurir* (Budapest daily), September 14, 1993, p. 20.

p. 236: *he believed that Kasparov and Karpov were actually agents of the Russian regime* Kurir, September 14, 1993.

p. 236: *"Everyone who is a Soviet, and everyone who is Jewish, cannot be trusted," he affirmed* Farkasházy, p. 29 ff.

p. 236: *"You can hardly turn around"* Letter from Regina Fischer to Bobby Fischer, December 15, 1990, MCF.

p. 236: *Zita remained in Los Angeles for six weeks and stayed at the home of Robert Ellsworth* "Has the Bad Boy of Chess Grown Up?" Los Angeles Times, September 19, 1993, pp. 13–15.

p. 237: *the real reason Bobby was interested in her was "because I didn't want anything from him"* Kurir, September 13, 1993, p. 20.

p. 237: *"He was ashamed of his poverty"* Seirawan and Stefanovic, p. 276.

p. 237: *He was also furious that although President Nixon had said he'd be invited to the White House* El Pais, April 3, 2001.

p. 237: *In the interview Zita later gave to Tivadar Farkasházy, she claimed that Bobby was still waiting* Los Angeles Times, September 23, 1993.

p. 238: *Besides offering Regina support, Bobby wanted to introduce her to Zita* Farkasházy, p. 29 ff.

p. 238: *"I wasn't thinking of that"* Kurir, September 14, 1993, p. 20.

p. 238: *He referred to Zita as his girlfriend* http:www.chessgames.com, May 3, 2008.

p. 238: *It took almost a year, but she finally located someone* "Zita's Story" and "A Short Story" in Seirawan and Stefanovic, pp. 275–76.

p. 239: *About a month later, in July 1992, Kubat, Zita, and two officials of Jugoskandic Bank were in Los Angeles* Independent, August 29, 1992.

p. 239: *He'd later learn that the banker was one of the most powerful men in Serbia* NYT, September 1, 1992, p. D1.

p. 239: *Kubat was afraid that Vasiljevic wouldn't release the advance payment* Contract between Bobby Fischer and Boris Spassky, Vladimir Miljavic for the Jugoskandik Company, signed July 11, 1992, FB.

p. 240: *Spassky agreed to everything in the contract* "Banker Lures Fischer to Play for Cheque," London Times, August 1992, p. 1.

p. 240: *Heavy fighting between forces* Associated Press, August 19, 1992.

p. 240: *The forty-nine-year-old Bobby Fischer was described by a reporter* NYT, August 30, 1992, p. A1.

p. 241: *After Bobby signed the contract to play* Farkasházy, p. 119 ff.

p. 241: *"At one pole, there is elation over Mr. Fischer's return from two decades of obscurity."* NYT, September 2, 1992, p. C14.

p. 242: *Bobby asked Gligoric ("Gliga") to play a secret training match* Chess in Translation, June 23, 2010, chessintranslation.com.

p. 242: *When asked at the time whether he'd like to engage Fischer in a match for the official championship, Kasparov snapped* NYT, September 2, 1992, p. C14.

p. 243: *Order to Provide Information and Cease and Desist Activities* Official Document from the Department of the Treasury to Bobby Fischer, August 21, 1992, FB.

p. 247: *He'd insisted that all questions be submitted to him in advance* Wire service reports of transcripts of chess conference, September 1, 1992.

p. 247: *"Let's start with some impudent questions from* The New York Times" NYT, September 2, 1992, p. A1.

p. 248: *Although a large number of reporters had been interested in attending Bobby Fischer's controversial press conference* CL, March 1993, p. 27.

p. 248: *He then spat on the letter, and applause broke out.* NYT, September 2, 1992, p. A1.

p. 248: *His anti-Americanism was lambasted* NYT, September 2, 1992, p. A18.

p. 249: *"I am bored and disgusted with him"* Ottawa Citizen, August 28, 1992.

p. 249: *"Yes, Fischer betrayed chess and everybody."* NYT, September 2, 1992, p. C14.

p. 249: *Denying that he was an anti-Semite* Wire service reports of first press conference, September 1, 1992.

p. 249: *"They have absolutely destroyed chess"* First press conference, September 1, 1992, reported in *The New York Times*, September 2, 1992.

p. 249 *"I like geniuses or crazy people"* Chronicle-Telegram, "The Man Behind the Chesspiece," September 23, 1992, p. A–7.

p. 250: *Twenty years of rust aside, Bobby played as masterfully as he had in 1972* NYT, September 3, 1992, p. C22.

p. 250: *Grandmaster Yasser Seirawan wrote* Seirawan and Stefanovic, p. 32.

p. 250: *"Playing forcefully, the American chess genius seems to be in top form."* NYT, September 3, 1992, p. 622.

p. 251: *"This was maybe an off-day for me."* Second press conference, September 3, 1992.

p. 251: *Lilienthal had never met Fischer, and at the conclusion of the fourth game, they were introduced at the hotel's restaurant* http://eidard.wordpress.com. (Fischer was also to have said: "Pawn e5 takes __6!" giving the precise moves.)

p. 251: *"My general approach was not to think about the result of the match"* Letter from Boris Spassky to the author, May 31, 2010.

p. 252: *"I think I am doing quite well, considering that I've been blacklisted for the last twenty years by world Jewry."* New York Daily News, September 2, 1992, p. 1.

p. 252: *"No, I have no regrets about spitting at that letter."* New York Daily News, September 2, 1992, p. 1.

p. 252: *"That man [Kasparov] is a pathological liar, so I wouldn't pay much attention to whatever he says."* New York Daily News, September 2, 1992, p. 2.

p. 252: *"So I consider that the United States government and Time Incorporated went into a criminal conspiracy"* Wire service reports for second press conference, September 2, 1992.

p. 253: *the greatest comeback since Napoleon Bonaparte sailed a single-masted fleet from the island of Elba in 1815* Time, September 28, 1992, p. 78.

p. 253: *"somewhere in the top ten in the world"* Seirawan and Stefanovic, p. 283.

p. 253: *"True, the match with Spassky was not all that great"* Interview of Arnold Denker by the author, December 2000, Boca Raton, Florida.

p. 254: *At this time Vasiljevic was making an arrangement for another match for Bobby* Letter from Isodoro Cherem to Bobby Fischer, August 5, 1992, FB.

p. 254: *Bobby had met Ljubojevic.* Vecerne Novosti (Yugoslavia newspaper), November 6, 1992.

p. 254: *Five hundred thousand depositors had funneled $2 billion into his sixteen bank* www.attacktheking.com.

p. 254: *Years later he was extradited to Serbia* March 29, 2010, NYT, p. A11.

p. 255: *On December 15, 1992, a single-count indictment in federal court in Washington, D.C., was handed down by a grand jury against Bobby Fischer* Copy of indictment from the U.S. District Court against Bobby Fischer, December 15, 1992.

p. 256: *"I have no friends here; only Gliga and the bodyguards"* Letter from Bobby Fischer to Zita Rajcsanyi, June 14, 1993, in DeLucia and DeLucia, p. 191.

p. 256: *"He was rough," she said.* *Kurir* (Budapest daily), September 13, 1993, p. 20.

p. 256: *She left a good-bye note indicating that her affair had nothing to do with why she didn't want to marry him.* Undated letter from Zita to Bobby Fischer, circa summer 1993, in DeLucia and DeLucia, p. 191.

p. 257: *"I was surprised to see how tall and big he was"* Interview of Zsuzsa Polgar by the author, May 23, 2009, Princeton, NJ.

p. 257: *She added that there he could socialize with some of the great Hungarian players he knew* Interview of Zsuza Polgar by author, May 23, 2009, Princeton, NJ.

p. 257: *The Polgars, thinking of everything, had taken a chance on their way across the border* *Lubbock Avalanche-Journal,* January 18, 2009.

p. 257: *"I think the Hungarians may arrest me as soon as I cross the border."* Faxed letter to Miyoko Watai from Bobby Fischer, June 19, 1993, in DeLucia and DeLucia, p. 192.

p. 258: *Entering the sparkling city of Budapest* Undated postcard from the Hotel Gellért, from Bobby Fischer to Regina Fischer, circa summer 1993, MCF.

Chapter 13: Crossing Borders

Interviews of Pal Benko, Olga Lilienthal (by Dimitry Komarov), Kirsan Ilyumzhinov, and Zsuzsa Polgar, in addition to others that appear in Tivadar Farkasházy's book *Bobby Vizzatér,* were invaluable sources for this chapter.

p. 259: *"You don't need bodyguards in Budapest"* Interview of Pal Benko by author, summer 2008, New York.

p. 259: *To protect himself, he bought a heavy coat made of horse leather* Interview of Pal Benko by author, summer 2008, New York.

p. 260: *As soon as he was settled at the Hotel Gellért, Bobby was invited to spend part of the summer with the Polgars* Interview of Zsuzsa Polgar by author, May 2009, Princeton, NJ.

p. 260: *about thirty-five miles north of Budapest, in the verdant Danube Bend section of the Slavic Hills of Hungary* "Seeking the Fischer King," *New York Daily News,* August 22, 1993.

p. 260: *All of the sisters played chess with him, but acceding to his preference, they played Fischer Random* Gligoric, *Shall We Play,* p. 86.

p. 260: *Zsuzsa played him "countless games"* Interview of Zsuzsa Polgar by author, May 2009, Princeton, NJ.

pp. 260–61: *"I tried to convince him in the beginning about the realities"* Interview of Zsuzsa Polgar by author, May 23, 2009, Princeton, NJ.

p. 261: *"He was like a big kid," Zsuzsa fondly remembered* Interview of Zsuzsa Polgar by author, May 2009, Princeton, NJ.

p. 262: *Even after living there for years, he referred to himself as a "tourist"* Calypso Radio interview of Bobby Fischer, January 13, 1999.

p. 262: *Although Olga was almost the same age as Bobby* Interview of Olga Lilienthal by Dmitry Komarov, circa 2008, letter courtesy of Magnus Skulasson.

p. 263: *"You are a good man, a good person, so you are not a Jew."* Farkasházy, p. 97.

p. 263: *Andrei had surreptitiously taken a photograph of Bobby at a New Year's Eve dinner party* Interview of Pal Benko by author, May 2010, New York.

p. 264: *He relayed a message to Lilienthal that he'd deliver the $100,000 in American cash to Bobby personally* Interview of Kirsan Ilyumzhinov by author, August 2002, Cherry Hill, NJ.

p. 264: *"I was struck by how Fischer was up on everything that was happening in our country."* Vladimir Linder and Isaac Linder, "From Morphy to Fischer—Who's Next?" Unpublished essay, Russia, no year.

p. 264: *Ilyumzhinov suggested that Bobby move to Kalmykia* Interview of Kirsan Ilyumzhinov by author, August 2002, New York.

p. 264: *Bobby thanked the president and asked about Kalmykia's medical care program* Sports Express, December 20, 1995.

p. 264: *Ilyumzhinov also offered to put up millions for another Fischer-Spassky match* Kasparov, p. 489.

p. 265: *"The old Jewish scoundrel Andrei Lilienthal"* From a book in progress by Bobby Fischer, *What Can You Expect from Baby Mutilators?* November 18, 1997. Extracts appeared in DeLucia and DeLucia, pp 248–61.

p. 265: *Incredulous, Bobby asked Sofia: "How can you even talk to those people?"* Farkasházy, p. 269.

p. 265: *When Zita told her mother what he'd said* Farkasházy, p. 135 ff.

p. 266: *"Single, tall, rich, handsome, middle-aged American man"* DeLucia and DeLucia, p. 236.

p. 266: *Once, when coming home late at night from an event* Farkasházy, p. 375.

p. 267: *To Kaltenbrunner the fact that the great Bobby Fischer was gracing his home* Farkasházy, pp. 382–85.

p. 267: *The film grossed more than $7 million and was nominated for an Academy Award* Internet Movie Database, imdb.com.

p. 268: *It's "a monumental swindle"* "Bobby Fischer Moves to a Satisfying Peace," *Chicago Sun-Times,* September 26, 1993.

p. 268: *Bobby felt safe enough to travel and eventually went to many countries* Interview of Pal Benko by author, April 2010, New York.

p. 268: *Mysteriously, he also journeyed to Italy to meet a member of the Mafia* Farkasházy, p. 198.

p. 269: *Some chess players in the state of Washington conjectured that he surreptitiously entered the United States* Chess, January 2001, p. 8.

p. 269: *Sometimes he'd vary his routine and go on long walks* Chicago Sun-Times, September 26, 1993.

p. 273: *Ellsworth actually realized his error in time to attend the auction and buy back $8,000 worth of the material* Böhm and Jongkind, p. 65.

p. 273: *He just wouldn't let it rest* Bobby Fischer live radio interviews, http://bobbyfischerpage.tripod.com.

p. 274: *One psychiatrist, Dr. Magnus Skulasson, who knew Bobby well toward the end of his life* Interview of Dr. Magnus Skulasson by author, October 2009, Reykjavik, Iceland.

p. 274: *Saidy added that the media were exploitative in publishing the most hideous of Bobby's statements* CL, June 1999, letter to Larry Evans in *Evans on Chess.*

p. 274: *He lambasted Saidy for living in the United States* Extract from Bobby Fischer's diary, August 5, 1999, in DeLucia and DeLucia, p. 285.

p. 275: *Bobby and Miyoko, both in their late fifties, lived a quiet life* http://www.anusha.com/paf690.htm.

p. 276: *One of his friends who observed them together said that he treated little Jinky with affection* Interview with Gardar Sverrisson by author, October 2009, Reykjavik, Iceland.

p. 277: *"Yes, well, this is all wonderful news"* Interview of Bobby Fischer on Radio Baguio, September 11, 2001.

Chapter 14: Arrest and Rescue

pp. 279: *He wanted the world to know about his devestating loss* DeLucia and De-Lucia, p. 275.

p. 279: *brought renewed scrutiny by the United States government* NYT, July 17, 2004, p. A1.

p. 281: *twenty-four new pages perfectly sewn in* http://www.canoe.ca/newsstand/columnists/ottawa.

p. 281: *It was dated December 11, 2003* Letter on "Embassy of the United States of America—Manila, Philippines" stationery, dated December 11, 2003, to Robert James Fischer, signed by Theodore Allegra, Consul of the U.S.A., FB.

p. 281: *being that the embassy had never sent the letter to Bern* Chessbase.com/newsdetail.asp?newsid=1852.

p. 282: *"He was so upset, and I didn't know what to say"* Interview of Miyoko Watai by Ev Mafurji on chessbase.com, January 9, 2004.

p. 283: *Miyoko, for her part, thought that U.S. authorities could have arrested Bobby anytime* AP wire story (Tokyo), July 18, 2004.

p. 283: *Another time, he purposely stepped on the glasses of a guard* Interview of Saemi Palsson by author, October 2009, Reykjavik, Iceland.

P. 283: *Fischer called it a "kidnapping"* Quoted in network news footage, March 24, 2005.

p. 284: *He also wrote to Secretary of State Colin Powell* AP wire story (Asia), August 17, 2004.

p. 285: *"permanently renounce my U.S. citizenship."* Bloomberg News Service. August 6, 2004.

p. 285: *Bobby's plea was based on his paternity* http://21-1-TW. Facebook.

p. 285: *North Korea . . . Libya . . . Iran . . . Montenegro . . . The Philippines* Undated e-mail from Miyoko Watai to Pal Benko, circa spring 2005 in DeLucia and DeLucia, p. 304.

pp. 285–86: *Venezuela . . . Switzerland.* "Freeing Bobby Fischer," a report by Einar S. Einarsson, June 6, 2008, FB.

p. 286: *he'd become part of the Icelandic sagas* NYT, (London), January 28, 2005, p. A7.

p. 286: *"Saemi, this is Bobby."* From the film *Me and Bobby Fischer,* 2009.

p. 286: *He was on a plane to the East* Interview of Saemi Palsson by author, October 7, 2009, Reykjavik, Iceland.

p. 287: *To not help them, they believed* "Freeing Bobby Fischer," a report by Einar S. Einarsson, June 6, 2008, FB.

p. 287: *they began lobbying the Icelandic government* Interview of Einar Einarsson by author, October 8, 2009, Reykjavik, Iceland.

p. 287: *"We feel obliged to express our deepest dismay"* Letter of March 15, 2005, by the RJF Committee, FB.

p. 287: *"the whole country has no culture, no taste"* Interview of Bobby Fischer on Bombo Radyo, August 12, 2004.

p. 287: *Fischer then announced that he was going to marry* AP wire story (Asia), August 17, 2004.

pp. 287–88: *"a pawn can become a queen."* NYT, August 20, 2004, p. A5.

p. 288: *"I'd rather not say"* Associated Press, December 4, 2006.

p. 288: *"It was already a de-facto marriage."* NYT, August 20, 2004, p. A5.

p. 288: *"We had been satisfied with our life before he was detained"* Interview of Miyoko Watai by Ev Mafurji on chessbase.com, January 9, 2004.

p. 288: *After months behind bars* http://www,channelnewasia.com.

p. 288: *Honorable Members of Althingi* From Bobby Fischer, January 19, 2005. FB.

p. 290: *These calls to Gardar* Interview of Gardar Sverisson by author, October 2009, Reykjavik, Iceland.

p. 290: *Bobby read some of the book* Letter from Richard Vattuone to author, January 2010.

p. 291: *Fukushima criticized Chieko Nohno* "Freeing Bobby Fischer," a report by Einar S. Einarsson, June 6, 2008, FB.

p. 291: *warning that if action weren't taken quickly* E-mail exchange between Einar Einarsson and John Bosnitch, March 21, 2005, FB.

p. 292: *"When the leader of a country"* Interview of David Oddsson by author, October 10, 2009, Reykjavik, Iceland.

p. 292: *A federal grand jury in Washington* AP wire story (Philadelphia), March 8, 2005.

p. 292: *suggesting that Iceland drop the offer of sanctuary* Japan Times, December 23, 2004.

p. 292: *Fischer's alleged crime of a violation of trade sanctions* Ibid.

p. 292: *"The Immigration Bureau must think"* Mainichi Daily News, March 22, 2005.

p. 293: *polled on whether to grant Fischer permanent citizenship* Act Respecting the Granting of Citizenship, no. 16/2005, FB.

p. 293: *a limousine supplied by the Icelandic embassy* AP wire story, March 23, 2005.

p. 293: *This was nothing but a kidnapping"* Watching America website, and various network sources. March 24, 2005, FB.

p. 294: *"It is not his beard"* Interview with Zita Farkasházy by Tivadar Farkasházy; *Bobby Visszater,* p. 369.

Chapter 15: Living and Dying in Iceland

A great amount of the source material for this chapter consisted of face-to-face interviews, telephone conversations, and correspondence with many Icelanders who knew Bobby Fischer during his residence in Reykjavik (2005–2008) and in 1972, and who were instrumental in freeing him from imprisonment in Japan. Additionally, correspondence with Bobby's lawyers resulted in the clarification of important information. Examination of documents and correspondence concerning his detention and the ultimate granting of his Icelandic citizenship also provided new facts.

p. 295: *blue denim work shirt and pants* AFP (Reykjavik), January 19, 2008.

p. 296: *As for what people thought about his dress* Interview of Gardar Sverrisson by author, October 2009, Reykjavik, Iceland.

p. 296: *he gave it as a gift to his new friend* Ibid.

p. 297: *"Fischer came close to being a moron"* Skeptical Inquirer, Vol. 33–5, September/October 2009.

p. 298: *and sometimes even falling asleep* Interview of Bragi Kristjonsson by author, October 2009, Reykjavik, Iceland.

p. 298: *"It's good to be free"* E-mail to Pal Benko from Bobby Fischer, April 20, 2006, in DeLucia and DeLucia, p. 305.

p. 298: *he pored over books on battles from ancient Greece to World War II* Interview of Einer Einarsson by author, October 2009, Reykjavik, Iceland.

p. 299: *"This is absolutely vicious, illegal and unfair"* *Morgunbladid,* July 29, 2005.

p. 299: *exchange of long, technical e-mails with UBS* Interview with Einar Einarsson by author, October 2009, Reykjavik, Iceland.

p. 299: *So he lost* Letter from UBS, "Termination Business Relationship Account," July 22, 2005, FB.

p. 299: *UBS liquidated all of his assets* Bank transfer statements from UBS to Landsbanki, various dates, May–August 2005, FB.

p. 300: *speculated that he was somehow prescient* Interview of Einar Einarsson by author, October 2009, Reykjavik, Iceland.

p. 300: *deep, serious study of history, philosophy, and other topics* *Iceland Review,* February 2008, p. 41.

p. 300: *Bókin reminded him of Dr. Albrecht Buschke's chess bookstore* *The Smart Set,* by Sara Blask, March 28, 2008.

p. 301: *Finally, he said he'd work for nothing* Interview of Bragi Kristjonsson by author, October 2009, Reykjavik, Iceland.

p. 301: *"You know, the fairy tale and the Brothers Grimm"* Interview of store clerk in Yggdrasil by author, October 2009, Reykjavik, Iceland.

p. 302: *Bobby answered in his typical Calvin Coolidge style* Telephone interview of Helgi Olaffson by author, October 8, 2009, Reykjavik, Iceland.

p. 302: *Sonja gently asked if he'd pose for a photo* Interview of "Sonja" by author, October 2009, Reykjavik, Iceland.

p. 303: *"Gee, they didn't know who I was"* Interview of Einar Einarsson by author, October 2009, Reykjavik, Iceland.

p. 304: *"as Fischer probably feels trapped in Iceland"* Interview of David Oddsson by author, October 2009, Reykjavik, Iceland.

p. 304: *Iceland was a "prison"* Interview of Gardar Sverrisson by author, October 9, 2009, Reykjavik, Iceland.

p. 304: *flagged to be arrested at any one of 368 airports* Interview of Bragi Kristjonsson by author, October 2009, Reykjavik, Iceland.

p. 304: *"Eating was very important to him"* Interview of Zsuzsa Polgar by author, May 2009, Princeton, NJ.

p. 305: *Bobby grimaced and agreed not to buy it* Interview of Einar Einarsson by author, October 2009, Reykjavik, Iceland.

p. 305: *"They were in love and showed it in many small ways"* Interview of Gardar Sverrisson by author, October 2009, Reykjavik, Iceland.

p. 306: *"But he also liked to study people when he was riding."* Ibid.

p. 306: *the driver keep both hands on the steering wheel at all times* Interview of Einar Einarsson by author, October 2009.

p. 307: *It became clear, however, that Titomirov had no interest.* E-mails from Joel Lautier, May 27, 2005, and Dr. Alex Titomirov, May 27, 2005, to Einar Einarsson, FB.

p. 307: *announced prize fund was $14 million* Undated five-page proposal, "Gothic Chess Match: The Clash of the Chess Legends," FB.

p. 308: *"These games are fake!"* Me and Bobby Fischer, 2009.

p. 309: *"Perhaps Fischer's ascent to world champion was part of some conspiracy"* Mark Segal, "Chess, Chance and Conspiracy," *Statistical Science* 22, no. 1, 2007, pp. 98–108.

p. 309: *Bobby began finding fault* Observer (London), February 10, 2008.

p. 309: *for the months of bodyguard work.* Interview of Saemi Palsson by author, October 2009.

p. 311: *"This is a film that is supposed to be about my kidnapping"* Interview with Saemi Palsson by author, October 7, 2009, Reykjavik, Iceland.

p. 311: *"I am Bobby Fischer!"* Ibid.

p. 311: *"This film is about the atom bomb."* Letter from Fridrik Gudmundsson to Bobby Fischer, January 28, 2007, FB.

p. 312: *Mr. Fischer wishes the group to draw attention* Press release issued by the RJF committee, May 4, 2007.

p. 312: *"I want to see the books."* Interview of Gudmundur Thorarinsson by author, October 2009.

p. 313: *Even key stalwarts felt his sting* Telegraph.co.uk, January 25. 2008.

p. 313: *Bobby's snit against him lasted only twenty-four hours* Interview of Gardar Sverrisson by author, October 2009.

p. 313: *"special but only in the negative sense"* E-mail from Bobby Fischer to Pal Benko, May 11, 2007, DeLucia and DeLucia, p. 308.

p. 313: *"I don't owe these [people] anything!"*   E-mail to Pal Benko from Bobby Fischer, May 10, 2007, as quoted in DeLucia and DeLucia, p. 308.

p. 314: *"Well, that's Bobby"*   Interview of Einar Einarsson by author, October 10, 2009, Reykjavik, Iceland.

p. 314: *"Never obey anyone's command"*   Wikipedia, accessed December 7, 2009.

p. 314: *"I am always on the attack"*   From *Me and Bobby Fischer,* 2009.

p. 314: *"I am a genius"*   From *Me and Bobby Fischer,* 2009.

p. 315: *Eventually, Bobby brought* him *a copy of* Basic Catechism   Interview of Gardar Sverrisson by author, October 2009.

p. 315: *Einarsson and Skulasson both concluded*   Letter to the author from Einar Einarsson, November 8, 2009, FB.

p. 315: *then professed that he thought "the only hope for the world"*   Interview of Gardar Sverrisson by author, October 2009.

p. 315: *"Unfortunately, we're not strong enough"*   quote from an unpublished 300-page manuscript by Bobby Fischer dated January 17, 1999, as reprinted in DeLucia and DeLucia, p. 272.

p. 316: *"The expressiveness of the eyes, my goodness, you can practically feel his sadness"*   Letter from David Surratt to Einar Einarsson, February 15, 2008.

p. 317: *His friend Pal Benko believed that to be the case*   Interview of Pal Benko by author, summer 2008, New York.

p. 318: *"Why didn't you bring the whole book!?"*   Interview of Fridrik Olafsson by author, October 2009.

p. 318: *contrary to reports that he had it perched on his bedside table*   Interview of Magnus Skulasson by author, October 2009.

p. 318: *He was at Bobby's bedside as a friend*   *Iceland Review,* February 2008, p. 43.

p. 318: *Bobby looked at him and said, "Nothing soothes as much as the human touch."*   Interview of Magnus Skulasson by author, October 2009, Reykjavik, Iceland.

p. 319: *became his attendants and guardians*   *Sunday Times* (London), April 20, 2008.

Epilogue

p. 320: *"My brother is dead"* E-mail to Einar Einarsson from Boris Spassky, January 18, 2009.

p. 320: *Only three weeks before Bobby's death* E-mail to Bobby Fischer from Boris Spassky, December 28, 2007.

p. 321: *"I have a brother's feeling"* Letter from Boris Spassky to author, May 31, 2010.

p. 321: *"Fischer just wanted to be buried like a normal human being"* "Requiem for the Black King," *Iceland Review,* July 4, 2008.

p. 323: *"Like him, he was buried with few present"* Ibid.

BIBLIOGRAPHY

Alburt, Lev, and Al Lawrence. *Three Days with Bobby Fischer, & Other Chess Essays: How to Meet Champions & Choose Your Openings.* New York: Chess Information and Research Center, 2003.

American Chess Journal: Premiere Issue (1992).

Andersen, C. *Barbra: The Way She Is.* New York: William Morrow, 2006.

Basalla, Bob. *Chess in the Movies.* Davenport, IA: TPI Wonderworks, 2005.

Berkovich, Felix. *Jewish Chess Masters on Stamps.* Jefferson, NC: McFarland & Company, Inc., Publishers, 2000.

Bisguier, Arthur B., and Newton Berry. *The Art of Bisguier: Selected Games 1961–2003.* Mitford, CT: Russell Enterprises, 2000.

Bjelica, Dimitrije. *Chess Meets of the Century.* Sarajevo, Yugoslavia: Zavod Za Izdavanje Udžbenika, 1971.

Böhm, Hans, and Kees Jongkind. *Bobby Fischer: The Wandering King.* London: B.T. Batsford, 2004.

Botvinnik, M. M. *Achieving the Aim.* New York: Pergamon Press, 1981.

Brady, Frank. *Bobby Fischer: Profile of a Prodigy.* New York: Dover Publications, Inc., 1973.

Bronstein, David. *Zurich International Chess Tournament, 1953.* Translated from the Second Russian Edition by Jim Marfia. New York: Dover Publications, Inc., 1979.

Burger, Robert E. *The Chess of Bobby Fischer.* Radnor, PA: Chilton Book Company, 1975.

Burgess, Graham. *Chess Highlights of the 20th Century.* London: Gambit Publications Ltd., 1999.

Canetti, Elias. *Auto-da-Fé.* New York: Continuum, 1981. (Originally published as *The Tower of Babel* in 1947.)

Chernev, Irving. *Wonders and Curiosities of Chess.* New York: Dover Publications, Inc., 1974.

Cockburn, Alexander. *Idle Passion: Chess and the Dance of Death*. New York: Simon & Schuster, 1974.

Collins, John W. *My Seven Chess Prodigies*. New York: Simon & Schuster, 1974.

Darrach, Brad. *Bobby Fischer vs. the Rest of the World*. Updated. New York: Stein and Day Publishers, 2009. New York: ISHI Press International, new edition.

De Groot, Adriaan. *Thought and Choice in Chess*. The Hague: Mouton & Co., 1965.

DeLucia, David. *David DeLucia's Chess Library: A Few Old Friends*. Second Edition. Darien, CT: David DeLucia, 2007.

DeLucia, David, and Alessandra DeLucia. *Bobby Fischer Uncensored*. Darien, CT: David DeLucia, 2009.

Divinsky, Nathan. *The Batsford Chess Encyclopedia*. London: B. T. Batsford, Ltd., 1990.

Donaldson, John. *A Legend on the Road: Bobby Fischer's 1964 Simul Tour*. Seattle, WA: International Chess Enterprises, 1994.

Donaldson, John, and Eric Tangborn. *The Unknown Bobby Fischer*. Seattle, WA: International Chess Enterprises, 1999.

Donner, J. H. *The King: Chess Pieces*. Alkmaar, the Netherlands: New In Chess, 2006.

Dunne, Alex. *Great Chess Books of the Twentieth Century in English*. Jefferson, NC: McFarland & Company, Inc., Publishers, 2005.

Edmonds, David, and John Eidinow. *Bobby Fischer Goes to War: The True Story of How the Soviets Lost the Most Extraordinary Chess Match of All Time*. London: Faber and Faber Limited, 2004.

Eisner, Will. *The Plot: The Secret Story of The Protocols of the Elders of Zion*. New York: W. W. Norton & Company, Inc.

Elo, Arpad E. *The Rating of Chessplayers, Past and Present*. New York: ARCO Publishing, Inc., 1978.

Euwe, Max. *Bobby Fischer—The Greatest?* New York: Sterling Publishing Co., Inc., 1979.

Euwe, Max, and Jan Timman. *Fischer: World Champion!* Alkmaar, the Netherlands: New In Chess, 2002.

Evans, Larry. *The Chess Beat*. New York: Pergamon Press, 1982.

Evans, Larry. *This Crazy World of Chess*. New York, NY: Cardoza Publishing, 2007.

Evans, Larry, and Ken Smith. *Chess World Championship 1972: Fischer vs. Spassky*. New York: Simon & Schuster, 1973.

Farkasházy, Tivadar. *Bobby Visszatér: avagy a Fischer-rejtély*. Budapest, Hungary: Adwise Media, 2008.

Fine, Reuben. *Bobby Fischer's Conquest of the World's Chess Championship: The Psychology and Tactics of the Title Match*. New York, NY: David McKay Company, Inc., 1973.

Fischer, Bobby. *My 60 Memorable Games*. New York: Simon & Schuster, 1969.

———. *I Was Tortured in the Pasadena Jailhouse!* CA: Bobby Fischer, 1982.

Fischer, Bobby, Stuart Margulies, and Donn Mosenfelder. *Bobby Fischer Teaches Chess*. New York: Bantam Books, 1989.

Freud, Sigmund. *The Basic Writings of Sigmund Freud*. Translated and edited by Dr. A. A. Brill. New York: The Modern Library/Random House, Inc., 1938.

Gaige, Jeremy. *Chess Personalia: A Biobibliography*. Jefferson, NC: McFarland & Company, Inc., Publishers, 2005.

Geuzendam, Dirk Jan ten. *Finding Bobby Fischer: Chess Interviews by Dirk Jan ten Geuzendam*. Alkmaar, the Netherlands: New In Chess, 1994.

———. *The Day Kasparov Quit, and Other Chess Interviews*. Alkmaar, the Netherlands: New In Chess, 2006.

Gladwell, Malcolm. *Outliers: The Story of Success*. New York: Little, Brown and Company, 2008.

Gligoric, Svetozar. *Fischer vs. Spassky: The Chess Match of the Century: World Chess Championship Match 1972*. New York: Simon & Schuster, 1972.

———. *Shall We Play Fischerandom Chess?* London: B.T. Batsford Ltd., 2002.

Golombek, Harry. *Chess: A History*. New York: G. P. Putnam's Sons, 1976.

Golombek, Harry, editor. *Golombek's Encyclopedia of Chess*. New York: Crown Publishers, Inc., 1977.

Grekov, Nicolai. *Soviet Chess*. Brought up to date by David Bronstein. New York: Capricorn Books, 1962.

Gufeld, Eduard, et al. *Bobby Fischer: From Chess Genius to Legend*. Davenport, IA: Thinkers Press, Inc., 2002.

Hammarskjöld, Dag. *Markings*. New York: Vintage Books, 2006.

Hannak, J. *Emanuel Lasker: The Life of a Chess Master*. New York: Simon & Schuster, 1959.

Hays, Lou, editor. *Bobby Fischer: Complete Games of the American World Chess Champion*. Dallas, TX: Hays Publishing, 1992.

Hilbert, John S. *Shady Side: The Life and Crimes of Norman Tweed Whitaker, Chess Master*. Yorklyn, DE: Caissa Editions, A Division of Dale Brandreth Books, 2000.

Hooper, David, and Kenneth Whyld. *Oxford Companion to Chess*. New York: Oxford University Press, 1996.

Horowitz, I. A., and P. L. Rothenberg. *The Personality of Chess*. New York: The Macmillan Company, 1963.

Horton, Byrne J. *Dictionary of Modern Chess*. New York: Philosophical Library, 1959.

Hurst, Sarah. *Curse of Kirsan*. Mitford, CT: Russell Enterprises, Inc., 2002.

Johnson, Daniel. *White King and Red Queen: How the Cold War Was Fought on the Chessboard*. London: Atlantic Books, 2007.

Kaikamjozov, Zhivko. *The Genius and the Misery of Chess*. Boston: Mongoose Press, 2008.

Karpov, Anatoly. *Karpov on Karpov: Memoirs of a Chess World Champion*. New York: Atheneum, 1991.

Kashdan, Isaac, editor. *Second Piatigorsky Cup: International Grandmaster Chess Tournament Held in Santa Monica, California, August 1966*. New York: Dover Publications, Inc., 1968.

Kasparov, Garry. *My Great Predecessors, Part IV*. London: Everyman Chess Series, Everyman Publishers, 2004.

Keres, Paul. *Grandmaster of Chess: The Complete Games of Paul Keres*. New York: Arco Publishing Company, Inc., 1977.

Koltanowski, George. *TV Chess*. San Francisco: KQED, Bay Area Educational Television Assn., 1968.

―――. *Chessnicdotes, Volume II*. Coraopolis, PA: Chess Enterprises, Inc., 1981.

Korchnoi, Viktor. *Chess Is My Life: Autobiography and Games*. London: B.T. Batsford Ltd., 1978.

Kotov, A. and M. Yudovich. *The Soviet School of Chess*. Moscow: Foreign Languages Publishing House, 1958.

Larsen, Bent. *Larsen's Selected Games of Chess, 1948–69*. New York: David McKay Company, Inc., 1970.

Lipnitsky, Isaac. *Questions of Modern Chess Theory: A Soviet Classic*. UK: Quality Chess UK LLP, 2008.

Mamet, David. *The Wicked Son*. New York: Schocken Press, 2006.

Margeirsson, Ingólfur. *Sæmi Rokk: Lifsdans Sæmundar Pássonar*. Reykjavik, Iceland: Bókaútgáfan Æskan ehf./ Almenna útgáfan, 2008.

Mednis, Edmar. *How to Beat Bobby Fischer*. Mineola, New York: Dover Publications, Inc., 1997.

Müller, Karsten. *Bobby Fischer: The Career and Complete Games of the American World Chess Champion*. Milford, CT: Russell Enterprises, Inc., 2009.

Münninghoff, Alexander. *Max Euwe: The Biography*. Alkmaar, the Netherlands: New In Chess, 2001.

Pandolfini, Bruce. *Bobby Fischer's Outrageous Chess Moves*. New York: Simon & Schuster, 1985.

Pandolfini, Bruce, editor. *The Best of Chess Life and Review, Vol. 1, 1933–1960*. New York: Simon & Schuster, 1988.

Piatigorsky, Jacqueline. *Jump in the Waves: A Memoir*. New York: St. Martin's Press, 1988.

Plisetsky, Dmitry, and Sergey Voronkov, compilers. *Russians Versus Fischer*. Moscow: Moscow Chess World, 1994.

Radford, John. *Child Prodigies and Exceptional Early Achievers*. New York: Macmillan, Inc., 1990.

Ree, Hans. *The Human Comedy of Chess: A Grandmaster's Chronicles*. Milford, CT: Russell Enterprises, Inc., 1999.

Russell, Hanon W. *A Chessplayer's Guide to Russian*. New Haven, CT: H. W. Russell, 1972.

Saidy, Anthony, and Norman Lessing. *The World of Chess*. New York: Random House, 1974.

Schonberg, Harold C. *Grandmasters of Chess*. Philadelphia and New York: J. B. Lippincott Company, 1973.

Schultz, Don. *Chess Don*. Boca Raton, FL: Chessdon Publishing, 1999.

———. *Fischer, Kasparov, and the Others: The Best of CHESSDON and Much More*. Highland Beach, FL: Chessdon Publishing, 2004.

Seirawan, Yasser, and George Stefanovic. *No Regrets: Fischer-Spassky 1992*. Seattle, WA: International Chess Enterprises, 1992.

Soltis, Andrew. *Karl Marx Plays Chess and Other Reports on the World's Oldest Game*. New York: David McKay Company, Inc., 1991.

———. *Bobby Fischer Rediscovered*. London: B.T. Batsford Ltd., 2003.

———. *The Wisest Things Ever Said About Chess*. London: B. T. Batsford, 2008.

Soltis, Andy, and Gene H. McCormick. *The United States Chess Championship, 1845–1996*. Second edition. Jefferson, NC: McFarland & Company, Inc., Publishers, 1997.

Sosonko, Genna. *Russian Silhouettes*. Alkmaar, the Netherlands: New In Chess, 2001.

———. *The Reliable Past*. Alkmaar, the Netherlands: New In Chess, 2003.

Steiner, George. *Fields of Force: Fischer and Spassky at Reykjavik*. New York: The Viking Press, 1974.

Sunnucks, Anne, compiler. *The Encyclopaedia of Chess*. London: Robert Hale, 1970.

Tal, Mikhail. *The Life and Games of Mikhail Tal*. New York: RHM Press, 1976.

Thorbergsson, Freysteinn. *Welcome to Iceland Mr. President!—A Short Work on Political Chess.* Reykjavik, Iceland: Freysteinn Thorbergsson, 1973.

Tiller, Terrence, editor. *Chess Treasury of the Air.* Harmondsworth, UK: Penguin Books, 1966.

Totaro, Lawrence. *Fisching for Forgeries.* Davenport, IA: Thinkers' Press, 2007.

Wade, R. G., and L. S. Blackstock, editors. *Interzonal Chess Tournament: Palma de Mallorca 1970.* Nottingham, England: The Chess Player, 1970.

Wade, Robert G., and Kevin J. O'Connell, editors. *Bobby Fischer's Chess Games.* Garden City, New York: Doubleday & Company, Inc., 1972.

Waitzkin, Fred. *Searching for Bobby Fischer: The Father of a Prodigy Observes the World of Chess.* New York: Penguin Books, 1988.

Winter, Edward. *Chess Explorations: A Pot-Pourri from the Journal* Chess Notes. London: Cadogan Chess, 1996.

———. *Kings, Commoners and Knaves: Further Chess Explorations.* Milford, CT: Russell Enterprises, Inc., 1999.

———. *A Chess Omnibus.* Milford, CT: Russell Enterprises, Inc., 2003.

INDEX